The Complete Guide to
BOWHUNTING DEER

by
CHUCK ADAMS

DBI BOOKS, INC.

DEDICATION

To my
pretty wife,
Joanne

ACKNOWLEDGEMENTS

There are several people I'd like to thank for assisting me with this book. Bill McIntosh of Bear Archery, Joe Johnston and Kathy O'Brien of Easton Aluminum, Sue McDonald of Martin Archery, Mike Murray of Ranging, Inc., Don Garbow of Buck Stop Lure Co., Chuck Saunders of Saunders Archery, and Colby Johnson of Bohning, Inc. were all abundantly helpful in supplying product photographs for this project. My good friends Ken Elliott of *Petersen's Hunting* Magazine and Russell Thornberry also contributed photographs which enhance this book considerably.

My special thanks goes to hunting buddies Bill Hom, Jeff Shimizu, Mick Roberts, Bob Smith, and Ron Hawkins for helping me with countless other photos which appear in this book. Without such good friends, bowhunting deer and writing books about this sport would not be nearly so much fun!

ABOUT OUR COVER

We are proud to have a Browning Drake Flight Master compound bow as the centerpiece on the covers of THE COMPLETE GUIDE TO BOWHUNTING DEER.

Browning's new Flight Master was fully designed by master bowyer Harry Drake and features a completely new reflex limb design. It's available in 28-30 or 30-32 inch draw lengths. Draw weight is 45-60 or 55-70 pounds with an axle-to-axle length of 46 inches.

The new Drake Flight Master has a sight window over 6 inches high and is capable of superb speed and accuracy, a result of Brownings new Helical-II cams that fully eliminate the need for a cable guard. The handle is of impregnated, laminated, epoxy finished birch.

Also seen is Browning's new rack and pinion bow sight complete with rangefinder and sight-light.

Arms and Armour Press, London, G.B., exclusive licensees and distributors in Britain and Europe; New Zealand, Nigeria, So. Africa and Zimbabwe, India and Pakistan; Singapore, Hong Kong and Japan. Capricorn Link (Aust.) Pty. Ltd. exclusive distributors in Australia.

ISBN 0-910676-73-9
Library of Congress Catalog Card # 84-070734

CONTENTS

Introduction

TO MY WAY of thinking, nothing quite matches a North American deer for pure bowhunting challenge and excitement. All big-game species on our continent are extremely worthwhile to pursue with bow-and-arrow gear, but there's definitely something special about a big-racked buck slipping warily through the undergrowth or gawking alertly and majestically from several hundred yards away.

According to biologists, there are six basic varieties of deer inhabiting our continent. Three of these—whitetail deer, mule deer, and blacktail deer—are traditionally regarded as deer by the average bow-shooting nimrod. Three other species—elk, moose, and caribou—are also called deer by animal experts because they grow and shed a fresh set of antlers each and every year. All six varieties of antler-growing animals share certain traits that make them stand out as bow-hunting targets.

One thing every deer has going for it is a full set of first-rate survival senses. Be it whitetail, blacktail, moose, or caribou, a deer has scalpel-sharp eyeballs, finely-tuned ears, and an incredibly sensitive nose. These senses are coupled with an inbred instinct for survival that far outstrips that of many other big-game species. Even the caribou, which is generally regarded as the least wary of deer, tends to be extremely alert and spooky unless hunted during the September rutting and migration period. The keen senses and basically nervous nature shared by all deer combine to make these animals a supreme challenge for any hunting archer.

In my mind, a handsome set of deer antlers is the ultimate bowhunting trophy. The horns of sheep and goats, the skulls of bears and cougars, and the hides of

A deer is an alert, wary prize worthy of any bowhunter's ability.

Bowhunting deer is a highly enjoyable pastime, especially when shared with good hunting companions.

Every deer rack is a unique, worthwhile trophy regardless of size. This nontypical mule deer is not large, but it will make an interesting addition to the trophy room of well-known bowhunter Russell Thornberry.

various American animals are extremely pleasing to view and own, but every set of deer antlers is a uniquely formed bowhunting prize. Normal horns from sheep or goats are extremely similar from animal to animal, bleached skulls are basically alike within a particular species, and tanned hides are more or less the same in shape and coloration from one animal to another of the same variety. By contrast, the trophy antlers of blacktail deer, whitetail deer, mule deer, elk, moose, and caribou grow from the skull in infinitely pleasing varieties of typical and non-typical conformations. Each rack is an individually interesting trophy no matter what the size of the antlers or what species of deer it comes from. Because of the tremendous antler variety North American deer produce, I feel these animals are the most interesting trophies our continent has to offer.

Deer have other things to offer a bowhunter as well. No matter what the species, a properly cared-for deer is incredibly good on the table. The meat from deer is also healthy to eat—a lean, tasty food lacking the high percentage of fat found in many domestic meats. Very few archers hunt deer to fill the freezer alone, but steaks and stews put on the table by successful deer hunters represent a pleasant bonus to a highly rewarding outdoor experience.

Fortunately for modern bowhunters, deer are not only the most challenging, interesting, and tasty game animals found in North America, but they are also the most widespread. Every state and province on our entire continent harbors at least one variety of deer, with many areas supporting two or three separate species. It is seldom the case that the best is also the most easily available, but bowhunting deer is a notable exception to the rule. Many serious archers are able to bowhunt deer within a few short miles of their homes, thanks to the ability of these sneaky animals to survive in proximity to man. At the very worst, a bowhunter may have to drive 3 or 4 hours to reach prime deer-hunting habitat. Couple this accessibility with the fact that most parts of the continent offer generous bow-hunting seasons and bag limits for deer, and bow-hunters are indeed sitting pretty when it comes to enjoying the challenge offered by antlered game. Given these pleasant deer-hunting realities, it is no great surprise that well over 90 percent of American bow-hunters concentrate on deer exclusively instead of other big-game species like bear, pronghorn antelope, or wild mountain sheep.

One reward of bowhunting deer is obviously a nice trophy in the bag, but there are more subtle rewards as well. An experienced bow-shooting deer hunter enjoys a rare intimacy with the game he hunts and nature at large. He becomes familiar with the most elusive traits of the wild things he encounters at close range on a day-in, day-out bowhunting basis. Such an intimacy with nature is seldom enjoyed by hunters who drop their game from several hundred yards away. A consistently successful bowhunter is an active part of nature, observing deer at eyelash-batting distance and learning to fully enjoy the animals he's trying to bag. This intimate appreciation and understanding of deer is one of the most gratifying rewards any seasoned bowhunter is likely to experience.

Consistently bagging deer with bow-and-arrow gear is an exacting test, requiring properly chosen and finely-honed shooting and hunting ability as well as intimate knowledge of each deer species being pursued. This is a test that any dedicated sportsman can pass with flying colors, but not without doing some serious homework and spending plenty of time thinking about the ins and outs of the task at hand. It is certainly true that much of what bowhunters learn can only be absorbed first-hand in the woods, the same as much of what workers learn must be discovered on the job itself—not from instructional manuals or books. However, the *basics* of bowhunting equipment selection and maintenance, accurate shooting on the range and in the field, pursuing various kinds of deer, and caring for the animals once they are down *can be* clearly and beneficially written down to eliminate slow, costly, and very frustrating trial and error. The purpose of this book is to lay a solid foundation of facts for you to build on with practical outdoor experience—a foundation of facts that should get you started smoothly and confidently in this most satisfying of all bowhunting sports.

Best wishes, and good bowhunting for deer!

A fine buck on the ground is the ultimate reward of careful bowhunting. Author Adams took this record-sized blacktail buck after a long, tedious stalk.

The Hunting Bow/1

THE MAJOR and most expensive piece of bow-shooting equipment any deer hunter is likely to purchase is the hunting bow. The amazing variety of bows designed to hit and bag deer is enough to boggle any beginner's mind, even if he spends several hours at a well-stocked archery pro shop with a knowledgeable salesman to help him make his choice. The choosing of that "just-right" deer-hunting bow is no easy thing even for an expert archer with plenty of practical experience behind him. The 40 or 50 major bow manufacturers in the United States are constantly changing product lines, offering unique new bow features, and distributing new sales literature with the hopes of tantalizing buyers into selecting *their* products instead of those of their competitors. This leaves the average bow-bending deer hunter in a bit of a dilemma at best.

Choosing a proper hunting bow for deer is really not all that difficult if a hunter goes about this process sensibly and systematically. There are three basic guidelines I would stress when choosing any bow for deer. If these are followed, the process of narrowing down the field should be enjoyable and stimulating instead of frustrating and intimidating.

1. First and foremost, a beginning bowhunter should purchase his bow at a well-stocked archery shop or sporting goods store rather than through one of the many mail-order discount houses or cut-rate department store outlets around the country. Buying gear at reduced rates from wholesale outfits certainly makes sense if an archer knows exactly what he wants from past experience, but the additional cost of bow-buying at a local archery retail outlet is an investment that can save a beginning or intermediate archer a whole lot of problems. A regular retail archery outlet is normally run by people qualified to suggest reasonable bow models with the proper draw weight, draw length, and other important specifications to match your particular

The very best place to buy a hunting bow is a well-stocked archery pro shop or sporting goods store.

Large, reputable archery factories like Bear Archery turn out top-quality hunting bows by the thousands.

physical size, muscle structure, etc. In addition, most archery pro shops have built-in facilities that allow you to shoot several bows before plunking down your hard-earned money. Looking through mail-order archery catalogs can be fun, but such "dream books" with their dozens of bows for sale can drive a prospective buyer absolutely crazy unless he already knows exactly which bow he wishes to use on deer.

2. A second basic guideline when choosing any hunting bow for deer is making sure you realize the specific advantages and drawbacks of every basic hunting-bow design. These design traits are fully covered a little later in this chapter. At present, the five basic types of hand-drawn hunting bows sold are longbows, recurve bows, round-wheel compound bows, compound cam-bows, and overdraw bows. Lord only knows what new hunting-bow designs will appear in the next few years as manufacturers experiment and marketing experts dream and scheme. However, a serious bow-buyer can always ferret out the pluses and minuses of new bow designs by asking dealers, talking to bowhunting friends, and reading the latest in magazines and books. Archery manufacturers will always exalt their latest bows to the heavens, but this doesn't necessarily mean these bows are the best designs for you. As in any other product, a bow's track record for accuracy and dependability should be something you look at before buying.

3. The third thing to remember when shopping for a hunting bow is the fact that most bows with good reputations will serve you well on deer. As in the purchase of a car, every bow offers slightly different features to consider, but top-notch manufacturers like Bear, Ben Pearson, Browning, Jennings, PSE, Martin,

Golden Eagle, Hoyt/Easton, Pro Line and others, all make bows that will get you deer on a regular basis. By all means shop intelligently for a hunting bow, but don't let the wide selection overload your mental circuits. Stick with well-known brands, consider traits of each bow design you feel will help you out, shoot a few bows at the archery store to determine which feels the best . . . and then get used to the bow you buy with confidence. There are probably dozens of bow designs you can get used to and do well with on deer—the key is choosing quality to begin with and then using the bow a lot to become accustomed to it.

Longbows

The longbow is the most basic, inexpensive deer-hunting bow available today. This simple design is ancient and relatively slow-shooting, yet it does a fairly good hunting job if a shooter learns to limit his shooting range to the bow's accuracy and trajectory capabilities.

Basically, a longbow consists of a fairly short hardwood handle section with a very long, relatively straight limb on either end. When strung, it describes an even, pleasant arc instead of the more complex lines of modern bows.

The longbows of yesteryear were made of various springy woods, including yew wood, osage orange, and ironwood. Many American Indians shot shortened versions of this bow design, and the longbow was the standard tool of war with Englishmen and other Europeans throughout the Middle Ages. In more recent times, old-time bowhunters like Saxton Pope, Art Young, Howard Hill, and Fred Bear shot such bows throughout the 1920s, 1930s, and 1940s with good results.

Although not the choice of many bowhunters, the

old-style longbow does have a following of serious deer hunters today. Such fellows stress the fact that a longbow is a simple, dependable tool with strong aesthetic appeal. They go on to say that challenge is the name of the game in bowhunting, and that nothing is more challenging to shoot than the good ol' longbow. On these points the longbow advocates are very certainly correct.

Modern longbows are without a doubt the most dependable ever produced, and several commercial and custom manufacturers sell these today. The current offerings are generally over 70 inches long from tip to tip in longbow tradition, but most have limbs made of modern maple-and-fiberglass laminations that prevent breakage and increase arrow speeds over all-wood limbs.

Despite the modern materials in longbows today, these bows still cast arrows at relatively slow speeds. An average 55-pound hunting longbow will cast the proper arrow to match at only 160 feet per second—a speed that results in a very arching arrow trajectory, making range estimation exceedingly critical on targets and game. Coupled with the fact that longbows are almost always shot without bowsights in traditional style, shooting these bows requires above-normal shooting skills beyond relatively close shooting ranges.

Two other drawbacks to consider when looking at longbows are the long length of these bows, and the fact that they seldom allow the use of a bow quiver, spring-loaded arrow rest, or similar amenities standard on other bow designs. An ultra-long bow of this type can be tough to load in a car, tough to maneuver in the woods, and darn near impossible to shoot in tree-stand locations with close-hugging limbs. Longbow shooting is traditional, back-to-basics fun, requiring among other things a shoulder or hip quiver, a regular old shelf rest for the arrow and feather fletching that flattens out when passing the primitive rest.

Longbows are a solid challenge to hit with—a challenge that can be fun if tradition and a difficult job well

(Right) Longbows are often sold with all the traditional accessories, including a fringed buckskin case, back quiver, and other old-style leather goods. This particular ensemble is offered by Martin Archery.

A longbow is a simple, dependable deer-hunting tool with long limbs and a simple, unpretentious grip (inset) often wrapped with leather.

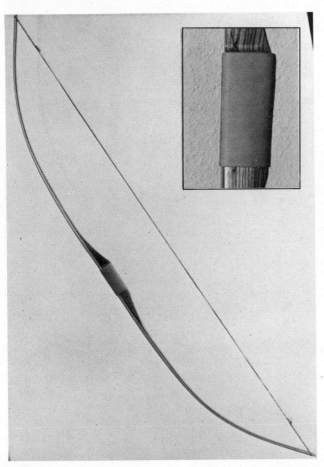

Longbows have been used for many years on deer with good results. This photo might well have been taken in the 1930s, when sport-hunting archery first gained momentum.

done are your main concerns. However, most deer hunters choose more efficient bow designs that enhance shooting accuracy and increase the odds of a buck in the bag.

Recurve Bows

During the 1950s and 1960s, the recurve was the most advanced deer-hunting bow available and the choice of most serious hunting archers. This bow design combines the dependable simplicity of the longbow with a shorter overall length, S-curved limbs that shoot more quickly and smoothly, and other design features like bow-quiver attachment, bow-stabilizer capability, pre-drilled holes for a bowsight, and acceptance of more tunable arrow rests that make accurate arrow flight less difficult to achieve.

Recurve hunting bows are still used by about 5 percent of modern bowhunters, according to official polls by the archery industry. The best of the lot have plenty going for them, and they sometimes cost as much or more than a top-notch compound hunting bow. The average recurve shoots about 180 feet per second when matched with a practical deer-hunting arrow, but a few well-designed, expensive recurve models cast arrows in the 200 fps class—right up there with more popular round-wheel compound bows. Recurves have a reputation for being extremely quiet to shoot when a bowstring is adequately silenced, and they measure on an average of only 60 inches from tip to tip to ensure decent maneuverability in the field. Some models "take down" or disassemble for ease of storage and transport—normally into a handle section and two separate limbs. Another advantage of the recurve is its extremely light physical weight that makes toting about the field a bonafide pleasure. Recurve bows are also less expensive on the average than more modern compound bows, although some top-notch

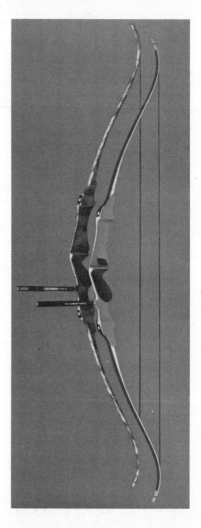

Top-quality take-down recurve bows like those by Hoyt/Easton have the good looks, fast performance, and practical transport design preferred by many deer-hunting archers.

(Opposite page) A one-piece recurve bow is a relatively inexpensive deer-hunting tool. ▶

(Left) Modern recurve bows are meticulously glued together at factories by first-rate craftsmen.

A recurve bow is a sturdy, dependable hunting tool. Famous bowhunter Fred Bear used one for years with excellent results.

The best recurve bows are drilled to accept bowsights, bow quivers, and other modern deer-hunting accessories.

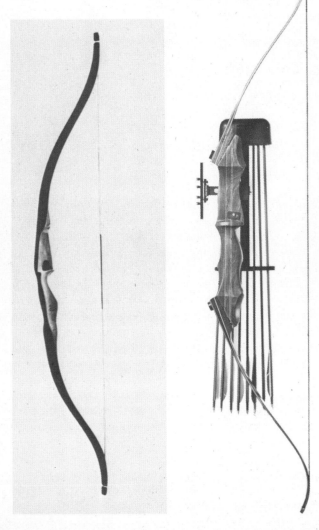

recurves carry extremely high price tags.

A recurve bow is a handsome, reliable shooting tool. However, it has one notable drawback that made it plummet from popularity when compound bows were commercially introduced in the late 1960s. You see, the recurve bow requires a shooter to hold the bowstring under full limb weight as he aims to take a shot. For example, a 50-pound deer-hunting recurve bow exerts a full 50 pounds on a hunter's fingers as he aims with a 28-inch arrow to take a shot. The compound bow eased finger and muscle tension with its unique mechanical design, and modern archers quickly converted to this wheel-and-cable bow en masse.

I personally enjoy bowhunting with recurve bows even today. However, they require more regular shooting practice to ensure toned-up muscles that won't quiver or wobble during a shot. Some deer hunters like the smooth, even way a recurve draws to full poundage, and many recurve advocates feel that such a bow draws and releases significantly faster than a bumpier-drawing compound bow. To each his own.

Round-Wheel Compound Bows

Round-wheel compound bows revolutionized hunting archery in 1968. The first such mechanical bows were touted by manufacturers to shoot lighter-weight arrows at incredible arrow speeds. Those first bows did not quite live up to their billing as super-fast-shooting machines, and they were plagued by handle breakage, cable breakage, and other mechanical problems to be

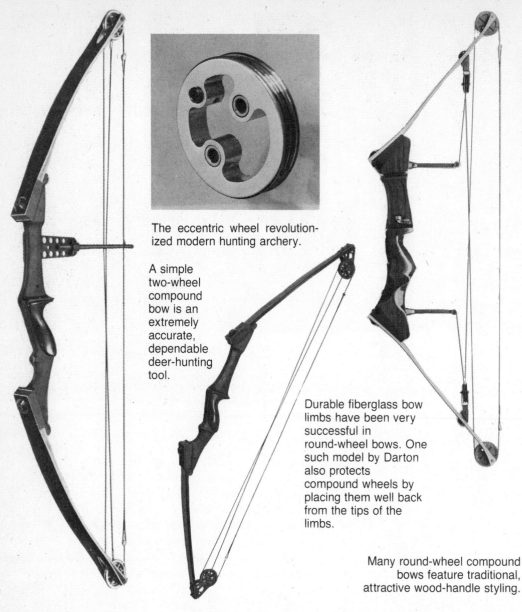

The eccentric wheel revolution-ized modern hunting archery.

A simple two-wheel compound bow is an extremely accurate, dependable deer-hunting tool.

Compound bows are available in both right-hand and left-hand models. This one is a right-hand model and is a so-called four-wheeler, which is ex-tremely fast-shooting but difficult for a begin-ner to tune.

Durable fiberglass bow limbs have been very successful in round-wheel bows. One such model by Darton also protects compound wheels by placing them well back from the tips of the limbs.

Many round-wheel compound bows feature traditional, attractive wood-handle styling.

expected in any brand new product design. However, such bows did indeed increase arrow velocities by an honest 10 percent over the velocities produced by average recurve bows. Compound manufacturers im-proved their wares over the next few years, ironing out the bugs and increasing arrow speed even more through subtle design alterations. By the mid-1970s, the round-wheel compound bow was the primary choice of serious deer-hunting archers—a bow that had proven itself to be a dependable performer in a wide variety of deer-hunting situations.

Basically, the first round-wheel compounds looked much the way they do today. They consisted of a fairly long wooden or metal handle section with relatively short, stubby bow limbs on either end. They offered the unique advantage of poundage adjustment over a 10- or 15-pound range, allowing a deer hunter to set his bow for a comfortable draw weight that yielded excellent accuracy. The early compound bows varied somewhat in appearance, physical weight, and exact mechanical

function, but they all provided several unique advan-tages never before enjoyed by deer-hunting archers.

Aside from poundage variation in a single bow, round-wheel compounds "let off" in draw weight at full draw to ease holding weight on shoulder muscles and bowstring fingers as a hunter aimed to shoot. For example, a 60-pound compound bow produced a full 60 pounds of bowstring pressure on the fingers at about half draw, but eased off in string pressure at full draw to 30 or 40 pounds. Such 40- or 50-percent draw-weight let-offs at full draw created a strange feel when a hunter, used to a recurve bow, first picked up a round-wheel compound and drew it back. However, archers quickly came to enjoy and appreciate the easy string-holding traits of the compound. Such bows al-lowed accurate shooting with minimal monthly practice and yielded somewhat flatter arrow flight than pro-duced by recurve bows of comparable draw weight.

Today, the round-wheel compound bow is still the favorite of most serious deer hunters. This design has

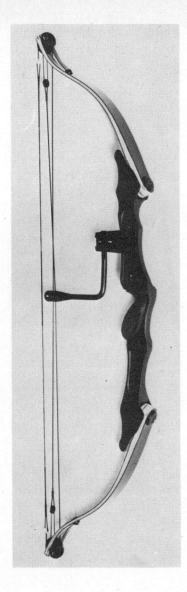

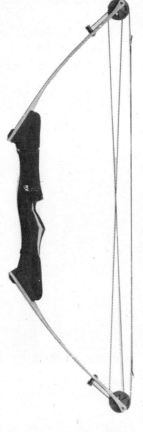

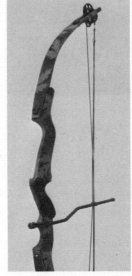

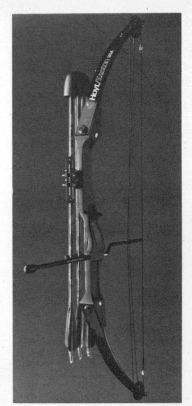

A few two-wheel bows feature draw length adjustment with the turn of small bolts on the limbs near the wheels.

(Below) Some factory compound bows are available in full attractive hunting camouflage. This one is sold by Pro Line.

Compound bows take many forms. This bow by Golden Eagle has recurving limbs and a dog-leg shaped cable guard.

The Hoyt/Easton Pro Hunter is a state-of-the-art two-wheel deer-hunting bow. This model features quick, simple shooting design; light carrying weight; full draw-weight adjustability; a low, out-of-the-way cable guard; and tapped holes to accept a bow stabilizer, bowsight, and bow quiver.

been perfected to the point where defects are rare and mechanical problems are something seldom encountered. Many round-wheel designs are seen on archery-shop racks, but most of these are simple, two-wheel bows that look quite similar to recurve bows in basic shape aside from the wheels on the limb-tips and the cables connecting these wheels together. Some such "two-wheelers" have wooden handles, some metal handles; some have so-called cable guards to hold cables away from arrows and to mute cable strum during shots; some have metal-alloy wheels, and some durable plastic wheels. Some are shorter than others; some lighter in overall weight; and some slightly faster or slower about casting an arrow. Some have wheels mounted inside notched-out limbs, and some have wheels attached to separate metal brackets. However, all such bows by reputable manufacturers are fine, well-made deer-hunting tools with a reputation for being quiet, dependable, and very, very accurate. The best have all the optional features a deer hunter needs

in a first-rate field bow (to be discussed later in this chapter).

Here are some general features to look for in a round-wheel deer-hunting bow. First, it should measure about 45 or 50 inches long from tip to tip. Any bow shorter than this will pinch your fingers with the string at full draw unless you use a mechanical bowstring release (bowstring releases are discussed in Chapter 5). Such string pinch can significantly degrade shooting accuracy.

Round-wheel compound bows with wood-and-fiberglass laminated bow limbs tend to shoot faster than such bows with solid fiberglass limbs. However, during the past few years the aerospace industry has made great strides in the manufacture of quality fiberglass, and some top round-wheel bows now carry solid-glass limbs instead of the more conventional laminated limbs. Fiberglass limbs are more durable than laminated limbs, more dependable in unusually wet weather, and close enough in speed-producing characteristics not to make a noticeable difference afield. Bows with solid fiberglass limbs are heavier to lug around than those with laminated limbs—a disadvantage in the minds of some. In times past a bow with solid glass limbs was considered second-rate by serious archers, but this is definitely not the case today.

The most versatile round-wheel compound bows available today allow a certain amount of draw-length adjustment to let a hunter experiment with slight variations in draw length which might or might not help his shooting comfort and accuracy. Such adjustment normally requires the shortening or lengthening of bow cables or threading these cables through different slots in compound wheels. Ask your archery dealer about this and other special features.

There are other deer-hunting bows on the horizon today, including compound cam-bows. However, it's tough to beat the basic round-wheel compound bow for shooting comfort, accuracy, and durable dependability. This design is without a doubt the most practical for most modern deer-hunting archers.

Compound Cam-Bows

The compound cam-bow is the latest brainchild of modern archery manufacturers. This bow looks a lot like a round-wheel, two-wheel compound bow except that conventional wheels have been replaced by egg-shaped cams. Such cams store more energy in bow limbs than regular wheels—energy which is transferred to the arrow during a shot in the form of faster arrow speed and/or deeper penetrating power in game.

The primary selling point of the cam-bow in deer-hunting circles is the fact that it shoots arrows an average of 10 to 20 percent faster than a conventional round-wheel compound bow. A hunting arrow flying at 220 to 240 fps can theoretically simplify hitting open-country deer like caribou and mule deer because it requires less precise range estimation to prevent high or low hits. However, the flat arrow trajectory produced by a cam-bow does not come for free, and many such bows currently have more disadvantages associated with them than a sensible deer hunter might wish to put up with. The increased arrow penetration in deer that a cam-bow provides is not a significant advantage because conventional round-wheel bows penetrate exceedingly well in the biggest moose that ever walked, when coupled with the proper broadhead-tipped arrows tuned up to fly with perfection.

At present, the compound cam-bow has the following disadvantages a potential buyer should seriously consider: First, cam-bows require considerably more physical power to draw, taxing muscles and making pinpoint shooting more difficult. Second, cam-bows tend to be significantly noisier to shoot than round-wheel bows because excess limb energy vibrates the limbs, cables, bowstring, and handle riser. Such noise can be an irritation to the shooter and can scare the

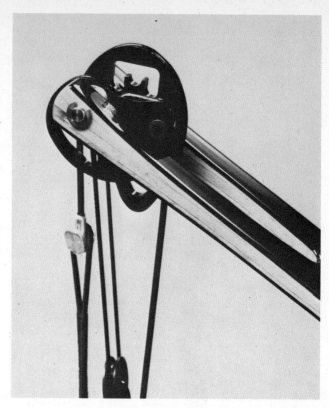

An oblong cam produces higher compound arrow speed than a traditional round compound wheel.

(Opposite page) At their best, compound cam-bows are sleek, streamlined hunting bows. These handsome Hoyt/ Easton Impalas are aptly named after the trim African antelope. ▶

beejesus out of deer. Third, cam-bows are potentially less accurate than round-wheel bows because their increased arrow speed makes arrow flight less stable. This is especially true when arrows are tipped by hunting broadheads. Fourth, cam-bows are currently less dependable than round-wheel bows because cables, bowstrings, and bow limbs tend to break under the tremendous pressures exerted by the egg-shaped cams. These particular strain-related problems are currently being worked out by manufacturers in the form of stronger cables, solid-fiberglass limbs, heavier bowstrings, etc. However, at present a cam-bow is not the dependable tool many serious deer hunters require on a long hunt afoot or a serious sit on stand.

Cam-bow enthusiasts are quick to point out that manufacturers are working on the bugs in this design. However, until the cam-bow proves itself to be dependable and quiet as well as fast, many serious hunters are continuing to stick by compounds with round instead of egg-shaped pulleys attached to the ends of limbs.

For deer hunters who already own cam-bows or like the thought of a bow that can produce more penetrating energy, such bows can be used quite effectively on deer if properly set up. At their best, cam-bows should

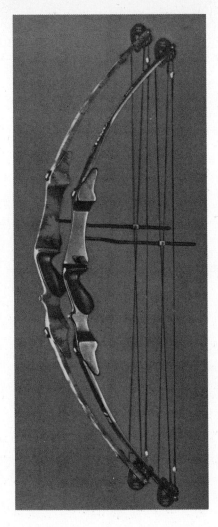

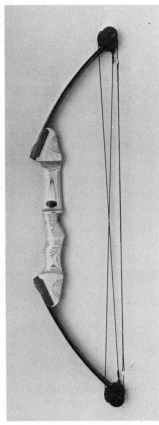

This top-of-the-line Martin cam-bow features an attractive laminated-maple handle riser plus cable guard, draw-weight adjustment, and attachment holes for a bowsight.

(Left) A lightweight, bare-bones compound cam-bow shot without sights can be an exceptionally quick-handling deer-hunting bow.

be used with very heavy arrows which absorb limb power most efficiently and penetrate deeply downrange. Such power can definitely help kill big deer like moose and elk that have been hit with poor shots that nick large bones or rake an animal from behind. Heavy arrows also quiet down a cam-bow considerably and reduce the chance of limb, cable, or bowstring failure by slowing down the speed at which these bow parts move.

Overdraw Bows

Another hunting-bow design commonly seen today is the overdraw bow which shoots a shorter-than-normal arrow at extremely high speed. Again, this design is meant primarily to flatten out arrow trajectory, thus making hitting animals easier at unknown distances.

Most overdraw hunting bows are simply conventional round-wheel compounds or compound cam-bows with arrow-rest carriages attached which sit behind the handle riser of a bow. This allows the shooting of a short, lightweight arrow that literally sizzles toward the target. A few unique forward-handle overdraw bows are designed especially for shooting truncated arrows.

Typically, an overdraw bow allows an average-sized man who would normally draw a 29- or 30-inch arrow to draw an arrow 24 or 25 inches long. This cuts down arrow weight and produces arrow speeds up to 10 or 15 percent above normal.

The overdraw bow has its deer-hunting fans, but like the cam-bow, this design has some serious deficiencies hunters should at least consider. Foremost is the fact that bow-shooting accuracy suffers anytime an arrow rides across a rest situated behind the grip of a bow. Such a rest placement amplifies rest torque during a shot, which in turn disrupts an arrow's flight as it leaves a bow by launching it off an unstable, moving rest. Secondary problems with overdraw bows include greater shooting noise associated with any ultra-light arrow and the somewhat unstable, touchy arrow flight that always accompanies arrow speeds much above 200 feet per second. Overdraw bows also tend to have a higher incidence of cable, limb, and bowstring failure because less limb energy is directly transferred to the arrow and more energy courses through the bow itself in the form of high-speed vibration.

One of the most practical applications of the overdraw bow is when bowhunters have extremely long

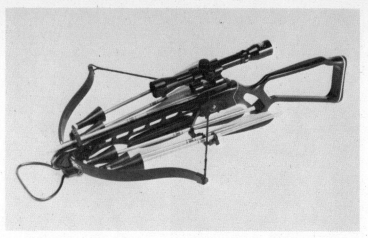

Some crossbows are particularly suited to hunting, like the quiver-attached line by Barnett International.

The unique-looking Martin Jaguar overdraw bow produces sizzling arrow speed because it shoots short, lighter-than-normal shafts.

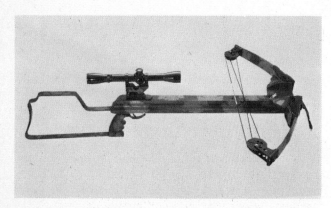

(Above and below) Crossbows come with traditional wooden stocks or lighter-weight skeletonized stocks, and some come fully camouflaged.

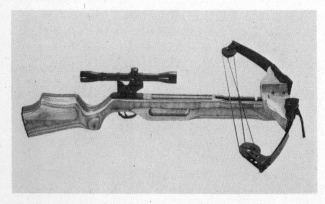

arms and correspondingly long draw lengths. In a few cases, such fellows cannot buy arrows long enough to draw in a normal bow, and in any event an overdraw bow allows such hunters to shoot shorter, lighter arrows that fly with normal trajectory instead of arching through the air like logs.

Let me point out here that some of my normal-sized bowhunting friends shoot overdraw bows with very good results. However, these pals are consciously and deliberately sacrificing quiet, accurate dependability in a deer bow in favor of flat trajectory. For open-country hunting when range estimation is difficult, such a tradeoff makes sense to some deer hunters.

Crossbows

Although not normally considered sporting in hardcore bowhunting circles, shoulder-shot crossbows with regular scope sights and rifle-like triggers are legal deer-hunting bows in several American states and Canadian provinces. Such bows shoot ultra-short arrows (called bolts) at extremely fast speeds with flat trajectories unequalled by conventional hand-drawn archery equipment.

Crossbows are in a hunting class all their own and are not particularly popular with the North American deer-hunting public. However, there is a certain fascination associated with shooting such "string guns," and if such shooting appeals to you, check your local deer-hunting regulations. Several reputable manufacturers sell top-notch hunting crossbows, including a few with extra-fast compound wheels and cables instead of more traditional recurving limbs. When properly set up and sighted in, such bows are extremely accurate out to 100 yards or more.

Special-Purpose Bows

In addition to normal adult hunting bows designed for deer and other big game, bow manufacturers also make other bows to meet individual needs. Among

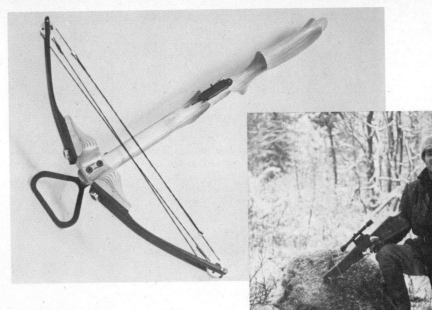

Hunting crossbows take many configurations, from recurves to round-wheel compounds with open or scope sights.

Crossbow hunting is legal in several states and Canadian provinces, and seems to be enjoying increased popularity today.

these are special scaled-down kids' bows, do-it-yourself kit bows, and extra-heavy draw-weight bows for the muscle-men among us who like the power and solid feel of bows drawing well over 70 pounds.

Both recurve bows and compound bows are available for junior deer hunters—quality shooting tools that are simply smaller and lighter in weight to match a youngster's weaker muscles and diminutive physical structure. Such bows are normally priced economically to match the short-term use they are likely to get.

The hobbyist might prefer to assemble and finish a deer-hunting bow himself. Several manufacturers offer recurve and compound-bow kits to satisfy the craftsman who takes pride in putting personal attention into his shooting equipment. Such bow kits are also less expensive than ready-made bows, a solid plus for an economy-minded hunter with the time to finish off a bow himself.

Special "elephant bows" with extra-heavy draw weights can be special-ordered by fellows with picnic-ham arms and drawing power to match. Shooting a 90-pound compound bow on deer definitely flattens

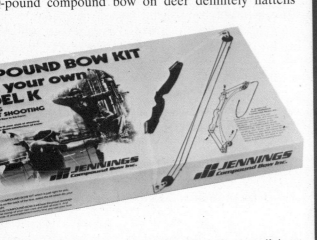

Compound bow kits are very popular with do-it-yourself deer hunters who want to save money and assemble a bow themselves.

Abbreviated hunting bows for kids are available through several companies, and can often be purchased in kits complete with armguard, finger glove, target quiver, target, arrows, and instructional manual. This little Bionic Ben is sold by Ben Pearson Archery.

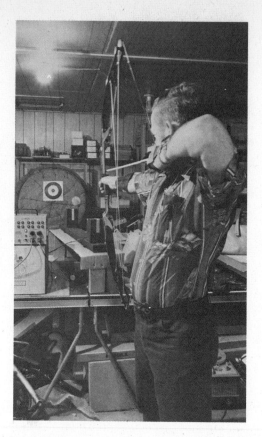

(Right) Chronographing bows to determine arrow speed can be fun, but raw arrow speed is not nearly as important in deer hunting as several other shooting factors.

(Left) For the strong-armed deer hunter, extra-heavy-draw "elephant bows" are sold by various archery companies.

arrow trajectory and increases penetrating ability in flesh, and a few beefy hunters can shoot such a bow with adequate deer-hunting accuracy. This and other custom features on hunting bows are something every archer should investigate prior to choosing a deer-hunting bow.

Notes on Bow Speed

I feel it's important to note here that bow manufacturers have always tended to stress the ability of a bow to shoot arrows fast over all other considerations. Shooting speed may indeed be the most graphic way to compare a bow with its competitors, but I believe the speed-mania drummed up by some bow manufacturers to promote their wares has been decidedly detrimental to the accurate, effective bowhunting of deer. This is not the fault of manufacturers alone, either. The American shooting public seems to have a strong appetite for projectile speed, just as the American driving public is totally fascinated by a fast, snappy automobile. Manufacturers capitalize on such appetites, but consumers are the ones who largely dictate what manufacturers produce and promote.

What most bowhunters do not realize is the indisputable fact that raw arrow speed and accurate arrow flight are almost always incompatible. An arrow traveling above 200 feet per second tends to become more and more unstable in flight as travel speed goes up—arrow vibrations against a bow increase as speed increases; any shooting mistakes an archer makes tend to be amplified; and the addition of a deer-hunting broad-

head to the front of an arrow makes high-speed shooting even more inaccurate.

The one plus of fast arrow speed is flat trajectory, but there are relatively few instances when the flatter trajectory of a 230 fps hunting arrow will make a notable difference in hitting accuracy over a more moderate 200 fps hunting arrow. The majority of deer are shot by archers at under 40 yards, and most whitetail deer are shot at under 30 yards. At such ranges, slightly flatter arrow trajectory is largely a waste of time.

It would be nice to see the bow-shooting public reevaluate its thirst for arrow speed. It is far more practical and far more productive in the deer woods to stress accurate arrow flight, bow dependability, quiet shooting, and clean, aesthetic bow lines. Reasonably fast arrow speed is certainly important in deer hunting, but not at the expense of exact arrow placement, trouble-free bow performance, near-silent shooting at game, and traditional, functional bow design. It is better to pick an average-speed deer bow that has a reputation for being an "old faithful" rather than buying a souped-up shooting machine that scatters arrows, sounds like a bucket of bolts, and blows up as you draw on the best buck you've seen all year!

Hunting-Bow Features to Consider

No matter what basic hunting-bow style you decide to use on deer, you should look for certain standard features that will probably make your hunting life easier. The following discussion does not apply to hunting crossbows, which are completely unique, special-purpose items.

Every good deer bow besides a longbow has a threaded stabilizer hole in the front of the handle riser a few inches below the grip. Some hunters use a short, stubby bow stabilizer and some do not, but it's nice to have this option in case a stabilizer promises to improve your shooting accuracy.

All reputable hunting bows also have handle sections drilled and tapped to accept bowsights and a bow-attached arrow quiver. The mounting holes for bowsights are normally on the off-side of the handle riser opposite the sight window area. Bow-quiver mounting holes are found in various places, depending on the bow manufacturer and the quiver recommended for a particular hunting bow.

Adjustable poundage within a 10- or 15-pound range is standard with all modern compound bows and should be expected in any potential purchase. Such draw-weight adjustment ensures accurate arrow flight and also lets a shooter find the draw weight that is most comfortable for him to shoot. Adjustable draw length is another desirable feature in a compound hunting bow, but not as essential as adjustable draw weight.

Some, but not all, good-quality hunting bows feature a selection of removable grip shapes to ensure comfortable, accurate shooting. Although not a requirement in a deer-hunting bow, many archers like to experiment with bow grips to find a combo that feels particularly good. In addition, some bows can be fitted with optional foam-rubber grips to help keep shooting hands warm in excessively cold deer-hunting weather. This particu-lar feature is especially necessary on metal-handle bows because metal is considerably colder to grip than wood in sub-freezing temperatures. Ask your archery dealer about hunting-bow models with replaceable custom grips.

Another option some modern bow makers offer is a camouflage bow finish instead of conventional solid, shiny limb and handle colors. A hunter can camouflage any bow himself with dull-surfaced bow paint or tape, but many commercial camo bows are extremely functional and very attractive to boot. The factory finish on your bow should not be an overriding choice consideration, but factory camouflage might be an option you'll want to consider to eliminate a do-it-yourself camouflaging job.

Other Considerations

A major key to shooting a bow accurately is matching your bow to your master or dominant shooting eye. Most right-handed people have a right master eye, and most left-handed people have a left master eye. However, a surprising number of shooters have master eyes opposite their favored hands. In order to shoot a bow with decent accuracy, a hunter must use a bow that lines up with his master eye. In cases where right-handed people have left master eyes or left-handed people have right master eyes, it is always best for the right-handers to shoot left-hand bows and the left-handers to shoot right-hand bows. Holding the bow-string with the off-hand will always feel awkward at first, but it is the only way to line up an opposite master eye with the arrow and the bowstring. Any left-handed,

(Right) Draw-weight adjustment bolts near the bow-limb butts are standard on all best-quality hunting compound bows.

Some first-rate compound-bow designs can be fitted with several different grip shapes to satisfy any archer's personal shooting druthers.

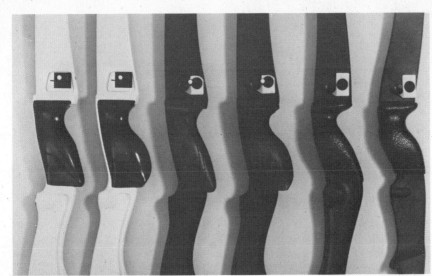

(Left) Be sure to determine your master eye prior to buying any deer-hunting bow by pointing at a distant object with your finger.

The yardstick-against-the-throat method of determining your draw length is very accurate and can be used alone.

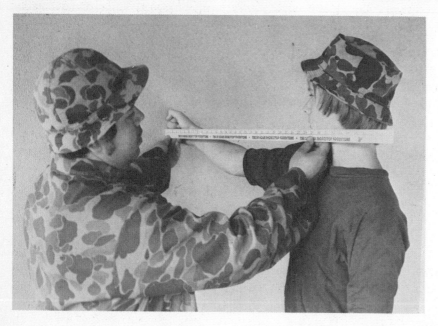

The knuckles-on-the-wall method of determining draw length is especially accurate if you have a friend to help.

right-eyed person can quickly learn to shoot a bow right-handed, and any right-handed, left-eyed person can quickly learn to shoot a bow left-handed. Do not make the mistake of buying a left-hand or right-hand bow based on your dominant hand—the more important thing is which of your *eyes* is dominant.

To determine your dominant or master eye, simply point your finger at a distant object *with both eyes open*. Close one eye and then the other while continuing to point. The eye that lines up with your finger and the object you're pointing at is your master eye.

When buying a hunting bow, always match the bow to your master eye. If you are right-eyed according to the pointing-finger test, buy a right-hand bow. If you are left-eyed, buy a left-hand bow. It is as simple as that.

A few bowhunters shoot bows opposite their master eyes. In order to do this accurately, they must close their master eye to forcibly line up the weaker eye with the arrow and the target. Closing an eye in this manner works okay in some cases, but invariably hampers a hunter's ability to judge distance and ruins his depth perception. It's far more effective to shoot a bow at deer with both eyes open, so it's best to match a bow to your master eye.

All compound bows must be purchased with wheels or cams of the proper size to drop off in draw weight at your proper draw length. To determine this draw length prior to buying a bow, simply place a yardstick against the base of your throat with arms and fingertips outstretched parallel to the ground. The distance from your throat to the tip of your middle finger will be your proper draw length. An alternate method of determining draw length is standing upright at right angles to a wall with your clenched fist against the wall. Turn your head to face the wall in this position and have a friend measure the distance from the wall by your fist to the corner of your mouth. The fist-against-the-wall method of measuring draw length requires two people but yields an especially accurate draw-length measurement.

You must choose a deer-hunting bow that matches your draw length, and you must also choose a bow of the proper draw weight to handle the size of deer you intend to pursue. Every deer hunter must settle on a specific draw weight that is most comfortable and most accurate for him to shoot, but he must also choose a bow that conforms to accepted draw-weight categories

Recommended Hunting Bow Draw Weights

		Deer Being Hunted					
		Blacktail Deer	Mule Deer	Whitetail Deer	Caribou	Elk	Moose
Draw Weight	40–50	X					
	50–60	X	X	X	X		
	60–70	X	X	X	X	X	
	70–80	X	X	X	X	X	X

for particular deer. The heavier-draw the bow, the deeper the arrows it shoots will penetrate in animals, and since different deer species grow to different sizes, a certain amount of weight-matching must occur for best results on game. A 40-pound bow will neatly kill a moose if the arrow happens to slip between the ribs, but a hunter can definitely be under-bowed for a particular kind of deer in particular circumstances. Study the accompanying draw-weight chart for recommendations on most effective bow weights for various kinds of deer.

Choosing a proper hunting bow is one of the most important steps in successfully preparing for deer season. When carefully selected, such a bow will yield maximum shooting pleasure and optimum success in the field!

2/Bow Accessories

THERE ARE several bow accessories which have become standard equipment with serious deer hunters around the country. Some are absolutely necessary to the accurate, effective shooting of a bow, and others are simply aids that have gained widespread popularity because they work well and enhance a hunting archer's shooting performance. A deer hunter is always best advised to keep his bow-attached accessories to a practical minimum to ensure simple and reliable shooting, but most of the following items are found on the bows of the country's most successful archery deer hunters. A few of the optional accessories described here might not appeal to you, but chances are you'll end up using most of them within a short time after you begin seriously bowhunting deer. All have stood the test of time, and most are apt to help you fill the freezer.

Bowsights

Bowsights were once scorned by traditional shooters of longbows and recurve hunting bows. Today, a bowsight is generally considered an essential part of every serious deer hunter's gear. There is no question that they help the vast majority of hunters hit what they aim at, be it targets or real live animals. In almost every official target-archery competition held, archers without bowsights are placed in a separate shooting class to prevent sight shooters from trouncing them thoroughly. That bowsights are potentially more accurate than no sights at all is really not even a debatable matter.

Most traditional modern-day longbow shooters do not use bowsights because they prefer the added challenge of shooting without such "new-fangled" aids. Some long-time recurve users also refrain from screwing, bolting, or taping sights to their bows, because either they're accustomed to shooting without sights, or they feel bowsights are not aesthetically appealing. I know a few compound shooters who also shoot "bare-bow" instead of using sights, because either they are too far-sighted to clearly see sights, or they have developed bad sight-shooting habits like freezing below the target (a phenomenon often called target panic) or jerking their sights across the target (often called pass-shooting). For such people, bowsights may not be the best way to aim at deer, but I believe it's safe to say that 19 out of every 20 bowhunters would be better off using some sort of bowsight to aim at targets and deer.

There are nearly as many bowsight designs on the market as there are variations in hunting bows. These run the gamut from simple, solid one-pin models, to complex and fragile sights with dozens of moving parts and worthless attachments.

The most popular bowsights for deer, and the ones I would recommend, attach solidly to a bow with screws or bolts and are made of sturdy metal or plastic with four, five, or six strong sight pins or aiming reticles. Bowsights for hunting vary considerably in configuration, and as long as pins or crosswires for different distances are easily adjustable, solidly locked in place, and mounted on a sturdy frame that cannot be easily bent or moved, a hunter cannot go very far wrong.

Most deer hunters attach their sights to the front of a bow to give them better sight definition or clarity as they aim at a target or animal. However, some nimrods place sights behind the handle because this sight area is better protected during rough-and-tumble use.

My favorite bowhunting sight is a typically good design. It attaches to the side of a bow with two stout Allen-head screws. The frame is made of sturdy aircraft aluminum, anodized to a dull, attractive black coloration. Two separate pin slides allow tight clustering of distance pins on a flat-shooting bow, and four strong, round-headed brass distance pins, fully adjustable for elevation and windage, come standard with this sight. Extra sight pins are sold separately, and I use a total of six pins set at 10-yard increments between 20 and 70

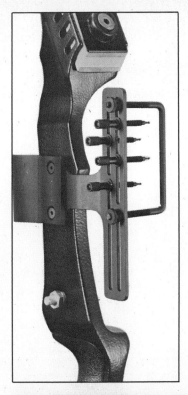

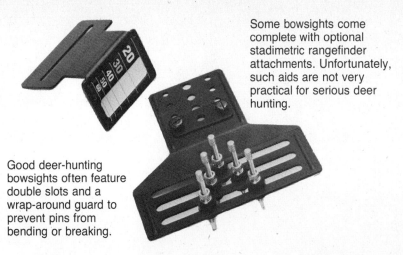

Some bowsights come complete with optional stadimetric rangefinder attachments. Unfortunately, such aids are not very practical for serious deer hunting.

Good deer-hunting bowsights often feature double slots and a wrap-around guard to prevent pins from bending or breaking.

Manufacturers are always trying to better help bowhunters estimate shooting range. This "trigger sight" was supposed to zero in on a deer's body size and move sights to compensate. It is now discontinued.

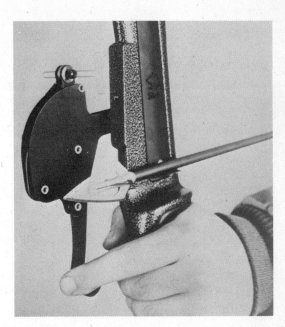

Bohning Glow-Ring bowsight pins are highly visible in low-light shooting situations to improve a deer hunter's odds.

yards. In addition, these pins are protected from most bumps to the front of my bow by a sturdy wrap-around pin guard. This is a typically good deer-hunting design.

Some bowsights have built-in rangefinding attachments of one sort or another to theoretically help a bowhunter get his deer. Although interesting to experiment with, I've found that most integral bowsight rangefinders are next to worthless in the majority of hunting situations. It is far more practical to use a separate belt-carried rangefinder to zero-in on the range.

One innovation worthy of mention here is the light-up or night-glow bowsight pin which either lights up with the aid of a small battery or chemically glows in the dark. Any bowhunter who has tried to aim at a late-moving whitetail buck or bull elk in dense, low-light mountain timber will fully appreciate the advantages this type of sight pin can offer. In extremely dim light, deer are sometimes difficult or impossible to aim at without a highly visible, brightly glowing bowsight

pin. Most bowhunters have only one such pin on their bows—usually the 20-yard pin. At longer shooting ranges, they hold high for dead-center hits on game.

Sophisticated Arrow Rests

Traditional longbowmen of yesteryear often rested the arrow across their knuckles or the upraised index finger of their bow hand. Later on, recurve users normally laid their arrows across bushy "rugs" glued to the wide wooden arrow-shelf sections of their bows. Today, bowhunters who emphasize accurate shooting rely on far more sophisticated arrow-rest designs with spring-loaded arms and buttons to cushion an arrow shaft as it launches out of a bow. The result is superior accuracy when such rests are properly used.

An arrow rest consists of a shelf that the bottom of the arrow rests upon, and a plate which the side of the arrow rests against. Such a rest theoretically gives a shaft accurate guidance as the bowstring comes taut and the arrow sizzles on its way.

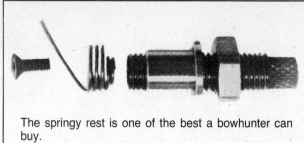

The springy rest is one of the best a bowhunter can buy.

Two common rests seen on deer-hunting bows from the factory are the springy rest (left) and a less desirable flexible plastic shelf combined with a solid screw-adjustable plate section (right).

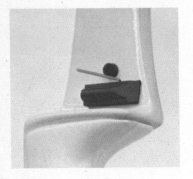

The ultra-accurate flipper rest holds a hunting arrow on a spring-loaded arm that flips out of the way as arrow fletching passes by during a shot.

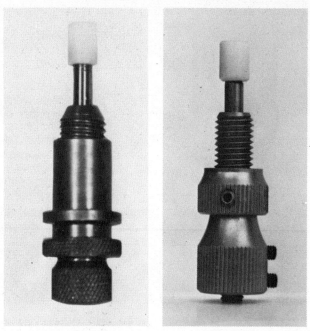

(Left and right) Cushion plunger arrow-rest plates screw into a bow and offer full adjustment in tuning arrows of various spines or stiffnesses.

Unfortunately, most hunting bows come equipped with el cheapo one-piece rests made of rubber or plastic—rests which are non-adjustable and are prone to producing dismal shooting accuracy at best. Even the most expensive deer-hunting bows on the market generally appear on archery-store racks with second-rate rests attached. Bow manufacturers often cut corners here and there to boost their profit margin, and one such corner is usually the arrow rest slapped on a bow at the factory. If your hunting bow has a one-piece rubber or plastic rest without arrow-plate adjustment, do yourself a favor and throw the rest away.

There are three adequate arrow-rest designs used by deer-hunting archers. The least durable and least desirable of the three is some sort of flexible plastic, rubber, or nylon rest arm which attaches near the threaded arrow-plate hole in a good-quality hunting bow. Such a rest arm is normally coupled with a solid, screw-adjustable arrow-plate that moves in and out of the bow's arrow-plate hole. Such a semi-rigid rest does not allow fine-tuning of arrow flight and tends to wear out as arrows slide across its surfaces, wearing grooves in the plastic, nylon, or rubber. This slowly changes point of arrow impact and ultimately requires the arrow rest to be replaced. However, a rest of this sort is adjustable in the plate and semi-flexible in the shelf arm, both of which allow tolerable arrow flight for the casual deer hunter.

The two arrow rests used by virtually all really serious deer hunting bow-benders are the flipper/plunger rest and the springy rest. The flipper/plunger consists of a Teflon-coated shelf arm which flattens out of the way under spring tension when an arrow passes, and a fully adjustable, Teflon-tipped arrow-plate button that plunges in and out to cushion the bending and vibrating arrow as it leaves the bow. The springy rest consists of a single, coiled piece of spring wire shaped to form a spring-cushion plate and a spring-wire shelf. It attaches to a fully adjustable threaded plug that screws in and out of a bow to provide complete

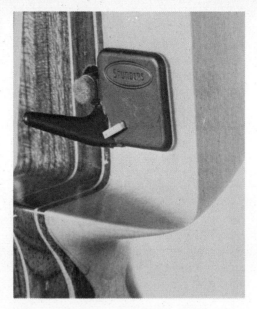

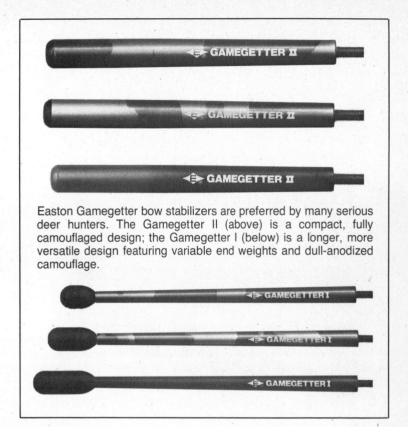

Easton Gamegetter bow stabilizers are preferred by many serious deer hunters. The Gamegetter II (above) is a compact, fully camouflaged design; the Gamegetter I (below) is a longer, more versatile design featuring variable end weights and dull-anodized camouflage.

This practical bowhunting rest by Saunders features a rugged, spring-loaded shelf area and a quiet felt-tipped plate section.

The Easton Vari-Weight stabilizer end weight allows bowhunters full stabilizer-weight versatility.

bow-tuning adjustability. Several spring sizes are available for both the cushion-plunger portions of the flipper/plunger rest and for the springy rest to accommodate any shooting need. Both arrow rests are extremely accurate when correctly installed and adjusted, and both give long service without wearing out or changing point of impact. More on adjusting these rests in the bow-tuning section of this book (Chapter 9).

Bow Stabilizers

A hunting-bow stabilizer is a relatively short, stubby bar that screw-attaches to the front of a bow several inches below the center of the grip. Such a stabilizer can weigh anywhere from a few ounces to a full pound, depending on the manufacturer and designer, but it is meant to accomplish two very important shooting tasks no matter what its exact shape or weight.

First and foremost, a hunting-bow stabilizer lowers a bow's center of gravity and gives it a weight-forward balance that helps prevent accuracy-destroying handle

torque when a hunter releases an arrow. The less a bow torques or twists in a shooter's hand, the less the arrow rest tends to move and throw an arrow off its course. Target archers often use one or more bow stabilizers up to 3 feet long to help their bows remain stationary during the course of a shot—the short, fat hunting-bow stabilizer helps do the same thing without protruding awkwardly to hang up on every tree and bush in sight.

A second important function of the hunting-bow stabilizer is to significantly dampen the vibration noise a bow makes when a shot is taken at game. A stabilizer tends to absorb such vibration and mute the hum any hunting bow makes when the bowstring comes taut and the arrow launches toward the target.

A wide variety of hunting-bow stabilizers are available at archery stores today. A few of these are illustrated here. My personal favorites are the simple 5¼-ounce Easton Game-Getter II stabilizer and the longer Easton Game-Getter I stabilizer with modular end weights which can be attached to suit any deer

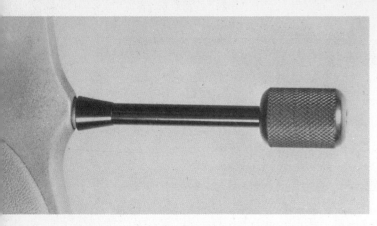

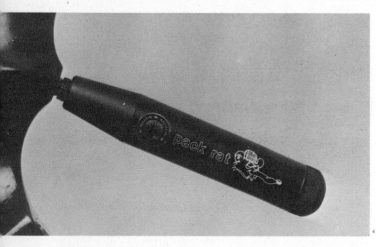

(Above and below) Bow stabilizers come in a wide variety of shapes and weights to suit every shooting taste.

This unique bow stabilizer by Martin is hollow to allow storage of small bowhunting items inside. However, stored items must be tightly packed to prevent rattling.

hunter's needs. One innovative hunting-stabilizer design is hollow to allow an archer to store odds and ends inside. However, this model is prone to rattle like a cupful of pebbles unless the contents are firmly padded with foam rubber, paper, or another vibration-dampening filler.

Bow stabilizers definitely improve shooting accuracy and quiet down a bow, but a fair number of bowhunters do not use this particular accessory because they feel it gets in the way and/or adds muscle-tiring weight to shooting equipment. In addition, a few hunters feel a stabilizer-weighted bow is slower to get into action, especially on moving deer. These are all debatable points, but in any event a hunting-bow stabilizer should be compact to prevent a bow from being awkward and cumbersome to carry. I hunt deer with a stabilizer a fair share of the time and feel this accessory helps my field shooting significantly.

Bow Quivers

Almost all bowhunters use some sort of bow-attached quiver to house their arrows as they move about the field or wait for deer on stand. A bow quiver is only one of several arrow-quiver designs available to deer hunters, but it has proven to be the handiest setup to carry about and pluck arrows from in the heat of the shooting action. Some hunters feel that such a quiver unbalances a bow, and there is no doubt that a bow quiver degrades shooting accuracy at least a little bit when compared to a bow used without any kind of arrow quiver attached. However, all things considered the bow quiver has been a resounding success in the deer woods since its invention over 30 years ago.

Commercial bow quivers vary in basic design and in the way they attach to the side of a hunting bow. However, the majority of good ones hold six or eight hunting arrows close at hand in snug, safe, and quiet fashion.

A deer hunter who decides to use a bow quiver should shop around carefully to find a model that perfectly suits his needs. Eight-arrow bow quivers are the most common ones available and are probably best for the average walking or stand-hunting archer who plans to be afield all day. A quiver holding more than eight arrows can be a solid plus for the fellow backpacking away from roads for several days on end, despite the fact that such a quiver adds considerable weight to the side of a bow. On the flip side of the coin, a morning and evening tree-stand hunter will generally have plenty of arrows if he uses a light, compact bow quiver holding three to five hunting shafts. No matter how many arrows your chosen bow quiver holds, it

(Left) One bowhunting stabilizer allows variable weight by the addition of internal weight collars. A heavy spring inside eliminates stabilizer rattle during a shot.

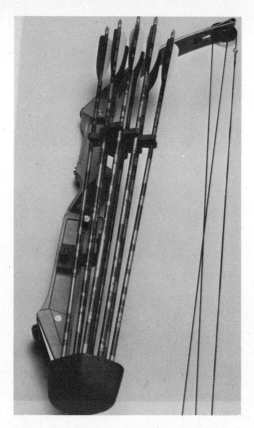

A top-notch bow quiver like this one by Hoyt/Easton features a safe, roomy arrowhead hood, positive rubber arrow grippers, and solid screw-attachment to a bow. The hood and grippers are spread far enough apart to prevent fletching rattle during a shot.

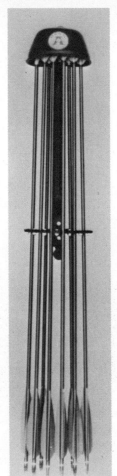

Noise-free bow-quiver hookup is a must for successful bowhunting of deer. This model locks quietly and solidly in place in a second.

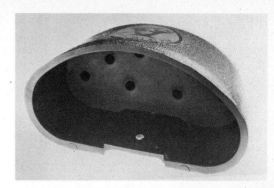

Most bow-quiver hoods hold arrowheads snugly and quietly apart in blocks of dense foam rubber.

At its best, a bow quiver is a compact, lightweight design holding six or eight arrows.

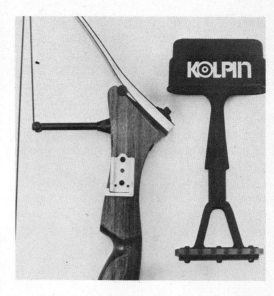

should have several other features to ensure quiet, safe and efficient performance. Here are some tips on choosing such a quiver wisely.

Every bow quiver should have a sturdy protective hood made of plastic, metal, or leather to protect the broadheads from moisture and grime and to protect the hunter from the razor-sharp edges. A few of the early bow quivers did not have a protective cover for the broadheads at all, and the results were many minor and serious cuts for the bowhunters who unfortunately purchased them. Today, most bow quivers have deep arrowhead hoods that fully enclose the large hunting broadheads. These hoods are normally filled with rubber, ethafoam, or other semi-rigid substance that broadheads slide into; they hold the arrows snugly and quietly apart as a hunter moves about the woods and hills. Some rubber or foam quiver-hood inserts have pre-molded holes for arrowheads to slip into; others are solid rubber or foam allowing the hunter to press in the heads wherever he desires.

One thing to consider when looking at bow-quiver hoods is the amount of room they allow for large hunting broadheads. A few otherwise sound quiver designs have hoods too small to hold six or eight deer-hunting broadheads without the broadhead edges grating together and quickly becoming dull.

On the opposite end of the bow quiver is some sort of a clip arrangement designed to firmly hold arrow shafts in place. The vast majority of bow quivers have a row of rubber arrow grippers that shafts press into tightly and quietly until they are plucked free with the flick of a finger. When buying a bow quiver for deer, make sure such arrow grippers indeed hold shafts quietly and securely to prevent shaft-to-shaft rattle, shaft-to-quiver clanking, or shafts from actually falling out. You do not want to make any unnecessary noises in the hunting field.

On the best bow quivers, the quiver hood and the rubber arrow grippers are between 12 and 24 inches apart to prevent the fletching from noisily rattling or rustling together during a shot. Most good bow quivers also fan the fletching ends of arrows slightly outward from the hood to give good clearance between them. There is nothing more frustrating than a bow quiver that mashes fletching; it is invariably noisy and mats or distorts the shape of the plastic vanes or feathers.

Modern bow quivers attach to bows in a variety of ways. A few attach in a semi-permanent fashion with bolts, screws, or tape, but most are quickly detachable to let a hunter store his quiver separately with arrows still in it or to remove the quiver from his bow when sitting in a tree stand with close-hugging foliage. The common misconception that a detachable bow quiver lets a hunter practice shooting without a quiver, put his quiver in place to hunt on foot, and then detach it whenever he so desires on stand is just that—a misconception. A bow tuned to shoot *without* a bow quiver should *never* be shot *with* a quiver, and a bow tuned to shoot *with* a quiver should never be shot *without* the quiver in place. Haphazardly attaching and detaching a bow quiver invariably ruins shooting accuracy, and is one of the main reasons archers miss shots at deer.

A few good bow quivers have additional features that might appeal to you. One quiver currently on the market can be attached to the bow at a backward angle, which provides a "quick-draw" capability if a second or third shot is required. Another can be mounted higher or lower on a bow to suit a hunter's personal arrow-grabbing needs.

No matter what its basic construction, a bow quiver must attach solidly to a bow to prevent game-spooking quiver-to-bow rattle during a shot. The best quiver/bow hookups are two-point arrangements that hold the quiver firmly in place.

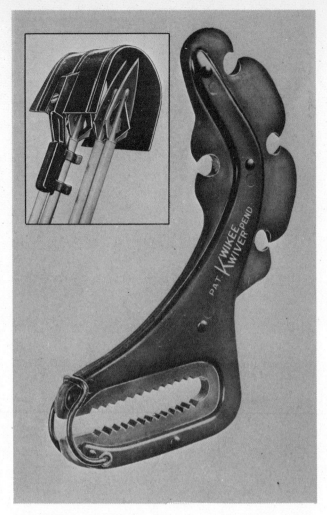

Kwikee Kwiver sells this inexpensive but safe four-arrow hood (inset)/arrow-gripper combo with budget-conscious deer hunters in mind.

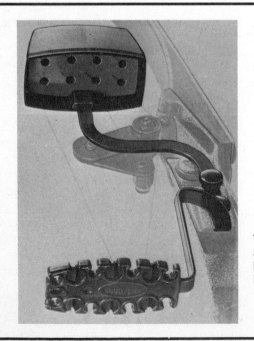

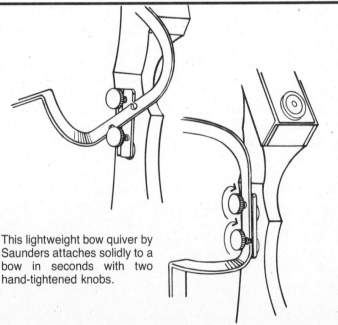

This lightweight bow quiver by Saunders attaches solidly to a bow in seconds with two hand-tightened knobs.

Spare Bowstrings and Bowstringers

Every new hunting bow comes complete with a durable Dacron bowstring. Though it will generally last for at least a year of regular shooting on targets and game, a serious hunter should always have at least one spare bowstring handy in case the original breaks or frays. Although a few bowhunters prefer to make their own from scratch, a spare factory-made bowstring costs just a few dollars and is every bit as dependable as the homemade kind.

When selecting a spare, make sure it is the same length as the original bowstring and has the same number of strands. If well-chosen, the spare will shoot the same as the original if, when put on the bow, it is left under tension to stretch to full length, and then set up with nocking point to ensure consistent arrow nocking. Nocking points are described later in this chapter.

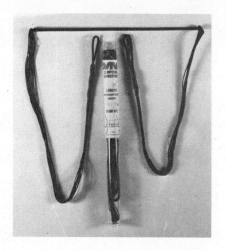

One popular bow quiver has a handy broadhead-tightening wrench molded into its plastic quiver hood.

Top-quality replacement bowstrings are available through many archery companies.

Every bow design requires some sort of bowstringer to aid in the replacement of a string. Many old-timers string their longbows and recurve bows by hand, but this method sometimes results in damaged bow limbs and/or personal injury to shooters when hands slip and bows go flying. A much better way to string and unstring longbows and recurves is a simple, inexpensive rope stringer with leather limb-tip cups on both ends.

All compound bows require a bowstringing tool for quick, easy removal and installation of strings. Different kinds of compound bowstringers are available to accommodate different bow models, so be sure you match your particular compound with the proper stringing tool. Discovering that your bowstringing tool won't work on your bow after a string breaks in the woods is very much like having a flat tire on your car and finding out your lug wrench won't fit the wheel nuts.

Bowstring Peeps and Kisser Buttons

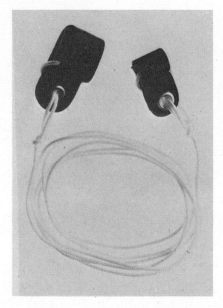

A bowstringing tool is absolutely necessary for replacing bowstrings plus stringing and unstringing recurve bows and longbows. The rope-type bowstringer shown here is designed for use with recurve bows.

Other bowstring-related accessories that are widely used by deer hunters include bowstring peeps and kisser buttons. A bowstring peep is a small metal or plastic gizmo that bisects the bowstring in exact alignment with your eye when you shoot. The hole in this peep ensures perfect aiming-eye alignment with the string from shot to shot, which in turn leads to superior shooting accuracy. Both hunting peeps and target peeps are available at your archery store—be sure to buy a regular hunting peep because it has a larger aperture to ensure good light transmission to the eye in early morning and late evening. The hole in a hunting peep should be at least ⅛-inch in diameter for clear, low-light visibility, with some hunters enlarging their peeps to this size or bigger with the aid of a hand drill and bit.

Using a bowstring peep takes some getting used to, and it is advised that a beginning archer learn to shoot without such an aid before attaching a peep to his

Target Peep

Hunting Peep

(Above and right) A peep ensures accurate eye alignment with a bowstring. Be sure you buy a regular hunting peep with a large aperture to ensure low-light shooting visibility.

(Left) The best nocking point consists of a clamp-on metal ring with a protective rubber cushion underneath.

bowstring. The primary problem is precise peep rotation during a shot to align the peep-hole with the eye—a skill that takes some time to master. Using a special peep-sight nocking point on the bowstring ensures correct peep rotation, and so does using surgical tubing to tie the peep to the bow. When the tubing stretches taut at full draw, the peep automatically rotates to proper position. Ask your archery dealer about the various bowstring-peep setups you might try for hunting deer.

A kisser button is a small, saucer-shaped piece of plastic that attaches to the bowstring at the point where the string anchors against a hunter's mouth. Such a kisser helps ensure consistent anchoring to the face because a hunter can press the kisser against his lips in the same place every time he draws. Normally

bowhunters don't use kisser buttons unless they anchor under their chins using a mechanical bowstring release (see Chapter 5). A kisser does not work with the conventional finger-in-the-corner-of-the-mouth anchor used by most deer-hunting archers.

Nocking Points and Related Gear

Bowstring peeps and kisser buttons are bowstring options some deer hunters prefer to use. However, a nocking point on the bowstring is not an option at all—it is a necessity for straight shooting.

A nocking point, sometimes called a nock locator, is a raised stop attached to the bowstring which the arrow butts up against during a shot to ensure a clean, consistent launch from the string. Nocking arrows in different places on a bowstring will dramatically change point of impact and will also cause hunting broadheads to dip and dive wildly. Finding the exact location where your nocking point should be attached to the bowstring is covered in Chapter 9. But make no mistake, you'll need a nocking point on the bowstring for sure.

There are several varieties sold at archery stores. Two common types are the clamp-on metal ring or the heat-shrink plastic model. The heat-shrink nocking point snugs about a bowstring when lightly heated with a match. The clamp-on consists of an aluminum ring, lined with rubber to protect the bowstring from abrasion. Although some hunters use heat-shrink nocking

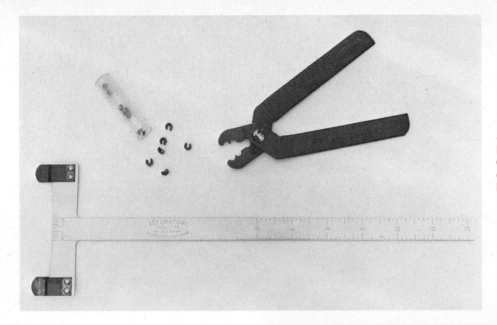

A bow square, nocking-point pliers, and a supply of clamp-on nocking points is essential for do-it-yourself bow tuning.

(Right) A bow square allows accurate placement of the nocking point on the string in relation to the arrow shelf on the bow handle.

(Below) Once a nocking point is placed on the string in correct position, it should be cinched down with nocking-point pliers.

points, the clamp-on variety is by far the most popular because it stays in place better and can be loosened and moved around several times during a bow-tuning session. I would strongly recommend the clamp-on nocking point to serious hunting archers.

Your archery dealer can fully handle nocking-point installation for you, or you can learn to do it yourself. Take a word from the wise and learn to do it yourself. I don't say this because the archery dealer doesn't know his stuff. It is simply that you need this versatility and know-how when you tune your bow for perfect arrow flight, set up new replacement bowstrings, or when you discover loosened nocking points that have moved out of place on the range or in the field.

To be properly set up, you should buy several clamp-on nocking points, an inexpensive pair of

nocking-point pliers to cinch them down, and a bow-string square to precisely measure nocking-point location on the string in relation to the arrow rest on your bow. You'll learn how to use these aids in detail in Chapter 9.

To initially begin shooting your bow on targets, the nocking point should be set about ⅜-inch above square with the arrow rest. The arrow is nocked directly beneath this point. Most factory bows are sold set up this way, but make sure your dealer sets the nocking point before you take your bow home so you can begin working on some bow-shooting basics prior to fine-tuning your bow for ultimate accuracy.

Other Bow-Attached Equipment

In addition to the hunting-bow accessories already discussed, many experienced archers judiciously attach one or more other accessories to their bows that they feel will help them shoot and hunt more effectively. Among the more common optional accessories seen in the field are **bow saddles**, **arrow holders**, and **cable guards.**

A **bow saddle** is a thin, soft piece of leather backed by good-quality, stick-on adhesive. Such a saddle is

A cable guard holds compound bow cables well away from an arrow and also hushes noisy cable strum during a shot.

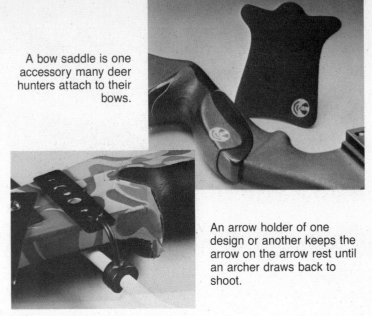

A bow saddle is one accessory many deer hunters attach to their bows.

An arrow holder of one design or another keeps the arrow on the arrow rest until an archer draws back to shoot.

normally affixed to the part of the bow the hand grips during a shot. This leather attachment has two basic functions. In severely cold weather, the leather protects and insulates the hand from an uncomfortably cold plastic or metal grip. In excessively warm weather, the saddle ensures a positive, no-slip grip in a sweaty bow hand. Some bowhunters shoot poorly with bow saddles on their bows because their hands adhere to the leather, and this accentuates accuracy-destroying torque during a shot. Other hunters with steady, non-torquing bow hands use saddles with good results. This particular bow accessory is one every archer must try out for himself.

A bow saddle has one unconventional use which works like a charm when hunting deer. The whole saddle or a smaller piece cut from it can be attached to the flat, hard shelf area of a bow just below the arrow rest. If an arrow accidentally falls off the arrow rest in the heat of the action, this soft leather will mute the sound of arrow colliding with bow and reduce the chance that a deer will hear the boo-boo and hightail it out of the country. Many good deer hunters cover all metal or wooden bow surfaces around an arrow rest to prevent noisy, accidental clanks between arrows and bow.

An **arrow holder** helps prevent a shaft from falling off the rest at an inopportune time. It also eliminates the need for a hunter to physically hold the arrow on the rest with his index finger as he walks around or waits in one place for deer. Hours of holding an arrow on the rest can completely poop out your finger and strain the muscles in your bow hand. Basically, an arrow holder is a small, spring-loaded finger that attaches to the back of a bow's handle in direct line with the arrow. Once an arrow is nocked and placed on the rest, this holder can be bent around and snapped on the shaft to hold it firmly on the rest until an archer draws. At the time of draw, the arrow holder releases from the shaft and snaps silently out of the way to allow an accurate shot. Such a holder is especially handy when a stand hunter wants to be ready to shoot in cold weather but also needs to hang up or lay down his bow and keep his hands buried in warm coat or pants pockets.

A **cable guard** on a compound hunting bow is a simple metal arm that holds the cables well away from the arrow shaft and fletching during a shot. Most good bows that need such a guard come complete with one from the factory, but a few deer hunters find they need to install a guard on a guardless bow to prevent wild, noisy arrow flight caused by the shaft and/or fletching colliding with cables during a shot. If you've shot for a while and suspect cable interference with your arrow, ask your archery or sporting goods dealer about various cable-guard designs.

Additional Bow-Related Gear

As time goes along, a bowhunter accumulates a wide variety of bow-related items he has discovered will help him out. These include Allen-wrench sets and screwdrivers for working on compound bows, oils and greases for lubricating the moving parts on a bow, and dozens of other beneficial accessories. The majority of serious deer hunters store their primary bow accessories and other gear in some sort of fishing tackle box or tool box so such equipment is close at hand in case it is needed to help a shooter out.

A few specific bow accessories are absolutely necessary for decent shooting performance. Several others are extremely popular options used by many successful bowhunters for deer. Carefully consider the bow accessories outlined here and choose wisely for maximum success afield!

Facts About Arrows/3

ALTHOUGH A bow is the single most expensive piece of shooting equipment a deer hunter needs to buy, the arrow he matches to that bow is really far more important to his target accuracy and ultimate success on various kinds of antlered game. A wide variety of bows will shoot arrows well for a particular bowhunter, but only one or two arrow sizes are apt to give him decent results on bull's-eyes and animals. To make matters even more critical, these acceptable arrow sizes must be precisely manufactured to ensure absolute straightness, stiffness, and weight that duplicates true, dead-center flight, arrow after arrow after arrow. A set of hunting arrows will not cost nearly as much as an average-priced hunting bow, but these arrows will generally make or break an archer's ability to hit what he aims at.

A deer-hunting arrow is composed of four basic parts—the shaft, the nock, the fletching, and the arrowhead. These four components must be well chosen and correctly combined to produce a hunting arrow that flies well, lasts long and does a quick, humane job on deer once it hits the mark.

Arrow Shafts

All parts of a hunting arrow must be right to yield the best results. However, the single most important choice in hunting-arrow selection is settling on a shaft of the correct material and size. The wrong shaft will never produce satisfactory shooting results, no matter how hard a bowhunter works on his equipment and his shooting form. The correct shaft can make arrow accuracy a breeze to achieve, even when the bow used might not be the best a nimrod could have chosen.

There are three basic arrow-shaft materials sold today—wood, fiberglass, and aluminum. Within these three materials are a wide variety of grades and sizes, but the first step in choosing a hunting shaft is deciding on one of the three basic materials.

Wood

Wooden shafts were used exclusively by the world's archers until a few short decades ago. They are still shot by a few bowhunters today, but are seldom employed for serious deer-hunting sport. The very best wooden shafts are made of top-grade, straight-grained cedar, logged and milled along the western edge of Oregon. In addition, special-order shafts of dense compressed cedar are also available to those who wish to use them. The primary selling point of cedar shafts is the fact that they are the least expensive to buy. However, this is about the only positive news. Cedar arrow shafts have several drawbacks every bowhunting deer enthusiast should ponder before making a choice.

First, wood is the most fragile of shaft materials, easily broken or splintered upon impact with solid objects like bones, rocks, and trees. Second, cedar is prone to warp and twist in wet weather, even when a hunter takes tender loving care to varnish his shafts and keep them as dry as possible. Cedar shafts are seldom completely straight to begin with, and a little rain or snow plays havoc with hand-picked shafts which seem to be straight.

Durability and lasting straightness are two positive traits cedar shafts do not have. In addition, they vary somewhat in physical weight from shaft to shaft, which in turn reduces arrow accuracy. Even more critical to accuracy is consistent stiffness within a group of shafts. Arrow stiffness is called "spine" by archers, and without consistent spine, arrows will never shoot to the same place. Unfortunately, wood density and flexibility vary considerably even within the same cedar tree, causing wooden shafts to differ significantly in spine.

A final problem with cedar shafts clearly makes them a second-rate choice in no-nonsense bowhunting for deer. This is the fact that a cedar shaft is not even consistent in stiffness completely around its circumference. Wood has grain, and grain is always stiffer when

The aluminum-shaft production facility at Easton Aluminum is a complex but efficient manufacturing operation.

Well-known bowhunters Jim Easton (left) and Joe Johnston are two leading innovators in the arrow-shaft industry, designing the lastest Easton aluminum shaft products for America's deer-hunting archers.

bent one way than another. Hunters can minimize this grain/stiffness problem by gluing on arrow nocks so the edge grain on every shaft rides against the bow. However, all in all, wooden shafts present a world of accuracy and maintenance problems for deer hunters.

Wooden arrow shafts have been used successfully on game for literally thousands of years, and many times more deer have been killed with them than with all the other shaft materials combined. Wood is still the primary shaft material used by traditional longbow shooters, and the arrows shoot with surprisingly good accuracy from these straight-limbed, relatively sluggish shooting tools. However, the faster a bow shoots, the more critical arrow straightness, stiffness, and weight consistency become in terms of accuracy. In the face of faster and faster recurve bows, round-wheel compound bows, compound cam-bows, and overdraw bows which have been produced in recent years, wood has truly become the dinosaur of deer-hunting shaft materials.

Fiberglass

Fiberglass is a much, much better shaft material. Manufacturers of fiberglass bowhunting shafts are using better and better compounds as time goes along —compounds that are stronger and more durable than those which were used in times past.

Fiberglass arrow shafts have the following positive features to consider. They are less expensive than top-grade aluminum arrow shafts. They are not affected at all by moisture, retaining their original straight-

ness level no matter what. They are strong, and as fiberglass enthusiasts point out, they are either straight or broken—no bending in this arrow-shaft material!

Despite its positive traits, fiberglass shafting does incorporate some problems that bother serious archery deer hunters. First, fiberglass is an extremely heavy shaft material, which causes two basic shooting problems: For one, the arrows tend to fly with more arching trajectory than those with aluminum shafts. For another, fiberglass shafts are relatively slow to straighten out once they leave a bow, the heavy ends causing a certain amount of back-and-forth flexing well in front of the bow. This can shed arrow energy to the sides and diminish accuracy as well as penetration on game.

A second drawback of fiberglass shafting is the regrettable fact that it is never perfectly straight, totally consistent in weight, or uniformly stiff completely around its circumference. This is due to the way it is manufactured. Anytime fiberglass is wrapped about a steel mandrel and allowed to set up, the walls of the shaft vary a bit in thickness, and the mandrel throws shafts somewhat out of straight. Variations in fiberglass density and thickness result in shaft weight variations, which in turn lead to slight changes in point of impact. Such deficiencies are not likely noticed by beginning and intermediate bowhunters, but they are there.

Aluminum

According to official studies, over 90 percent of American deer-hunting archers use aluminum shafts

Every aluminum shaft begins as a 1-inch tube of top-quality aluminum stock.

(Above and right) Once drawn down to proper size, aluminum arrow shafts are specially heat-tempered to ensure durability and strength.

All top-grade aluminum deer-hunting shafts are dull-anodized in chemical tanks to ensure good field camouflage and to guard against messy surface oxidation.

(Above and below) The two most popular grades of aluminum bowhunting shafts are 24SRT-X Gamegetter Green and higher-strength XX75 Autumn Orange, Smoke Gray, or Green-and-Black Camo-Hunter.

(Right) Aluminum shafts are incredibly uniform in stiffness within a given size—a uniformity which can be tested on a shaft-spining tool.

for all their serious shooting. There are definite reasons for this. Although top-grade aluminum shafts cost a bit more than the best-grade fiberglass, they are well worth the price to most dedicated hunters. To understand why aluminum shafts are so desirable to shoot, a person must know a few basic facts about how such shafts are manufactured.

An aluminum arrow shaft begins as a 1-inch tube of good-grade material. It is drawn down to size in a series of steps by extremely sophisticated machines that produce an exact, uniform wall thickness and diameter. This also ensures that the arrows are precisely the same physical weight from shaft to shaft. Once the shafts are drawn to exact size, they are heat-tempered to high alloy strength, chemically anodized on the surface to prevent oxidation and to produce a dull, camouflage color, and then individually hand-straightened to perfection on sophisticated shaft straighteners. This complex process results in shafts that are unequalled in straightness and uniformity of weight and stiffness. The result is superb arrow accuracy within a particular aluminum shaft size. All shafts of a given size are the same, and they shoot the same. It is as simple as that.

Aside from pinpoint accuracy and nifty dull-anodized hunting colors, aluminum arrow shafts have other important characteristics in their favor. They are completely waterproof and extremely durable. The best hunting alloys—24SRT-X (Game-Getter Green) and XX75 (Autumn Orange, Smoke Gray, and Black-And-Green Camo)—will take considerable abuse be-

fore bending or breaking and can generally be re-straightened again if a mild bend does occur. In addition, aluminum shafts are available in more hunting sizes than any other shaft material, which translates into total bow-tuning versatility. Multiple shaft choice also allows a hunter to select arrows best suited to particular jobs like deeper-than-normal penetration, extra-flat arrow flight, or unusual durability. At present, there are well over 30 aluminum arrow-shaft sizes suitable for bows of deer-hunting draw weight.

Which arrow shaft you decide on will probably depend on how much money you want to spend. The only practical choices for hunting deer are fiberglass and aluminum, and aluminum clearly offers the most advantages. Some hunters would even argue that aluminum is cheaper than fiberglass because a broken glass shaft is a worthless shaft whereas a bent aluminum shaft can often be salvaged. The ultimate choice is up to you.

Once you decide on a deer-hunting shaft material, the next step is choosing a shaft size to match your draw length and the draw weight of your bow. This is accomplished by consulting a manufacturer's shaft-selection chart. Your archery dealer should have such a chart on hand, and the standard Easton Aluminum Hunting Shaft Selection Chart used by most bowhunters is included in this chapter.

Choosing a proper arrow shaft is no real chore, but remember these helpful hints when making your selection. When choosing among aluminum shaft sizes,

EASTON ALUMINUM HUNTING SHAFT SELECTION CHART

(Most popular size selection is shown in the unshaded area of each box)

ACTUAL BOW WEIGHT (At Your Draw Length)	CORRECT HUNTING ARROW LENGTH (Your Draw Length Plus ½ to ¾ Inch Clearance)																COMPOUND BOW PEAK WEIGHT	
	26½ - 27½ (27″)		27½ - 28½ (28″)		28½ - 29½ (29″)		29½ - 30½ (30″)		30½ - 31½ (31″)		31½ - 32½ (32″)		32½ - 33½ (33″)		33½ - 34½ (34″)		30% Let-off	50% Let-off
	Shaft Size	Arrow Weight	Shaft Size	Arrow Weight	Shaft Size	Arrow Weight	Shaft Size	Arrow Weight	Shaft Size	Arrow Weight	Shaft Size	Arrow Weight	Shaft Size	Arrow Weight	Shaft Size	Arrow Weight		
35-39	1913* 1815 1816	415 424 440	1913* 1915□ 1916 1818	426 447 471 490	2013* 1916 1917□	451 481 501	2114 2016 8.4M 1917□ 1918	486 507 508 511 537	2114 2016 2115□ 1918 8.5M	496 517 524 549 565	2213* 2115□ 2018 8.6M	505 535 583 619	2213* 2117	514 587			41-46	47-52
40-44	1913* 1915□ 1916 1818	415 438 461 478	2013* 1916 1917□ 1820**	442 471 490 530	2114 2016 8.4M 1917□ 1918	476 496 497 501 526	2114 2016 2115□ 1918 8.5M	486 507 513 537 553	2213* 2115□ 2018 8.6M	495 524 571 612	2213* 2117 2018 8.7M	505 575 583 675	2117 2216	587 587			47-52	53-59
45-49	2013* 1916 1917□ 1820**	433 461 479 517	2114 2016 8.4M 1917□ 1918	466 486 487 490 514	2114 2016 2115□ 8.5M 1920**	476 496 502 541 559	2213* 2115□ 2018 8.6M	485 513 558 598	2213* 2117 2018 2020 8.7M	495 563 571 609 660	2117 2216 2020 8.7M	575 575 622 675	2216 2217□	587 609	2219	658	53-58	60-66
50-54	2114 2016 1917□ 1918	456 475 479 503	2114 2016 8.4M 2115□ 1920**	466 486 487 492 546	2213* 2115□ 8.5M 2018 1920**	475 502 541 546 559	2213* 2117 2018 2020 8.6M	485 551 558 595 598	2117 2216 2020 8.7M	563 563 609 660	2216 2217□ 8.7M	575 596 675	2216 2217□ 2219	587 609 644	2219	658	59-64	67-72
55-59	2114 2016 8.4M 2115□ 1920**	456 475 477 481 534	2213* 2115□ 8.5M 2018 1920**	465 492 529 534 546	2213* 2117 2018 2020 8.6M	475 539 546 582 585	2117 2216 2020 8.7M	551 551 595 645	2216 2217□ 8.7M	563 584 660	2216 2217□ 2219	575 596 631	2317 2219	634 644	2317 2219	648 658	65-70	73-79
60-64	2213* 8.4M 2115□ 2018 1920**	455 477 481 522 534	2213* 2117 8.5M 2018 2020	465 527 529 534 568	2117 2216 2020 8.6M	539 539 582 585	2216 2217□ 8.7M	551 571 645	2216 2217□ 2219 8.7M	563 584 617 660	2217□ 2219	596 631	2317 2219	634 644	2317	648	71-76	80-86
65-69	2213* 2117 2018 2020	455 515 522 555	2117 2216 2020 8.6M	527 527 568 571	2216 2217□ 8.7M	539 558 629	2216 2217□ 2219 8.7M	551 571 603 645	2217□ 2219	584 617	2317 2219	621 631	2317	634	2317	648	77-82	87-93
70-74	2117 2216 2020	515 515 555	2216 2217□	527 546	2216 2217□ 2219	539 558 589	2217□ 2219	571 603	2317 2219	607 617	2317	621	2317	634	2419	685	83-88	94-100
75-79	2216 2217□	515 533	2216 2217□ 2219	527 546 575	2217□ 2219	558 589	2317 2219	594 603	2317	607	2317	621	2419	670	2419	685	89-94	101-107
80-84	2216 2217□ 2219	515 533 562	2217□ 2219	546 575	2317 2219	580 589	2317	594	2317	607	2419	656	2419	670	2419	685	95-100	108-114
85-89	2217□ 2219	533 562	2317 2219	567 575	2317	580	2317	594	2419	641	2419	656	2419	670			101-106	115-121
90-94	2317 2219	553 562	2317	567	2317	580	2419	627	2419	641	2419	656					107-112	122-128
95-99	2317	553	2317	567	2419	612	2419	627	2419	641							113-118	129-135
100-109	2317	553	2419	597	2419	612	2419	627									119-129	136-149
110-119	2419	583	2419	597	2419	612											130-142	150-163

*Available in XX75 only. **Available in GAME GETTER only.

□ Indicates Jim Dougherty "Naturals"

†NOTE: The shaft sizes 1815 through 2419 are contractions of actual physical dimensions of the tubes—example: **2016** has a **20/64″** outside diameter and a **.016″** wall thickness.

‡NOTE: The arrow weight in grains (437.5 grains per ounce) includes a 125 grain broadhead, 30 grain insert and 35 grains (average between plastic vanes and feathers) for nock and fletching.

there are normally several sizes that will fly accurately from your bow. For most deer-hunting tasks, choose a moderately heavy shaft to strike a compromise between flat trajectory and deep arrow penetration in game. For shooting big deer like elk and moose at moderately close range, a heavier shaft produces optimum penetration in flesh. For hunting open-country deer, like high-country mulies and caribou where shots are apt to be long, select a lighter-than-average shaft to flatten arrow flight and reduce the chances of a long-range miss or crippling hit.

All else being equal, arrow manufacturers have found that larger-diameter, thinner-wall shafts like the 2016, 2117, 2213, 2216, and 2317 tend to fly most accurately from compound bows, while the smaller-diameter, heavier-wall shafts like 1920s, 2018s, and 2020s tend to fly most accurately from recurve bows and longbows. This is one more factor to consider when selecting an arrow size to shoot. (In aluminum arrow-shaft sizes, the first two numbers indicate the shaft diameter in 64ths of an inch and the second two numbers indicate the wall thickness in thousandths of an inch. For example, a 2117 shaft is $^{21}/_{64}$-inch in outside diameter and has walls .017-inch thick.)

Here's one other extremely important hint about choosing a deer-hunting arrow shaft. If you're a beginner, don't rush out and buy dozens of arrows at once. Purchase half a dozen and shoot them awhile to see how they fly. Shaft-selection charts are at best rough guides to actual shaft selection, especially in hunting situations when arrowheads often deviate dramatically in weight from the standard head weight of 125 grains. You may discover that your originally chosen shaft size will absolutely not fly well from your bow, forcing you to choose a shaft of stiffer or weaker spine or to retune your bow to fit the arrow (see Chapter 9 for details). If

you must change the shaft size, it is much easier to cope with if you don't already own several dozen arrows.

For you experienced bowhunters who are having trouble with arrow flight, consider this. For every 15 grains of arrowhead weight above and beyond the standard 125 grains, you must shoot one shaft size stiffer than recommended to achieve decent arrow flight. For example, if you prefer to shoot 140-grain broadheads on deer and the chart says you need a 2117 arrow, you actually need a 2216 arrow to achieve acceptable accuracy with your equipment.

Nocks

Sensibly choosing an arrow shaft of the proper material and size is the primary key to accurate arrow flight. However, the arrow nock is also an extremely important part of any hunting arrow. It must be the proper size and configuration for best performance on deer and must also be attached correctly to ensure good accuracy.

A variety of arrow nocks are found on hunting arrows sold today. The best of the lot are made of tough, durable plastic and snap snugly on a bowstring to prevent them from falling off at the wrong time and spoiling a chance at deer. Such snap-on nocks often have a slightly raised index on one side to allow a hunter to nock an arrow with the fletching in proper rotation without actually looking down at the fletching. Some bowhunters learn to rely on such a nocking index, but this isn't a necessary trait of an accurate arrow nock.

When choosing hunting arrows at the store, visually inspect the nocks to make sure they are all glued on straight to the shafts. Extensive tests by Easton Aluminum, this country's largest arrow-shaft manufacturer, have concluded that a crooked nock is one of the

Easton Camo-Hunter aluminum shafts are very popular with serious archery deer hunters.

primary causes of erratic arrow flight. Most factory-assembled hunting arrows are fitted with well-aligned nocks, but once in a while a defective nock pops up or one slips during the gluing process and ends up off center. Such a nock can produce absolutely wild arrow flight—a tragic happenstance if that particular arrow is the one you shoot at a deer.

If your archery dealer allows, try snapping an arrow on the string of your bow to check the fit. The proper nock snaps in place with a faintly audible click, will hold the arrow on the string when the arrow is allowed to hang down vertically, yet will disengage from the bowstring with a light tap on the rear with your finger. If a snap-on nock is glued on straight and fits the string with this level of snugness, it will shoot arrows accurately and give you trouble-free service in the field.

Top-quality snap-on arrow nocks are available in a wide variety of sizes and colors to match any deer-hunting need.

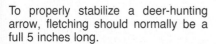

To properly stabilize a deer-hunting arrow, fletching should normally be a full 5 inches long.

Fletching

The majority of modern factory hunting arrows are fletched with plastic vanes instead of older-style feather fletching. Vanes have proven far more durable and long-lasting than feathers and are also completely impervious to rain and snow.

Feather fletching provides slightly better arrow stability with large deer-hunting broadheads because it creates more flight drag on the rear of an arrow. Feathers are the primary choice of longbow and recurve shooters because such bows are designed so arrows pass extremely close to the handle section as they sizzle on their way. Feathers flatten out as they pass a bow closely to prevent wobbly arrow flight, whereas plastic vanes tend to bump a longbow or recurve bow and send arrows helter-skelter. For the hunter who has chronic broadhead-flight problems or prefers to shoot a recurve bow or longbow, feather fletching is probably the best choice to make.

Most compound-bow shooters achieve excellent accuracy with modern plastic arrow fletching. Regardless of which fletching material you choose, on hunting arrows it should be long enough to properly stabilize an arrow in flight. Standard arrows with three fletches should carry 5-inch long fletching for optimum accuracy. Less common four-fletched arrows should carry fletching 4 inches long for best arrow flight. A few bowhunters prefer four-fletched arrows because they clear compound-bow cables better, allow easy arrow-nocking in an overdraw bow with an arrow rest less than 5 inches from the bowstring, or because a four-fletched arrow cannot be nocked backwards on the bowstring the way a three-fletched arrow can. Both fletching styles shoot well as long as other fletching requirements are met.

One such requirement is a fairly strong spiral around the arrow shaft. Far too many otherwise good factory hunting arrows have fletching which spirals very little if at all. This degrades arrow accuracy because a hunting arrow must spin as it travels through the air to stabilize it properly. Hunting broadheads for deer are especially apt to steer an arrow off course unless the arrow rotates strongly as it flies. When buying arrows, insist on fletching that spirals instead of aligning exactly with the shafts.

A fine point of fletching that many archery perfectionists pay attention to is whether fletching spirals to the left or to the right around an arrow. This is especially important with plastic vanes, which do not flatten out if they bump a bow in flight. For best accuracy, a right-handed shooter should select vanes that spiral from left to right when viewed from the rear of an arrow. For a left-handed shooter, vanes should

A wide variety of arrowheads is available, including the time-tested old-style slip-over or glue-on heads shown. From top are: Zwickey Black Diamond broadhead for big game; three-blade Bodkin small game broadhead; a Shocker blunt; steel field point; a simple steel blunt; Judo Point; and the HTM Rubber blunt. Quite effective, these are not as easy to attach as the more modern screw-in models usually favored now.

spiral from right to left. By doing so, vanes more perfectly clear an arrow rest and wobble less as they leave a bow.

As a hunter becomes more and more familiar with using archery equipment, he often tackles more and more do-it-yourself phases of this sport. One of the most common is fletching arrows instead of buying them pre-fletched from the factory. This process saves money and also ensures that fletching is of the ideal size and spiral to promote first-rate accuracy. For more details on do-it-yourself fletching, consult Chapter 6.

Arrowheads

The kind of arrowhead that an archer uses on deer is called a broadhead. This is a relatively large-diameter arrowhead with multiple, shaving-sharp blades designed to penetrate and disrupt a deer's vital organs. Broadheads will be discussed in detail in Chapter 4.

A bowhunter uses broadheads only when actually pursuing deer, but he uses several other types of arrowheads for target practice, stump-shooting, and honing up his skills on small animals like ground squirrels and woodchucks. Among the most common kinds of secondary arrowheads used by deer hunters are field points, blunts, and Judo points.

Field points, often called target points by hunters, are simple steel arrowheads used for target practice and shooting very small animals and birds. These are the most aerodynamically accurate arrowheads used by hunters, and are the primary heads used for target shooting during off-season months.

Blunt arrowheads are usually made of steel, rubber or plastic. Large flat frontal surfaces prevent deep arrow penetration and effectively stun animals and birds under 3 pounds. A blunt-tipped arrow is ideal for shooting at rotten stumps, dirt banks, and other natural targets a hunter can tune up his skills on while wandering about the woods. Unlike a field point, a blunt arrowhead will not wedge tightly in wood, making it relatively easy to extract after a shot.

Judo points are touted by their manufacturer to be completely unlosable, and this claim is not very far from the truth. A Judo point consists of a steel body with four short spring-wire arms protruding from it at right angles. This head absolutely refuses to skip and bury under grass or leaves, something that field points and blunts are notorious for doing in areas with hard ground topped by heavy cover. A Judo's spring-wire

(Right) A variety of arrowheads can be shot from a deer-hunting bow, provided all heads weigh the same and the bow is properly tuned for accuracy.

Simple steel field points are best for most target shooting practice prior to deer season.

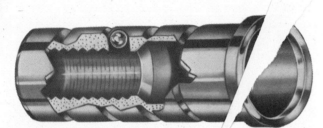

A female insert is glued in the end of a tubular arrow shaft to allow easy attachment of all screw-in arrowheads.

Various arrowhead-hookup designs are used with aluminum hunting shafts (top to bottom): old-style glue-in broadhead adapter, threaded R.P.S. (Replaceable Point System) shaft insert, short 35-grain screw-in broadhead adapter, and long break-off 45-grain screw-in broadhead adapter.

arms catch the ground and tumble an arrow, making this head a real arrow-saver in places where foliage or ground litter can gobble up normal shafts time after time after time. Judo points are equally good for taking potshots at natural targets like stumps and for hunting small animals like squirrels and rabbits.

All of the secondary arrowheads generally used by deer hunters can be purchased in either a glue-on or screw-in configuration. The older-style glue-on heads have a few practical applications in archery, but the screw-in heads are far more convenient to use, and they work the best in most shooting situations. Broadheads are a different matter. If you like a particular head, it is generally either a glue-on head *or* a screw-in head—not available in both configurations.

A serious bowhunter generally keeps a good selection of field points, blunts, and/or Judo points on hand at all times in addition to his favorite bowhunting broadheads. When purchasing such heads, it is very important to make sure they *all weigh the same*. Mixing 125-grain heads with 135-grain heads and 145-grain heads is pure poison to accuracy because only one head weight will fly well from a bow tuned a particular way. Mixing arrowhead weights is one of the primary reasons many archers have arrow-accuracy problems.

To begin with, an archer should buy 125-grain field points and let it go at that. Until he begins tuning his hunting bow, he won't know what arrowhead weight will work best with his bow/arrow combination, and until he selects a deer-hunting broadhead he won't know what exact field-point weight to choose to match this broadhead. As in arrow-shaft selection, a bowhunter should start with a few field points and hold off on mass-buying heads until the bow-tuning process is complete (see Chapter 9).

Arrow Cut-Off and Point Installation

Once you select your hunting arrows, your archery dealer will cut them off to the proper length (your draw length plus about ¾-inch to clear the front of the bow). Once this is done, he will install either screw-in or glue-on arrowhead inserts to the ends of these arrows, and then affix glue-on heads to old-style inserts with hot-melt cement. For easy arrowhead interchangeability, the screw-in route is definitely best.

Do-it-yourself, home-grown arrow cut-off can cause real problems unless an archer knows exactly what he's doing. Top-grade aluminum arrow shafts can be completely ruined when self-appointed "pros" cut these off with tubing cutters or hacksaws, and fiberglass shafts can be cracked or splintered beyond repair with similar self-invented cut-off methods. Hunting shafts should be cut to proper length on a high-speed arrow cut-off tool to ensure clean, functional cuts. The most wide-spread arrow cut-off abuse is the use of a squeeze-down tubing cutter to snap off the ends of shafts. In aluminum, this misguided technique places tremendous outward pressures on tubing walls. When a point insert is then glued into the end of a shaft, the walls break out then and there, or more commonly, arrow-wall cracks appear weeks or months later.

Do-it-yourself gluing is no big problem with arrow points and inserts, but the proper glues should be used for best results. In fiberglass shafts, point inserts must be attached with epoxy. In aluminum, hot-melt archery cement is the standard adhesive for attaching screw-in or glue-on arrow-point inserts to shafts.

A hunting arrow is the single most important part of any deer hunter's gear. If the shaft, nock, fletching, and arrowheads to be attached are all carefully chosen, such an arrow has the potential to shoot the centers out of targets and drop deer with pinpoint vital hits!

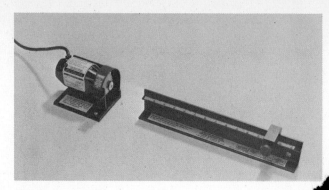

To properly cut arrow shafts to length, an archer must use regular shaft cut-off tool like this model from Easton.

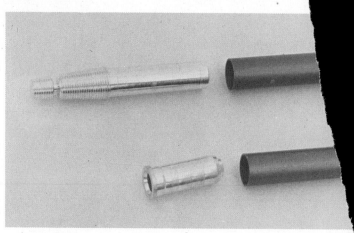

Old-style glue-on arrowheads and modern screw-in arrowheads require different insert designs in the ends of arrow shafts.

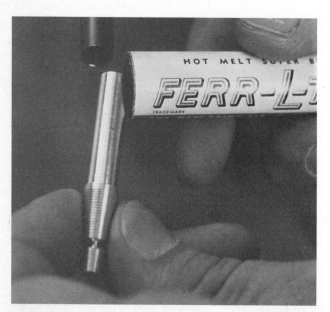

Hot-melt ferrule cement similar to that used to assemble fishing rods is normally used to attach arrow inserts to tubular aluminum shafts.

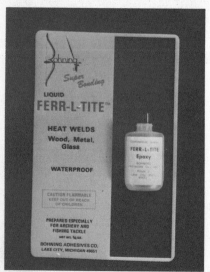

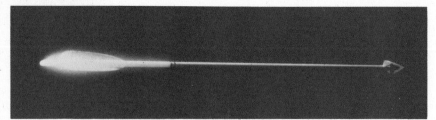

One unique "Tracer Arrow" sold at archery stores glows at the rear end for good low-light arrow-flight visibility.

Epoxy is the preferred glue for attaching arrow inserts in the ends of fiberglass bowhunting shafts.

The Hunting Broadhead/4

A BIG-GAME hunting broadhead is a truly remarkable cutting tool. The average deer-hunting arrow travels at something close to 200 feet per second with a total "muzzle energy" directly in front of the bow of only 50 or 55 foot-pounds. This is approximately half the energy of a tiny .22 Short cartridge, yet the arrow will easily pass through a deer's broadside chest cavity for a clean, humane kill when tipped by a well-designed broadhead. By contrast, a .22 Short is hard pressed to drop a stunted chipmunk with the same lethal effect, and a .30-06 bullet with several *thousand* foot-pounds of energy won't kill a deer one whit faster than a broadhead-tipped arrow.

The broadhead is clearly the key to a hunting arrow's dramatic deer-killing ability. The same arrow tipped with a rubber blunt would bounce harmlessly off a buck deer's shoulder instead of sizzling through the vitals, completely wasting the meager energy the shaft has as it flies from the shooter to the target. A broadhead utilizes this small energy with high efficiency, slicing deep with little or no friction to stop its deadly travel. It is nothing short of amazing what a deer-hunting broadhead can do.

A broadhead normally kills a deer in one of two basic ways. If it directly hits a vital organ like the heart or lungs, it slices through this organ and completely stops the animal's vital functions for a near-instantaneous kill. If the broadhead slices the liver or another body area rich in arteries or blood vessels, it promotes massive bleeding which quickly weakens the animal and causes it to ultimately pass out and die. Contrary to popular belief, the majority of deer hit vitally with arrows do not bleed to death at all—they drop for the same reason they drop when hit properly with a big-bore rifle bullet. The lung center or the heart simply stops working, and the animal dies from lack of oxygen to the brain.

Every serious archery deer hunter wants a broad-head that drops animals with maximum killing efficiency. This minimizes tracking and trailing hassles after a shot is made and ensures a quick, humane end to a magnificent big-game creature. Unfortunately, not all of the 40 or 50 major hunting broadhead designs sold today are equally suited to neatly bagging deer. Most are at least adequate for this task, but the truly conscientious deer hunter carefully considers the traits of various big-game broadheads, experiments with a few of the more appealing configurations, and settles on one that seems to dispatch animals with particular speed and efficiency. Factors of primary importance in deciding which head kills the best are how accurate it is, how deeply it penetrates, how big a hole it cuts, and how well the blades take and hold an edge.

In addition to sheer deer-dropping ability, bow-hunters must also consider a few other broadhead traits that will directly affect the quality of their sport. These are what I call convenience traits—things like how quickly a head attaches to a shaft, how easily the blades can be sharpened or replaced, and how well a broadhead withstands impact damage. The raw killing ability of a deer-hunting broadhead is always of foremost importance to a dedicated nimrod, but secondary niceties of particular broadhead designs might certainly influence the ultimate choice of that just-right deer-hunting head.

Here are some solid facts about modern deer-hunting broadheads that should help you choose a design which is likely to serve you well. As in the selection of automobiles and friends, the choice of a deer-hunting broadhead is a highly personal thing with no one model suiting every hunter's individual requirements and unique personal druthers. However, some broadhead models are definitely better for deer hunting than others, and it's every hunter's duty to discard the marginal designs, carefully compare the better ones, and zero in on one that seems especially sensible to use.

Accuracy

Broadheads in general are notorious for flying with very poor accuracy. By far the most common complaint I receive from readers of my bowhunting articles and books is that their field points fly pretty well, but their broadheads dip, dive, zoom upwards, and otherwise wander unpredictably through the air.

The most common cause of poor broadhead accuracy is simply the lack of bow tuning. In Chapter 9 we will discuss the tuning method in detail. If an arrow leaves a bow wobbling instead of flying straight, it will still shoot fairly well if tipped by a field point. However, a wobbling arrow tipped by a broadhead will seldom fly accurately because the blades of the head catch air unevenly and steer the arrow off course like a rudder steers a ship. This tendency is called "planing" and is a problem every bowhunter has experienced at one time or another.

The primary cause of broadhead planing is usually a poorly tuned bow. However, it is a fact that some broadhead designs are more inherently accurate than others. There are two basic factors that determine how potentially accurate a broadhead will be.

The first factor is the physical size of a particular

Streamlined broadhead design ensures accurate flight.

Top broadhead design gets the game! The author's wife Joanne takes nice deer each and every year with sharp, streamlined heads shot from a 40-pound compound bow.

head. More specifically, accuracy is determined by how much surface area there is on a broadhead's cutting blades. All else being equal, a four-blade head that measures 7/8-inch in diameter will fly more accurately than a four-blade head that measures 1½ inches in diameter. Similarly, a three-blade head 1-inch in diameter is potentially more accurate than a four-blade head measuring the same 1-inch in diameter. The more flat blade surface there is to catch air and amplify arrow wobble, the more apt a head is to wander at least slightly off course. Even if a bow is perfectly tuned, a

hunter does not achieve a perfect string release every time, and even if he releases a good, clean shot, other factors like crosswind and foliage that bump a flying arrow can start an arrow wobbling and result in less than decent accuracy.

You certainly can't kill deer that you can't hit in the first place. As a result, a hunter should choose a broadhead of reasonable size that isn't likely to fly erratically whenever a mountain breeze kicks up or a cloud passes overhead. As a general rule, three- or four-blade broadheads between 1 inch and 1¼ inches in diameter have proven the most practical compromise between good killing size and decent shooting accuracy.

Despite the general broadhead-size rule, manufacturers have produced several excellent deer broadheads of larger diameter that minimize planing through the incorporation of large cutouts in the blades. These cutouts reduce the surface area of blades, allowing air to pass through sideways instead of pressuring a head off its intended path. One problem that some blade-cutout broadheads have, however, is the tendency to hiss as they fly, a noise that can scare deer away. Regardless, several big-game broadheads currently available measure up to 1½ inches in diameter and still fly with excellent accuracy from a well-tuned bow.

As arrow speed goes up, everything about a bow-shooting setup becomes more critical when it comes to accuracy. Arrow vibration increases, bow torque increases, and air pressure on broadhead blades also increases. As a result, many hunters using ultra-fast cam-bows, overdraw bows, and more conventional bows with excessively heavy draw weights are forced to use smaller-than-normal broadheads to achieve suitable accuracy on targets and game. The faster an arrow flies, the more prone it is to plane when tipped with a

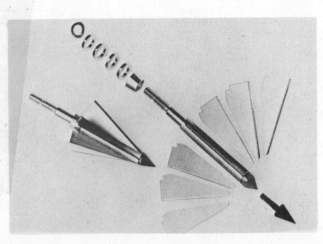

Some of the best modern deer-hunting broadheads are composite designs like this Kolpin Modular.

broadhead. As a result, it is not surprising that long-bows and recurve bows produce fewer broadhead-planing problems and are less finicky about the size and configuration of heads they shoot. There is no such thing as a free ride in bowhunting—you always give up something to get something else.

Broadhead size is a significant factor in accuracy. Even more important is the precision with which a broadhead is manufactured. If a head does not exactly align with the shaft it is attached to, it cannot cut air cleanly and will inevitably sail off course. Most popu-

A jagged-edge broadhead is not known for its ability to penetrate deeply.

lar, name-brand, deer-hunting broadheads are precisely manufactured to ensure good alignment with shafts, particularly the newer screw-in, replaceable-blade models. However, never take broadhead alignment for granted. If a broadhead attached to a shaft will not spin precisely on its tip without wobble, it will surely fly off course. To check various broadhead designs for true alignment, attach them to straight arrow shafts, spin them on their tips like tops, and watch for wobble *where the broadhead meets the shaft.* There are several popular broadheads on the market that will not attach precisely to shafts no matter what, wobbling noticeably when spun as described. Avoid such sloppy manufacturing attempts like the plague—they will cost you deer in the field.

The majority of old-style glue-on broadheads can be jockeyed around on a shaft at the time of gluing until they align with the shaft precisely. However, a few are so poorly welded together that no amount of effort can true them up. Use your common sense to inspect and discard such visibly shoddy broadhead models.

The final test of broadhead accuracy is shooting broadheads for a while on targets. Never pass judgment on a broadhead until your bow is properly tuned. If a particular design gives problems even after tuning, you should discard it and find a model that works well. Remember, without decent shooting accuracy, there is really no sense in going deer hunting in the first place.

Broadhead Cutting Ability

It is fairly obvious that the more tissue a broadhead cuts after it hits a deer, the faster it is likely to kill the animal. This is particularly true with hits that do not directly penetrate vital organs like the lungs or heart.

As a general rule of thumb, a bowhunter after deer should shoot the largest broadhead he can achieve good accuracy with. A tiny head measuring less than 1 inch across the blades will neatly drop a deer if it centers the chest cavity, but such a head will produce a slower death than a larger broadhead if it smacks the ham, paunch, or another less instantly vital part of a deer's anatomy. This is taking for granted that both sizes of broadheads are shaving sharp to begin with to promote maximum blood loss in an animal.

The one-piece welded-steel Snuffer broadhead is a popular, extremely rugged glue-on arrowhead for deer.

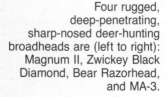

Some broadheads, like the PSE Brute, come in several configurations to match any deer hunter's tastes.

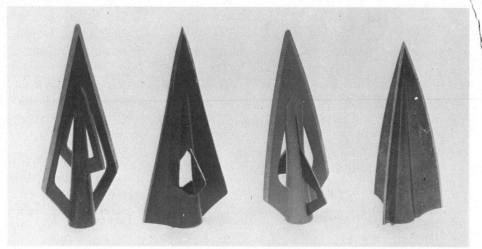

Four rugged, deep-penetrating, sharp-nosed deer-hunting broadheads are (left to right): Magnum II, Zwickey Black Diamond, Bear Razorhead, and MA-3.

Similarly, a three-blade broadhead of a particular size cuts precisely one-quarter less tissue than a four-blade broadhead of the same size—a factor which can definitely make a difference with marginal hits. Arguments among bowhunters will probably go on forever about whether three blades are as good as four or whether smaller heads kill as well as larger heads. As far as I'm concerned, such debates are meaningless when comparing arrows that puncture the lungs or heart. In such cases, the animals invariably drop—and drop quickly.

Where broadhead size and blade number really come into play is when arrows do not hit the vital chest. The problem of non-chest hits is compounded in larger deer like elk, moose, and caribou because these animals have a lot more blood to lose before going down.

If you think about the ins and outs of broadhead-size selection, you must logically conclude that the larger a head is once it hits, the better it is from a blood-loss point of view. There are no two ways about it. There

are plenty of hunters who regularly kill elk with little broadheads, but in my mind these fellows get the job done *in spite of* their broadheads. Some of these hunters simply cannot get larger heads to fly well, and without major equipment changes or dropping bow poundage to reduce arrow speed, they are pretty well stuck with what they're currently using. However, many hunters shoot broadheads smaller than necessary to achieve accurate flight from a well-tuned bow. These nimrods are needlessly handicapping themselves and dropping their chances of killing deer by at least a few percentage points.

The same thing can be said for deer hunters using two-blade broadheads. I know that there are diehard hunters out there who swear by their two-blade broadheads, but these shooters are dropping deer in spite of their broadheads—not because of them. The only excuse I can see for shooting a two-blade broadhead on deer is when a hunter feels the two-blade head is the only kind he can properly sharpen by hand. A few

A simple, one-piece three-blade head like the Black Copperhead Talon is tough to beat for durability and accurate arrow flight.

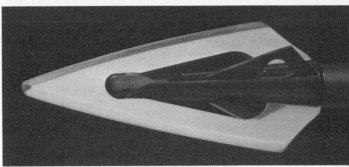

The screw-in Super Bear Razorhead S/S is factory-sharpened, rugged, and sharp-pointed for deepest penetration in deer.

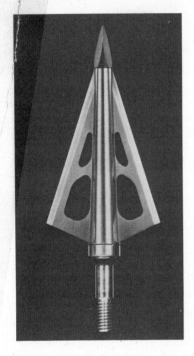

The Razorback Thunderhead measures nearly 1½ inches in diameter but maintains decent accuracy with large blade cutouts.

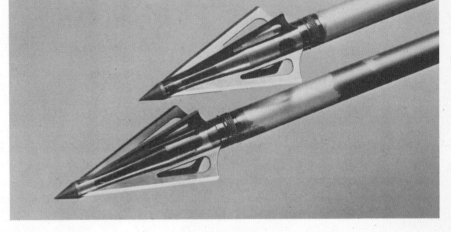

The new Hoyt/Easton Camo-Hunter Broadhead combines all the traits of a first-rate hunting head—streamline design with cutouts in the blades, shaving keen edges, and positive screw attachment. It also has a unique camouflaged aluminum center section.

large two-blade, hand-sharpened broadheads kill pretty well compared to smaller, factory-sharpened heads with three or four blades. Since it is usually easier to sharpen a two-blade head, hunters operating on this theory do have a valid point.

As mentioned before, a well-designed broadhead with three or four sharp blades measuring 1 inch to 1¼ inches in diameter is sufficient to drop any deer that ever walked the woods, even when hits are not precisely in the heart/lung area. As a result, the majority of in-the-know archery deer hunters use heads of this basic configuration. Such heads have stood the test of time and are a safe bet for any conscientious bowhunter.

Penetrating Ability

One of the least understood aspects of broadhead design is its ability to penetrate deeply in flesh. There's a lot of mumbo jumbo written on this subject each and every year, but actually testing and comparing the penetrating abilities of various kinds of broadheads is extremely difficult because flesh is a completely unique substance for heads to slice through. All the shooting into concrete blocks, styrofoam target butts, and other artificial substances really doesn't prove a thing about how broadheads will penetrate the chest, ham, or paunch of a broadside or quartering-away deer.

As mentioned before, one of a broadhead's primary functions should be to utilize an arrow's meager energy to best advantage. I was amazed not too long ago when one of the foremost broadhead manufacturers in the country told me he didn't believe that broadhead design had any significant effect on depth of penetration in game. This could not be farther from the truth! Any old-time deer hunter with plenty of broadhead shooting experience will tell you that certain broadhead designs dramatically out-penetrate others—and he can probably tell you which ones penetrate best and why. A fellow who shoots 50 or 75 deer with various broadheads and spends some time thinking about the results

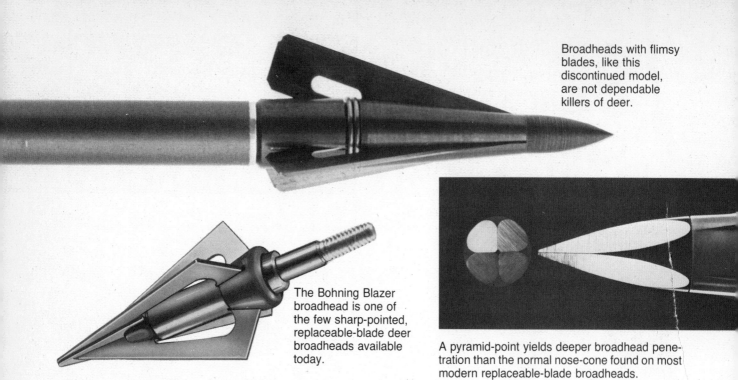

Broadheads with flimsy blades, like this discontinued model, are not dependable killers of deer.

The Bohning Blazer broadhead is one of the few sharp-pointed, replaceable-blade deer broadheads available today.

A pyramid-point yields deeper broadhead penetration than the normal nose-cone found on most modern replaceable-blade broadheads.

will be able to draw some definite conclusions about which heads penetrate best.

As near as I can figure, I have personally shot over 300 deer-sized big-game animals with a bow and have seen at least that many taken by other archers over the course of the years. From my experience, there are two major factors that influence how well a broadhead penetrates flesh: The first is how streamlined the broadhead happens to be. The second is what kind of frontal point or nose it has. Let me explain.

A hunting broadhead with jagged or saw-tooth edges produces blade-to-flesh friction as it rips into an animal. Similarly, a head with an excessive number of blades, a center section that does not slide smoothly through flesh, or other design features that obviously cause friction will never penetrate very well. The best heads are relatively friction-free designs with sharp, smooth blades and no obstacles in their design to impede smooth, slick penetration.

Another major factor affecting deep broadhead penetration is the type of frontal tip or nose incorporated in its design. As far as I'm concerned, this is the number one factor, making some broadheads poor penetrators, some fair penetrators, and others superior penetrators. It is also a factor generally overlooked by broadhead manufacturers and the general shooting public alike.

There are two basic kinds of broadheads sold at archery stores today—heads with sharpened slicing tips and heads with nose-cone or pyramid-point tips. The sharpened-tip broadhead has a spade-like point that begins cutting the instant it touches flesh. The nose-cone or pyramid-point on the other hand plows through flesh for a fraction of an inch before the blades make contact and start to cut a larger hole.

Until a few years ago, almost all deer-hunting broadheads were one-piece, hand-sharpenable designs with cutting edges extending to the very front. These sharpened-nose heads were extremely good at penetrating because they sliced exclusively instead of punching through with a cone-shaped nose. Computer studies have shown that the very best of these sharp-point heads are approximately three times as long as they are wide—the 3-to-1 shape ratio coupled with a keen slicing tip promotes deep penetration in flesh with very little friction.

In recent times, the so-called replaceable-blade broadhead has swept the marketplace because it eliminates the need to hand-sharpen broadhead edges. Characteristically, such a head also screws to an arrow instead of requiring time-consuming hand-gluing in place—another convenience for bowhunters. However, almost all replaceable-blade broadhead designs incorporate a nose-cone or pyramid-shaped point ahead of cutting blades—a point that creates considerable friction as it plows through flesh. Replaceable-blade broadheads are used successfully by many bowhunters today, but they penetrate poorly compared to older-style sharp-around-the-end type broadheads.

This is not to say that replaceable-blade broadheads of the nose-cone or pyramid-point design are unacceptable for hunting deer. A hunter should simply be aware that he is giving up penetrating ability when he uses such heads. The smaller the frontal cone on a broadhead and the closer the blades are to the front, the better it will penetrate. The larger the cone and the farther back the blades, the poorer it will penetrate. Tests have shown that a pyramid-shaped point with three or four edges creates somewhat less friction in

POPULAR DEER-HUNTING BROADHEADS

Name	Weight	Diameter	Number of Blades	General Description
Ace Rocket	130 grs.	1 3/16"	2	Hand-sharpenable blades. Solid one-piece sharpened-point design.
Ace Standard	140 grs.	1 3/16"	2	Hand-sharpenable blades. Solid one-piece sharpened-point design.
Ace Super-Express	150 grs.	1 3/8"	2	Hand-sharpenable vented blades. Solid one-piece design.
African 4-Blade	175 grs.	1 5/16"	4	Hand-sharpenable blades. One-piece sharpened-point design.
Alaskan 4-Blade	190 grs.	1 3/8"	4	Hand-sharpenable blades, replaceable auxiliary blades, both vented. Sharpened point.
Anderson Magnum 245	2-Blade: 114 grs. 4-Blade: 134 grs.	1 1/2"	2, 4	Replaceable presharpened vented stainless blades. Pyramid-point design.
Bear Super Razor Head	125 grs.	1 1/8"	2, 4	Presharpened vented stainless blades. Accepts vented auxiliary blade, chisel point.
Ben Pearson Switch Blade	125 grs.	1 1/8"	4	Presharpened vented blades. Replaceable auxiliary blade. Sharpened-point design.
Black Copperhead Magnum	130 grs.	1 1/8"	3	Hand-sharpenable blades with saw-tooth edges. Solid one-piece design.
Black Copperhead Shrike	125 grs.	1 1/8"	2	Hand-sharpenable blades. Solid one-piece sharpened point design.
Black Copperhead Slicer	125 grs.	1 1/8"	4	Hand-sharpenable blades. Solid one-piece design.
Bodkin	125 grs.	1 1/4"	3	Hand-sharpenable blades. Solid one-piece design.
Bohning Blazer	140 grs.	1 1/8"	4	Replaceable presharpened vented stainless steel blade units, sharp around the end for deep penetration.
Butterfield Brute	135 grs.	1 1/2"	2, 4	Hand-sharpenable vented main blades, accepts vented auxiliary blade. Sharpened point.
Catclaw-RZ	—	—	4, 6	Hand-sharpenable vented carbon-steel main blade. Two or four razor-blades fit in slots around back of main blade, sharpened point.
Eagle-4	150 grs.	—	4	Hand-sharpenable vented blades. Sharpened point design.
Hunter	138 grs.	—	2	Hand-sharpenable blades. Long, slender sharpened-point design.
Kolpin Modular	3-Blade: 110 grs. 4-Blade: 120 grs. 6-Blade: 140 grs.	—	3, 4, 6	Replaceable presharpened stainless blades. Unique off-center blade design takes 10-grain weight collars.

Name	Weight	Diameter	Number of Blades	General Description
MA-2	110 grs. 125 grs.	1 1/16"	2	Hand-sharpenable blades. Solid one-piece sharpened-point design.
MA-3	100 grs. 125 grs.	1 1/16"	3	Hand-sharpenable blades. Solid one-piece design.
Magnum I	140 grs.	—	4	Hand-sharpenable vented stainless blades. Solid one-piece sharpened-point design.
Magnum II	125 grs.	—	4	Hand-sharpenable vented stainless blades. Solid one-piece sharpened-point design.
Martin Blue Streak 5	130 grs.	—	5	Hand-sharpenable blades. Replaceable presharpened stainless or carbon blades. Nose-cone design.
Martin Bowlo	115 grs.	—	2	Hand-sharpenable blades. Long, slender sharpened-point design.
Missile Spike	135 grs. 165-grs.	—	4	Unique spike-point design with small, rear-mounted blades.
Premium I	125 grs.	1"	4	Presharpened vented blades. Long, slender sharpened-point design.
PSE Brute	104 grs. To 140 grs.	7/8" To 1 1/4"	3, 4	Replaceable presharpened stainless blades. Nose-cone design. Seven configurations.
Razorbak 4	142 grs.	1.05"	4	Replaceable presharpened blades set in cartridge that rotates freely. Pyramid-point design.
Razorbak 5	142 grs.	.916"	5	Replaceable presharpened blades set in cartridge that rotates freely. Pyramid-point design.
Razorbak Thunderhead	180 grs.	1.4"	3	Replaceable presharpened vented stainless blades. Pyramid-point design.
Rocky Mountain Razor	3-Blade: 130 grs. 4-Blade: 140 grs.	1 1/4 And 1 1/2	3, 4	Replaceable presharpened vented stainless blades. Nose-cone design.
Satellite	120 grs. To 145 grs.	—	3, 4	Replaceable presharpened stainless or carbon blades. Nose-cone design. Several sizes.
Savora Super-S	3-Blade: 117 grs. 4-Blade: 126 grs.	1 1/8"	3, 4	Replaceable presharpened stainless or carbon blades. One-piece aluminum nose-cone center.
Snuffer	160 grs.	1 1/2"	3	Hand-sharpenable vented spring-steel blades. Solid copper-welded one-piece design.
Wasp Cam-Lok	3-Blade: 130 grs. 4-Blade: 140 grs.	—	3, 4	Replaceable presharpened vented blades. Nose-cone design.
Zwickey Black Diamond	110 grs. And 125 grs.	1 1/8" And 1 3/8"	2, 4	Hand-sharpenable blades. Solid one-piece sharpened-point design. Triple-layer steel tip.

flesh than a regular round nose cone, but both point styles impede friction-free penetration in flesh.

For many bowhunters, the reduction in penetrating ability of the pre-sharpened, nose-cone or pyramid-point broadheads is more than offset by convenience factors like blade replacement and instant screw attachment. Such a conclusion is especially valid if a hunter concentrates on smaller deer species like whitetails and mulies, which require shallower arrow penetration for fast kills. With 400-pound caribou, 800-pound elk, and 1500-pound moose, the arguments for using a replaceable-blade, nose-cone-type head are not nearly so convincing. On elk, why use a nose-cone head that penetrates an average of 12 inches from a 70-pound bow, when a broadhead sharpened completely around the tip is apt to leave the same bow, completely pass through the animal's 2-foot-thick body and bury itself in a log on the far side? Those who have shot plenty of big deer with both broadhead styles know that the difference in penetration is often at least this dramatic, and also know that twice the broadhead tissue damage plus two holes in the hide instead of one can often make the critical difference between finding and losing an animal.

There's one other important thing to consider when choosing between a deep-penetrating broadhead and a moderate-penetrating broadhead. A hand-sharpened head that cuts to the very tip might be a pain to sharpen, but the 25- or 30-percent increase in this head's penetrating ability will let you significantly drop your bow's draw weight and still match the performance of a nose-cone broadhead shot at a heavier poundage. For example, my wife Joanne regularly kills blacktail deer with a little 40-pound round-wheel compound bow coupled with arrows tipped by hand-sharpened, extremely low-friction broadheads. This combo almost always shoots completely through broadside deer out to 40 yards, and easily penetrates 2 feet on quartering-away shots in the ham or flank. In order to achieve equal penetration with a less efficient nose-cone broadhead, I'm sure Joanne would have to increase her bow's draw weight to 50 or 55 pounds. She'd have to shoot more regularly, work out with weights, and do one-handed pushups all day long to handle such a bow . . . and she wouldn't gain a thing over the more efficient combo she's shooting today!

If you cannot sharpen broadheads well, or if you like the convenience of a replaceable-blade hunting broadhead, be sure to choose one with a relatively small frontal cone or pyramid-point and with blades that extend as close as possible to this point. If the ability to hand-sharpen a conventional head is your only hangup, there are a few excellent factory-sharpened broadheads on the market that are sharp completely around the tip. If hand-sharpening is no problem for you, there are quite a few old-style, unsharpened broadheads available at archery stores that work admirably on game.

Broadhead Durability

Some deer-hunting broadheads are more durable than others. Durability is desirable because it saves money in the long run and also contributes to killing ability when a head collides with heavy animal bones.

Some broadheads are solid, one-piece welded designs that have a sterling reputation for holding together even when they miss the mark and smack rocks, trees, or seasoned deadwood. Others are notoriously fragile, giving a bowhunter only one shot before bending, breaking, or cracking into totally unusable condition.

Within reason, almost any broadhead sold by a reputable manufacturer will hold up well enough for bowhunting deer. A few models with serious design flaws come and go as time passes, and these generally disappear fairly fast as hunters discover their inadequacies. One such broadhead sold a few years back incorporated regular razor blades set into a center nose-cone section. As often as not, the blades shed from the broadhead before it entered an animal, leaving the cutting parts of the head lying on the ground and driving a bladeless pencil point into the deer. That particular head, like most duds, quickly fell by the wayside.

I really have nothing against replaceable-blade, nose-cone-type heads, but these tend to be fairly fragile in general because they have aluminum center sections that bend out of shape on impact. Some manufacturers of such heads attach hardened-steel nose-cones or pyramid-points in a futile attempt to reduce this tendency to bend. In reality, such steel tips generally drive back into the aluminum on impact or bend to one side like a broken nose. Such replaceable-blade broadheads are extremely accurate and very convenient, but most can be considered one-shot heads if they collide with anything solid.

The thicker the blades on a broadhead, the less apt they are to shatter on impact. The best replaceable-blade broadheads today have full .015-inch to .025-inch thick blades to ensure cutting dependability. Heads with thinner blades usually kill deer well enough with broadside chest hits, but collision with heavy bones in the shoulder, spine, or ham areas can literally blow up such heads and severely hamper killing ability. Make darn sure that your deer-hunting broadheads have stout, sturdy blades.

The most durable broadheads are various one-piece welded designs made of steel. These most commonly have three or four blades which must be sharpened by hand. Although not necessary for most kinds of deer hunting, such heads can usually be shot over and over again without experiencing any damage other than dulled edges that need to be resharpened. Broadheads of this sort are best for bowhunting rocky areas where missed shots absolutely destroy less durable models—

A bowhunter should make sure that broadheads are shaving sharp at all times.

Modern replaceable-blade broadheads contrast sharply in size and design with ancient volcanic-glass Indian arrowheads.

especially if a hunter is backpacking far away from roads and cannot afford to carry 20 pounds of broadheads in his pack. My favorite optimum-durability broadhead has a triple sandwich of welded steel in the tip area, and I have killed as many as three different deer with the same broadhead of this type before it bent or broke.

Sharpness and Edge-Holding Ability

Even if you forget everything else said here about deer-hunting broadheads, do not forget this—*a broadhead must have shaving-sharp edges to do a decent job on deer.* There is absolutely no excuse for hunting deer with dull-edged broadheads because such a shoddy procedure does a disservice to the game you hunt as well as to yourself. A dull broadhead is a maimer and a crippler—not a killer—and should never be found in a deer hunter's quiver.

A sharp broadhead edge does two important things in animals: For one thing, it penetrates with a minimum of friction for maximum penetration. Even more important, it slices off blood vessels cleanly to promote massive bleeding with a minimum of flow-constricting coagulation. A sharp instrument cuts tissue without releasing blood-clotting catalysts in the wound, which results in a fast, free flow of blood that drops animals fast. If you've ever accidentally cut yourself with a razor blade while shaving, you know the cut bleeds and bleeds and bleeds. By contrast, a cut with a dull knife bleeds a little bit and then clogs up. Ideally, a broadhead produces the same effect as a razor cut, giving you every chance to recover a solidly hit animal.

If you score a marginal hit that doesn't drop a deer, sharp broadhead edges will cause a strong blood flow that cleanses a wound before the cut seals up. This guarantees rapid wound-healing for the animal that a dull edge is not likely to provide.

American Indians were quite successful at killing deer with their crude bows and arrows, and one major reason was the fact that these early Americans used razor-keen arrowheads chipped from various kinds of volcanic glass. Theoretically, glass takes an even finer

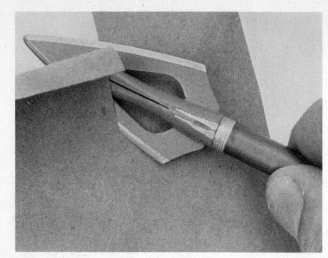

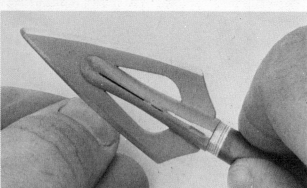

(Left, below left and below) To check the sharpness of each broadhead edge, slice paper, run edges lightly across a thumbnail, or slice edges across stretched rubber bands. A truly keen edge slices paper and rubber bands easily, and grabs a thumbnail instead of sliding easily across it.

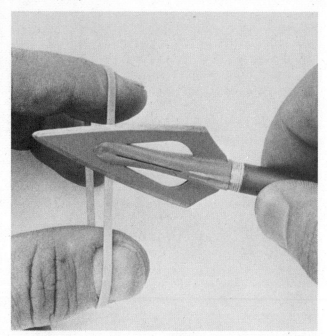

edge than steel because of its denser molecular structure—a fortunate happenstance for native bow-hunters of yesteryear.

How sharp is sharp enough? Unfortunately, many hunters who fancy themselves expert broadhead sharpeners cannot adequately sharpen an edge to save their lives! Three primary tests of edge sharpness will settle this question once and for all. Drag an edge across your thumbnail *lightly* to test the edge—if the edge slides instead of grabbing into the nail solidly, it is too dull to hunt with. Carefully, try shaving hair off your arm or leg with a broadhead edge—if hair cuts away easily as if with a razor blade, the edge is sharp enough to hunt deer with. If you have to scrape and work at shaving hair, the edge is not adequate. Stretch a medium-sized rubber band between two fingers and slide a broadhead edge over it with very light pressure—if the rubber band does not instantly cut in two without friction, the edge is not up to snuff.

In most cases, top-quality factory-sharpened broadhead blades will pass these sharpness tests with flying colors. Every edge on every broadhead you hunt with should be adequately sharp along its entire length to ensure quick, humane kills on deer. A hunter who prefers factory-sharpened edges should make darn sure he uses a broadhead model with uniformly sharp edges and he should check these edges frequently, replacing any blades that become dull.

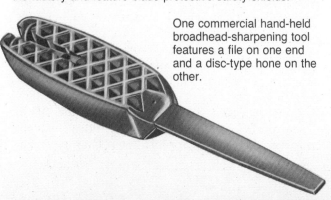

The Razorback 4 and 5 broadheads come ultra-sharp from the factory and feature blade-protective safety shields.

One commercial hand-held broadhead-sharpening tool features a file on one end and a disc-type hone on the other.

The fellow who prefers to sharpen broadheads himself should practice the sharpening art until he has it down pat. If he can't seem to get the hang of hand sharpening, he'll do himself a favor by going to a keen factory-sharpened model. Part of the hand-sharpening skill depends on the type of broadhead being sharpened, and a hunter who cannot seem to sharpen one model adequately might try one or two others on the theory that the original broadhead's steel was second-rate or that the shape of this head presented a too-difficult sharpening challenge. Most hand-sharpenable broadheads incorporate excellent steel, but a few do not. On top of this, it's a fact that some such heads are considerably easier to hand-sharpen than others because of the way blades fan out from the central sections of these broadheads. For example, a two-blade head is the easiest type to sharpen properly, whereas a four-blade head is difficult to manipulate on a stone. Among the best hand-sharpenable deer-hunting broadheads are four-blade heads with two main blades plus two "auxiliary blades" that remove to facilitate easier hand-sharpening.

Here are a few other important facts about broadhead-blade sharpness. The two major enemies of a sharp steel edge are abrasion and rusting caused by moisture. Anytime a blade is shot, or when it is bumped against a rock, tree, car door, or another hard object, the edge is dulled and must be replaced or

(Above and left) Broadhead wrenches allow snug attachment and easy detachment of broadheads without danger to a bowhunter's fingers.

The items necessary to hand-sharpen a broadhead are (clockwise): honing oil, mill file, broadhead attached to a shaft, edge-stropping leather, medium- and fine-grain honing stones.

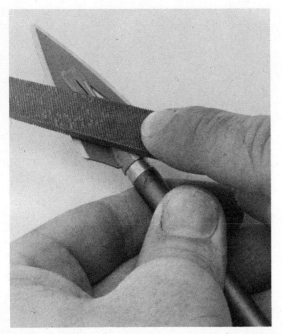

1. To sharpen your own broadheads, file all edges to an approximate 22-degree angle, using the ferrule (center section) of the broadhead as a file guide.

resharpened. Anytime rust forms on an edge, it dramatically loses its keeness.

There are two basic kinds of steels used in broadhead blades, and each has specific advantages worth considering. Stainless steel does not normally take and hold an edge as keenly as high-carbon steel does, but the stainless is far more resistant to edge-dulling moisture. In contrast, high-carbon steel takes a keener edge initially and is less prone to chip or flatten out when it bumps obstacles during the course of a hunting day, but such steel needs regular oiling to prevent microscopic edge-dulling from fog, rain, or snow. Both steels work well on deer, but the high-carbon variety is better if you want to put up with keeping it oiled and totally rust-free.

Two other quick notes on broadhead sharpness. First, to keep broadhead edges keen and rust-free, and to protect you and others from dangerous accidental

2. (Above) Lightly spade the end of the broadhead to strengthen the tip and allow stone sharpening completely around the nose.

3. Carefully hone all edges on a well-oiled, medium-grain knife-sharpening stone, using the broadhead ferrule as a guide to ensure an approximate 22-degree edge angle.

4. Hone the broadhead a second time on a fine-grain stone to polish edges and enhance sharpness.

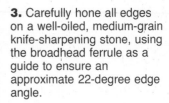

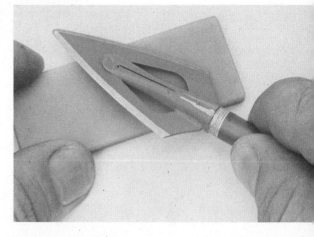

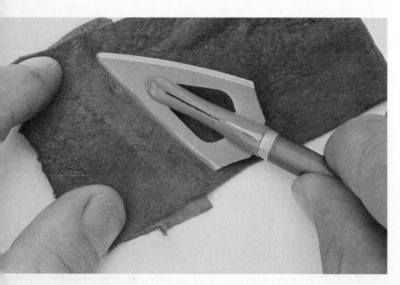

5. Strop each side of each blade edge by running the edge *backwards* across buckskin or another kind of leather. This refines an edge even further.

So-called "shaft locks" are little spring rings that attach between a broadhead and a shaft to ensure snug, consistent arrowhead alignment.

(Right) Old-style glue-on broadheads can be excellent deer-getters, but only when carefully glue-aligned to shafts to ensure accurate flight.

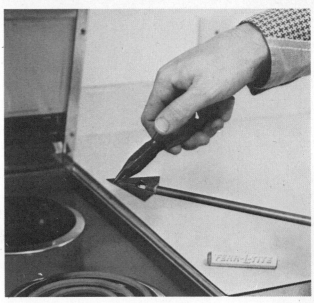

cuts, always store sharp broadheads in some sort of durable container. Second, always use a commercial broadhead wrench to attach and detach screw-in broadheads instead of your fingers—using your hands to do so can result in severe cuts if your grip on a broadhead accidentally slips.

Other Important Broadhead Traits

At this point, we've covered the primary things to look for in an effective deer-hunting broadhead. However, other specific factors might influence your final choice.

Most factory-sharpened, replaceable-blade hunting heads screw-attach quickly and conveniently to hunting arrows. By contrast, most hand-sharpenable heads must be glued to tapered inserts that in turn attach to hunting arrows. Any glue-on broadhead can be converted to a screw-in broadhead by epoxying it to an aluminum, screw-in broadhead adapter sold by several different companies. The alternative to this is gluing each head directly to a shaft, a process that prevents quick arrowhead replacement in the field and does not allow a hunter to store and transport sharp broadheads in a separate compact container. In most cases, a deer hunter is best advised to epoxy glue-on heads to screw-in broadhead adapters. However, in any event the glue-on heads require extra work to prepare them for the field—work some bowhunters would prefer to do without.

Obviously, replaceable-blade hunting broadheads are far handier to use than those which require tedious hand sharpening. Even the best broadhead sharpeners

usually spend 15 minutes per head to ensure razor-keen edges—a per-head time span that rapidly adds up when a hunter has to prepare eight or 10 heads for deer season. Even hunters who are fully capable of sharpening steel to scalpel perfection sometimes opt to use pre-sharpened blades for the sake of convenience.

If there are several deer-hunting broadheads available you feel will do a fine job for you in the field, consider the foregoing convenience factors to help you make a final choice.

Unusual Broadhead Designs

With all due respect to archery manufacturers, hunting-head designers occasionally introduce off-the-wall broadhead models that deviate dramatically from tried-and-true norms and absolutely insult the intelligence of any experienced hunting archer. Two such heads currently on the market are designed to penetrate shallowly in deer and then stop dead as blades fly open like switchblades, or high-friction center sections jam solidly against meat or bone. Such misbegotten broadheads fly in the face of all practical broadhead-design knowledge, perhaps making their creators a few quick bucks but inevitably causing unsuspecting consumers a great deal of grief. Offbeat broadhead designs are fun to theorize about and experiment with, but a bowhunter should stick with time-tested, traditional styles to ensure success and satisfaction in the field.

A sharp, well-designed deer-hunting broadhead will drop game with astounding effectiveness and speed. To ensure optimum success afield, choose your hunting heads with care!

5/Shooting Equipment

IN ADDITION to basic bow-and-arrow equipment, a deer hunter needs some important accessories to help him shoot well and make this shooting an optimally enjoyable and productive experience. These important shooting items include some sort of bowstring release aid to protect the fingers, an armguard to protect the bow arm from the string, a target-arrow quiver and/or other kind of quiver, a good-quality optical bowhunting rangefinder, and a complement of practical target-range equipment. In addition, a hunter may opt to add a few other things to this gear collection which will help him in his bow-shooting both at home and in the field. Here are these important shooting accessories discussed and described in detail to help you make sensible choices.

Bowstring Release Aids

Every bowhunter needs some sort of protection for his bowstring fingers which also helps him achieve smooth, accurate arrow release. A few misinformed hunters shoot a bow bare-fingered, but the friction of bowstring against skin can cause discomfort and blisters plus sloppy, inaccurate arrow releases.

The two traditional bowstring release aids used by hunters are the finger glove and the shooting tab. The plastic or leather finger glove fits snugly over the archer's three string-gripping fingers and is held in place by a snap-on or Velcro-closing wrist strap. The tab is a smaller, more compact piece of flat leather or plastic which attaches to the middle finger of the bowstring hand with a simple slip-over loop. Both designs are popular with deer hunters, and both adequately protect bowstring fingers during a shot.

A good-quality leather finger glove usually feels most natural to a beginning archer because it fits snugly over the fingers like a regular glove. However, it is inherently less accurate than a shooting tab because the leather eventually grooves deeply where the bowstring meets the glove during the aiming process. This deep grooving tends to hang the bowstring up when an arrow is released, cutting down on release smoothness and slightly scattering arrows. Some excellent bow shots like the feel of a shooting glove and use one in spite of its tendency to groove, but these hunters must keep close watch and replace their gloves whenever the grooves begin to seriously hamper smooth shooting.

Although a few companies make plastic shooting gloves, these have no practical applications in serious deer hunting. Plastic gloves never last as long as leather gloves, are seldom as comfortable to wear, make more noise when an arrow is released, and tend to groove more deeply than good-quality leather does.

For hunters who decide to stick with a shooting glove, there are dozens of models sold in a myriad of finger sizes. Some of these are even camouflaged to help a hunter hide from the wary eyes of deer.

Several varieties of good-quality shooting tabs are sold at archery stores, but the near-standard choice of experienced shots is the so-called "Kant-Pinch" design. This tab provides two or three separate layers of finger-cushioning material between the string and a shooter's hand and has an integral finger-spreading block that prevents the index and middle fingers of the hand from pinching and torquing an arrow nock when the draw is made. One shooting-tab design I prefer consists of a heavy leather backing that lies against the fingers, a middle layer of tough, cushioning rubber on top of that, and a third layer of smooth, leather-backed calf hair that lies against the bowstring. Such a cushioned calf-hair tab provides an incredibly slick bowstring release, does not groove at all like a glove, and fully guards the bowstring fingers against bruising or abrasion. Such a tab is used by virtually all tournament shooters who opt to hold the string with their fingers, and provides the silkiest, most accurate string release possible with the fingers.

Another thing I like about a finger tab is the fact that it allows a hand to breathe in warm weather instead of sweating inside a glove. A tab can also be rotated 180 degrees on the middle finger when it is not in use, allowing a hunter to eat, drive a car, or do anything else with his hands while the tab is still instantly ready to be rotated and used.

A shooting tab feels a bit strange to some hunters when they first try one out, especially when they anchor against their faces and aim prior to a shot. However, after a little practice a tab fits as comfortably as an old, well-worn shoe.

Although the majority of deer hunters use shooting gloves or tabs, an increasing number of hunters are turning to mechanical bowstring release aids to grip and release a string. Such mechanical releases have advan-

tages and disadvantages every shooter should consider prior to trying them out.

The mechanical bowstring release was first used in tournament-shooting circles a few years back, and it almost immediately boosted target scores considerably. Such a release snaps snugly on a bowstring directly below an arrow and holds the string firmly during the draw, anchor, and aim. When a shooter is on the target, he simply pulls or pushes a gun-like trigger on the release, and it lets go of the string with incredible crispness.

Mechanical bowstring releases vary somewhat in the way they are held in the hand, from T-shaped models held like hay hooks, to "concho" models gripped in a closed fist, to wrist-strap models that are actually buckled around the shooter's wrist. However, all pro-

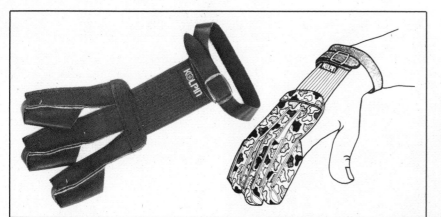

A shooting glove protects the bowstring fingers and is also comfortable to wear. The best models are made of leather, and a few are actually camouflaged.

(Left and above) A "Kant-Pinch" type shooting tab allows the most accurate finger release of a bowstring and becomes easy to use with a little bit of practice.

(Left and below) A wrist-strap mechanical bowstring release is ultra-accurate and especially easy to use with heavy-draw deer bows.

A mechanical bowstring release is deadly accurate in practiced hands.

vide the major advantage of holding the bowstring at one point and releasing it with gun-like precision when the trigger is gently pressed. Bowstring release triggers vary from conventional index-finger triggers to buttons pushed with the thumb or little finger. However, all top-quality designs provide a clean, consistent bowstring release.

There is no question that in expert hands, a bowstring release is more accurate on targets than a standard three-finger release. A person simply cannot hold a string in three separate, quivering fingers and expect to let go exactly the same from shot to shot. As a result, some bowhunters feel that they are better off using a mechanical bowstring release instead of a regular three-finger draw.

Before you rush out and buy one, consider these significant hunting disadvantages: First, a release is noticeably slower to use than the fingers. Second, it must be carried constantly in the hand. Third, it tends to clank arrows and/or bow noisily when a hunter is grabbing for backup shots in his quiver. Fourth, it tends to wear out bowstrings quite rapidly in the area where it latches on. Fifth, it makes considerably more noise when it releases the string than three fingers do. Sixth, it does not allow the level of arrow control on the arrow rest provided by two fingers hugging the nock of an arrow. If a release-drawn arrow falls off your rest, you cannot put it back on without letting down the bowstring, going through considerable body gyrations, and then drawing the bow once more. Seventh, a mechanical release can malfunction like any other mechanical device, giving a hunter one more thing to worry about in the field. And eighth, setting up a bowstring to use with a release requires two nocking points instead of one plus considerable experimentation to find out exactly where these two nocking points must go for clean arrow flight. Using a bowstring release may be potentially more accurate than using your fingers, but exercising this option is certainly no free lunch.

On the positive side of the coin, a bowstring release

(Left and below) A T-shaped bowstring release is one popular hunting design. Several trigger-button placements are available on such releases, including thumb buttons like the one shown here.

(Above and left) A baggy bow-arm sleeve can ruin shooting accuracy. To flatten out a sleeve and also protect a forearm from painful bowstring slap, experienced bowhunters always use some sort of armguard.

is very accurate, especially for hunters who have serious problems achieving a decent finger release. In frigid weather, a release functions well even when fingers are nearly numb from the cold. A release also completely eliminates finger bruising—a problem some archers have when shooting heavy-draw bows.

As a general rule, I recommend that deer-hunting archers learn to shoot with a finger glove or tab prior to trying out a bowstring release. In most cases, archers can become extremely accurate with a three-finger draw—more than accurate enough to take deer at fairly long shooting ranges. A bowstring release aid is certainly beneficial to some hunters who are not satisfied with their finger-shooting ability, but I feel that for most hunters the slight target-accuracy edge of using a bowstring release in no way compensates for the built-in disadvantages of this alternate string-release method. In a nutshell, shooting at archery targets and shooting at serious big-game are two entirely different sports.

Armguards

In addition to some sort of bowstring release aid, a deer hunter needs an inexpensive armguard which attaches firmly to his forearm between the elbow and wrist. An armguard does two basic things—it protects the shooter's arm from extremely painful bowstring slap during a shot, and it also holds down the baggy sleeve on a hunting shirt or coat to ensure accurate shooting. Nothing sends an arrow wild more surely than a bowstring hitting a sleeve during a shot, thus disrupting the string's travel and making the arrow wobble badly.

There's nothing complicated about choosing a bow-hunting armguard. Various models are available, including good-quality leather guards and skeletonized plastic guards that breath well in hot hunting weather. The best hunting armguards are about 6 inches long and 4 inches wide—just large enough to fully cover the vulnerable part of a shooter's forearm. I personally

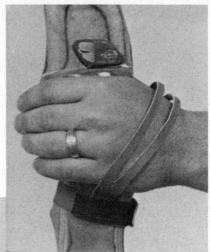

(Left) In warm bowhunting weather, a ventilated armguard like this model from Saunders is cool and very effective to wear.

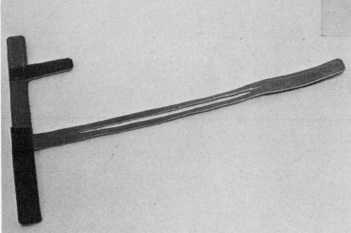

(Left, above and right) A wrist sling allows a hunter to shoot with a loose, open hand to prevent bow-grabbing which results in poor accuracy. This Martin Twin-Sling allows two hand-holding configurations to satisfy individual shooting tastes.

prefer a solid leather armguard over one made of plastic because the leather makes less noise when the bowstring occasionally smacks it during a shot.

Other Shooting Aids

Two other bow-shooting aids that are widely used by bowhunters are wrist slings and powder pouches. Both can improve shooting accuracy when properly employed.

A wrist sling is a leather or braided nylon strap assembly which physically ties an archer's hand to a bow. This gizmo can be a pain to leave attached throughout the course of a hunting day, but it performs one very important function. If a bowhunter has a difficult time holding his bow in a loose, torque-free grip during a shot, a wrist sling allows him to shoot with an open hand and eliminates the chance that he will grab or squeeze the bow as the arrow launches on its way. Bow-grabbing is a major bow-shooting problem of many hunters, and a wrist sling can help a shooter lick

this problem and improve his score on deer.

A powder pouch is a simple commercial container that clips or ties to a hunter's belt. It has a porous frontal window that leaks out talcum powder when a hunter traps it with his bowstring fingers. A little Johnson's Baby Powder or similar talc dusted on a shooter's glove or tab will most definitely provide a slicker-than-normal string release and a higher level of shooting accuracy. I use a powder pouch at all times when target shooting and hunting, and know for certain that it helps my field accuracy significantly. An added plus in hunting is the fact that a little talc tapped from this pouch instantly drifts away on the prevailing breeze, letting me monitor wind direction as I sit on stand or sneak around the woods.

Arrow Quivers

The bow quiver has been fully described in Chapter 2. However, there are other quivers a deer-hunting archer should know about and experiment with.

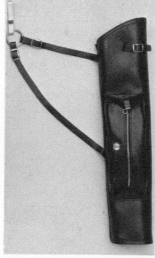

A powder pouch gives a deer hunter easy access to dry lubricant for a shooting glove or tab.

A fairly expensive target-shooting hip quiver usually has ample arrow capacity plus a side compartment for small shooting accessories.

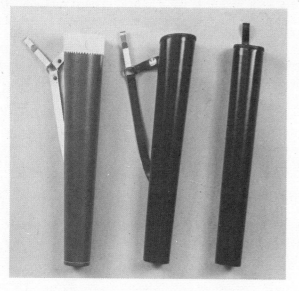

Simple, inexpensive tube-type hip quivers are handy to use on a backyard shooting range.

This hunting hip quiver is camouflaged for the field.

Every bowhunter should own some sort of inexpensive target quiver to conveniently carry field-point arrows on the range. The kind of quiver I'm referring to is a simple tube that clips on an archer's belt along his side. Such a quiver need not be elaborate, but a hunter can purchase some pretty fancy target hip quivers if he so desires. Practically speaking, an inexpensive plastic model will work just fine as long as it is large enough in diameter to loosely carry eight or 10 arrows with ease.

In addition to a simple target quiver, some deer hunters prefer to use hip or back quivers for carrying deer-hunting arrows instead of the more popular bow quiver. Although a bow quiver is most convenient to use in the majority of hunting circumstances, it is not the ideal quiver for all archery deer hunters. Shooters who get nitpicky about shooting accuracy and bow balance know that a bow quiver slightly degrades accuracy and slightly unbalances a bow, and such fellows sometimes go to alternate hunting quivers to ensure best bow accuracy and balance. I personally use

a hip quiver a fair share of the time for this reason, especially when I'm carrying a fast-shooting, accuracy-critical bow, or when I'm using extra-large, extra-touchy hunting broadheads to ensure quick kills on moose, elk, or caribou. A separate belt-carried arrow quiver is a nuisance, but results in the best bow accuracy in some special-purpose situations.

Several archery companies sell hip quivers that hold hunting arrows close at hand along a hunter's side. Such quivers actually require less obtrusive hand movement to pluck out backup arrows when shooting at deer than bow quivers do although the difference is slight and seldom, if ever, alters the outcome of a shooting situation. A hip quiver is slightly tougher to maneuver through brush than is a hand-carried bow and bow quiver, but a hunter rapidly learns to weave in and out of foliage with a belt-mounted quiver.

A back quiver normally attaches to a bowhunter's body with a network of straps and rides directly in the middle of a shooter's back. Such a quiver rides well out

61

of the way as a hunter moves around and, in the larger models, lets him carry many more than the standard eight arrows for extended treks in country where lots of long-range shooting is the exception instead of the rule. Back quivers are most popular with backpacking bowhunters who wish to carry a dozen or more arrows into the wilderness with them and want to have all of these arrows close at hand when game is spotted and stalked.

No matter what kind of hip or back quiver a bowhunter buys, it should share the same safety features that are standard in a good-quality bow quiver. Broadheads should be fully enclosed beneath a protective hood, and arrows should be snugly held in rubber grippers. It is easier to fall on a body-attached quiver than on a bow-attached model, so such a quiver must fully protect the hunter from the razor-keen broadheads.

The old-style shoulder quiver seen in Robin Hood movies is every bit as outdated as wooden arrow shafts. It was never a particularly practical design, rattling shafts together noisily, dulling sharp broadhead edges quickly, and hanging up on every overhead limb and vine in sight. A few longbowmen carry shoulder quivers for old times' sake, but modern bowhunters intent on nailing deer steer well clear of these antiquated items.

Bowhunting Rangefinders

Next to the compound bow, the quality bowhunting rangefinder is without a doubt the single most important deer-hunting item to be introduced during the past few decades. Unless a person is fully aware of the arching trajectory of an arrow in flight, he cannot begin to appreciate how critical range estimation is in hitting deer-sized objects.

Bowhunters justifiably worry about how accurate their shooting is on targets, striving to achieve consistently smooth bowstring releases and other polished aspects of top-notch shooting form. However, when compared to accurate range estimation, a hunter's ability to hit objects at known ranges is not nearly as important.

Consider the following facts about the arching trajectory of a hunting arrow. A 522-grain, 1918 aluminum arrow shot from a moderately fast-shooting round-wheel compound bow of 55 pounds leaves the bow at about 185 feet per second. This arrow, which is typical of what the average whitetail deer hunter will shoot, hits dead on at 15 yards, hits 5 inches low at 20 yards, hits 13.1 inches low at 25 yards, hits 23.8 inches low at 30 yards, hits 53.1 inches low at 40 yards, and hits 73.1 inches low at 45 yards. These staggering drop statistics clearly illustrate what shooting problems a deer-hunting archer is up against when he heads for the field. With the bow/arrow combo just described, a hunter who mistakes 20 yards for 15 will clip the 10-inch-deep vital zone on a broadside deer extremely low with the very good possibility of a lost, lightly crippled animal. If he mistakes 25 yards for 15 or even 20, he will miss the deer he is shooting at completely. At ranges past 25, our bowhunter will have to accurately judge shooting distance within 1 or 2 yards for vital hits on deer! Such pinpoint range estimation is virtually impossible to pull off the majority of the time, even when a bowhunter practices eyeballing ranges on a regular basis.

Flatter-shooting round-wheel compound bows, cambows, and overdraw bows somewhat increase an archer's capability for mis-estimating range and still hitting deer in vital areas. However, the majority of deer missed by archers are still missed high or low. It is simply all too easy to badly blow distance estimation on deer in the field, even under ideal terrain and lighting situations. Add to this the fact that shooting often occurs across canyons, up and down hills, out of high tree stands, and/or in the dim light of early morning or late evening, and a bowhunter without some sort of rangefinding aid is apt to mis-guesstimate a majority of hunting shots that come his way.

Bowhunters have been trying to improve their range-estimating abilities for years, both by practicing range estimation by eye and by employing various mechanical devices. Eye-estimating practice helps a lot, and some hunters have also claimed to benefit by so-called stadimetric rangefinders attached to bowsights. To use a stadimetric rangefinder, a hunter has to draw his bow, fit the chest depth of a broadside deer perfectly between a set of bars or in a correct-sized metal ring, and then use the bowsight distance pin that corresponds to this particular set of bars or rangefinding ring. There have always been three problems with this particular method of determining bowshooting distance.

First, a deer seldom stands broadside in one wide-open place long enough to let a hunter line up bars or rings. Second, the time it takes to use a stadimetric rangefinder at full draw tires a hunter's shooting muscles to the point where he might well blow a shot even if he correctly figures the range. Third, using a stadimetric rangefinder results in relatively crude distance estimation because deer vary considerably in body depth and because holding a bar or a ring on an animal is a wobbly proposition at best.

So much for stadimetric bowhunting rangefinders. Thank goodness there are better rangefinders now available. The pioneer in the development of quality bowhunting rangefinders and the undisputed leader in this field is Ranging, Inc., of East Rochester, New York. Over the past several years, Ranging, Inc., has continued to upgrade their already fine belt-carried optical rangefinders, improving reading accuracy and also its compact design. The most current bowhunter's models are the Model 50/2 Mini-Rangefinder and the Model 80/2 Pro Rangefinder. Both zero in on deer with

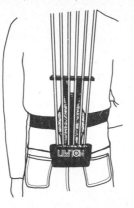

A back quiver rides well out of the way and allows unobtrusive behind-the-body arrow access.

(Below and right) Hip quivers for hunting are sold by several companies. The best of these provide the same roomy broadhead hoods and secure rubber arrow-shaft grippers found on good bow quivers.

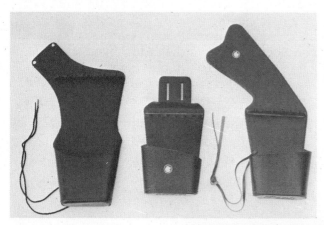

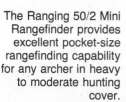

The Ranging 50/2 Mini Rangefinder provides excellent pocket-size rangefinding capability for any archer in heavy to moderate hunting cover.

The Ranging 80/2 Pro Rangefinder is the choice of most serious open-country bowhunters because it allows pinpoint distance estimation at longer shooting ranges.

A hip quiver frees a bow of unwieldy bow-quiver weight, which can sometimes improve field-shooting accuracy and lead to more deer in the bag.

the turn of a dial, bringing two separate images of an object together into one and providing the exact distance to that object on a highly visible distance scale. Such rangefinders have revolutionized deer-hunting archery, giving the hunter a reliably accurate means of determining the exact distance to the animal he's shooting at.

The Ranging Model 50/2 and Model 80/2 offer the precision of distance measurement absolutely necessary for hitting deer with a bow. The 50/2 measures ranges from 15 to 70 yards and is accurate to within 1 yard at 50 yards. The 80/2 measures ranges from 20 to 100 yards and is accurate to within 2 yards at 80 yards. Both units are even more accurate at closer bow-shooting distances. The Model 50/2 weighs only 5 ounces, measures less than 6 inches in length and can be carried on its factory neckstrap or in a shirt pocket. An optional belt-attached commercial camouflage case is also available for this model. The Model 80/2 weighs only 10 ounces, measures less than 10 inches in length and is designed to be carried in a trim camouflage belt pouch. These two bowhunting rangefinders are the state of the art in optical aids for distance-conscious archers.

Ranging, Inc., also manufactures an excellent little hand-held stadimetric rangefinder that has the bow-mounted type beat in every way. Although not the accurate tool that the models 50/2 and 80/2 are, this little, palm-sized rangefinder is used successfully by many deer hunters each and every year.

Accurate optical bowhunting rangefinders are used by deer hunters in two basic ways. When used from tree stands or ground blinds, these optical aids let a hunter take readings on nearby logs, rocks, tree trunks, and similar landmarks along the trails where game is likely to appear. This eliminates the need to pace off ranges around a stand—a practice which takes time and energy and which also tends to saturate a stand area with deer-spooking scent.

A bowhunter who moves about on foot can use his rangefinder to take readings on both nearby landmarks and target deer themselves. In a stalking situation, a hunter can sometimes actually lift his rangefinder slowly from the pouch and get an accurate reading on the animal's antlers or the sharp edge of its body against contrasting foliage. In situations when a deer's outline is not clearly visible enough to accurately line up images, a hunter can usually zero in on a weather-bleached snag, tree trunk, or other definite object at the same range as the game and accurately determine the distance. Bowhunting rangefinders work like a charm when properly used!

To ensure accurate distance readings in bowhunting situations, a deer hunter should properly calibrate his rangefinder according to directions, check these calibrations periodically, and practice with his rangefinder to learn how to bring double images together sharply.

Target-Range Equipment

To be well-set-up in the shooting-equipment department, a deer hunter needs a simple, functional backyard target range. This allows him to practice his

A serious deer hunter learns to quickly use and rely on his belt-carried bowhunting rangefinder.

Bowhunting rangefinders are best carried in handy commercial belt pouches.

The palm-sized Ranging Sure Shot optical stadimetric rangefinder is an economical deer-hunting choice.

shooting skills and keep his archery muscles in tip-top shape.

Of primary importance is a good, quality target butt. There are several fully portable commercial butts available through your archery store if you wish to put away a butt when it isn't in use or want the option of carting it along to the hunting camp when deer season is open. In addition, the homemade straw bale target butt is a solid favorite of knowledgeable bowhunters. Here are some details on both commercial and do-it-yourself target butts.

One long-standing favorite among commercial bow-hunting target butts is the Indian rope-grass matt. This round, brown-colored butt is available in several diameters from 12 inches up to 48 inches. The smaller sizes are fully portable and can be leaned up against a tree, fence, or similar backstop as long as matts are kept damp, according to instructions, to prevent the natural grass they are made of from drying out, loosening up, and letting arrows penetrate completely through. In addition, regular commercial matt easels are available for these target butts. Rope-grass matts will take a fair amount of abuse before giving up the ghost and can be shot with any kind of field point. Broadheads cannot be used with rope-grass matts.

Two other popular portable field-point target butts are what I call "bean-bag" butts and "pass-through" butts. The bean-bag butt is any kind of butt which consists of a burlap-like bag loosely stuffed with cotton or other impact-absorbent material. Such a butt can be shot over and over again without damage to the

An Indian rope-grass matt is one of the best portable target butts available.

A bean-bag butt like this one from Calmont Archery provides excellent portability and durability. This particular model has bull's-eyes on one side and a deer target on the other. It is easily reversed on its compact metal easel.

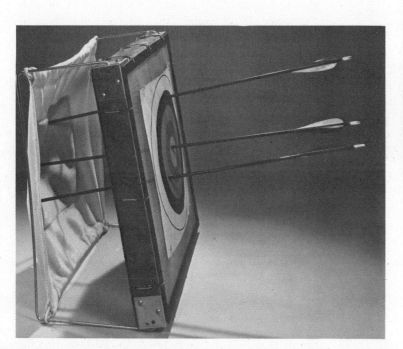

This pass-through butt by Promat Archery allows enjoyable target shooting at home and in the field.

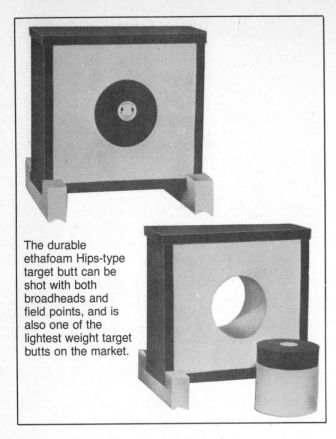

The durable ethafoam Hips-type target butt can be shot with both broadheads and field points, and is also one of the lightest weight target butts on the market.

stuffing. A pass-through butt has a woven face made of nylon strands or strands of a similar impact-resistant material. Arrows hit a target attached to such woven mesh, pass through the mesh between the strands, and collide with a loosely hanging, heavy-fabric curtain several inches behind the face of the target. This sort of butt is also fairly durable when shot with field-point hunting arrows.

The only durable, portable target butt I know about that can be shot with broadheads as well as field points is the Hips-type ethafoam target. Several companies manufacture such a butt, and the space-age, self-healing ethafoam it is composed of takes broadhead abuse surprisingly well. The best of such target butts feature replaceable center sections to salvage a butt when broadheads finally chew the center to shreds. Ethafoam is incredibly light in weight, making it the ideal material for a butt you want to throw in the hunting rig or carry into the garage when a shooting session is done.

A simple straw-bale butt is by far the most practical homemade target for backyard shooting. This is assembled by stacking three large, tight straw bales on two old automobile tires. The tires hold the bales high and dry, and do not damage arrows that accidentally hit low. Such a butt setup can be made especially stable by driving a wooden post on either side of the bales to wedge them in a rigid upright position. Although any kind of straw works well in such a setup, wheat straw is most durable and least prone to shred and disintegrate with regular shooting. I like big, three-wire bales the best for such a setup. A straw-bale butt costs less than $15 to erect and lasts an incredibly long time. When the middle bale wears out, simply rotate it to top or bottom and keep on shooting until all three bales are thoroughly thrashed. In the winter, cover the bales with inexpensive plastic to keep them dry and serviceable.

(Left and below) A straw-bale butt consisting of several bales atop old auto tires is one of the cheapest and most durable target butts available. A simple bow rack alongside a butt makes a shooter's life a little easier.

A single bale of straw can make a decent target butt, too. Simply stand it up on end and lean it against a homemade easel or an existing object like a tree or fence.

A wide variety of archery targets can be attached to your backyard butt. Among these are commercial gold-centered American Round faces, black and white field-shooting faces, blue and white PAA faces, and many, many others. Homemade archery targets work as well if you want to make them. One excellent and extremely cheap do-it-yourself target face is a regular white paper pie plate with a black circle drawn in the center with a broad-tipped felt marker. Such bull's-eye targets are best for beginners to shoot at, and also best for experts to use when working on their bow-shooting form. In addition, there are many deer targets sold through archery stores—both printed on paper and sculpted in 3-D. There is more on deer targets in Chapter 10.

Aside from a suitable target butt and some kind of target to aim at, a hunter needs very few other things to set up a comfortable and practical shooting facility. Most hunters pound pegs in the ground on a backyard range to mark shooting increments like 20, 25, and 30 yards. A few invest in some kind of bow rack for their range, although a nail pounded in a tree for bow-hanging or a table to lay a bow on will suffice. Archery manufacturers sell some nifty little target-range gizmos worth looking at next time you go to the archery shop or sporting goods store—things like a foam-rubber arrow gripper that makes pulling arrows from a tight bale easy on the hands. There really isn't much range gear needed to enjoy shooting at your house.

Chapters 1 through 5 have outlined most of the gear you'll need to shoot a bow and shoot it well. Now it's time to move along to the basics of sound bow-shooting on targets and game.

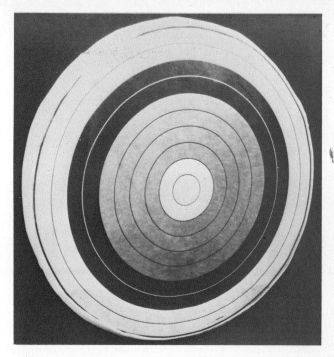

A variety of standard bull's-eye targets are sold at archery stores.

A simple foam-rubber arrow puller can help a hunter remove stubborn arrows from a tight target butt.

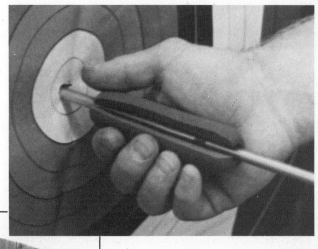

Three-dimensional foam animal targets like those sold by Martin Archery provide realistic backyard shooting fun.

6/Equipment Care

MODERN bow-shooting equipment is extremely dependable and trouble-free. However, it does require a certain amount of upkeep and repair for optimum shooting performance. Very little is written on the subject of care for hunting bows and arrows, and I encounter dozens of examples of inadvertent shooting-equipment abuse each and every year. Proper care does not require much time, effort, or thought, but often goes begging because archers do not know how to baby their gear to prolong its life and keep it shooting well.

Whenever you buy a piece of bow-shooting equipment, read the accompanying manufacturer's literature for hints on how this equipment should be handled. In addition to those specific tips, here are some basic guidelines on how to care for and repair your equipment.

Bow Cases

One of the smartest things any hunter can do is purchase some sort of protective bow case that fully encloses a bow and shields it from bumps, moisture, heat, and grime. Far too many archers dispense with this precaution and subject their bows to direct abuse that could easily be prevented. Bow cases run the price spectrum from cheap to terribly expensive, but a semi-soft case costing less than $20 is smart protection for a valuable shooting tool even if a hunter is pinching pennies.

The most commonly seen cases are the semi-soft variety just mentioned. These are typically made with a vinyl or fabric exterior, a soft flannel lining, and some kind of batting in between to cushion and protect. A case of this sort normally has handles for carrying and a zippered closure. Bow cases matching this general description are sold to fit compounds, older-style recurves and longbows, and hunting-grade crossbows.

Semi-soft cases come in many colors, several sizes and designs. Color is strictly a matter of personal taste, but the most practical shape for compound hunting bows is the square-end design. This particular configuration is tapered to a point on one end to conform to a compound bow limb and is more or less square on the other end to loosely cover not only the bow but also an attached bow quiver full of arrows. This square-end design makes transport easy because the bow-quiver

(Below and opposite page) This camo-print bow case by Saunders is easily carried over a shoulder.

68

(Above) A really well-padded semi-soft case will adequately protect a compound bow from almost any reasonable abuse. This overstuffed model has foam rubber walls well over 1-inch thick.

(Below and right) The most practical soft compound cases are square on one end to cover a bow-attached quiver.

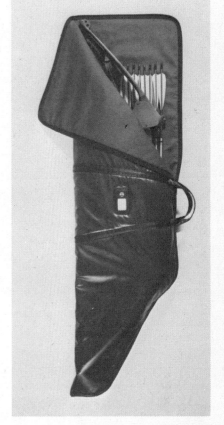

Semi-soft protective cases are available for all kinds of bows. This fine fleece-lined case holds a hunting crossbow and accessories.

(Right) A hard plastic or metal case offers ultimate protection from shock and moisture. Such a case often holds ample hunting arrows and accessories, too.

Placing a bow in a hot car is a sure way to ruin laminated limbs in short order.

setup remains intact. All a hunter needs to do to hunt deer is pull his assembled shooting setup from the case.

When shopping for a semi-soft bow case, pay attention to some beneficial special features. Some cases include integral compartments for a stabilizer, and others have additional handles or backpack straps attached to allow over-the-shoulder carrying. The most important thing, however, is checking out the quality of case construction and making sure a case has adequate padding to protect bowsights and other more fragile parts.

For better bow protection during transport—particularly on long automobile trips or commercial airlines—there are several more expensive bow cases available through archery or sporting goods stores. Some of these are merely modified semi-soft cases with thick foam-rubber padding instead of the thinner, less shock-absorbent materials. Others consist of hard plastic or aluminum shells fully padded inside with good-quality foam rubber. Some such cases are roomy enough to hold not only a hunting bow but also a couple of dozen arrows, a bow quiver, and all the shooting accessories needed on a hunting trip.

One of my favorite compound-bow cases is the

Saf-T-Case, a rugged, fully waterproof, solidly padded aluminum unit, made primarily for rifles and shotguns. The Saf-T-Case has a strong, full-length piano hinge, four latches to hold the lid in place, and padlock loops to lock these latches closed. It is large enough to hold most compound bows, and represents the ideal choice for long-distance airline transport.

Protection from Heat, Moisture, and Stress

Aside from general knock-around abuse, hunting bows are susceptible to damage by heat, moisture, and stress. Here's how to protect your favorite bow from these three enemies.

Heat

Excessive heat can ruin the limbs on quality bows in a few short minutes. Laminated wood-and-fiberglass limbs are especially sensitive to heat and will literally come apart at the seams if they become too hot and the industrial-grade epoxy they are glued together with disintegrates and fails.

Anytime bow limbs become too hot to easily touch, they are apt to come apart. The most common cause of heat-related failure is leaving a bow in a hot, unventilated automobile—especially in the super-hot area directly beneath the windshield. Even if limbs subjected to heat do not fly apart on the spot, they can fail weeks or months later as shooting stress completes the breakdown process.

Any other heat source will have a similar effect. Laying a bow too close to a campfire, fireplace, or wood stove can quickly ruin the limbs. Bow limbs occasionally blow up even in ultra-hot hunting situations when a nimrod accidentally leaves his bow lying on the steel bed of a pickup, a hot rock, or other hot surface. A hunter should take pains to keep his bow reasonably cool at all times to prevent obvious or hidden damage to the limbs.

Moisture

Moisture can be as devastating to bow limbs as heat can. Generally, it takes days and days of hunting in wet conditions to take its toll, but eventually steady moisture can creep through the commercial finish on bow limbs and soak into wooden core laminations. This softens and deteriorates wood to the point where it simply breaks apart under the tremendous tensions of bending to cast an arrow. Solid-fiberglass bow limbs found on some modern, good-quality compound bows are not susceptible to damage by water.

To protect laminated limbs from moisture, simply dry them off whenever possible and keep a bow inside or covered up instead of hanging out all night in torrential downpours. Don't worry about hunting in the rain—bow limbs are finished to protect them from such contact with the elements. It is excessive moisture over many days that can damage laminated limbs.

Moisture will also quickly rust the steel parts of a compound bow unless precautions are taken. If you have camouflaged your bow with dull paint, most exposed steel parts are at least partially protected from water. However, it's a good idea to use WD-40 or other penetrating oil on draw-weight adjustment bolts, wheel or cam axles, quiver and bowsight mounting screws, and similar steel parts that might rust if neglected. One part of a bow that *will* rust unless oiled periodically is the spring in a cushion plunger arrow plate. A little penetrating oil squirted around the plunger shaft will keep this button functioning smoothly and accurately.

Stress

Stress is the third major enemy of hunting bows. Again, the parts of the bow generally hurt most are the upper and lower limbs. Stress takes on several forms in bow limbs, weakening them or causing them to break. Dry firing (drawing and letting go of the bowstring without an arrow being nocked) is one of the worst things anyone can do. Such abuse stresses limbs by sending tremendous shock waves coursing through them—waves which can weaken wood, fragment laminating glue, and/or splinter fiberglass laminations. Archers can sometimes get away with accidental dry fires when arrow nocks break or arrows accidentally disengage from the bowstring prior to shooting. However, dry firing should be avoided whenever humanly possible. Such stress can also break a bowstring or a compound cable in addition to a fragile limb.

Almost as damaging to laminated bow limbs, cables, and strings as dry firing is shooting ultra-lightweight arrows for long periods of time. Ultra-lights do not adequately absorb a bow's shooting power, and the result is excessive vibration and stress applied to every moving part of a bow. Manufacturers' tests have clearly shown that a bow shot with moderately heavy arrows will outlast a bow shot with faster-flying, lighter-weight arrows. This is one reason deer hunters should think twice before becoming caught up in the "speed-mania" that drives many modern archers. A lightweight "toothpick" arrow like those shot from overdraw bows is not only noisy to shoot and inherently less accurate than a slower, more stable shaft—it is also slowly but surely vibrating a bow's moving parts toward stress fatigue and failure. This is solid, tested fact—not conjecture on my part.

One common form of stress that ruins bows is simply storing them with pressure on one or both limbs. Such pressure can be the physical weight of a recurve or longbow limb as it sits upright for months in the corner, or it can be the constant bending pressure on bow limbs never relieved by being unstrung or relaxed during off-season months.

A recurve bow or longbow should always be unstrung when not in use to prevent limbs from eventually weakening in draw weight. Careful bowhunters un-string such bows at the end of every hunting day and string them again the next time they go afield. Such bows should be hung horizontally across pegs or nails to keep bow weight evenly distributed on limbs—standing bows upright in a corner will eventually twist limb tips and completely ruin them.

Compound hunting bows need not be unstrung each hunting day—to do so would result in a hopeless tangle of cables, limbs, and bowstring. However, manufacturers recommend that the limbs on compound bows be relaxed by backing out draw-weight adjustment bolts whenever they are to be set aside for more than a month. To leave a compound bow at full limb weight will inevitably result in drops in bow poundage as limbs take a slight permanent set or bend. The hunter who shoots year round must live with steadily weakening limbs, retuning his bow every so often and tightening limb bolts to regain lost poundage. Such stress-caused limb weakening is nothing to worry about and will not usually result in breakage. It just needs to be monitored and compensated for as time goes along.

Bow Lubrication

A hunting bow requires a few other maintenance details from time to time to keep it in top functioning condition. One of the most important is periodic lubrication of various moving parts.

Of primary importance is the bowstring. Bowstrings

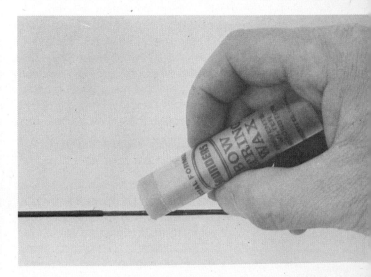

(Above and below) Waxing a bowstring lubricates individual strands and also prevents surface fraying. Most commercial bowstring waxes come in handy tubes.

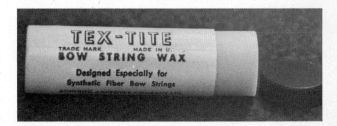

are normally composed of 14, 16, or 18 Dacron strands assembled to a particular length to match a particular size and style of bow. Although few realize it, there is considerable friction between dry Dacron strands as they stretch and bend during the shooting process. This friction will fray and eventually break a bowstring with plenty of shooting unless it is reduced with some kind of bowstring wax.

In addition to strand-to-strand friction, an unwaxed string is also prone to snagging and fraying as it rubs against limbs, car seats, a hunter's clothing, and other rough-surfaced things. A liberal coating of bowstring wax protects it from such wear, prolonging its life several times longer than if it were kept in completely dry unwaxed condition.

There are several kinds of bowstring wax available through archery and sporting goods stores. Most do an excellent job. My favorite, however, is tough to get these days. This is regular beeswax, which can still be purchased at many hardware stores, general stores, and feed stores. Most modern bowstring waxes are slightly too thin and smeary for my tastes and wear off the surface of a string rather quickly when a bow is regularly handled and carried through heavy brush. Beeswax, by contrast, has a stiffer consistency that provides long-term protection. Any bowstring wax will properly lubricate Dacron strands—the newer synthetic waxes must merely be applied more frequently.

Compound bows require lubrication in the axle areas for the quickest, most consistent shooting. As mentioned before, lubrication with oil is especially important in damp hunting environments. In addition, several companies sell dry silicone-type lubes that spray-apply to the wheel/axle areas. For dry environments where moisture-fighting is not a main concern, the dry lubes, which are carried into moving parts with an evaporating liquid agent, are less messy to use than oils.

Serving the Bowstring

Another maintenance requirement of hunting bows is the occasional replacement of the central serving or wrapping around the Dacron bowstring. This serving is generally made of heavy nylon monofilament similar to that used for fishing line. Though commercial bowstrings are usually well made with top-grade materials, the central serving tends to wear where the arrow nocks on the string, where the bowstring hits an armguard during shots, or where a mechanical bowstring release snaps on. These serving pressure points eventually flatten and threaten breakage, requiring a hunter to replace the entire bowstring or remove old serving and wrap on some more. It is far cheaper to re-serve a string than it is to replace it.

To attach new serving, you need a spool of monofilament serving and a serving tool. These items are quite inexpensive and last for years. The serving tool is a simple gadget that allows an even wrap around the string at any pressure you desire.

There is an added advantage of serving strings yourself besides the simple economy. An archer can buy serving monofilament in several different diameters, which allows him to vary how tightly arrow nocks snap to a bowstring. Varying the tightness of monofilament wrap with a serving tool also gives nock-tightness flexibility. Ensuring first-rate snap-on nock attachment to a bowstring prevents a too-tight nock from falling off the string at the wrong time and also prevents a too-tight nock/string union that can degrade accuracy. Remember this from Chapter 3—a properly fitting snap-on arrow nock will allow an arrow to hang vertically from a bowstring without falling off, but can be disengaged with a fairly gentle finger tap to the rear end of the hanging nock.

Bow Refinishing

A hunting bow is usually coated with plastic or oil finish at the factory. Like a gunstock, a bow used heavily for several years might require home refinishing to restore its beauty and guarantee protection from moisture.

Some archery companies offer bow-refinishing kits to rejuvenate the wood and fiberglass surfaces. One of the very best such kits is sold by Bohning, America's number one manufacturer of adhesives for bows and arrows.

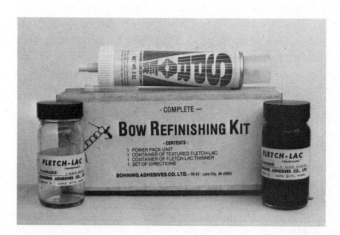

To refurbish the surfaces on a well-worn bow, several companies offer complete bow-refinishing kits. This one is offered by Bohning.

Replacing Arrow Nocks

One of the most common forms of arrow damage is a broken or disengaged arrow nock. During regular target practice, a good shot occasionally smacks a nock with another arrow and breaks or cracks it. Arrows that hit hard objects like rocks, stumps, or trees also sometimes shed their nocks—the terrific forces and vibrations within the arrows popping nocks completely off nock tapers. Do not despair; nocks are easily replaced if a bowhunter knows how.

To replace a nock, first remove any remaining bits of the nock with a sharp knife and then scrub the nock taper thoroughly with acetone or other solvent to remove old glue. Next, replace the damaged nock with an identical one sold at any archery or sporting goods store. A bead of good-quality fletching cement like Bohning Fletch-Tite is first placed on the nock taper, and then the nock is rotated clockwise in place to ensure an even coat of glue between nock and arrow. At room temperature, such a bond will be dry enough to shoot within an hour or two.

Repairing Damaged Arrow Fletching

Arrow fletching inevitably becomes tattered with regular shooting on targets. Feather fletching wears down where it contacts a bow and becomes matted from moisture and deep penetration in target butts. Plastic vanes develop ragged holes where other arrows have hit and passed through, and also become matted or scrunched down when jammed in a bow case or hip-type target quiver. Such fletching must be repaired or replaced to ensure accurate shooting on targets and deer.

Feather fletching which is merely matted down will neatly bounce back to its original shape when lightly steamed over the spout of a teapot. If feathers are

ly affect arrow flight unless it is huge. A tattered plastic vane left unrepaired invariably hisses through the air and slows down faster than other arrows—which results in low hits and noise-frightened deer.

Misshapen plastic vanes can usually be returned to their original shape if gently warmed by a fire or a stove and rubbed back to shape with your hand. Caution: Vanes that become *hot* instead of warm can crinkle and become permanently distorted.

If arrow fletching becomes too tattered, if vanes begin to fall off, or if you simply want to bring your arrows back to spanking-new condition, you'll need to have your archery or sporting goods dealer remove old fletching and fletch your arrows again. An even better route to go if you have the time, money, and ambition, is purchasing a good-quality fletching tool and doing the job yourself. Fletching arrows yourself will save you considerable money in the long run if you shoot a lot and is also an enjoyable pastime. The ability to fletch arrows yourself also gives you total flexibility to experiment with fletching colors, different degrees of fletching spiral, etc.

To do your own fletching, you'll need a fletching jig, a supply of feathers or vanes 5 inches long, and a tube or two of top-grade fletching cement. If you shoot right-handed, you should buy a jig with a right helical clamp. This clamp will spiral vanes the proper direction for best flight characteristics from a bow. If you shoot left-handed, purchase a jig with a left helical clamp.

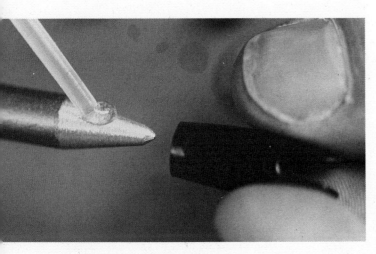

Broken nocks are easily replaced with new ones using a little top-quality fletching cement on the nock taper.

bloody from passing through a deer, they should be washed out in warm water and allowed to dry before the steaming process. Once dry, steamed-out feathers are as good as new.

A plastic vane with a hole from another arrow can often be repaired by carefully snipping out the tattered area with a sharp pair of scissors. This leaves a triangular notch in a vane, but such a notch will not significant-

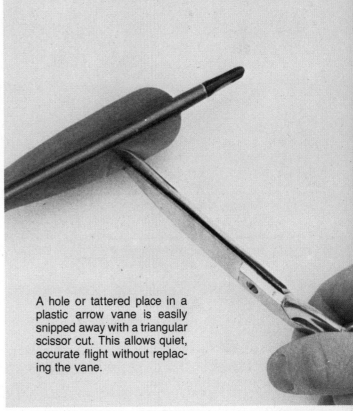

A hole or tattered place in a plastic arrow vane is easily snipped away with a triangular scissor cut. This allows quiet, accurate flight without replacing the vane.

The Martin fletching jig is a rotating model that provides easy single-vane gluing.

Cabela's Fletcher is a tough, cast-metal design which allows all three vanes on an arrow to be glued in place at once.

(Below) The Bitzenberger arrow fletcher is the Cadillac of these tools, producing precise, professional fletching each and every time.

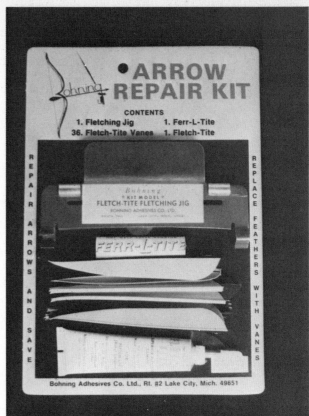

Bohning's arrow-repair kit includes everything needed to replace fletching and install arrow points.

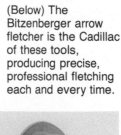

Fletching arrows is not difficult at all. Aluminum and fiberglass arrow shafts must be thoroughly cleaned with a warm-water Ajax scrub or a scrub with acetone on a clean paper towel. The glue-bases of plastic vanes must be similarly scrubbed with acetone on a Q-Tip or paper towel because vanes straight from the factory are coated with a microscopic layer of casting wax that degrades a good vane/arrow bond. Once gluing surfaces are thoroughly scrubbed and dry, fletching can begin.

To fletch an arrow, simply follow the manufacturer's instructions. A uniform bead of fletching glue is run along the glue base of a vane after it is positioned in the fletching clamp. This vane is then pressed firmly against the arrow shaft, which is resting in the rotating carriage of the fletching jig. After the glue dries, the fletching clamp is removed and the arrow shaft rotated to accept another vane. It's as simple as that!

Once an arrow is fletched, dab a bead of glue on each end of each vane where it meets the shaft. This provides extra glue-down strength and prevents straw or fabric from a target butt jamming under the end of a vane and forcing it to lift away from the shaft. When properly glued down, plastic vanes, gripped and pulled by pliers, will tear in pieces before they separate from a shaft.

(Above and right) Several excellent fletching glues are sold at archery stores. The most popular is Fletch-Tite. One company has invented a little wire-arm gizmo to allow the smooth spreading of glue on the base of a vane.

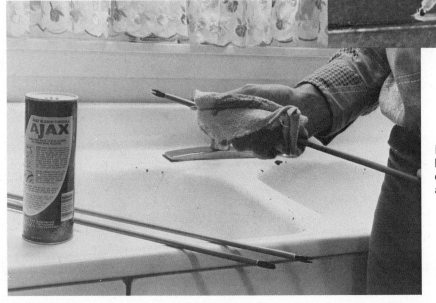

In preparation for fletching shafts, a bowhunter should scrub the back third of a shaft with Ajax and warm water or an evaporating cleaner like acetone.

Shaft Cleaning and Repair

Aluminum and fiberglass arrow shafts are exceedingly easy to clean after getting bloody or dirty. Simply give them a thorough scrub with warm, soapy water and dry them off with a towel.

Fiberglass shafts which become cracked or splintered must be discarded so they don't explode in a bow and fill your skin with painful fragments. You avoid this danger problem with aluminum shafts, but occasionally they will become bent or broken after solid impact with animals or rocks and trees.

A broken aluminum shaft must be thrown away. A bent shaft can usually be returned to brand-new condition with the use of a arrow-shaft straightener. First, you need to cull out crooked aluminum shafts by spinning them over a fingernail. Your archery or sporting goods dealer probably has a pro-shop straightener which will restore these culls to original straightness. Arrow straightening is usually well worth the expense. An even more economical way to go in the long run is buying a moderately priced arrow straightener for use at home. It will do a fine job on bent shafts once you get the hang of using it.

In addition to using a mechanical shaft straightener, some archers become proficient at straightening arrows

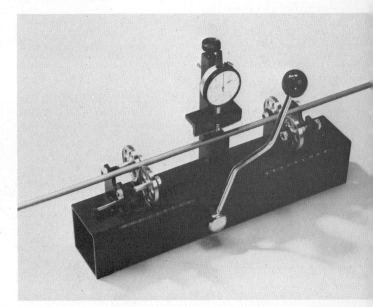

Bent aluminum hunting shafts are best straightened on a precise arrow straightener like this model by Easton.

A bowhunter can hand-straighten mildly bent aluminum shafts with a little time and practice.

Spare broadhead blades are best stored in a vial or pill container to keep out rust-causing moisture.

The author prefers to store and transport razor-sharp broadheads in an oil-soaked styrofoam block inside an airtight freezer jar.

by hand. To do this, a shooter must look down a bent shaft in good light, determine the direction of the bend, and correct this bend by bending the shaft by hand in the opposite direction. Hand-straightening requires some time and well-developed skill, but a persistent person can straighten shafts by hand with a fair degree of accuracy. This is especially handy if you suffer an arrow-bending spree in a remote deer camp and get low on factory-straight hunting arrows.

Care for Arrowheads

Bowhunting arrowheads require little or no care except for the periodic oiling of broadhead edges and occasional blood scrub-up whenever a hunter gets lucky on deer. The blades on some welded broadhead designs can be carefully straightened with pliers if they become slightly bent out of alignment. Most replaceable-blade broadheads with machined-aluminum center sections are impossible to salvage once they become bent.

To protect replaceable broadhead blades or keen hand-sharpened broadheads in the hunting camp and during the off-season months, it's a good idea to enclose them in waterproof containers that protect edges from rust and also protect you from accidental cuts. One excellent container is a clean plastic vial or

Bowhunters often store arrowheads, wrenches, and other bow-related gear in soft or hard protective cases.

A little oil on keen broadhead edges keeps them sharp in moist hunting conditions.

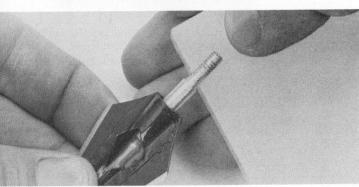

(Left) To prevent the aluminum threads on screw-in arrowheads from jamming in the aluminum threads of arrow inserts, rub a little paraffin on them.

pill dispenser. It can be carried in a shirt or pants pocket in the field as well as safely stored away at home. For sharpened broadheads without removable blades, there's no better way to store these safely than jamming them into a large, oil-soaked block of ordinary styrofoam. The styrofoam can be cleanly and neatly enclosed in a large Tupperware container or plastic garbage bag to keep oil in and moisture out. I generally carry and store broadheads in a big Tupperware freezer jar filled with a form-fitting piece of oil-soaked styrofoam I cut to shape with a sharp knife. Such a setup fully encloses broadhead blades with the screw-in male part of each broadhead exposed for easy attachment to arrows. Once I screw on a shaft, I pull the entire shaft/broadhead unit free.

One other note on arrowhead care. The threaded aluminum male part of some arrowheads will permanently jam in the threaded aluminum female insert in the end of an arrow if these parts become slightly oxidized from exposure to the elements. This is not generally a problem when arrowheads have steel attachment threads, but aluminum screwing into aluminum often seizes up as if welded in place. Usually, this frustrating occurrence will waste an expensive broadhead, requiring that the whole jammed arrowhead/arrow-insert unit be heated loose from the shaft and

thrown away. To prevent seizing and jamming, simply oil or otherwise lubricate the threads of every arrowhead before screwing it into a shaft. I personally use ordinary grocery-store paraffin, rubbing the threaded part of every arrowhead across a block of this stuff before screwing the head into an arrow. This precaution completely eliminates the hassle and waste of seizure between arrowheads and arrows.

Taking Care of Other Shooting Gear

Most other bow-shooting equipment requires little or no special care or maintenance. A hunter should conduct a common-sense check of incidental shooting gear from time to time to discover any problems which might need repair. The hoods on bow quivers occasionally break, leather in shooting tabs or gloves eventually dries and cracks, and the elastic fasteners on shooting armguards sometimes lose their snap and holding ability. However, a hunter needs no special instruction to repair or replace such worn-out gear.

A smart bowhunter mothers his shooting equipment like a hen watches out for a young brood of chicks. He learns how to care for shooting equipment at the outset, keeps close tabs on the condition of his gear, and makes repairs and adjustments as required to guarantee accurate, trouble-free shooting.

7/Clothes and Gear

PROPER bowhunting clothes and footwear must satisfy three important requirements. If a particular article of clothing does not conform to all three, it must be considered marginal at best for hunting deer. First, bowhunting duds must be quiet-surfaced to prevent deer from hearing a hunter move. Second, apparel must be properly camouflaged to blend well with the habitat. Third, clothing and footwear must be comfortable to wear, to move about in, and shoot a bow in. If a hat, jacket, pair of trousers, set of hunting boots, or other piece of bodywear fulfills these requirements, it should help instead of hinder an archery deer hunter get his game.

Bowhunting Clothes Must Be Quiet

All species of deer have incredibly keen ears, tuned to hear the tiniest scrape or crackle of danger. With this in mind, bowhunters must select clothes which make as little noise as possible. Many otherwise excellent garments are made of ripstop nylon, hard-weave 60/40 cotton and synthetic blend, or other fabric guaranteed to startle deer completely out of their hides. Generally clothing made of these materials scrapes or whines noisily when brushed against branches, bushes, rocks, and other natural objects a hunter passes or leans against in the woods. Noisy fabrics can actually alert and scare away deer at moderate bow ranges when a hunter draws to take a shot or simply moves about, the clothing rustling quite audibly. Such garments should be avoided at all cost.

The best fabrics for bowhunting deer are usually soft-weave cotton or wool. A few soft synthetics and synthetic blends are also quiet-surfaced enough. It never ceases to amaze me how many so-called bowhunting clothes are totally ill-suited for this task because they make too much surface noise. They may look great and feel great to wear, but they'll frighten any sharp-eared deer. A dependable noise test of any

potential article of wear is dragging your fingernails lightly across the cloth. If it shrieks or scrapes loudly, it should be left on the clothing rack or shelf.

Clothing Camouflage

In addition to being quiet, bowhunting clothes must blend well with the backgrounds they are to be used against. A deer's eyes are every bit as sharp as its ears, and any standout garment worn by a bowhunter will warn deer away as surely as a white flag flapping in the breeze.

Many bowhunters operate under the misconception that standard leaf-print World War II camouflage is ideal for all deer hunting environments. We live in a time when camouflage clothes are extremely popular, and a person who looks around a bit can find darn near any garment in this particular type of camouflage print. World War II camouflage, small dark-green, dark-brown, and/or black leafy shapes against a lighter field of tan or green, and the somewhat less common Vietnam camouflage, larger splotches of contrasting color, will blend well with a relatively dark forest background. However, as often as not both are completely ill-suited to bowhunting deer.

The key to buying and using camouflage clothing is choosing garments which blend well with the environment you expect to be hunting in. Regular leaf-print garb blends quite well with most medium to dark deep-woods settings, but absolutely stands out like a sore thumb against lighter-colored environments where deer often hang out. Such dark-camo clothes do not work well in snowy settings, sagebrush country or hills covered with dead grass. A hunter must match his camouflage to the basic colors of the country he expects to bowhunt in.

Aside from basic color-matching to surrounding terrain, a bowhunter must choose clothes that consist of sharply contrasting colors. Actually, I should say con-

(Left and below) Conventional shirts and jackets in traditional World War II leaf-print patterns blend well with many deer-hunting environments. These particular garments are distributed by Jim Dougherty Archery.

Head-to-toe camouflage is best when bowhunting sharp-eyed deer.

A bowhunter must match his camouflage clothes to existing backdrops. This archer's snow-camo pants and darker top blend quite well in his hunting area.

Well-known bowhunter and arrow-shaft manufacturer Jim Easton exhibits well-chosen deer-hunting camouflage here. The solid pants and mottled shirt matched rock-strewn country with lots of bushes and trees above the ground.

A bowhunter should match clothes to weather conditions to ensure hunting and shooting comfort.

trasting *shades of gray* because all deer are completely color-blind. They see only shades of black, gray, and white—such shades should contrast in a garment to blend best with surrounding terrain. Contrast breaks up a hunter's basic human outline to trick a deer's eyes, and blends much better with a variety of backgrounds than does a solid-colored garment. Although it goes against tradition, such contrast need not be in the form of leafy shapes, either. Regular plaid clothing blends every bit as well as World War II camo or other "natural" camo patterns—the key is sharp contrast in the basic shades of individual checks in the plaid.

If you are not sure how well a colorful garment contrasts in black and white, simply take a black-and-white picture of it against an average deer-hunting background. Some of the very best deer-hunting garments in terms of camouflage are brightly colored reds, blues, and yellows. Although such clothing does not look in place to the human eye, it can blend quite nicely with a hunting background of a matching overall shade of gray.

To summarize, when choosing your basic deer-hunting clothes, remember to insist on plaid or leaf-print color patterns that contrast well in black and white. Match the overall shade of such clothes to the backgrounds you intend to hunt—not to some preconceived notion you have about what bowhunting clothes are supposed to look like. If you do these two basic things, you should blend reasonably well with deer habitat.

Importance of Clothing Comfort

Deer-hunting clothes must be soft-surfaced and well camouflaged. They must also be comfortable to wear and shoot in. This necessitates some careful forethought by a garment-shopping bowhunter.

First, you should match clothes and footgear to the weather you plan to encounter. Don't buy an insulated pair of camouflage coveralls to hunt in 90-degree weather. Don't outfit yourself with thin camo T-shirts if temperatures might plunge below freezing. Don't wear camouflage sneakers into areas where snow covers the ground. These simple-minded tips may insult your intelligence, but all too many bowhunters forget about weather comfort as they shop excitedly for nifty-looking duds.

Equally important in deer hunting is how well a garment fits. There are two reasons for this. First, an ill-fitting shirt or pair of trousers can chafe and torment you to tears in the woods as you walk around in search of deer. Second, clothing that fits too loosely or too tightly is difficult or impossible to shoot in accurately, the baggy folds slapping a bowstring or ultra-tight sleeves impeding free arm movement. Unfortunately, many regular leaf-print bowhunting clothes are not offered in enough sizes to fit everyone well.

What a bowhunter must remember when searching for clothes is that he does have proper choices besides the conventional garments sold at archery or sporting goods stores. Plaid shirts are excellent garments for

In hot weather, an archer can wear a camo T-shirt to match daytime hunting temperatures.

A camouflage bill cap is the choice of many successful deer-hunting archers.

The traditional Jones-style bowhunting hat is a practical choice for most hunting situations.

bowhunting deer, and anyone can find such shirts that fit to a T. Similarly, a deer hunter can make homemade bowhunting pants out of ordinary blue jeans or similarly good-fitting pants by tie-bleaching or tie-dyeing. These techniques are discussed later in this chapter. If you can't readily find good-fitting camouflage clothes, consider alternatives which do yield comfort in the field.

Headgear for Bowhunting

Let's start at the very top of a bowhunter's head and work downward from there. Most deer hunters wear hats of some variety to keep out the elements, keep their hair in tow, and/or hide a blond head of hair. Hat or cap selection is largely a matter of personal preference, but a hat should be quiet, camouflaged, and comfortable as discussed earlier. Unfortunately, some commonly seen bowhunting hats do not conform to all three criteria.

Some bowhunters opt to wear a regular baseball-type bill cap with a camouflage-print coloration. This hat type shields the face from sun and rain, and is relatively quiet to hunt in. One problem connected with a bill cap is its tendency to collide with a bowstring as a hunter draws and anchors against his face. Whether or not the bill touches the string depends largely on a bowhunter's shooting and anchoring style, and everyone must check out this potential problem for himself. There are few things that can ruin a shot at a deer more than knocking off your hat or having it get in the way of a shot.

One excellent bowhunting hat, if a shooter does not hit the rim with his string, is the standard beaver-felt western hat. When chosen in a medium-brown color, it blends closely enough to serve fairly well. One problem with a cowboy-style deer-hunting hat is that it is prone to rub against dense foliage as a hunter moves, but felt does not make much noise and the brim keeps rain and snow well away from the face and back of the neck.

If anything could be called the "standard" deer-hunting hat among archers, it would be the Jones-style cap. This design is basically an inverted bowl of cotton cloth with the rim folded up in back. This is the same basic hat preferred by many avid duck hunters. The Jones-style hat is an excellent choice as long as the fabric is not too stiff. All too many are coated with a stiffening waterproofer that sings a loud song when branches rub across it. Because a Jones hat does not have a widely protruding brim, it seldom gets in the way of the bowstring when hunters draw to shoot.

My personal favorite in a bowhunting cap is the good ol' standard stocking or watch cap. They can be purchased in a wide variety of sizes, colors, and materials and offer certain advantages that make sense in bowhunting. A stocking cap hugs the head to completely clear the bowstring and is made of soft-woven wool or synthetics that make no noise in the undergrowth. It is adequately warm for very cold weather when made of

A rigid camo face mask hides an archer's light and shiny complexion but makes anchoring to shoot somewhat difficult.

A stocking cap is a versatile bowhunting headgear choice, providing head and ear warmth in the chilliest bowhunting situations.

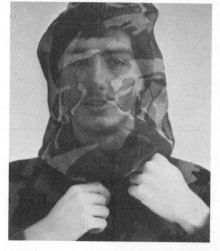

(Left and below) A headnet is decent face camouflage for bowhunting deer. Headnets with large eye slots allow much better visibility than those without.

heavy fabric and sheds rainwater well when made of wool. It can be pulled down over the ears for extra warmth, and some varieties feature full face-protective masks that pull down from inside to combat really chilly weather and camouflage the face when the need arises. Stocking caps are available in camouflage patterns from several clothing manufacturers although a garment this small need not be multi-colored to avoid the prying eyes of deer. To each his own, but I prefer the stocking cap for serious deer hunting.

Aside from pull-down ski masks, there are several other forms of face coverings used by bowhunters. These are primarily to hide a light-colored complexion from a deer's very keen eyesight. The most common are camouflage headnets and rigid face masks. I've always had some reservations about the masks because they severely impede a hunter's ability to anchor the bowstring against his face. Headnets work fairly well as long as they fit the face snugly to allow a decent anchor and as long as they feature an eye slit which allows clear visibility. Several loose-weave headnet designs are sold without an eye slit, requiring a hunter to look through the mesh. This seriously impedes a nimrod's ability to see during the middle of the day and cuts down on light transmission enough to completely ruin visibility in early morning and late evening when deer are most likely to be around and about. One innovative headnet setup I like incorporates an empty set of eyeglass frames in its construction. The net is attached to the frames, letting a hunter look out through two large windows at the world. This particular headnet avoids the common problem of the viewing hole in a headnet slipping around the head and thus impeding one or both eyes. Such an occurrence can prevent or ruin a critical shot at a deer.

Another bit of bowhunting headgear for the ladies can help hide a female archer's shiny, wind-blown hair. This is a camouflage scarf which can be purchased through many archery equipment stores.

Shirts, Jackets, Sweaters, and Vests

There is probably a greater variety of upper-body wear in camouflage patterns than in any other clothing category. Shirts, jackets, sweaters, and vests in camouflage colorations abound at archery and sporting goods dealerships. Many of these are excellent for bowhunting . . . and many more should be avoided like the plague.

Remember, bowhunting garb must be quiet and good-fitting as well as properly camouflaged. Commercial upper-body camouflage is best used for bowhunting elk or moose in piney forests or mule deer, blacktail deer, or whitetail deer in similarly dark surroundings. Almost all available upper-body garments are the standard World War II camouflage.

The best commercial leaf-print bowhunting shirts are made of cotton flannel or standard soft-weave cotton. For warm or hot hunting weather, there are short-sleeve T-shirts in a variety of sizes. For cooler weather, there are long-sleeve T-shirts and regular, heavier button-up shirts. In addition, an enterprising bowhunter who needs something other than the standard camouflage or simply can't find a shirt that fits well can have a ball looking through the plaid, soft-cotton work shirts at a department store.

For really cold or wet weather, nothing matches wool-plaid shirts for warmth and comfort. Wool stays warm even when wet—something which cannot be said for cotton—and is available in many pleasing, contrasty plaids including black-and-green and black-and-red. You should have no trouble at all finding good-fitting shirts for hiding from the eyes of wary close-range deer.

For really cold-weather bowhunting, deer hunters will need to wear a jacket or sweater to maintain a reasonable level of comfort. As with shirts, there are myriad jackets available with camouflage colorings. Some are quiet-surfaced, but most I have seen are a bit too noisy to suit my deer-hunting tastes. Manufacturers feel that rugged jacket construction requires a very durable outer shell of hard-weave fabric, but such fabric is unfortunately prone to make telltale noises as a hunter walks through foliage. As a general rule, plaid

A camouflage scarf helps cover a lady bowhunter's light or shiny hair.

The author took this nice 4×4 mule deer buck while wearing a light-colored leafprint shirt and equally light-colored tie-bleached pants. This getup blended well with the wide-open, dead-grass area where Adams stalked the deer.

wool jackets are far more quiet than the leaf-print models sold at sporting goods outlets, and blend every bit as well with deer terrain.

It is hard to beat a good-quality wool or synthetic-blend sweater for hunting in really cold weather. Sweaters with pleasing camouflage patterns are available from several manufacturers, and these hold in heat extremely well. They also fit tightly to the body, giving when a hunter moves, but staying well away from the bowstring in the arm and chest area when he draws and anchors to shoot. The U.S. military also issues excellent cold-weather sweaters you can use to good advantage—check for these at your local Army-Navy surplus store.

Goose-down vests with leaf-print, ripstop-nylon shells are commonplace items at sporting goods stores. They provide excellent upper-body warmth in cold weather but tend to make lots of noise like all nylon garments. A bowhunter can make good use of any vest despite the nylon or hard-weave cotton surfaces, provided he wears this vest *under* other soft-surfaced clothing. This eliminates the noise problem and provides first-rate warmth when hunting temperatures drop to icy levels.

Upper-Body Rain Gear

Some of the best bowhunting a deer hunter can ever experience occurs when rain is falling at a steady pace. This quiets the woods and covers the sounds of a hunter's movements. However, such hunting is not very comfortable unless a woodsman is properly clad in rain-protective gear.

Rubber raincoats have been the standby of riflemen and shotgunners for years. Unfortunately, such jackets crinkle like dry newspaper, rattle against the tree limbs and brush, and shine like beacons when wet. The only feasible wet-weather, upper-body clothing is good-quality wool. This stuff sheds water well, and retains its warmth when moisture does penetrate to inside layers of clothing. Wool gets the game in rainy weather, while rubberwear scares it away.

Tips on Wearing Upper-Body Garments

If a hunter gets cold, he generally gets cold in the upper body first. To prevent this, a bowhunter should dress in layers and add or shed clothing as the need arises. For example, you might dress in a cotton T-shirt, flannel shirt, goose-down vest, and wool jacket to combat the nippy early-morning hours on a deer stand. As temperatures warm in late morning, you can shed the jacket and vest to remain comfortable as you wait for deer. If midday weather gets downright hot, the flannel shirt can go as well. If the stand-hunting vigil lasts until dark, clothes can be slipped on again as temperatures fall. It is a fact that multiple layers of clothing trap warm air around the body better than a single padded garment, and dressing in layers also allows a hunter to achieve a constant comfort level which is never possible with only one or two heavier upper-body garments.

No matter what upper-body wear you prefer or how many layers you put on, make darn sure this clothing is not too bulky to allow a crisp, clean shot. One common shooting hindrance with shirts and jackets is a flap-closing pocket on the side of your chest nearest your bow arm. It can catch a bowstring and send a shot wild, especially if other clothes are layered underneath to bulge the pocket out more than normal. Being a right-hander, I generally remove the pockets from the left sides of all my bowhunting shirts and jackets to eliminate accidental bowstring snag.

Trousers for Bowhunting Deer

There are three kinds of acceptable bowhunting trousers for deer—commercial camouflage pants, homemade camouflage pants, and conventional single-color pants. Let me elaborate a bit on each type.

A limited selection of commercial camouflage pants is available at archery or sporting goods stores. Not surprisingly, most of these pants are regular World War II leaf-print garments. Manufacturers have avoided widespread production of camo pants because so many individual sizes are needed to have a complete inventory. Three or four sizes of jackets or shirts fit all, but bowhunters come in myriad waist sizes and leg lengths, requiring dealers to carry dozens of different trouser sizes to give customers a decent selection. As a result, there are plenty of shirts and jackets but relatively few bowhunting pants available.

If you can find a comfortable, well-made pair of trousers, more power to you. If you cannot, do not worry. It is extremely easy to make your own camouflage pants by tie-dyeing or tie-bleaching ordinary cotton pants sold at any department store or dry goods store.

To tie-dye or tie-bleach pants, first tie one or two loose knots in each leg and bind together the waist area with a cord or rubber band. If your chosen pants are white or relatively light in color, dye the tied-up pants in good-quality clothing dye of a sharply contrasting darker color like deep green, dark brown, or black. Once the dying process is complete, untie the pants and wash them in cold water. The result will be a mottled, two-tone pair of trousers that fit you well. Experiment with color combinations that match the country you prefer to bowhunt.

A process I feel yields even better results is something I developed myself. I call this tie-bleaching. This works best on denim pants of various dark colors like blue and brown. Tie up these pants as earlier described and immerse them in a solution of ½-cup laundry bleach (such as Clorox) to 1-gallon water. Let the pants soak until the exposed fabric fades to a light color. This generally takes 2 or 3 hours. Remove the pants, untie the legs and waist, and wash out the bleach in a cold-water cycle. The result is a mottled pair of pants with dark blotches on a lighter background. Unlike tie-dyed pants, the dark contrasting colors are original with the fabric and fade very slowly if at all with repeated washings. The bleach does not deteriorate cloth if washed out right away, and such pants wear like iron in the denim tradition. A hunter who wants lighter-colored camouflage can start with older, faded pants or new pants of a lighter color. Experiment a bit to see what you like.

Solid-colored pants have a place in bowhunting deer. Fortunately, deer usually see a bowhunter's upper body more clearly than the area below the belt in

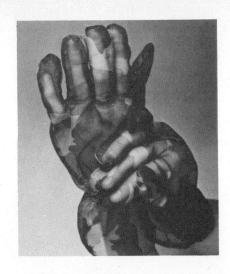

Camouflage gloves are favored by some archers, but tend to hamper the accurate shooting of a bow.

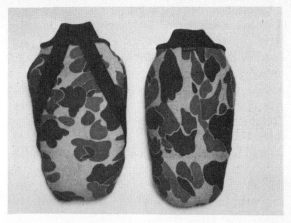

Warm mittens will keep a stand hunter's hands toasty and can quickly be removed if a shot is to be taken.

terrain with bushes, grass, and other low-growing plants. In addition, forest settings usually have mottled leafy backgrounds over 4 feet above the ground and more solid-colored tree trunks, rocks, stumps, and other natural objects closer to the ground. For these reasons, I've found that a bowhunter in camouflaged upper garments and solid-colored pants can still take deer on a regular basis.

Camouflage trousers are generally better than solid colors, but you can get by with solid medium-color pants. At times, there is no other option. Almost all good-quality wool trousers suitable for bowhunting in rain and very cold weather are of solid color, forcing you to go this route. I prefer two-tone pants, but wouldn't stay home if my only trousers were Levi's or one-color wool.

Suitable Footwear

Bowhunting boots or shoes are too small to require camouflage. As long as footwear is a medium color like brown, the primary considerations in selection are comfort and quiet construction.

I am nothing short of amazed at the number of deer hunters I encounter who wear Vibram-soled boots as they attempt to sneak about the woods. If an archer can ease up on a deer with such a handicap, my hat is off in honest admiration. Vibram is one of the best-gripping, most durable boot-sole materials known to man, but it is also one of the most inflexible and noisy. As a result, it is completely ill-suited for stalking and stillhunting wary deer. Where Vibram boot soles come into their own is high above the ground on stand. They give unexcelled grip on a tree-stand platform and make little noise unless an archer stomps around aloft.

For sneaking around the woods, I prefer boots with soft crepe-rubber soles. Such boots are sold by virtually every major outdoor shoe manufacturer, and they do an excellent job because they give to cushion every step on crackly footing and also let a hunter feel twigs,

limbs, and other noisy debris underfoot before he steps down with full body weight. Soft-rubber soles do not wear quite as well as Vibram, but they wear plenty good enough and provide an excellent grip on everything but snow or slimy mud.

Aside from boots, bowhunters use a variety of other footwear including tennis shoes and regular soft-soled street shoes. As long as the color is right, the wearing comfort is there, and the soles are quiet, such shoes are no handicap to the wearers.

There is really no such thing as a fully waterproof leather boot. Some models billed this way come reasonably close, but enough regular moisture exposure will ultimately seep through the best-treated leather and dampen the feet inside. As a result, hunters who frequent swampy areas or expect uniformly wet or snowy conditions are sometimes best served by waterproof rubber boots. Such boots are generally not as comfortable to hike in seriously, but they are quiet to wear and can get a specific wet-weather job done when leather footwear fails. The one drawback some good-quality rubber boots have is very shiny surfaces, but these can be easily dulled by a rubdown with medium-grit sandpaper.

Miscellaneous Deer-Hunting Garb

A variety of clothing odds and ends are used on occasion by archery deer hunters. These include gloves or mittens, one-piece coveralls, and less practical items like camouflage suspenders and leaf-print jockey shorts.

I have mixed feelings about using gloves for bowhunting deer. A few deer hunters don gloves in cold weather, holding the bow in one gloved hand and shucking the other glove to shoot or actually leaving it on. Using gloves in this manner can slow a shooter down or degrade his shooting ability. However, cold fingers would probably retard accuracy even more.

Some bowhunters wear cotton-mesh camouflage

gloves to hide their light-colored hands from deer. In many situations this is going overboard on camouflage, especially when a hunter is sitting in a tree stand high above a deer's line of sight. If hand camouflage seems appropriate, smearing on a little camouflage makeup makes more sense to me because it doesn't hamper natural bow-shooting like gloves are prone to do.

For truly cold-weather hunting, I prefer to wear mittens instead of gloves. Mittens are warmer than gloves because they pool the body heat of all the fingers and are much easier to pull off if a quick shot needs to be taken. Several archery companies sell leaf-print mittens for the cold-weather bowhunter, and one sells a unique belt-attached handwarmer for the bowstring hand which looks like a giant mitten. A deer hunter who moves about in cold weather can generally keep hands warm by simply jamming them in his pockets, but sitting on stand requires more efficient protection from the cold. I feel the best answer to this problem is a warmly constructed mitten.

An archer can shoot fairly well with practice by leaving a mitten on his bow hand. This is what I do in freezing tree-stand conditions. I pull off the other mitten prior to a shot and use a bare hand and finger tab to release the bowstring. For moderately cold weather I wear standard GI wool mitten liners, which are simply heavy-duty wool mittens. When things really cool down, I add a pair of down-filled ski mittens or commercial camouflage mittens over these warm wool liners.

I personally dislike one-piece coveralls for hunting because they never seem to fit right in the waist/crotch

A small, handy drop-point folder like this Easton belt-buckle knife is ideal for most deer-hunting needs.

area. Most such clothing is also too warm for early-fall hiking, and cannot be easily layered with other upper-body wear to control comfort. However, a heavy-duty pair of coveralls is just the ticket for many cold-weather tree-stand hunters, holding in body heat well as an archer waits motionlessly for deer. If camo coveralls appeal to you, several companies offer them in World War II leaf-print patterns.

If camouflage *everything* turns you on, you can go whole-hog with suspenders, underwear, neckerchieves, socks, and similar duds. These items won't put any more deer in your freezer, but they can be fun to wear and show off to friends. Check out such offerings at archery shops and general sporting goods stores.

Other Bowhunting Gear

As a general rule of thumb, a bowhunter should carry only a few well-selected items on his person as he walks or waits for deer. Too many gadgets hanging from an archer's body can hinder a lot more than help, weighing him down like an over-decorated Christmas tree and clanking or scraping noisily as he moves about. This mistake is made by far too many archery deer hunters—hurting their chances of hunting success.

Aside from shooting equipment, clothing, stands, and a complement of odor-masking scents, a bow-hunter does need a few personal items on every outing to help him hunt and improve his level of comfort. If properly chosen, they will not get in the way and will

Fixed-blade hunting knives like these drop-point models will perform any cutting chore on a deer to perfection.

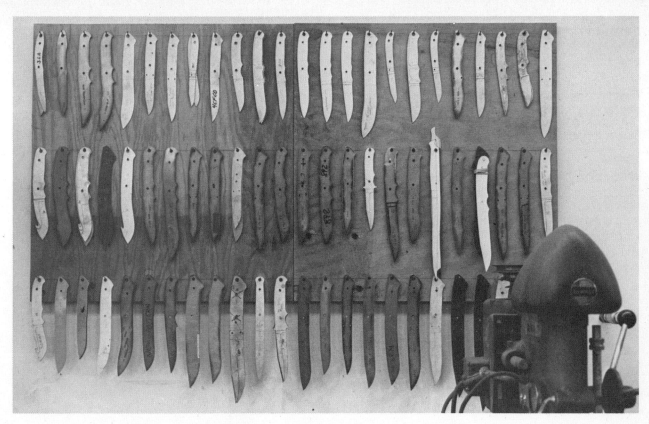

Custom knifemakers offer a tremendous variety of blade/handle configurations to well-heeled clients.

not make game-spooking noise.

When selecting gear, select it with the idea of keeping equipment to a bare-bones, smoothly functioning minimum. For example, when I bowhunt for a full day in deer country, I usually carry a rangefinder, knife, canteen, pair of binoculars, spare arm to hold my bow as I glass, roll of fluorescent trail-marking tape, and a cigarette lighter for an emergency fire. That is all, aside from basic shooting gear. I have no day pack, no small tool kit, no bone saw, and no other equipment I really do not need. By contrast, I know fellows who positively tire themselves out lugging around a whole store full of gizmos they never use to good advantage.

Here are some of the more common items bow-hunters use to help them get their deer or make their lives more comfortable. All of these may not be for you, but they certainly deserve consideration.

Knives and Knife Accessories

Every deer hunter needs a knife to field dress game and to complete necessary skinning and butchering chores. Actually, some hunters own several knives for specialized deer-care purposes, from drop-point gutting knives to curved-blade skinning knives to extra-stout butcher knives. However, for practical deer-hunting purposes a single blade will do everything that needs to be done to a deer from the moment it drops to the moment it reaches the butcher shop or freezer.

When choosing a practical knife for deer hunting, an archer should consider four basic things—how long the knife blade should be, what basic blade shape would be best, whether the knife should be a folding or rigid model, and how good the blade steel should be. Unless he's a knife fancier on top of being a hunter, he should leave the finer points of knife selection to collectors and connoisseurs.

No deer hunter needs a field knife with a blade longer than 3 or 4 inches. A moose, which is America's biggest deer, can be nicely gutted, skinned, and quartered with such a knife alone, provided the user knows his stuff.

If there was only one basic blade shape available for deer hunters, this shape would ideally be the drop-point. One of the strongest blade shapes made, it keeps the point of the knife well away from the innards of a deer during the field-dressing process. A drop-point also has a nicely curving edge well suited to skinning.

Next to the drop-point, the standard clip-point blade, found as a main blade in most folding pocket-knives, works on deer, too. It does not hold the point away from the paunch during gutting, but a hunter can use his fingers to do that.

A major decision when selecting a field knife is whether to buy a folding model or a rigid, nonfolding design. Each has its fans, and I'm not about to start an argument by siding with one or the other. I personally prefer a folding model carried in a leather belt case, mainly because a folder is only half as long as a

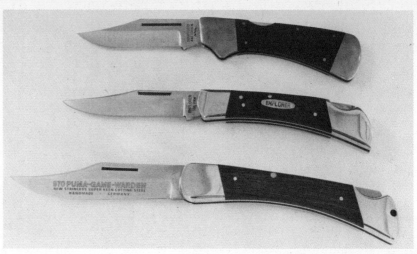

(Right) Folding clip-point knives with lock-open blades 3 to 4 inches long are versatile deer-hunting companions.

(Below) Good-quality stainless-steel blades are excellent deer-hunting choices. Though prone to chip more than high-carbon steel, as evidenced by this closeup photo, the advantages of stainless outweigh the chipping disadvantage.

A good deer-hunting knife takes a hair-shaving edge and holds this edge very well.

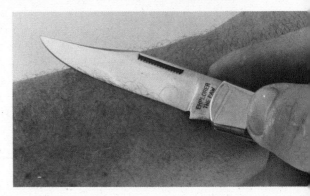

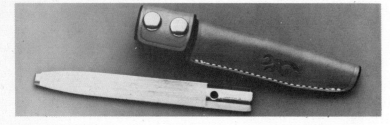

(Left) A compact knife-sharpening steel can be a handy deer-hunter's companion if an edge becomes dull during the field-dressing or skinning chore.

fixed-blade model. A good-quality pocketknife with a reasonably long blade that locks on opening is also a safe-to-use, easy-to-carry blade for deer. A rigid, fixed-blade field knife, stronger in basic construction than a folder, usually consists of one central piece of steel with two grip halves attached. Take your pick.

Quality of blade steel is probably the most important consideration of all. There are a number of knife steels touted by knife connoisseurs—stainless to prevent easy corrosion, tough steels that seldom chip or break, and hard steels that hold an edge for an excessively long period of time. For the average deer hunter with an average bank account, nothing can beat a name-brand knife with a 440-C stainless-steel blade. Stainless is rust-resistant, hard enough to hold a fine edge, and fairly resistant to edge chipping with normal use. For the fellow who wants to spend big bucks on a knife, there are dozens of custom knifemakers around the country offering a wide variety of deer-knife designs in fine steels to suit any need.

The important things to remember when choosing a knife steel are edge-holding ability and corrosion resist-ance. Many high-carbon steels, particularly in pocketknives, are very good about taking and holding an edge, but begin rusting like crazy whenever a damp-looking cloud passes overhead!

Naturally, a deer hunter needs a good-quality honing stone and/or sharpening steel to keep his knife fully sharp and serviceable. Ask your sporting goods dealer about various knife-sharpening aids and the skills necessary to use them properly.

Binoculars and Spotting Scopes

I feel positively naked in the hills without a good-quality binocular within easy reach. It can expand a bowhunter's outdoor enjoyment immensely, but more importantly, improve his chances of scoring on deer.

Many beginning archers feel binoculars are not important in bowhunting because shooting ranges are short. This feeling is especially predominant among whitetail hunters because these animals are usually taken at close range in heavy cover. Why use a binocular in bowhunting when animals are generally taken under 40 yards?

I'll tell you why. In the majority of bowhunting situations—both long- and close-range—deer are not in the wide open where they can be easily identified and sized up. When bowhunting moose, elk, caribou, mule deer, and blacktail on foot, a hunter is as apt to spot animals at 300 yards as 30, necessitating the use of a binocular to spot deer on distant slopes, size up their racks if a trophy is important, and figure out approach routes by carefully scanning terrain. When stand-hunting whitetail or other species in dense, close cover, a binocular is still important because it lets a nimrod spot or identify deer parts like ears, antlers, noses, and hooves that are not easily discernible to the naked eye. A bowhunter who uses a good-quality binocular in all deer-hunting situations will see far more deer before they see him, giving him an edge in putting these animals in the bag.

In close-range situations, a magnified view can also help locate holes in brush, otherwise invisible to the unaided eye, that arrows can slip through. In addition, obstacles an arrow cannot penetrate are revealed. I have started to draw on several animals in my bow-hunting life, decided to check things out first with a binocular, and discovered that small networks of twigs or other things in the way would have careened an arrow well off the mark. In several of these instances, I waited for deer to move into the clear and dropped them with true-flying arrows.

What is a good bowhunting binocular, anyway? There is no pat answer to this question, because everyone's tastes and pocketbooks are different. However, for serious deer hunting I feel that a medium-sized, top-quality glass of 7 to 10 power is the very best choice. Many bowhunters opt to buy mini-binoculars that weigh under 16 ounces and easily fit in a shirt pocket or the palm of a hand, but these optics embody serious drawbacks. Even the best of the lot have narrow fields of view, diminished light-gathering qualities, and fairly low magnification levels, seldom exceeding 6x. In addition, they are less stable to view through *because* of their light physical weight, wobbling with every quiver of flesh and beat of the heart.

By contrast, a full-sized binocular of 20 to 30 ounces has a wide field of view, excellent light-gathering qualities, necessary in low-light situations, and the magnification needed for a truly close-up view. In addition, they are heavy enough for stable viewing.

My favorites are all of the rubber-coated variety, sometimes called "armored" binoculars. These dampen sounds considerably when accidentally bumped against a bow, tree limb, tree-stand support arm, or other hard object. Rubber-coated glasses are quiet—a necessity in serious bowhunting.

Spotting Scopes

Although not necessary for many kinds of bow-hunting, a spotting scope is an important aid for sizing up the antlers of distant deer. Animals like caribou and mule deer inhabit the sort of terrain that sometimes requires a telescopic glass in the 15x to 25x range—otherwise, an archer might spend half a day moving into binocular range only to discover that the animal he is looking at is below acceptable trophy size. That amounts to half a day down the tube that could have been salvaged with one careful look through a good-quality spotting scope.

Rubber-coated binoculars like these 8× Zeiss provide the ultimate in quiet bowhunting use.

Good-quality, medium-weight binoculars like these Leupold 9× glasses are excellent deer-hunting choices.

(Left and right) Camouflaged frameless backpacks are favored by many archery deer hunters.

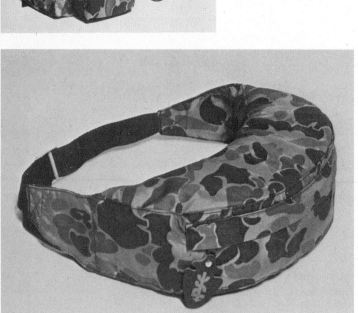

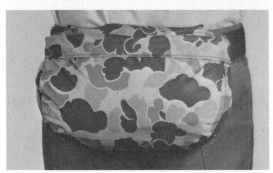

(Above and right) Fanny packs of various sizes provide ample room for carrying day-use items on most deer-hunting trips.

Because they are fairly bulky to carry and use, and because they require a tripod or at least a steady rest over a rock or log for clear viewing, spotting scopes are only worthwhile in specialized long-range looking for trophy heads. A clear 10x binocular will do everything most trophy hunters require, so don't run out and buy a spotting scope unless you are really sure you need one.

Backpacks and Belt Packs

Bowhunters tend to have more equipment to carry around than do gun hunters, and as a result many opt to carry small frameless backpacks or belt packs to hold spare broadheads, a spare bowstring, a bowstringer, and other items they might need in the field. In addition, some bowhunters prefer the solitude and excellent game opportunities often found in remote places reached only by horse train or serious back-packing with a regular frame-and-sack backpack unit. Since few of us own horses, most of us opt to backpack instead.

The frameless backpack is almost an institution among bowhunters, a place to carry a lunch, meat saw, spotting scope, and smaller items required for using bow-and-arrow gear. You can find backpacks at archery stores and general sporting goods stores, the majority of which are sturdy units that strap comfortably to the shoulders. The primary drawback of carrying such a pack is noise. Of the dozens of frameless pack designs available today with well-camouflaged leaf-print patterns, virtually all are made of heavy-duty nylon or similar rough-surfaced fabric that sounds like a string quartet whenever an archer slips through heavy brush or trees. Frameless backpacks are more suited to bowhunting deer in relatively open terrain, provided you want to pack around the bulk and the weight.

A small zippered belt pouch allows a bowhunter to carry a lunch and a few key archery accessories into the field.

A regular backpack with frame is sometimes necessary for walking into remote areas where big bucks abound. This particular camo model is sold by PSE.

(Right) A backpack frame is often essential for carrying out the meat, hide, and antlers of large animals taken a long walk from the nearest road.

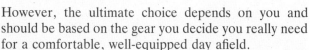

However, the ultimate choice depends on you and should be based on the gear you decide you really need for a comfortable, well-equipped day afield.

From my experience, the most logical application of the frameless backpack is when the larger species are the target animals. Moose and elk usually inhabit large country requiring substantial walks—which means transporting more food and water. Moose and elk hunters are often trophy hunters, too, dictating the need for a spotting scope. When down, these big animals are best cut up with a bone saw or hatchet, best jockeyed around with a small block-and-tackle outfit, and best protected with large meat bags. The extra items necessary for hunting and handling deer over 500 pounds are best carried in a roomy frameless packsack.

For most bowhunting needs, the belt or fanny pack provides all the carrying space an archer really needs. Most are made of scratchy, noisy nylon, but many are made of leaf-print, camouflage materials that blend well with a hunter's body. With the exception of large models, belt packs can be carried in the middle of the back above the hips to avoid noisy collision with foliage if a hunter plans to move through brushy areas. I sometimes carry a medium-sized belt pack on strenuous all-day bowhunts requiring a large lunch in addition to normally carried items.

To find out about regular frame-type backpacks, your best bet is visiting the nearest backpacking or sporting goods store. A backpack setup with a frame is ideal for walking into remote, game-rich areas for several days of hunting, and is also excellent for packing out game you are lucky enough to bag. Although good bowhunters seldom stalk or stillhunt deer carrying a full-sized backpack, a few companies offer frame-type models with fully camouflaged packsacks instead of the more common single-color varieties.

Camouflage Makeup

Many deer hunters prefer camouflage makeup on the face and hands instead of alternatives like headnets and gloves. There are several types and colors of camouflage makeup available and all have their advocates. My personal favorite is the old GI-type that comes in stick form inside a short metal tube. Two separate colors are usually in every tube—one at each end—and this particular type of makeup seems to stay on the face better in warm weather without melting or mixing with perspiration and running all over the place. The genuine GI face camouflage also has insect repellent in it, a plus in some deer-hunting situations.

Bowhunting makeup is also offered by manufacturers in cream form, coming in tubes or little compact-type containers. Some compacts have mirrors to let a hunter view the face-painting job he is doing. This type is normally applied with a finger or a soft piece of cloth.

When choosing makeup, be sure to remember that all deer are entirely color-blind. A nifty pattern of green and brown streaks on the face may impress your hunting buddies, but to deer all those smears and smudges will look basically alike. I generally use only one dark color to dull and two-tone my light, shiny mug—preferably dark green, dark brown, or black. A little lighter color thrown in here and there won't hurt, but it probably won't help, either.

In a pinch, you can do an excellent job with charcoal from a fire or mud from a stream bank or lakeshore. Such do-it-yourself techniques are inferior to using store-bought camouflage because they are far messier to begin with and a real pain to clean up. Most commercial camo makeups wash away with warm soap and water or dissolve when rubbed with cold cream. Charcoal and mud will get the camo job done, but charcoal in particular can be very difficult to remove.

Canteens

On-the-go bowhunters need drinking water, and this usually means carrying some sort of canteen. Unfortunately, conventional belt-carried canteens or plastic backpacker's water containers slosh noisily once a drink or two is taken, making plenty of noise anytime a hunter walks, shifts his weight, or even draws his bow.

The bota bag is a perfect solution to the problem. This particular canteen has a flexible rubber-like waterproof interior, a soft leather exterior, a plastic screw-off cap, and a handy carrying cord or strap. Because the bota bag is fully flexible, a hunter can force all the air

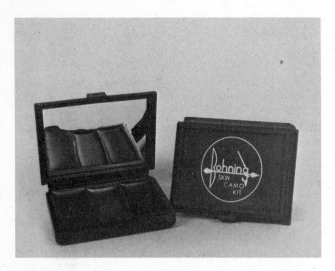

Skin-camo compacts like this one from Bohning usually include two or three colors of makeup plus a handy mirror to aid in application.

(Right) A bota bag is the ideal bowhunting canteen because it is quiet and easy to carry out of the way.

out of it after a drink, screw the cap tight, and be assured of slosh-free travel. The soft flexible leather exterior also prevents noise if the bag bumps a rock, tree, or similar unyielding object.

I normally carry one slung behind my back with the carrying strap under one armpit, across the chest, and over the other shoulder. This carrying method does not impede shooting at all, and yields maximum water-carrying comfort. Available through sporting goods stores and archery shops, bota bags come in sizes to match any hunter's level of thirst, including one magnum model that holds a full 3 liters.

Game Trackers

A game tracker is a relatively new invention designed to aid bowhunters in finding deer that run away hard-hit but leaving very little blood. This gizmo consists of a cartridge full of fine, strong thread that attaches to the front of a bow, the thread wrapped so it will pay out freely when the end is pulled. The free end is normally attached to the broadhead so that when a hunter shoots at a deer, the thread pays out of the tracker cartridge. If a hit is scored and the deer runs off, the animal leaves several hundred feet of thread behind it to aid in the follow-up process. If a hunter can

find the thread, he theoretically will find his deer at the other end.

Game trackers work fairly well on close-range shots in very heavy cover. Such cover makes recovering arrow-hit deer more difficult than normal, especially when leaves are deep and prone to turn over as a deer runs off, hiding a lot of blood under leaves and making recovery difficult. Game trackers are most commonly used on whitetail deer hunted from tree stands, some archers swearing by them.

However, there are two built-in drawbacks. First, this is strictly a one-shot setup; if the first shot misses the mark, a hunter does not have a tracker thread for backup shots. Second, shots should be limited to ranges under 25 yards because the thread places significant drag on an arrow and reduces both its flat-shooting capabilities and its ability to penetrate much past 20 or 25 yards.

In most cases, a tree-stand bowhunter who properly tunes his bow and scores a solid hit on a deer will achieve complete broadhead penetration, yielding good blood flow out the lower half of the deer's body. However, if a blood trail is meager or nonexistent, a tracker thread attached to the arrow could make the difference between finding and losing the animal.

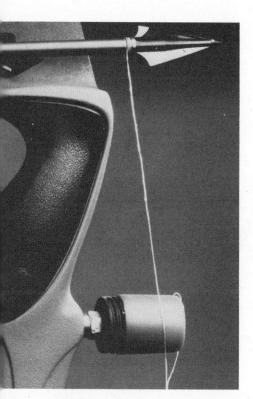

Some game trackers attach directly to the stabilizer hole in front of a hunting bow.

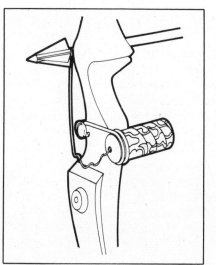

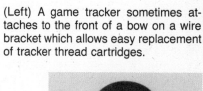

(Left) A game tracker sometimes attaches to the front of a bow on a wire bracket which allows easy replacement of tracker thread cartridges.

(Above and left) The Bohning "Game Finder" is a tracker complete with broadhead wrench on the back end.

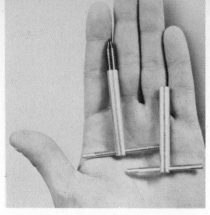

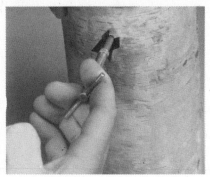

(Above and below) An arrowhead puller is a simple gizmo that allows an archer to work loose arrowheads buried in wood.

A compact, belt-attached spare arm lets a deer hunter hang his bow at his side while he uses binoculars or otherwise utilizes both hands.

(Right) Well-known bowhunter and archery manufacturer Jim Dougherty puts his double-hook spare arm to good use.

Spare Arms

Occasionally someone comes up with a nifty little invention that really works well. The spare arm is such an invention. There is nothing complex or expensive about it, but it provides a welcome service in the woods.

A little, fabric-covered metal hook, the spare arm attaches to the belt of your hunting pants. When you wish to use your binoculars or otherwise engage both hands with something besides your bow, you simply hang the bow horizontally by the bowstring or the handle riser in the upturned hook of the spare arm. This frees the hands yet leaves the bow at your side within easy reach. The less desirable alternatives are to hug a bow between your knees or lay it down on the ground. A spare arm is much, much easier to use.

Another arm design is a simple shoulder harness with two fabric-covered hooks that hold a bow higher on the body under the arm. Although not as convenient to use for hunting on foot, the higher-riding version is ideal for carrying a bow while riding a horse or holding a bow while sitting down. Check out both designs at your local archery or sporting goods dealership.

Arrowhead Pullers

No matter how well a deer hunter happens to shoot, he will invariably smack trees, logs, and stumps from time to time with misdirected arrows. Unless these arrows are tipped by steel blunts, a shooter normally has trouble extracting them from wood by hand. The bowhunter who yanks and twists a shaft in an attempt to pull it free, most likely will bend both shaft and arrow beyond repair. For this reason, archery manufacturers have introduced several types of arrowhead pullers.

Arrowhead pullers only work on screw-in arrow points. If a glue-on arrowhead deeply buries in wood, the shaft must be heated off the head with a cigarette lighter, match, or another heat source that melts arrowhead ferrule cement. In such cases, the arrowhead is lost. However, with screw-in points the outcome is usually better. First, a hunter unscrews the shaft and puts it aside. Next, he screws the puller tightly to the arrowhead, grips the T-handle, and carefully works the arrowhead free. The same solid grip and pulling leverage are not possible with a fragile, slippery arrow shaft attached to a point. Since an arrowhead puller is a simple, inexpensive, and extremely compact item, most deer hunters carry one in the field or at least have one handy around camp.

Bone Saws and Hatchets

Bone saws and hatchets are not really necessary for basic field care, but certainly help in actual butchering because it is always easier to saw or chop through the spine, legs, pelvis, and other large bone areas than jockeying around with a knife to find joints between sections of bone. For details on butchering deer, see Chapter 20.

One popular arrowhead puller doubles as a screw-in tree-stand bow hanger.

Versatile bowhunters own a wide selection of outdoor camping gear to suit any occasion.

A bone saw or hatchet is especially important in the field care of large, heat-retaining animals like elk and moose that require quick quartering to prevent meat spoilage. I have completely dismembered several elk and moose with a 3-inch knife alone, but this job takes far longer with a knife than it does with a sawing or chopping tool.

Normally, a saw or hatchet should be left in camp and retrieved when an animal is finally downed. However, in warm bowhunting weather typical of early-fall archery deer seasons, it is sometimes advisable to carry a compact saw or hatchet in a small frameless backpack or belt pouch to quarter and hang large deer.

A hatchet is a hatchet. When choosing one for carting around, the only suggestion I would have is to select a well-balanced and fairly light model. Super-light hatchets lack the power-swinging characteristics of a moderate-weight hatchet, so don't go *too* light.

Bone saws come in several handy designs. The most common for field carrying are the push-type saw with a T-shaped handle and the folding pull-saw. Of the two, I much prefer the pull-saw because it folds into a more compact package and draws instead of pushes to completely prevent the blade from binding and bending during use. There is nothing more frustrating than getting halfway through a pelvis bone or spine and having your push-saw blade hang up and buckle. This is an annoyance at best, can break a saw blade if you're cutting with gusto, and can result in cut or barked knuckles if your hand slips on the saw handle. Check

out folding pull-type bone saws at sporting goods dealers to compare these with the more conventional push-type models.

Miscellaneous Equipment

As time goes along, bowhunters usually accumulate a wide variety of gear that might or might not improve the deer-hunting experience. Some items, like compasses, first aid kits, fluorescent tape for trail marking, firestarting kits, and block-and-tackle setups for hoisting deer are time-tested things which are very important to most deer-hunting archers. Other things, like ornamental bowhunting belt buckles, shoulder patches, and the like are primarily fun items that proclaim to the world that a person loves to bowhunt deer and is proud of it. Pleasant hours spent perusing archery catalogs and general sporting goods catalogs will show you what is available in the way of miscellaneous bowhunting gear for practical application and fun.

Most long-time bowhunters own a raft of hunting equipment accumulated over the years. Some of this ends up permanently in a dusty corner, some like camping gear sits ready for those occasions when it really comes in handy, and some is used every time an archer goes afield. An archer must choose his hunting equipment with care, test this equipment thoroughly to see if it really works, and settle on a trim, smoothly functioning ensemble of gear that improves his personal comfort and ability to put deer meat in the freezer and antlers on the wall!

8/Bow-Shooting Basics

THE BOW-SHOOTING styles of experienced deer hunters vary greatly from individual to individual. However, the step-by-step basics of good shooting outlined in this chapter are the most accurate for nearly everyone who gives them a serious try. Once a hunter masters these basic steps, he can then experiment with mild modifications in style which might or might not stand him in good stead. However, to prevent bad shooting habits from developing, he should have these basics down pat before modifying his shooting form.

Long-time bowhunters as well as beginners would do well to carefully study the photos and text of this chapter. Most experienced hunters have learned to shoot a bow "by the seat of their pants" instead of following detailed instructions or enlisting the services of a professional shooting coach. As a result, many have ingrained flaws in their form that hamper their full accuracy potential.

Before an archer begins careful step-by-step bow-shooting practice, he should make sure his bow is set up properly for such initial shooting. Such a setup is approximate at best, but it should produce at least fair arrow flight and give you an accuracy incentive to perfect your bow-shooting form.

Double-check your bow to make sure it has a nocking point clamped on the bowstring. The nocking point should be situated at a right angle to and approximately ⅜-inch above the arrow rest position.

If you shoot a compound bow, the arrow plate portion of your arrow rest should be adjusted to about ¼-inch away from the bow itself to ensure decent fletching clearance. If you shoot a longbow or recurve bow, your rest is probably adhesive-backed and non-adjustable.

The vast majority of bowhunters use some sort of bowsight. If you have one on your bow, move the top-most pin or crosswire to a point about 3 vertical inches above the arrow rest. This pin placement should put your arrows reasonably close to the bull's-eye if you stand 10 to 15 yards away from the target and anchor in the corner of your mouth.

Once these initial steps are taken, place a bull's-eye target on your target butt and shoot an arrow step by step. Here's how:

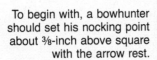

To begin with, a bowhunter should set his nocking point about ⅜-inch above square with the arrow rest.

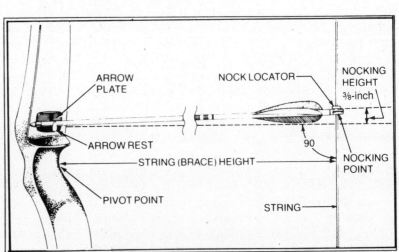

STAND PROPERLY

To begin with, stand very close to your target—10 or 15 yards away at the most. Long-distance accuracy is not the important thing now. To stand properly, your body should be at approximately a 90 degree angle to your target with feet spread comfortably, between 12 to 18 inches apart. Hold your bow loosely in your left hand if you are a right-handed shooter. Most archers enjoy the best accuracy if their feet point slightly toward the target—in other words, a right-handed shooter's right foot should be slightly ahead of his left foot. Once such a stance is achieved, turn your head to face the target.

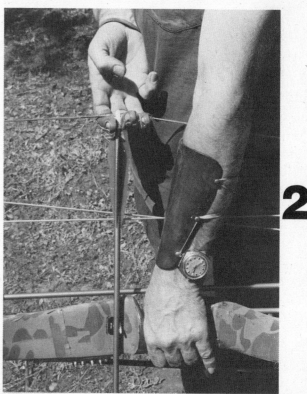

GRIP THE BOWSTRING

Nock an arrow directly under the nocking point on the bowstring, place the arrow on the arrow rest and cant the bow slightly to keep it in place. Grip the bowstring with your index finger above the arrow nock and your next two fingers below it. At this point, the bowstring should be cradled in the first joints of these three fingers with the fingers bent enough to securely hold the string. When gripping the bowstring properly in this manner, your bowstring fingers will form a modified Boy Scout salute.

BEGIN THE DRAW

Gripping the bowstring as described and holding the bow in a relaxed but closed-finger hand, fully extend your bow arm toward the target and begin drawing back the string. During the draw, be sure to keep the wrist of your bow hand as straight as possible with most of the bow-grip pressure on the web between your thumb and forefinger. Beginning shooters often have trouble keeping the arrow on the arrow rest at this point—if you experience this problem, cant your bow slightly during the draw and also hold the arrow on the rest with the index finger of your bow hand. Shooters quickly learn to rotate the bowstring in their fingers during the draw to pressure the arrow against the rest.

4

FINISH THE DRAW

Draw the bowstring smoothly back to the right side of your face (left side if you're a left-handed shooter). Continue to look at the target as you draw, using your back and shoulder muscles to pull back the string. Continue to keep most of the pressure of the bow grip on the web of your hand—not the palm or heel. Such a straight-wrist grip is most accurate for the majority of shooters. Throughout the draw, make sure your bow is vertical to the ground unless you need to cant it initially to keep the arrow on the rest.

ANCHOR THE BOWSTRING HAND

Once your bow is fully drawn, anchor your bow-string hand solidly against your face with the index finger pressed in the corner of your mouth. The thumb of the string hand should be dropped beneath the point of the jaw with the jaw cradled firmly in the pocket formed between your index finger and thumb. In this position, your shooting eye should align closely with the bowstring—the string should be an out-of-focus bar to the left or right of your eye. With a little practice, this particular anchor is very consistent from shot to shot and leads to excellent accuracy. Shooting without a solid anchor against the face is very much like shooting an open-sighted rifle with the back sight removed—shots hit different places! Anchoring solidly also transfers a percentage of the bowstring pressure to the neck muscles for a steadier aim and shot.

5

6

GRIP THE BOW PROPERLY

How you grip the bow for a shot is one of the most critical parts of bow-shooting form. If the bow is clenched tightly, the muscles in the hand and forearm tend to bunch up and jerk a shot off target when you release the bowstring. The proper hold for a hunting bow prior to a shot is a relaxed, closed-hand grip. Bowhunters who shoot with an *open* hand and grab at the bow as they release generally shoot even more poorly than those who hold a bow death-grip tight. It is difficult for beginning shooters to hold a bow so it won't fall out of the hand, yet hold it in a relaxed, non-jumpy fashion. Most of the best-shooting bowhunters touch one or more fingertips to their thumb as they grip a bow, letting the bow rattle loosely in this encircling grip when the shot is made. As you aim at the target, you should consciously concentrate on relaxing your bow hand from the wrist on forward.

7

CHECK FINGER PRESSURE

There are infinite ways an archer can hold a bowstring in his three shooting fingers. Exactly how you hold the string will partly be determined by the shape and length of your three drawing fingers, but it will be largely determined by conscious effort on your part.

Some hunters place equal string pressure on all three fingers, and some place more pressure on one finger than another. Deciding what grip feels most comfortable takes time and practice. To begin with, try to hold the string with equal pressure. When this is done, the forearm and elbow of your bowstring arm should align almost exactly with the arrow. Such arrow alignment places a minimum of stress on shooting muscles and contributes to good accuracy. Have a friend visually check your forearm alignment from time to time to make sure you are exerting equal pressure on your drawing fingers. Consistency of string hold is one key to accurate shooting.

AIM AT THE TARGET

Once you have drawn and anchored to your face, smoothly bring the bowsight pin toward the target and center it as best you can. Focus your eyes on the target when aiming—not on the sight pin. Learn to be consistent in the way you approach the bull's-eye with the sight. If coming up on the target feels most natural, do this every time. If coming down feels better, stick with that method. A few bowhunters move on target from the side instead of up or down, and this is fine as long as they aim the same from shot to shot. Because it allows maximum visibility of the target above the sights during the draw and aim, most bowhunters draw slightly low and come up on the target.

Bowhunters who prefer to shoot without sights usually use the arrow tip as a conscious or subconscious bowsight, "gapping" this tip below the target to achieve dead-center hits. The further away the target is, the higher the arrow tip is held and the smaller the gap is between target and tip. At one distance down range, the arrow actually hits the target when the arrow point is placed directly on the target. This distance is called point-on distance, and usually falls somewhere between 50 and 90 yards with a conventional index-finger anchor in the corner of the mouth.

Plenty of practice will help the non-bowsight shooter to hit fairly well, using the arrow point as a crude form of sight. However, gapping off the arrow point is never

8

as accurate as bowsight shooting, so the vast majority of deer hunters use sights.

One other note on aiming at the target. If you do use bowsights, your bow must be held vertically for decent accuracy at all shooting ranges. A few shooters who prefer to hunt without bowsights cant their bows slightly, and as long as they do this the same from shot to shot, accuracy will not suffer. However, it's a lot easier to hold a bow vertically than trying to cant it to the same angle on each and every shot.

9

RELEASE AND FOLLOW THROUGH

The bowstring release is the most critical part of good shooting. A bowhunter must strive to achieve as smooth a release as is humanly possible to send the arrow cleanly on its way.

For smooth release, simply relax your fingers when you are on target and let the string slide free. When this is properly done, your bowstring hand will slide backwards slightly *and stay against your face.* It is improper to deliberately throw open your hand to release the string—let the string pressure on your fingers do the work as you simply relax your hand.

Once you release the bowstring, follow through the shot by holding the bow in a relaxed, stationary position with the sight remaining on the target. *Try to hold the sight on the target until the arrow hits the target.* The bow will naturally recoil to one side as the bowstring is released, but by consciously trying to hold the sight in place, you'll allow the arrow to launch accurately before the bow recoils out of the way. Following through a shot in this manner is vital to tight groups on targets and consistent hits on deer.

Good shooting form yields accurate results.

Sighting-In Your Bow

Unless you luck out, your initial bowsight setting will be somewhat off when you start shooting. After a few shots to establish a point-of-impact pattern, sight-in your close-range pin *by moving it in the direction arrows are hitting.* If arrows hit high and right, move your sight up and to the right. If they hit low and left, move your sight down and to the left.

After some target practice, you'll want to begin shooting from 20 yards and even farther away. At this point, it is easy to resight your bow by shooting two or three arrows at 20 yards and moving the sight to where

(Right) To sight-in a bow, simply move the sight pin to where the arrow has hit. For example, if you hit high and left, move your pin up and to the left.

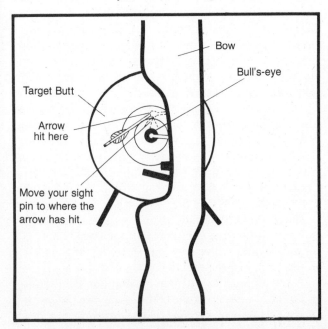

Bow

Bull's-eye

Target Butt

Arrow hit here

Move your sight pin to where the arrow has hit.

these arrows hit. The same procedure should be repeated for 30 yards, 40 yards, and other normal sight-pin distances. Most deer hunters carry four, five, or six sight pins on their bows set at 10-yard increments for 20 yards, 30 yards, 40 yards, 50 yards, and so on. For shooting at intermediate ranges like 25 yards, they simply gap between the pins.

Conscious Practice Makes Perfect

All bowhunters experience shooting problems from time to time. Beginners seldom shoot well overnight, and advanced shooters go into slumps and develop bad habits like any other athlete. The major key in learning to shoot well and maintaining a high level of accuracy is *consciously* following the basic steps of good shooting just outlined. As you learn to shoot a bow, analyze your form step-by-step to make darn sure you are not doing something wrong that could turn into a bad habit that is hard to break. Eventually good habits will become unconscious reflexes, but even the most advanced shooters should reevaluate their shooting techniques from time to time to prevent poor habits from creeping in. When an experienced bowhunter's shooting begins to drop off unexpectedly, or when a shooter reaches a particular level of accuracy that he simply cannot seem to improve upon, it is time to go back to basics. Deer hunters seldom think about their form as they shoot at game, but they can keep this form ideal through conscious analysis and correction on the target range.

Here are a few other bow-shooting practice tips. To begin with, shoot only 20 or 30 arrows per day to prevent tired, sore fingers and muscles. Two or three shooting sessions per week is plenty—more can keep muscles tired and prevent you from shooting well. Ease into the physical demands of shooting a bow—to rush in will wear you down and lead to bad shooting habits caused by wobbly muscles and a negative or frustrated mental attitude. It normally takes a full 3 months of twice-weekly practice to fully strengthen a shooter's drawing and aiming muscles—after that, once-a-week shooting of 60 to 100 arrows will keep you ready to punch the centers out of bull's-eyes and drop deer in their tracks.

Common Shooting Problems

Here are some common shooting problems experienced by beginners and experts alike. Learn to look for these problems and correct them before they get out of hand.

Hitting Your Chest or Armguard with the Bowstring: This problem is most noticeable when you smack the back of your armguard with the string. By contrast, many hunters hit baggy chest clothing or lightly snag an armguard with the string and never know it. However, when this happens, the arrow normally hits to the left (for a right-handed shooter). To correct this problem, open up your stance. In other words, face the target more directly. By pointing your toes more toward the target, your chest and bow arm automatically move away from the string and eliminate perplexing hits to the side. Many bowhunters stand away from the target at 45 degrees instead of 90 degrees to prevent string contact with the chest and arm.

Gripping the Bow Too Tightly: We've already discussed this one in the step-by-step shooting section. Do not grip your bow tightly! This tenses up muscles and causes erratic shooting. Work on making your hand feel like a *club* when you aim to shoot—if it is this relaxed, your arrows should go on course. If you continue to grip the bow in white-knuckle fashion, or if you develop a habit of grabbing the bow at the instant you release even if you begin with a loose grip, try using a wrist sling that lets you shoot with an open hand.

The Arrow Falls Off the Rest: This is a common problem with beginning shooters. To prevent this, grip the bowstring in very deep, tightly curled finger grooves and roll the string by opening the fingers slightly as you raise your bow to draw. This will torque the arrow into the bow and hold it on the rest.

Inconsistent Anchor: A solid bowstring anchor is as important as the back sight on a hunting rifle. Floating your anchor all over your face will always cause big arrow groups. With practice, most bowhunters learn to anchor consistently from shot to shot. If you have troubles achieving a consistent, comfortable anchor, put a bowstring peep on your string and position it in line with your master eye. Looking through such a peep will force you to anchor the same from shot to shot.

Target Panic: Target panic is a subconscious, psychological shooting problem. When this descends upon a shooter, he begins to freeze off-target and absolutely cannot move the bowsight to the bull's-eye. Target panic can be caused by many things, including overtired shooting muscles, too much bow weight, or simply a mental block against aiming directly at the bull's-eye.

Hopefully, you'll never experience this frustrating bad habit. However, many, many shooters do. The best way to lick the problem is shooting for awhile at close range at a fairly large bull's-eye. At first, simply draw your bow without an arrow and aim at the bull's-eye for several seconds. Do not let go of the bowstring! Let off on the draw and repeat this several times. Next, shoot a few arrows at the close-range target, concentrating on aiming at the exact center of the bull's-eye. The closer your sight pin is to the bull's-eye when you draw, the less trouble you are apt to have with freezing off-target. With lots of close-range practice, you'll eventually be able to move back to longer ranges without freezing.

Target panic is a common problem with bowsight shooters who try too hard and worry too much about how well they shoot. One key to overcoming the tendency to freeze off-target is simply not worrying excessively about how well you shoot. By all means work on improving your groups, but don't fret about doing so!

Plucking the Bowstring: A bowstring pluck occurs when a shooter strums the bowstring with his fingers instead of releasing by fully relaxing his hand. When you pluck the bowstring, your hand normally flies away from your face instead of sliding back against it smoothly. A plucked arrow always hits in the direction the bowstring hand flies—to the right if the shooter is right-handed. Plucking the bowstring is a problem every finger shooter experiences from time to time and can only be corrected by consciously relaxing the string hand and keeping it against the face during the release. String plucking is especially common when a shooting glove becomes deeply grooved and tends to hang up a smooth bowstring release, and occurs with some frequency among tab-shooters.

Caving In: When a shooter caves in, he drops his bow prematurely instead of following through a shot. Most often, the bow drops down and to the right for a right-handed shooter. The result is usually a hit low and to the right. Caving in is often caused by tired shooting muscles and can always be cured by only shooting when you're rested and consciously following through on every shot.

Variations in Shooting Style

As a hunter perfects his bow-shooting ability, he should experiment with variations in shooting style to help improve accuracy. Here are a few common variations you might want to try.

Variations in Stance: As a normal rule, a shooter is most accurate when standing at a 90 degree angle to the target or facing the target slightly as he shoots. A few hunters find that they shoot best by facing the target at a greater angle than normal. I personally stand at 45 degrees to the target instead of the conventional 90 degrees. As a general rule, facing *away* from the target more than 90 degrees is bad business because the bowstring usually brushes a shooter's chest and/or arm during a shot. If you shoot a right-hand bow, make sure your right foot is not planted behind your left foot as you shoot.

Variations In Bowstring Grip: Although most deer

Some good bowhunters prefer to stand with feet pointing at a 90-degree angle to the target. Others shoot better with a

more open stance, slightly facing the target with their feet at a 45-degree angle.

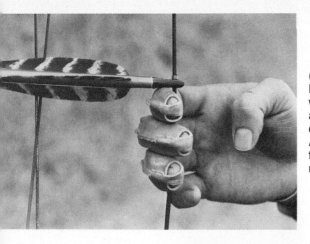

(Left and right) Most bow-hunters grip the bowstring with one finger above the arrow and two below. However, a few prefer the Apache draw with all three fingers below the arrow nock.

(Right and far right) A hunter should experiment with different three-finger grips on the bowstring and find one that is most accurate. Some archers deep-hook a string with all three fingers, others float the third or lowest finger because this gives them a smoother string release.

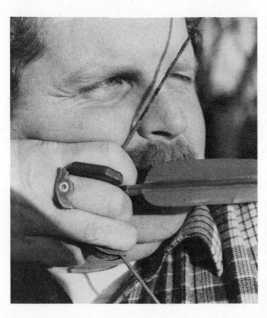

hunters grip the string with one finger above the nock and two below it, a few use the so-called "Apache draw" with all three fingers underneath the arrow. The Apache draw offers no advantage to a bowsight user, but it helps some non-sight shooters aim directly down the arrow because this string-holding method raises the arrow closer to the eye. Shooting down the arrow with an Apache draw is sometimes called "gunbarreling" because the shooter uses the arrow like a shotgun barrel to aim on close shots. Apache drawing is generally a disadvantage in shooting situations over 30 or 40 yards because the arrow drops below the line of sight at these longer ranges. As a result, it is used primarily by archers hunting close-range deer from tree stands.

No matter where you put your string fingers in relation to the arrow, you should settle into a smooth, comfortable way of holding and releasing a bowstring. Placing equal pressure on all three fingers may or may not be your ideal shooting grip. For example, I shoot best by placing about 80 percent of string weight on my two top fingers and slightly floating the third. This raises my elbow somewhat out of line with the arrow

and places extra strain on the two top fingers, but my holding method feels most comfortable due to the shape of my hand and length of my fingers.

I also tend to ease open my string fingers slightly as I aim to make my hold on the string shallower at the time of the release. When I'm ready to release, the bow-string is riding on the balls of my fingers and slips away with very little finger movement or friction. This release method requires more finger strength and thicker bowstring calluses on the balls of my fingers, but it yields ultimate accuracy for me. Experiment with bow-string grips to settle on one that works for you.

Variations in Anchor: Although most bowhunters anchor with the index finger in the corner of the mouth, a few use other solid anchors with good results.

Some archers who prefer to shoot without bowsights use a higher-than-normal anchor to move the arrow closer to the eye and help them use the arrowhead as a crude form of sight. The most common high anchor is the middle finger in the corner of the mouth. When combined with the Apache-draw method of holding the bowstring, this anchor moves the arrow upward to

(Far left and left) Exactly where you anchor to your face is a matter of personal preference. Some bowhunters like excessively high face anchors; others like to anchor under the chin.

nearly in line with the eye—an aiming advantage for some shooters on close-range deer and targets.

One common problem some sight shooters experience is the inability to get more than two or three sight pins on their bows in the area above the arrow. To solve this dilemma, a hunter must anchor lower on his face to increase the upward angle of the arrow in relation to the eye. This raises arrow trajectory considerably, often allowing a hunter to add distance pins to his sight for ranges out to 70 or 80 yards.

The most common low anchor used by hunters is the under-the-chin anchor. With this anchor, the shooter's index finger butts up under his chin and the tip of his nose lightly rests against the string. When used with a bowstring peep, this anchor is one of the steadiest and most accurate because an archer has three separate reference points to ensure a consistent anchor—his chin, his nose, and the peep on the string.

Variations in Bow Grip: Although all good shots grip a bow loosely to eliminate muscle tension and bow torque, there are three loose grip variations commonly seen on the target range.

The straight-wrist grip is most common and most accurate for the majority of shooters. When viewed from the side, this grip keeps the top of the hand more or less in line with the top of the arm. In other words, the wrist and hand are not cocked up or down significantly when the shooter holds his bow.

A high-wrist grip is sometimes preferred by shooters. Some hunters I know use this grip simply because it feels more comfortable. Others use it because it fits the shape of their bow handles the best. Such a grip is achieved by cocking the bow hand sharply downward and wrist sharply upward as you hold the bow and draw. With this grip, most of the pressure of the bow handle against the hand falls against the top of the web between the thumb and forefinger. The high-wrist grip

THE STRAIGHT-WRIST GRIP

THE HIGH-WRIST GRIP

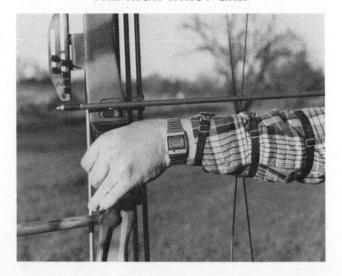

THE LOW-WRIST GRIP

is every bit as accurate as the straight-wrist grip, provided a shooter holds the bow consistently from shot to shot.

A low-wrist grip is the least accurate of bow-holding methods. However, a few hunters shoot well with this one despite its inherent disadvantages. A low-wrist grip is assumed by cocking the bow hand sharply upward and wrist sharply downward to apply pressure to the bow handle along the full length of the palm and butt of the hand. Most shooters who use this grip originally fell into the habit because it spread out bow-hand pressure across a larger portion of the hand. The trouble is, with so much bow-to-hand contact associated with this grip, it is more difficult for a shooter to consistently hold a bow from shot to shot. A little more or a little less pressure against the heel of the bow hand will cause arrows to fly high or low and wobble in the process. The low-wrist grip is extremely comfortable, but is best left alone if you can adapt to a straight-wrist or high-wrist grip on the bow.

Learning to shoot a bow is not all that difficult, provided you take the process step by step and consciously work on doing everything right. The best shooting accuracy will not come until you gradually strengthen shooting muscles over several months and fine-tune your bow as described in Chapter 9. After your shooting habits are formed, your muscles toned for steady and comfortable shooting, and your bow tuned to produce perfect arrow flight, you'll be absolutely amazed at how good your bow-shooting becomes. Most bowhunters never realize more than a fraction of their accurate shooting potential, but you *can* reach full potential if you practice step by step and carefully tune your bow. The inevitable result will be more deer in the bag and the great feeling of a job well done!

9/Step-By-Step Bow Tuning

AS FAR AS I'm concerned, this is the single most important chapter in this book. What I'm about to discuss here has never appeared anywhere in the past. It is my own personally devised bow-tuning method, and if I do say so myself, it is completely foolproof.

This method evolved over the past 15 years as I shot dozens of bows and sought to find a fast, easy way to achieve perfect arrow flight. I've been through all the frustration most serious archers experience as they fight and grapple with getting their bows to shoot. I, too, have agonized for hours over combos that wouldn't shoot broadheads and field points to the same point of aim, that seemed to shoot field points well but wouldn't shoot broadheads worth a darn, or simply wouldn't shoot any kind of arrow without wobble, noise, and a notable lack of accuracy.

Most deer-hunting archers are not overly concerned with achieving perfect arrow flight because they do not know what they're missing. If arrows lob into the general area of the target, they figure they're doing as well as can be expected. Unfortunately, I'm convinced that at least 99 out of every 100 American bowhunters are currently shooting poorly or at least marginally tuned bows that do okay but don't do great on targets and game.

Arrow flight does not usually concern most bow-hunters until they attach broadheads to their shafts. Now, all of a sudden, point of impact changes and arrows often fly wildly as the broadheads plane radically through the air. This phenomenon can be confusing at best, and a hunter can adjust his arrow rest, nocking point, draw weight, and other things until the cows come home without accidentally finding the accurate tune point of his bow. It's no more than a one-in-a-million chance that a hunter will end up with a perfectly

tuned-up bow by random tinkering—which is why I'm writing this chapter.

A well-tuned bow/arrow combination yields several important advantages: First, it will dramatically and instantly improve accuracy, turning 8-inch, 20-yard groups into 3-inch, 20-yard groups without any shooting style change. Second, it will ensure that arrows with points of the same weight will hit the exact same place with excellent accuracy—even fairly large hunting broadheads. Third, the bow will immediately become quieter to shoot because every part of the shooting gear is properly working together. And fourth, arrows will fly a little bit faster and penetrate a whole lot better because no arrow energy is shed to the sides due to wobble.

I call the following step-by-step bow-tuning procedure "modified bare-shaft tuning." This procedure was devised after hundreds of hours of theorizing, trial-and-error shooting on the range, and using the computer information of various bow and arrow manufacturers. If you carefully follow these steps, this procedure is guaranteed to produce better arrow flight than you've ever experienced in your life. It works equally well on any kind of bow, be it longbow, recurve, round-wheel compound, or compound cam-bow.

One other note on bow-tuning. Do not attempt to tune your bow until you have mastered the basic shooting steps outlined in Chapter 8. Every change you make in your shooting form will change the tune of your bow, so become relatively consistent about shooting before fine-tuning your equipment. Changes in bowstring grip, bow grip, stance, and other parts of good shooting will all change the way an arrow flies and will render careful tuning a completely worthless endeavor.

1 Pre-Set Arrow Rest

The first step in bow-tuning is setting your arrow rest to a ballpark starting position. The best bow rests for tuning are the flipper/plunger combination and the springy rest—if your bow will accept one of these, it's best to use one, the flipper/plunger being best of all. To set your rest, move the cushion plunger button or springy rest about ¼-inch away from the bow to provide good fletching clearance. Set the plunger's spring tension at a moderate setting. If you're using some sort of arrow rest that doesn't screw in or out—like many longbows and recurve bows have—no rest adjustment need be made.

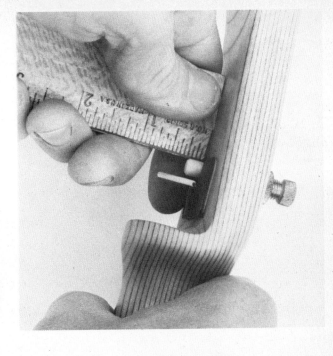

(Right) The arrow-rest plate on a bow should be set initially about ¼-inch away from the bow. From here, it can be adjusted in about ⅛-inch or out about ⅛-inch without shooting problems occurring.

(Right) A one-piece adjustable springy rest should be initially set with the plate area about ¼-inch from the bow.

2 Pre-Set Nocking Point

Set the nocking point at a 90-degree angle to the arrow rest and ⅜-inch above that point. This location, like the arrow-plate location, is only approximate but represents a place to begin tuning from.

Set your bowsight for about 10 yards by shooting a few field points. Most of the shooting during the tuning process will be done from this short range.

3 Decide on Draw Weight

You should decide on a comfortable draw weight prior to tuning your bow. An accurate bow scale helps you precisely match bow weight to arrow-shaft size for best tuning results.

This step applies only to bows with adjustable draw weights. Hunters who use adjustable-draw-weight bows have the habit of changing draw weight to experiment with different comfort levels of shooting. Prior to tuning your bow, decide what draw weight you prefer and leave your bow set there. Some bowhunters own regular archery scales for measuring bow weight, but it isn't absolutely necessary to know the exact poundage setting as long as it feels good to shoot. However, you *should* know your bow poundage within a pound or two to ensure proper shaft selection—if you don't, your archery dealer or sporting goods dealer will have a bow scale or necessary literature on your bow to help you determine this draw weight.

Remember this: If you tune a bow for a particular draw weight, you cannot change this weight without tuning the bow all over again.

4 Check Arrow Size

Before you begin tuning your bow, it's a good idea to refer to an arrow-shaft selection chart to double-check your choice of arrow size. If the arrows you are shooting do not fall within the recommended sizes to match your draw length and approximate draw weight, you will not be able to properly tune your bow.

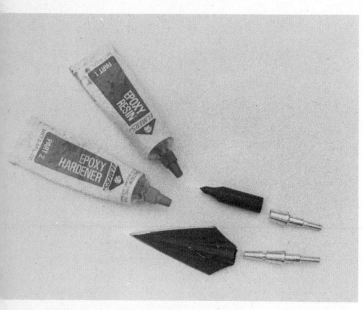

Matching up arrowhead weight often requires combining component parts of known weight. For example, a short broadhead adapter plus a 125-grain glue-on field point and a long adapter plus a middle-sized Zwickey Black Diamond broadhead both equal 165 grains when epoxied together.

5 Arrowhead Weight

The only way you'll ever get arrows to fly properly is by using arrowheads of a single weight. Mixing 145-grain broadheads with 125-grain field points almost certainly guarantees inaccurate arrow flight and a different point of impact for each different arrowhead weight.

Manufacturers offer several field-point weights to choose from, including 125 grains, 140 grains, 145 grains, and 150 grains. You can make up arrowheads of your own to achieve even heavier grain weights by gluing aluminum, screw-in broadhead adapters to old-style glue-on field points and broadheads. For example, a 125-grain glue-on field point epoxied to a full-length Easton Break-Off Broadhead Adapter weighs 175 grains (125 grains for the head, 45 grains for the adapter, and 5 grains for the glue). Similarly, the same basic combo with the 10-grain tip of the Easton adapter broken off weighs exactly 165 grains. You must decide what point weight you want to shoot before tuning your bow because even a 10-grain change in point weight will ruin the bow tune.

The best way to decide on an arrowhead weight is by selecting the broadhead you want to hunt deer with and matching its weight with a commercial or home-assembled field point. For instance, I usually hunt deer with 165-grain broadheads, so I glue up 165-grain field points to match, and tune up my bow with this point weight. If you haven't yet chosen a deer-hunting broadhead, go ahead and tune your bow with standard 125-grain field points. You may have to re-tune later on if you select a broadhead of a different weight, but at least your bow will shoot well in the meantime.

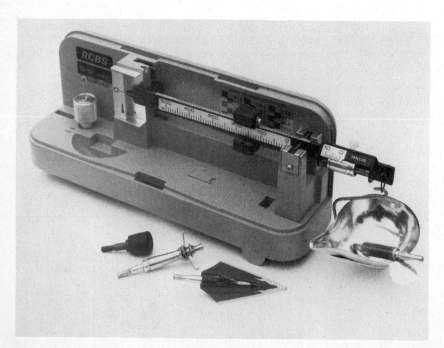

All arrowheads an archer uses must weigh the same to produce accurate, well-tuned arrow flight.

6 Reduce Draw Weight

Now you're through with preliminary preparation and ready to begin tuning the bow. Almost all compound bows can be adjusted in draw weight by turning Allen-head bolts holding the butts of upper and lower limbs. If your bow is of this design, and if you plan to shoot arrows with plastic vanes, reduce bow weight exactly one full turn on both top and bottom limbs. This is a *vitally* important step; I'll explain why later on.

Before tuning a compound bow for arrows with plastic vanes, reduce draw weight one full turn at each limb butt.

7 Prepare Bare Shaft

In order to tune up your bow, you'll need one or two arrows exactly like your regular arrows except *without* fletching. These must be identical in shaft size and length to the fletched arrows you intend to shoot at targets and deer. You can either strip away the fletching and fletching glue from one or two arrows with a sharp knife, or buy bare shafts complete with nocks and point inserts from your sporting goods store or archery dealer. Note: Such shafts must be perfectly straight with nocks glued on straight. Triple-check this before shooting because a bent bare shaft or one with a crooked nock will fly absolutely crazy and won't help you one little bit.

Attach field point arrowheads of the weight you decided on in step 4 to your straight bare shafts. You are now almost ready to shoot.

One way to prepare bare shafts for bow-tuning is simply stripping off plastic vanes and fletching glue with a sharp knife.

8 Make Tuning Target

When tuning your bow, you'll be watching bare shafts fly toward the target. The best target background to see these shafts against is white paper. With this in mind, take a large white piece of butcher paper or some other pure-white paper and make a small black bull's-eye in the center with a felt-tipped pen. This paper should be at least 2 feet square for best results. In a pinch, a regular paper bull's-eye target can be turned backwards to form a white tuning target. Tack this tuning target on your target butt, and you're ready to tune your bow.

A tuning target is necessary for shooting bare shafts. Such a target can be made of white paper or cardboard with a black aiming spot drawn in the middle.

9 Shoot Bare Shaft

This is the step that tells you what adjustments need to be made to perfectly tune your bow. Stand 10 yards from the target butt and shoot a bare shaft at the small black bull's-eye, trying to follow the good steps of bow-shooting. As the bare shaft flies, the rear end will yaw in a particular direction—it will probably yaw badly. Shoot a few bare shafts to determine visually which way the tail end of the arrow is leaving as it flies. You can do this yourself, but it helps to have a friend stand behind you to watch the bare shafts in the air.

A perfectly tuned bare shaft flies like a dart with the rear end in exact line with the point. An out-of-tune shaft flies tail high, tail low, tail right, tail left, or with a combination of vertical and horizontal misalignment. This will be readily evident when you shoot bare shafts. It is fairly easy to identify a tail high and right shaft or a tail low and left shaft when that shaft is watched against a white paper background.

A good way to double-check your eyes is by determining the angle the shaft has entered your target butt. Although not a surefire method because target butts sometimes flip arrow tails different ways *after* entry, the entry angle of a bare shaft in a target butt will often confirm what you thought you saw flying through the air.

Tail High-Right Shaft

Tail-Right Shaft

Tail-Low Shaft

Tail-Left Shaft

Tail-High Shaft

Tail Low-
Left Shaft

How a perfectly
tuned shaft strikes
the target.

10 Adjust the Nocking Point

To eliminate a tail-high or tail-low tendency in a bare shaft, you must move your nocking point up or down. Such a tail-high or tail-low tendency in a bare shaft tells you that regular fletched arrows will wobble up and down in flight. To eliminate up-and-down wobble, which is often called porpoising, move your nocking point in the *opposite direction* the bare-shaft tail is flying. If the shaft flies tail high, move the nocking point down. If the shaft flies tail low, move the nocking point up. Tinker with such nocking-point movement until bare shafts appear to have no tail-high or tail-low tendencies.

Although many hunting bows shoot best with nocking points in the normal position of about ⅜-inch above 90 degrees to the arrow shelf, variations in shooting style and individual factory bows can require nocking-point placement quite a ways away from the ⅜-inch location. I've seen bows that shot perfectly with nocking points placed over 1 inch above 90 degrees, and other bows that shot best with nocking points that were actually below 90 degrees to the arrow shelf. You must move a nocking point around until you find the tune point for your bow . . . don't become discouraged if this point is nowhere near ⅜-inch above 90 degrees with the arrow shelf.

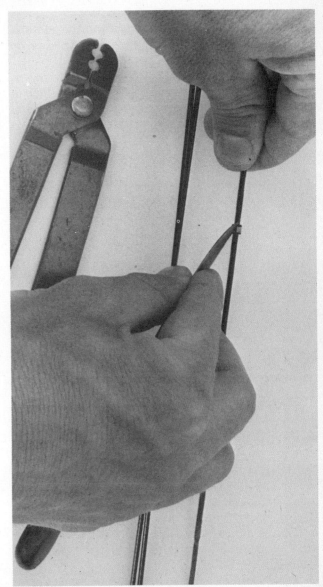

To eliminate tail-low or tail-high bare-shaft flight, simply move the nocking point up or down.

11 Adjust the Arrow Plate

Tail-left and tail-right tendencies in a flying bare shaft can usually be removed by adjusting the plate portion of an adjustable arrow rest. Such tail-right or tail-left tendencies result in side-to-side arrow wobble with regular fletched shafts. Wobble is called fishtailing, and severely hampers bow-shooting accuracy.

If you have a spring-loaded cushion plunger on your bow, weaken the spring tension if shafts fly tail right or tighten spring tension if shafts fly tail left (reverse this procedure for left-hand bows). In similar fashion, if you shoot a right-hand bow and have access to different springy-rest springs of different tensions (springy springs are normally available in hunting tensions of 15, 20, and 25 ounces), you can put on a weaker spring if shafts fly tail right or put on a stiffer spring if shafts fly tail left. Sometimes, such spring-tension adjustments alone will completely eliminate the tail-right or tail-left flight of a bare arrow shaft. If not, you'll have to move your rest plate in or out as well.

If you have a rest on your bow with no tension-adjustable arrow plate, or if adjusting spring tension on your cushion plunger or springy rest will not completely eliminate tail-right or tail-left bare-shaft tendencies, you must move the arrow plate in or out of the bow to straighten out bare-shaft flight. To do this properly, move the arrow plate *in the direction the arrow tail is yawing*. For a tail-right shaft, move the cushion-plunger button, spring rest, or another adjustable plate to the right until bare shafts straighten out. For a tail-left shaft, move the arrow-rest plate to the left until bare shafts straighten out. In most cases, such adjustments will result in excellent bare-shaft flight. If they do not, and you run out of arrow-plate adjustment room, continue on to step 12.

When I say "run out of arrow-plate room," I mean

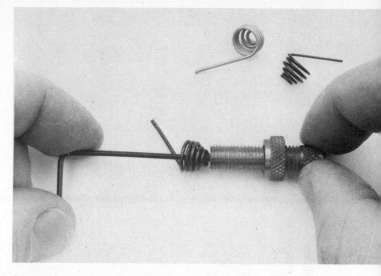

Changing spring tension will often solve tail-right or tail-left bare-shaft problems. A springy rest with multiple spring sizes makes such tension changes easy.

moving the arrow plate more than 1/8-inch to 3/16-inch in or out from the original 1/4-inch placement from the bow. An arrow plate too close to a bow will disrupt arrow flight as plastic vanes collide with a bow, and an arrow plate too far out will precariously perch an arrow on the very end of the arrow-rest shelf.

If your bow does not have an adjustable arrow-rest plate, tail-right or tail-left bare-shaft flight will be difficult to correct with the rest. This is a common problem on longbows and recurve bows. The best a hunter can do with such a rest is replace it with one that *is* adjustable. If this is not possible on your bow, go on to Step 12.

12 Alternative Bow-Tuning Procedures

If you have a compound bow fitted with a plunger/flipper rest or springy rest, Steps 10 and 11 will normally straighten out bare-shaft flight. It is important to note here that shooting a bare shaft perfectly each and every time is difficult or impossible for most shooters because such a vaneless shaft amplifies any little variations in shooting form. If you tune your bow to a point where bare shafts fly nearly perfect and exhibit no consistent tail-misalignment direction, you can consider these shafts tuned as well as can be expected.

If bare shafts have not straightened out by step 11, it

is almost certain that you are shooting the wrong arrow-shaft size for good arrow flight. Arrow-shaft selection charts are rough reference aids at best, and they occasionally fail to recommend the proper shaft size to match a particular bow and a particular shooting style. You may have to change shaft sizes to compensate for these variables, but do not despair yet. Two other tuning procedures may allow you to tune up with your original arrows.

If arrows fly tail-right from a right-hand bow and cannot be straightened out by moving the arrow plate to the right, your arrow is not bending enough in the bow to properly stabilize it. A too-stiff arrow of this sort flies tail-left from a left-hand bow. To cure this problem without selecting weaker, more limber arrow shafts, you can do one of two things. First, you can raise the poundage of your compound bow steadily until using steps 1, 9, and 11 will make bare shafts finally straighten out. Second, you can attach heavier and heavier points to your bare arrow shafts to force them to bend more as they leave the bow. After attaching heavier points, you must go through steps 1, 9, and 11 all over again to see if these points will tune up properly. If you cannot raise your bow's poundage enough to straighten arrow flight, or if no amount of extra arrowhead weight straightens out bare shafts, you'll have to try shooting weaker arrow shafts to cure the tail-right problem (tail-left in a left-hand bow). On an arrow-shaft selection chart, shaft sizes are weaker the higher up on the chart columns you look.

If your bare shafts fly tail-left from a right-hand bow or tail-right from a left-hand bow, the arrows you are using are bending too much as they leave the bow. To cure this problem when steps 1, 9, and 11 do not work, reduce the poundage of your compound bow or attach lighter-weight arrowheads to your shafts and repeat steps 1, 9, and 11. In similar fashion to tuning a too-stiff shaft, a too-weak shaft that will not straighten out must be replaced by a stiffer shaft on an arrow-shaft selection chart. Stiffer shaft sizes are found in the lower columns of an arrow-shaft selection chart.

Obviously, altering your bow poundage or changing field-point weight is not an acceptable tuning alternative if you are dead-set on shooting a particular bow-poundage or completely sold on a deer-hunting broadhead of a particular weight. If you wish to leave both draw weight and arrowhead weight the same, your only option is changing arrow-shaft sizes until you find the proper one to match your chosen draw weight and arrowhead weight.

Although recurve bows and longbows seldom have adjustable arrow plates, they can always be tuned by changing point weights or arrow-shaft sizes. In addition, shortening a bowstring on such bows by twisting it will *reduce* arrow speed; conversely, lengthening the string by untwisting it or buying a slightly longer string will *increase* arrow speed. Changing bowstring length on recurves and longbows will often straighten out tail-left or tail-right bare shafts in similar fashion to raising or lowering compound-bow draw weight. To cure a tail-left bare shaft from a right-hand bow, shorten the bowstring. To cure a tail-right bare shaft from a right-hand bow, lengthen the bowstring. Reverse these directions for a left-hand bow.

13 Final Tune

When bare shafts fly well from your bow, your bow is nearly tuned up. However, when bare shafts fly perfectly, fletched arrows do not fly perfectly because fletching weighs up to 10 percent of a hunting arrow's total weight. This slows the flight of a fletched arrow and makes it bend slightly less as it leaves a bow.

Plastic vanes and fletching glued on an arrow shaft weigh up to 50 grains and *significantly* slow down and stiffen an arrow as it leaves a bow. As a result, my experiments have shown that a compound bow using plastic vanes requires about one full turn on draw-weight adjustment bolts to raise bow poundage enough to compensate for the weight of these vanes and match bare-shaft speed and flexibility. This is why you turned your vane-shooting compound down one turn in step 6 and tuned bare shafts at that setting. Once your bare shafts fly perfectly from such a bow, *raise your bow weight back up to where it originally was and your bow should be in perfect tune with vane-fletched shafts.*

Virtually all longbow and recurve-bow shooters with experience use feather fletching on their arrows. So do some compound shooters. Feathers are exceedingly light in weight compared to vanes and seldom slow fletched shafts enough to untune a bow. Any slight adjustments for feather fletching can be made in step 14.

14 Check Final Tune

The ultimate test of a tuned-up bow is shooting broadheads and field points of your chosen weight attached to regular fletched hunting arrows. Note:

The results of proper modified bare-shaft bow-tuning are superior arrow groups on targets and better accuracy on game.

Never shoot a broadhead attached to a bare shaft—such a shaft can fly wildly enough to be potentially dangerous.

If you have properly tuned your bow, and if broadheads are attached perfectly straight to shafts, both field points and broadheads should hit the exact same place with superb accuracy. In the unlikely event that broadheads group slightly away from field points, the added weight of feathers or vanes on the fletched arrows may be the culprit. Make the following fine-tune adjustments to finish the bow-tuning process.

If broadheads hit to the right of field points, move the arrow-plate portion of your arrow rest slightly to the left or slightly lower the poundage of your bow until all arrows hit together. If broadheads hit to the left of field points, move the arrow-plate portion of your rest slightly to the right or raise the poundage of your bow slightly. If broadheads hit above field points, raise your nocking point slightly. If broadheads hit below field points, lower your nocking point slightly. When broadheads and field points of the same weight hit the same point of aim, your bow is perfectly tuned and should shoot groups you never believed possible.

Final Notes on Modified Bare-Shaft Tuning

The foregoing bow-tuning method is virtually infallible if you follow the step-by-step procedure faithfully. Tuning may become a time-consuming hassle if you are forced to experiment with bow poundage, arrowhead weight, or arrow-shaft sizes before achieving decent bare-shaft flight. However, the end result is well worth the trouble because you'll reach a plateau of shooting accuracy you'd never have dreamed possible.

Because bow limbs on all bows tend to let down slightly in draw weight over many months of shooting, because compound cables sometimes slip, because bowstrings lengthen throughout their life, because archers usually alter their shooting styles over time, and because of many similar change factors, a bow-hunter should double-check and alter the tune of his bow from time to time with broadheads as outlined in Step 14. And anytime he changes draw weight, arrowhead weight, or any other part of his bow/arrow combo, he must retune his bow with Steps 1 through 14. The end result will be perfect, non-wobbly arrow flight and all the nifty advantages that go with it!

Advanced Shooting/10

ONE QUESTION asked by most beginning archers is how accurate can they really become with bow-and-arrow gear? The answer to this is virtually impossible because every person has a unique level of hand/eye coordination and a unique drive to practice and excel at a particular task. However, the average shooter who pays careful attention to proper bow-shooting form, properly tunes up his bow/arrow combination, and spends ample time on the target range can shoot far better than most armchair experts with poorly tuned bows and limited experience could ever imagine.

As a rough rule of thumb, an in-shape shooter with the proper basics under control should be able to put nine out of 10 arrows in a 5-inch bull's-eye at 20 yards. Mathematically, this means that he should be able to put nine out of 10 arrows in a 10-inch bull at 40 yards and the same number of arrows in a 15-inch bull at 60 yards. Longer shooting ranges often psyche out a shooter who is confident with his gear at 20 or 30 yards, but if he aims solidly and follows through his shots, he'll be able to shoot the group sizes just mentioned. Many bowhunters shoot even better than this, placing the majority of their shots in 3- or 4-inch groups at 20 yards and most in 9- to 12-inch groups at 60 yards.

The most important thing a hunter should realize about his shooting ability is that no matter how well or how poorly he shoots at a particular stage of his deer-hunting career, he can always take animals with consistency if he refrains from shooting at ranges beyond his effective hitting ability. If he cannot consistently hit a whitetail deer's 10-inch vital zone at ranges past 25 yards, he should not shoot beyond this effective killing distance. If he can hit a 10-inch circle at 60 yards nearly every time, there is no good reason why he shouldn't exercise this skill on deer if they are calmly standing at known distances. By all means try to improve your basic shooting skills, but don't worry excessively about these skills. Limit shooting distance to your own capabilities and enjoy hunting deer!

Once a hunter learns the basics of good bow-shooting, fine-tunes his hunting bow to shoot arrows with optimum wobble-free accuracy, and tightens backyard target groups through careful practice, he is well on his way to being a successful shot on deer. However, shooting at backyard bull's-eyes and shooting at deer are two entirely different things, and all the time in the world spent on the target range will not fully prepare a bowhunter for casting arrows at big-antlered bucks.

To be honest, nothing can teach a bowhunter everything about shooting at deer but the experience itself. There is no substitute for the adrenaline-charged experience of drawing down on a buck at such a short distance that you can actually see its eyes flutter and watch the flies crawl across its shoulder blades. A bowhunter never knows for sure how he will react in such a situation until he is actually there. No matter how much other shooting practice you have behind you, there is nothing quite as electricity-charged and mentally unsettling as having a big-game animal within solid killing range of your bow.

Despite this fact, a serious bowhunter can practice several advanced shooting techniques which will greatly improve his odds of scoring at the genuine moment of truth. Practicing such techniques lacks the high level of excitement and uncertainty involved in shooting at game, but it does teach the bowhunter some mental and physical skills he needs to hit animals solidly in field-shooting situations.

Shooting from Unorthodox Positions

Shooting at targets from a classic upright stance sharpens the eyes and strengthens the muscles, but hunters are not always allowed this luxury when shooting at real, live deer. At certain times, a bowhunter must kneel down, bend over, or twist his body dramatically in order to clear foliage with his bow as he draws or to put an arrow through a small opening in the trees. Regular range practice is a must for successfully bow-hunting deer, but a hunter must branch out from this and practice less polite shooting that just might get him his buck.

Once you master the step-by-step shooting basics, begin practicing from a kneeling position, from a squat, and from various sitting poses on the ground or from stable objects such as chairs, boxes, and upside-down buckets. You can do this in your own backyard, shooting at the same targets you normally practice with. Face at various angles to the target and learn to twist your body around and still hit close to the bull's-eye. Deliberately cant your bow to one side as if a low-hanging limb prevents you from holding your bow in the classic upright position. Try to anticipate awkward shooting positions you might encounter in the field and learn where to hold your sights and how to alter your form to make such shooting situations pay off big. In my experience, an archery deer hunter in the field can generally set up an upright, standing shot at a deer instead of a shot requiring an unorthodox body position. However, every so often a hunter has to sit, squat, kneel, twist around, or bend over to shoot. If he has

practiced such maneuvers ahead of time, he'll often nail deer that otherwise would get away.

One very interesting and enjoyable game helps teach hunters to shoot well from non-classic shooting positions. This game requires two or more participants. To play, shooters take turns dreaming up awkward body positions to shoot from at various deer-hunting yardages. For example, if three archers decide to play this game on a backyard range, the first might decide to shoot one arrow from a kneeling, twisted position 25 yards away from the target. The other two shooters would have to follow suit, and the one who hit the closest to the bull's-eye would get one game point. Then it would be the second shooter's turn to pick an awkward or unorthodox shooting position at a random distance. All players would shoot from this position and distance, and the closest hit to the bull's-eye would get the game point. Such follow-the-leader shooting is loads of fun and a pleasant break from upright, traditional target practice. When my friends and I play this game on the backyard range, we normally keep on shooting until one of us reaches 25 game points. The contests are usually tight, and everyone learns a lot.

Learning to Control Arrow Trajectory

Being able to hit the bull's-eye from various known and unknown yardages is well and good, but the most successful deer hunters also become intimately familiar with the entire flight paths of their arrows. They practice shooting at oddball ranges between their set sight pins, and also practice shooting closer and farther away than their sight pins are set for. Such practice can help nail deer in unusual shooting situations.

There are three situations that instantly come to mind where intimate knowledge of your arrow trajectory can put deer down that would otherwise get away. These are at extra-long shooting ranges, ultra-short shooting ranges, and when obstacles like bushes, rocks, logs, or low hills happen to come between you and a deer, blocking a clear view of the deer's vital zone or actually threatening to impede the course of an arrow. Knowing exactly where your arrow flies all the way from bow to target can make a really big difference in your chances of making good in such situations. Let me explain what I mean.

Shooting at Extra-Long Range

Every bowhunter must decide for himself how far away he can competently shoot at deer. A whitetail's vital chest zone is only 10 or 12 inches in diameter, and an elk's is only 18 or 20 inches across. As discussed earlier, most dedicated, year-round bow-shooters can hit stationary targets of these sizes out to 60 or 70 yards if they tune up their bows properly and concentrate on good shooting form. I know serious eastern whitetail hunters who will literally come unglued when someone talks about shooting at deer past 20 or 25 yards, but

A lot of shooting practice with a well-tuned bow can produce superb accuracy. Occasionally, a hunter actually drives one shaft inside another, which is called a "Robin Hood." The author holds one such Robin Hood here. (Photo by Mick Roberts)

Impact Point of an Arrow

When using the 20 yard aiming pin and shooting at various distances. Figures given assume a perfect shot.

Bow & Arrow Combination	10 yds.	15 yds.	20 yds.	25 yds.	30 yds.	35 yds.	40 yds.
55 Lb. Compound/2016 Arrow 28″ Draw	5.0″ High	3.8″ High	◉	6.3″ Low	15.4″ Low	27.0″ Low	41.4″ Low
60 Lb. Cam/2117 Arrow 30″ Draw	3.8″ High	2.8″ High	◉	4.8″ Low	11.5″ Low	20.0″ Low	30.6″ Low
65 Lb. Compound/2117 Arrow 30″ Draw	4.1″ High	3.1″ High	◉	5.2″ Low	12.4″ Low	22.0″ Low	33.5″ Low
70 Lb. Cam/2219 Arrow 30″ Draw	3.2″ High	2.4″ High	◉	4.0″ Low	9.7″ Low	17.0″ Low	26.1″ Low

The shooting data above shows how inability to guess the correct distance causes missed shots. When a deer shows up give yourself the best chance to nail it. Use a Ranging 50 Rangefinder to measure around your stand ahead of time. You'll bag a trophy for sure!

Even flat-shooting compound bows and cam-bows require pin-point range estimation and aiming adjustments for solid hits on deer. (Illustration courtesy Ranging, Inc.)

An archer who knows the exact trajectory traits of his bow/arrow combo can sometimes nail deer even when mid-range obstacles seem to be in the way.

most of these fellows have never had the chance to shoot at long-range deer and generally shoot poorly tuned bows that would be hard pressed to hit a deer beyond 30 yards. Most good bowhunters with some long-range experience and well-tuned bows regard any shot at a stationary deer under 30 yards as a *gimme shot,* and I agree. There is no good excuse for missing such a shot if the deer is calm, broadside, and in the open. All of us have missed such shots, for sure, but it is usually because we get excited and blow the setup.

With this in mind, let's talk about knowing your long-range arrow trajectory to cope with special hunting problems. Most bowhunters do not have sights on their bows for ranges past 60 or 70 yards, so they cannot accurately shoot past these distances unless they practice long-range shooting often and learn how to gap-shoot off their lowest sights and arrow points. Although a hunter should usually refrain from shooting at deer past 70 yards—even if he is a good shot—there are a few circumstances when I feel such shooting is entirely justified.

Let's say for the sake of speculation that you hit a

At times, a long-range shot puts venison in the bag. The author nailed this excellent record-sized blacktail buck at precisely 70 yards when he realized a closer shot was impossible.

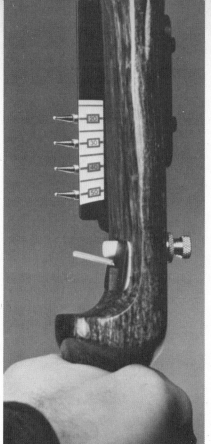

A bowhunter learns to use a rangefinding tool to help him make long, short, or tricky shots at deer.

(Right) A color-coded bowsight that corresponds to colors on a rangefinder dial simplifies and speeds up range estimation and shooting in the field.

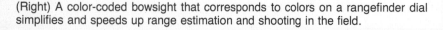

deer in the paunch area by mistake because the animal jumps the bowstring (spooks from shooting noise) as you release the arrow from your tree stand. The animal runs off and stands broadside at 80 yards, obviously hurt but by no means down and out. Up the ridge, two of your hunting buddies will be walking in for lunch within a few minutes, and you know that they are likely to bump right into the deer and scare it out of its hide. If you have an accurate rangefinder on your belt and the basic skill to hit a washtub at 80 yards, you probably have a 50-50 chance of nailing the deer with one or more extra long-range shots before the animal runs away. In such a situation, I say you should shoot and hope for the best.

Let's look at another example of justified long-range shooting: It is the very last afternoon of elk season. You have traveled 1200 miles to go on a once-in-a-lifetime, out-of-state archery hunt, and you still don't have your animal. A nice bull is feeding out of the timber 90 yards away, turns broadside, and walks between two Volkswagen-sized boulders. The animal is feeding on grass, its entire ribcage exposed and its antler tips bobbing up and down. As you take the first step to stalk in closer, a big cow elk strolls out of the timber behind the bull and freezes as she sees you move. You know from 9½ days of hard hunting that the cow will cut and run within a few seconds, taking the bull away with her. Do you pass the shot at the unalerted, stationary bull, or do you shoot? I say shoot!

Both of the foregoing examples illustrate what I call

low-percentage shots. You probably have no more than a 50-50 chance of scoring in these situations, even if you're a top shot with a bow. However, if you try several such shots over a couple of years, the percentages will catch up, and you'll nail one or more nice, long-range animals. If you have nothing to lose and everything to gain, why not go ahead and try?

Because of these views on long-range deer shooting, I believe it is very important for a hunter to practice at longer ranges to learn the trajectory peculiarities of his bow/arrow combo. Two things to pay particular attention to are the point-on distance of your bow, and where to hold the last sight pin in order to hit various long-range targets at 10-yard increments beyond the distance range of that sight pin.

Take my favorite round-wheel compound bow as an example: If I am shooting well, my arrow hits the target when I stand at exactly 90 yards and point aim the tip of the broadhead on the bull's-eye. With this point-on distance of 90 yards, and the fact that my last (lowest) regular sight pin is set for 70 yards, I can hit fairly well out to 90 yards if I know the exact range. At 80 yards, I gap about halfway between my 70-yard sight pin and my arrow point. At other ranges between 70 and 90 yards, I compensate my aim slightly to put the arrow in the right place.

Shooting at Ultra-Short Range

I'd be willing to bet that deer hunters miss almost as many bow shots at ranges under 20 yards as they do at ranges over 60. It is painfully easy to miss a deer completely at 10 or 15 yards if you rely totally on your 20-yard sight pin. This problem is minimized with flatter-shooting bows, but many, many hunters glance arrows harmlessly off the backs of deer each and every year because they aim dead-center with their 20-yard sights for shots that are less than 20 yards in distance.

Most hunting bows shot with a standard bowstring-hand anchor point in the corner of the mouth shoot dead on at 20 yards, 4 to 10 inches above the 20-yard sight pin at 15 yards, 2 to 8 inches above the 20-yard sight at 10 yards, about dead on at 3 yards, and a couple of inches low at 1 yard. For instance, I must hold about 6 inches low on the target with my 20-yard pin at 15 yards with one bow I own, and must aim with my 40-yard pin when shooting at a penny-sized target spot 1 yard away. Knowing your bow's trajectory can help you hit deer solidly at intermediate ranges like 10 or 15 yards and can also help you hit deer when you are trying to clear obstacles that exist between you and the target animal.

Using Trajectory Knowledge to Clear Obstacles

We'll consider a close-range shooting example first to illustrate how knowing your exact arrow trajectory can save your deer-shooting day. Let's say a nice whitetail buck walks past your deer blind only 20 yards away. Unfortunately, the animal stops broadside to feed with two obstacles between you and it—a leafy tree branch hanging down 3 yards in front of you and a dense bush thrusting up 15 yards away. The deer is clearly visible through the bush, but there are no gaps in its tight-knit branches. You carefully eyeball the distances to these obstacles, realize that the deer will be in solid cover soon, and decide to try a shot.

There is no way a hunting arrow can accurately shoot through tight brush or limbs. The shaft will invariably glance off course amid a series of loud, game-spooking clatters. With this in mind, you find a small, open hole through the leaves and limbs 3 yards away directly in line with the bush. At this range, you know your arrow will hit exactly where the 20-yard sight pin is aimed, and since the deer is standing 20 away yards, you will get past the limb in front of you if you aim directly at the deer through the gap in the leafy limb.

Now the only problem is the bush. At 15 yards, you know from past experience that your arrow will be about 7 inches above your 20-yard sight pin, and the bush is 15 yards away. Since the buck's backline is barely below the top of the bush, you decide to hold for a high lung shot on the deer in an attempt to clear the bush. You draw, aim behind the buck's shoulder slightly high, and let go. Your arrow shoots high through the hole in the 3-yard limb, sails over the bush by a scant inch, and drops into the buck's chest cavity for a quick, clean kill. Such mental calculations are made by

trajectory-conscious deer hunters all the time, and many deer that hunters cannot clearly see are cleanly harvested. Knowledge of trajectory does pay off.

At longer shooting ranges, clearing mid-range obstacles with your arrow is usually easier to figure out. If a 40-yard deer is barely hidden behind a low 20-yard bush, the arrow will easily clear the bush by a couple of feet as it rises above line of sight and drops back down again. The quickest way to check obstacle clearance at normal shooting ranges is simply drawing on the partially obscured animal and checking your sight-pin placement as you aim. On the 40-yard deer just mentioned, your 20-yard sight pin would be well above the obstacle bush halfway between you and the deer—which tells you the arrow would pass well above the bush, too. Remember, your arrow will fly where your sight pin is for any given yardage. If your 20-yard sight is above a 20-yard bush as you aim, the arrow will be above the bush at 20 yards, too.

In some circumstances, a deer hunter cannot get an arrow into an animal even when he sees that animal clearly. If a 40-yard deer is in the wide open but a low-growing limb juts out 20 yards from you and overlaps with your 20-yard sight as you aim, you'll hit the limb and blow the shot. Similarly, if you peek over a big rock and see a buck 20 yards beyond, the arrow might collide with the top of the rock even if your 20-yard sight pin is above the edge of the rock and on the deer. Remember, an arrow hits below the 20-yard sight at ranges of 2 or 3 feet, so shooting over close-range barriers like a rock can be extremely tricky or completely impossible. If you realize you can't make a particular shot because of obstacle placement and the trajectory of your arrow, you must change position or wait for the target animal to move.

Shooting Up and Down

Unfortunately for bowhunters, a bow's trajectory and resulting point of impact is not the same when shots are taken at downward or upward angles. This is mainly because the earth's gravitational pull affects a projectile differently when it flies upward or downward instead of on a dead-level path.

A second factor that influences upward and downward shooting is a hunter's altered body position as he bends to aim uphill or downhill at a target. Only regular practice at non-level shooting will teach him how to alter his aim for those types of shots.

Despite the highly individual nature of impact changes caused by upward and downward shooting, there are certain strong rules to follow when faced with these types of shots. Arrows always hit higher than normal on downward shots because arrows do not arch as much as they speed downward toward a target. Such high point of impact is exaggerated at longer downhill shooting ranges, requiring you to hold significantly lower than normal to hit deer 30, 40, or 50 yards away

Shooting sharply down from a tree stand can be tricky business unless a hunter practices such shooting prior to season.

Shooting downward from a stepladder can help teach an archer how to compensate on shots at deer below him.

on a severe downhill slope. Serious bowhunters practice shooting downhill in the field a lot to develop a feel for such tricky shooting.

One of the most common reasons for misses from tree stands is the higher impact point of an arrow shot downward from a stand. A hunter who bends at the waist to take downward shots can more or less retain the upper-body form he uses for flat-ground shooting, and bending at the waist certainly minimizes the chance of hitting extra-high on deer that are below a stand or on a downhill slope. A tree-stand hunter using a safety belt can lean into the belt and achieve a near-perfect bend at the waist which helps him shoot accurately despite the downward angle. Nonetheless, hunters shooting downward must always aim at least a little low to compensate for the effects of gravity on an arrow.

There are several ways a bowhunter can practice downward shots. Many shoot from tall, steady stepladders or the flat top of a garage or patio roof. Others actually erect tree stands in the backyard to shoot at objects on the ground or attached to portable target butts. In the field, an archer can shoot from hillsides at soft, natural objects like rotten stumps and dirt banks below. More on such shooting later in this chapter.

Shooting upward produces less dramatic changes in point of impact because arrow flight is slowed instead of accelerated by the tug of gravity. Usually, bowhunters shoot slightly high on uphill shots under 25 or 30 yards, and shoot slightly low on longer uphill shots. However, much of where a hunter hits on uphill targets is determined by how he stands and bends his body on uneven sidehill slopes. As a result, such shooting takes the same diligent in-the-field practice as downhill shooting to learn how to properly compensate for changes in point of impact.

Unless a bowhunter bends at the waist to align his eye with the target on uphill and downhill shots, his draw length is apt to change and thus slow down or speed up arrow flight. As a general rule, a hunter who fails to bend at the waist properly draws longer than normal when shooting down and draws shorter than normal when shooting up. This will accentuate the tendency to hit high on downward shots and the tendency to hit low on upward shots. When confronted with an upward or downward shot, try to bend at the waist instead of the neck to align your eye with the target.

In-the-Field Shooting Practice

In-the-field shooting practice is one of the most beneficial ways of mastering advanced shooting. Such practice takes two basic forms—roving or stumpshooting, and bowhunting small game.

Roving, sometimes called stumpshooting, can be practiced in any reasonably remote section of the woods that allows a shooter to move about and take random shots at various natural targets like rotten stumps, dirt banks, leaves or grass clumps on embankments, etc. Such in-the-field practice completely familiarizes a hunter with the peculiarities of shooting in actual deer habitat, teaching him how to hit targets up and down hills, across ravines, around bushes and tree limbs, etc. At its best roving or stumpshooting should be practiced in the same clothing you plan to use when hunting, and with any other gear you might consider carrying along. Roving provides the ideal opportunity for a nimrod to learn to use his bowhunting range-finder, to get the feel of carrying binoculars while shooting a bow, etc.

For roving and stumpshooting, a bowhunter should use the very same shooting equipment he plans to use on deer—*except* for the arrowhead. The best arrow-heads for roving are steel blunts, rubber blunts, or Judo points. Broadheads are too fragile for multiple shooting at natural targets, and also tend to wedge tightly in stumps, roots, and any other form of wood. Regular field points are durable enough for stump shooting, and work in a pinch, but also tend to wedge tightly in wood. By contrast, blunts and Judo points characteristically stick in wood but allow easy removal by hand. These ideal roving points also minimize arrow skipping or glancing off the ground or other surfaces. By contrast, field points are notorious for skipping.

It is important when choosing field-shooting arrow-heads to match the exact arrowhead weight of your broadhead points. This ensures the good arrow flight of a properly tuned hunting bow (see Chapter 9). You may be able to match arrowhead weight with a standard steel blunt or screw-in Judo point, or you may have to assemble your own points at home. For example, I match my 165-grain broadheads and field points with steel blunts and Judo points by epoxying the glue-on, 125-grain versions of these heads to 35-grain, break-off Easton Aluminum screw-in broadhead adapters. With an average of 5 grains of epoxy, these heads weigh about 165 grains and shoot extremely well. Matching

the 165 grains with rubber blunts is not so easy. I buy rubber blunts, weigh them on a grain scale, and then hacksaw or grind down the noses of regular 125-grain steel screw-in blunts until the combined weight of a rubber blunt and steel blunt equals 165 grains. I screw the cut-down steel blunt into an arrow, slip the rubber blunt over it, and head for the hills!

Although roving, or stumpshooting, is good practice and great fun when pursued alone, it is even more enjoyable and more interesting when several shooters make it into a contest. To do this, shooters take turns picking random targets in the woods and shooting at them, a variation of the follow-the-leader shooting game mentioned earlier in this chapter. As the hunters move about the woods and take pot shots at various targets, they not only enjoy the challenge, not to mention good, clean fun with friends—they also devel-op a feel for shooting arrows at unknown distances in a deer-hunting environment.

The only kind of in-the-field shooting that even more closely resembles actual deer hunting is bowhunting various kinds of small game like ground squirrels, prairie dogs, or jackrabbits. Such pests abound in one form or another across the country, and provide excel-lent off-season shooting practice for anyone who cares to sneak around on foot. Such bowhunting adds an element of excitement and challenge that only comes from trying to shoot at an alert, living target. Nothing completely prepares a bowhunter for encounters with deer, but small-game hunting comes closer than any-thing else to doing so.

Organized Shooting Practice

Shooting alone and enjoying casual target practice with friends helps a hunter prepare for experiences with deer. However, various forms of organized shooting

Organized archery-club shoots provide fun, competition, and comradery with other serious shooters.

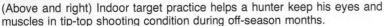

(Above and right) Indoor target practice helps a hunter keep his eyes and muscles in tip-top shooting condition during off-season months.

Bowhunter silhouette shooting is good practice for deer hunting and fine competition as well.

practice also sharpen archery skills and help a hunter learn to handle the tensions of a pressure shooting situation. Although competing for a prize and shooting at a deer are in many ways completely different from each other, there is an element of sameness in how a shooter controls his excitement and emotions to put the arrow where it belongs.

There are many forms of official shooting competition available through local archery clubs and larger state and national archery organizations. Official competition is not absolutely necessary to sharpen up your abilities, but it certainly helps if you happen to enjoy organized events and the special tensions and thrills of head-to-head competition. To find out about organized archery competition in your area, ask your archery or sporting goods dealer.

One of the most beneficial forms of organized shooting competition is the week-in, week-out indoor shooting that many archery clubs sponsor throughout off-season winter months. Indoor archery lanes are not available everywhere, but most larger towns offer such shooting to archers who wish to keep their muscles fit and their aiming-eyes sharp. Every indoor archery setup is slightly different, ranging from casual pay-and-shoot facilities to regular winter archery leagues similar to bowling leagues with individual and team prizes. Indoor winter shooting is one of my favorite off-season pastimes because it keeps me fit and lets me enjoy the company of other serious deer-hunting friends.

A wide range of outdoor bow-shooting events can also be enjoyed by serious hunters. Among popular events are official shoots put on by local and state chapters of the National Field Archers Association, National Archers Association, and other well-established organizations dedicated to quality archery. Some archery clubs affiliated with such parent organizations hold annual competition shoots with prizes for winners in various classes. A few such shoots are regular animal rounds with three-dimensional or flat paper or cardboard animal targets that make this type of shooting a relatively realistic hunting simulation. Again, your archery dealer or sporting goods dealer can give you details on such shooting events.

One relatively new form of shooting competition is extremely exciting for many serious archers. This is bowhunter silhouette shooting—a fast-paced competitive game which requires archers to shoot 12 arrows at 12 silhouette targets within a 2-minute time span. These silhouettes are the same standard chickens, pigs, turkeys, and rams used in rifle and pistol silhouette shooting, but are made of tough, self-healing ethafoam which will not damage a hunting broadhead. It is pure fun to shoot at these targets between ranges of about 25 and 75 yards; with any solidly hit silhouette jumping in the air and falling over in spectacular fashion. There are prizes and money to be won, and the practice of launching arrows at animal silhouettes out to longranges will sharpen a bowhunter's field-shooting skills.

If organized shooting competition turns you on, check out the possibilities offered by various state and local archery tournaments.

Animal Target Shooting

One problem many deer hunters have is learning to shoot at a specific vital spot on a deer-sized target. Hunters who have absolutely no trouble hitting a grapefruit-sized bull's-eye at 20 yards often miss a deer's vitals at the same distance because they shoot at the whole deer instead of picking a small, vital portion of the animal at which to aim. It is a natural tendency to shoot better on smaller targets than larger ones because a smaller target forces a shooter to concentrate his efforts. A deer hunter must overcome the tendency to regard the whole animal as a large target and, instead, pick a small aiming spot on the animal.

Shooting at a regular commercial animal target can help you master this skill. The target need not be a deer target; shooting at a variety of animal targets on a backyard range helps to keep things interesting. However, at least part of a deer hunter's shooting time should be devoted to aiming at likenesses of deer to fully develop his spot-picking skills. Such practice will carry over into real deer-shooting situations and result in solid hits instead of fringe hits or clean misses.

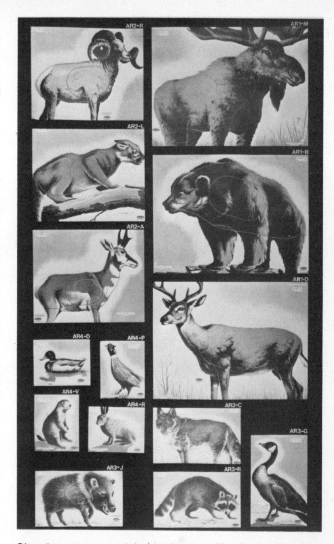

Shooting at commercial animal targets like these offered by Martin Archery will help a hunter learn to hit the exact vitals of deer.

Some bowhunters rely completely on commercial animal targets for this sort of shooting, and some prefer to make their own targets to save hard-earned money. Excellent deer-silhouette targets can be made from large sheets of paper or cardboard, and provide a large, uniformly colored shooting surface similar to a deer's side. Even a brown paper grocery bag flattened out and tacked to a target butt can train a shooter to put arrows in particular spots on a non-bull's-eye target.

A variety of bow-shooting practice is required to fully prepare an archer for going after deer. The hunter who varies his shooting intelligently can learn a world about arrow trajectory and advance his accuracy to expert levels. The ultimate result will be maximum enjoyment and plenty of deer in the bag!

*11/*Pre-Hunt Preparation

OVER THE course of several months of active shooting, a deer hunter will work most of the bugs out of his bow/arrow combination and his own shooting style. He will tune up his bow properly for ultimate accuracy, sight it in to his maximum accurate shooting ranges, and otherwise arrive at a satisfactory shooting-equipment setup. However, prior to actually heading after deer, a hunter should do several other things to his shooting setup to give him an optimum chance of putting meat in the freezer. Here is how to systematically proceed.

Silencing Bow Vibration

In most cases, how quiet your bow-and-arrow shoots has little to do with how accurate it is. A well-tuned bow is normally somewhat quieter than an untuned bow, but many well-tuned bows still make a considerable shooting racket. This noise might not hamper your performance on the target range, but it certainly will hamper your success ratio on deer.

A deer of any species has incredibly well-refined reflexes. This comes from being a prey species pursued by a variety of predators like wolves, coyotes, and mountain lions in addition to the ultimate predator, man. When a bow launches an arrow, a deer, even as large as an elk or moose, can duck, leap in the air, whirl sideways, or turn and run with such speed that the result is a missed shot or a very poor hit. I have had animals take arrows through the lungs from the *opposite* side I was originally aiming at. By the time the arrow had arrived on target, they had entirely swapped ends. I have also had other animals, including elk, sidestep accurately placed arrows after they heard the twang of a bowstring, the rattle of compound cables, or the hum of high-performance bow limbs. Side-stepping oncoming arrows happens as often as not at ranges under 40 yards, and until you've experienced a deer "jump string" in such fashion you simply cannot appreciate the very quick reflexes these animals are born with.

Nothing aside from a high-powered hunting rifle can completely eliminate the chance that a deer will jump string and escape before the arrow arrives. The faster a bow shoots, the less theoretical chance a deer has of running off unscathed. However, faster bows often create more noise than slower bows, at least partially canceling out this theoretical advantage. Similarly, the closer you are to a deer when you shoot, the less time the animal has to move out of the arrow's path. An average hunting arrow shot from an average round-wheel compound bow takes about 1 second to travel 70 yards and about ½-second to travel 35 yards. Being close helps ensure hits if a deer jumps string, but such a shooting-distance advantage tends to seem less important when you consider that deer at close range are more apt to hear bow noise and run than deer farther away.

The best thing a hunter can do is make his bow as quiet as humanly possible. There are several parts of a bow which normally need to be silenced—be sure you take care of this very important task prior to heading into the woods.

A vibrating bowstring is a major culprit. To prevent your bowstring from strumming like an off-key guitar string during a shot, you should silence it with some sort of commercial or homemade bowstring silencer. Most commercial string silencers are made of rubber and shaped to soak up vibration. My personal favorites, and the ones most commonly seen on bowstrings today, are so-called "catwhisker" silencers. They resemble and are made of the material as the skirts on bass plugs and are normally slipped between the strands of a bowstring to permanently hold them in place. Many other commercial bowstring silencers work well, too, and for those interested in cutting costs, several rubber bands tied to the bowstring will also work. Try out one

(Left) "Catwhisker" bowstring silencers dampen string vibration and resulting noise incredibly well.

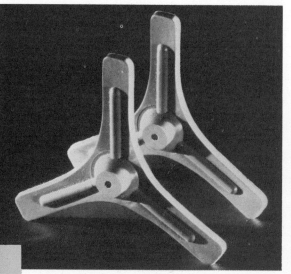

(Left and below) Solid rubber bowstring silencers of various sorts are excellent choices for hushing a noisy bowstring.

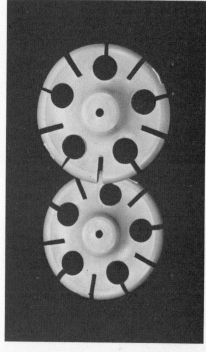

One commercial bowstring silencer looks like a wad of filaments from a living room carpet.

or more models and listen to see how much they cut down bowstring twang.

On recurve bows, bowstrings sometimes slap limbs noisily near the tips during shots. This problem is especially prevalent with very sharply recurving limb tips. To dampen string slap, a hunter can glue moleskin or felt to both upper and lower limbs in the area where string meets limb. Another solution is installing rubber "brush buttons" in the areas where string slap is occurring.

Cables on compound bows often rattle together noisily during a shot. Many bowhunters attach rubber bowstring silencers to cables to mute vibration, and this practice most definitely helps to quiet a compound bow. However, the chief source of noise is usually at the point where two cables cross near the center of the bow. One way to silence crossing bow cables is to cover both with moleskin, felt, or similar dampening agent at the point the cables cross. Several archery companies sell adhesive-backed cable silencers of this sort. Another way to stop noise in this cable region is by using one of the several soft-plastic cable connectors offered by

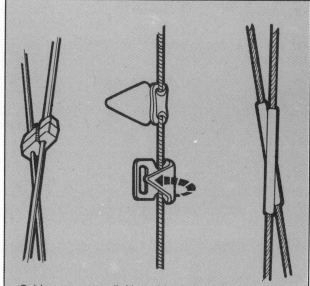

Cable separators (left) and loop-around rubber bowstring silencers (middle) both help quiet down a noisy compound bow. Commercial moleskin cable silencers (right) dampen vibration where compound cables cross and also reduce cable wear in such high-friction areas.

archery manufacturers. These actually tie cables together to keep them from rattling against one another —a principle that works quite well if the plastic cable joiners stay in place. Unfortunately, some designs fly off after a few dozen or a few hundred shots. A third way to quiet cables is by installing a cable guard to hold cables off to one side and hold crossing cables tightly together to greatly minimize rattle noise during a shot.

In the relatively new compound cam-bows and overdraw bows, stresses run so high that limb vibration itself can make significant noise when these bows are shot. Several shooters I know actually tie long strips of rubber band or catwhisker material around the limbs to dampen limb-vibration noise. The key to such limb silencing is leaving plenty of rubber ends hanging loose to absorb vibration during a shot.

Aside from the foregoing vibration-dampening techniques, one of the best things any hunter can do to hush bow noise is attaching a shooting stabilizer to the front of his bow. A bow stabilizer soaks up noisy vibration like a sponge.

Silencing Other Bow-Related Noises

Aside from string, cable, and limb vibration, bows often make a variety of other sounds which can alert and scare away deer.

One of the most common correctable bow noises is the squeak or creak of plastic-coated compound cables rubbing against the tracks in compound wheels. This noise is easily eliminated by dusting a little powdered graphite or ordinary baby powder in the offending areas. Note: It is never a good idea to oil cable-to-bow contact points because oil often makes plastic-coated cables squeak worse than before.

The axles that hold compound-bow wheels or cams sometimes become dry and squeak like rusty door hinges. To correct this problem, simply squirt a little penetrating lubricant like WD-40 in the axle/wheel area and let the lube creep into moving parts. This easy maintenance step generally wipes out axle squeak after a few draws of a bow.

Two other common sources of unnecessary bow noise are a loose bow-quiver connection or loose

(Above) Bow-limb socks are one means of covering the light-reflective limbs of a bow.

Compound-bow lubricant is just the ticket for silencing a squeaky compound-wheel axle.

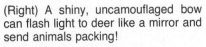

Leaf-print tape will effectively camouflage a hunting bow, but takes plenty of time to apply.

(Right) A shiny, uncamouflaged bow can flash light to deer like a mirror and send animals packing!

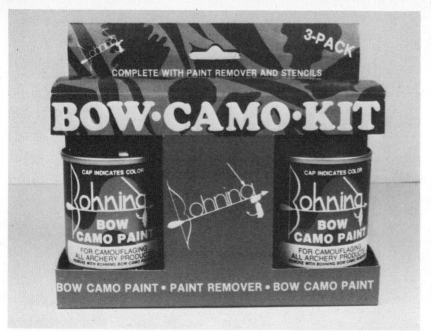

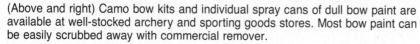

(Above and right) Camo bow kits and individual spray cans of dull bow paint are available at well-stocked archery and sporting goods stores. Most bow paint can be easily scrubbed away with commercial remover.

bowsight pin. The best way to locate these noise problem areas is by thudding the grip area of your bow with a closed fist and listening for rattle points. To quiet down a quiver, tighten all connection points, use moleskin or felt between connection point and bow or, hold contact points snugly in place with plastic tape. If your bowsight pins tend to vibrate loose—a common problem—they should be carefully tightened with pliers and/or glued in place before a hunt with regular arrow-fletching cement. This cement is easily removed with solvent, yet holds bowsight adjustments firmly in place on a hunting trip. Anything loose on a bow will rattle obnoxiously. Before hunting, be sure all nuts, bolts, and other parts of a bow are snug.

No bow is dead quiet. As a general rule, the slower-shooting models and bows shooting fairly heavy arrows are the quietest of the lot. However, the shooting-noise level of any hunting bow can be effectively reduced if a hunter takes the time to locate and correct problem areas that buzz, clank, or rattle.

Camouflaging the Bow

The eyes of deer are incredibly keen. As a result, a hunting bow, bow quiver, and any related equipment must be camouflaged to mute shiny surfaces and hide light-colored areas that might attract attention. A few hunting bows come completely camouflaged from the factory, but most are left bright as a new silver dollar to attract a customer's eye across the counter.

There are several decent ways to camouflage a deer-hunting bow. The quickest and easiest, but not necessarily the best, is simply encasing bow limbs in commercial leaf-print bow-limb socks made of soft-surfaced cotton or similar fabric. This cuts the bulk of bow shine, and takes about 2 minutes to accomplish. However, a couple of things about commercial limb socks bother me. For one thing, the shiny handle riser of a bow is left in the wide open for deer to see. For another, limb socks are bulky, prone to snag on foliage, and are guaranteed to soak up rainwater and give you a shower when you finally do get a shot. For these reasons, I prefer to camouflage my bows in more time-consuming ways.

The *most* time-consuming bow-camo method I know is covering a bow, quiver, and other shiny or light-colored shooting equipment with adhesive-backed camouflage tape. This job is especially tedious on compound bows because there are so many nooks and crannies to cover. However, a bow camouflaged with leaf-print camo tape is quite effective to hunt with because of the two-tone pattern and non-glare nature of the tape. Unless you cannot abide the thought of spraying paint on your bow, this particular process is by far the best method of giving shooting gear a dull, two-tone hunting finish.

Several companies offer excellent bow-camo paint that can be peeled away or removed with a mild solvent and some elbow grease. I'm sure that someone, somewhere has removed camouflage paint from a bow to restore shiny surfaces, but I've never once seen this happen. After a hunter builds up his courage to dull down a bow with paint, he generally leaves it that way because it works so well.

To my taste, a neatly spray-painted bow is every bit

127

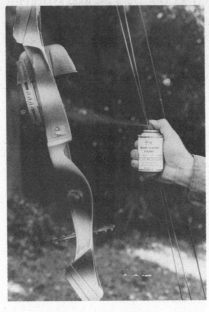
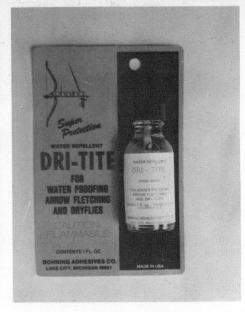

To spray-paint a bow, first scrub it down with rubbing alcohol to remove oil and grime. Next, apply a light base coat, then add dark contrasting stripes.

Bohning sells excellent water-proofer for feather fletching on arrows.

as attractive as the shiny over-the-counter variety. Spraying a bow with good-grade commercial camouflage paint does not take nearly the time that taping does, and paint covers the complete bow evenly right down to compound wheels and cables.

There are two basic ways to effectively camouflage a bow, quiver, and other gear with bow paint. Both require the hunter to first rub down all surfaces with a paper towel dipped in rubbing alcohol to remove any oil, grease, or grime which might prevent paint from adhering well. The first method requires you to simply clean your bow, let the alcohol evaporate, and then spray the entire unit with a light brown or a green base coat of camo paint. Once this coat dries, spray a few horizontal bands of contrasting black or dark brown across the limbs and handle riser. The result is a pleasant two-tone paint job that blends quite well with most deer-hunting backgrounds.

A more time-consuming method is to spray on a dark green, brown, or black base coat first, and after it thoroughly dries, cut leafy shapes out of wide masking tape and lightly attach them to the surfaces of bow limbs and handle riser in a pleasing pattern. Next, spray the entire bow with a lighter contrasting shade of brown or green. Let the second coat dry, then peel off the masking-tape leaves. The result is a pattern of dark leaves against a light-colored background. This particular camo job won't hide you from deer any better than the first, but it is more fun to create and looks more pleasing to the eye.

Other Shooting-Gear Preparation

A meticulous bowhunter covers several other equipment get-ready bases before the opening day of deer

season rolls around. Some of these are little odds and ends that take only a minute to do, and others require a little more time and forethought.

If you plan to hunt with feather fletching and expect to encounter rain or snow, you should waterproof this fletching with commercial fletching waterproofer or silicone-base dry-fly floatant. In a pinch, a thorough coating of ordinary hair spray will do.

Another arrow-related chore a deer hunter should tackle before hunting season is checking all his arrows for straightness and having the dealer straighten any that are not. Arrows sometimes bend with regular rough-and-tumble target practice, so don't take for granted that all your "ammo" is in tip-top condition.

There are several ways to check for shaft straightness, from using a commercial arrow straightening tool, to rolling shafts across a flat tabletop to detect slight wobble, to spinning shafts across a thumbnail to feel any "bump" as the shaft spins. Ask your dealer to show you the thumbnail spinning method—it is easy to master and extremely reliable once you develop the knack.

Prior to hunting, an archer should also make sure his deer broadheads are in tip-top condition. This includes inspecting every edge for keeness and resharpening or replacing any blade that doesn't pass the sharpness tests covered in Chapter 4. Broadheads can become dull just sitting around if they aren't coated with oil because microscopic corrosion can destroy cutting edges within hours if the air is slightly damp.

You should also try to anticipate what spare equipment you might need during deer season and purchase necessary spares. For example, I always carry an extra flipper rest and bowsight pin with me when I hunt in case my original flipper snags and breaks off or I fall on my bowsight and bend or snap a pin. Such simple spare-part protection can save the day if you happen to be deep in the woods when minor equipment trouble develops.

Just before deer-hunting season opens up, a bowhunter should double-check his bow's tune on the target range by shooting broadheads and field points at a bull's-eye target. If both varieties of heads hit the same place, equipment is still in tune and ready to hunt with. If not, a shooter should retune his hunting bow using the steps in Chapter 9. Never assume that broadheads will hit where target points do just prior to hunting season—bows sometimes drift out of tune and require readjustment. Remember, too, that if you use a bow quiver, you should always practice shooting and check your bow's tune with a quiver full of arrows attached. A bow with a quiver never shoots the same as one without, and a bow with an empty quiver never shoots the same as one with a full quiver.

Double-Check and Record Adjustments

It can be a bonafide disaster if you travel many miles to a deer-hunting hotspot, pull out your bow, and discover that the bowsights are loose, the cushion plunger has rattled out, or the bowstring has frayed nearly in two. Such things happen with fair frequency as vehicles bounce over rough back roads and bows are repeatedly transferred from one location to another. There are several ways to keep such occurrences from ruining in-the-field accuracy and rattling your confidence in your shooting gear.

Before you go afield, simply measure and mark certain key adjustments on your bow and write them down. Using an accurate ruler, measure how far out your bowsight pins protrude from the body of the sight and write this measurement down on a piece of paper. With a strip of masking tape, mark sight pin placement on the bracket with an ink pen or lead pencil. If one or more pins are knocked loose in spite of glue-down precautions, you can put them exactly back in place by referring to your penned windage and elevation marks. In similar fashion, measure how far out your arrow-rest plate protrudes from the bow. Write this measurement down, too, just in case the arrow plate rattles loose.

A third measurement of importance is the shortest distance from the valley of the bow grip to the bowstring. This measurement, taken at right angles to the bowstring, is called the brace height measurement. If a bowstring breaks or frays badly enough to need replacing, you'll have to twist or untwist the replacement string to match this brace height to avoid changes in the

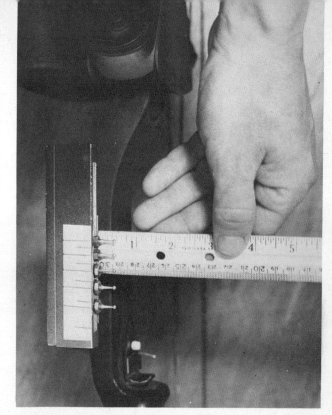

A careful bowhunter should measure and record sight-pin positions and other settings on his bow which might rattle or bump out of kilter on a hunt.

way your bow shoots. Since a string continues to stretch quite a bit for several weeks after it is installed—thus lowering a bow's brace height—you'll have to double-check the brace-height measurement several times after replacing a string. To raise brace height, twist the string tighter to shorten it. To lower brace height, untwist the string to lengthen it, or buy a slightly longer bowstring.

Aside from writing down the aforementioned measurements, you should carefully measure your nocking-point location with a bow square and record this in case a nocking point slips on the string or you need to replace a string.

By double-checking and recording these important bow adjustments, you can be assured of accurate shooting even if something rattles loose or moves unexpectedly on your hunting bow.

The careful, meticulous deer hunter leaves no stone unturned in his quest for the ultimate bow-shooting setup. The end result of such time-consuming care is a bow/arrow combination that is quiet, camouflaged, and accurate. Such a shooting setup will be a joy to use and a consistently successful performer on both targets and deer. What more could anyone ask for?

12/Tree Stands and Blinds

ONE OF THE most effective ways of bowhunting deer is ambushing them from a well-placed stand. Because deer have excellent eyesight and also display a distinct tendency not to look upward for danger, the most popular and most successful stands are usually elevated well above ground level. An added advantage of elevated stands is the fact that they generally carry away deer-spooking human odor on upper-air breezes. In states where tree-stand hunting is illegal, bowhunters enjoy good deer-hunting success with ground blinds which block out, at ground level, the prying eyes of deer. Good archery deer hunters thoroughly investigate available elevated stands and ground blinds plus optional stand accessories to give them maximum flexibility in getting close to deer.

Rigid Climbing Tree Stands

One of the most popular and most traditional bowhunting tree stands is the rigid climbing stand. Basically, it consists of a sturdy platform which attaches to a straight-trunked, relatively limbless tree with a metal gripping frame. Many come complete with some sort of hand-climbing tool that grips a tree above the stand, eliminating the need for a hunter to hug a tree as he climbs with the stand.

To get the rigid tree stand aloft, the bowhunter straps the stand platform to his feet or legs and uses his arms or hand-climbing tool to inchworm up a tree. He lifts his feet, drawing the platform up the tree, settles his weight back down on the platform section, attains a higher grip on the tree with arms or the climbing tool, pulls the stand up with his feet once more, and continues until he reaches the height he wants. Practice at using such a stand allows a hunter to rapidly ascend and descend a limbless tree trunk to practical deer-hunting heights of 12 to 30 feet.

A wide variety of rigid climbing tree stands are available to bowhunters through archery and sporting goods stores and discount houses. Most are sturdy, dependable designs, ranging from tiny platforms suitable for barely allowing support for the feet to roomy platforms several feet square. Naturally, the larger-platform models weigh more and require more muscle-power to pack them in and set them up. However, once aloft the larger models are more comfortable for the hours spent waiting and watching for deer.

The best rigid climbing tree stands on the market feature stout aluminum frames, tree-gripping blades that will not slip, and sturdy platforms made of all-weather plywood. Many have integral seats for comfort, and most come with hand-climbing tools that keep a hunter's chest and arms away from rough, abrasive bark as he climbs. One important feature to look for in such stands is a sturdy bolt-together design that will not lead to bolt-assembly breakage and a dangerous fall to the ground.

One unique product Baker Tree Stand has recently added to their line is the tree-stand seat climber. It is used in the same manner as a regular tree-stand hand-climbing tool, but lets a hunter sit down comfortably as he inches up a tree. This particular design coupled with a top-quality rigid stand platform is the climbing Cadillac of bowhunting tree stands, requiring virtually no physical exertion to inch a hunter up a 20- or 30-foot tree trunk.

Ask your archery or sporting goods dealer about available climbing tree stands. They might be ideal for you if your hunting is done in areas where tall, straight trees with very few low-growing limbs are standard.

Conventional Tree Slings

Although not as comfortable as a tree stand, the so-called tree sling is among the most versatile of all elevated deer stands. It requires a hunter to climb to a desired stand height and then attach the sling to the tree. Once accomplished, the hunter sits in the sling,

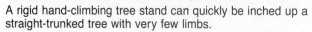

A rigid hand-climbing tree stand can quickly be inched up a straight-trunked tree with very few limbs.

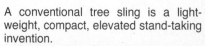

(Above and left) Many hand-climbing tree stands can be carried in and out of the woods on commercial backpack straps. The Baker seat climber allows easy tree-climbing with little or no muscle strain.

A conventional tree sling is a light-weight, compact, elevated stand-taking invention.

(Left) Well-known bowhunter Ted Poper displays his unique "Ultimate" climbing tree sling here. It weighs only 6 pounds and is easily packed across an archer's back with its own nylon seat assembly. (Middle) The rope and hardware for Poper's climbing tree sling is first unpacked from its own seat assembly in preparation for climbing. (Right) The stout nylon rope is tossed over a sturdy limb at a desired climbing height, then passed back through a climbing ratchet box.

which resembles a hammock for the derriere. The hunter can then pivot to see and shoot in several directions.

A tree sling's flexible strap construction, compact size, and light weight make it ideal for packing into remote mule deer and elk hunting areas. It can only be used spontaneously in trees that have limbs close to the ground although with some forethought a bowhunter can carry a few screw-in tree-stand steps with him to help him reach suitable tree-hunting heights. More about tree-stand steps later in this chapter.

Climbing Tree Slings

One of the most exciting tree-stand innovations to hit the market in recent times is the climbing tree sling. This unique product combines self-climbing versatility with excellent sitting comfort and unequaled shooting flexibility. At present, the climbing tree sling design is sold only by Hunter's Products, Inc. of Reading, Pennsylvania. It is available through many archery and sporting goods stores and should be seriously considered by any bowhunter who wants ultimate tactical leverage on forest-dwelling deer.

As shown in the accompanying photo sequence, the entire tree-sling assembly is conveniently stored in its own padded seat and is easily carried across a walking

hunter's back. It weighs next to nothing, yet unfurls into one of the niftiest tree-stand designs going. A hunter simply tosses the loose end of the climbing rope over an overhead limb, runs the rope through the climbing ratchet box, sits down on the padded seat with the nylon safety harness around the legs and midsection, and then ties his shooting gear to the loose end of rope. Using an easy pull-and-climb motion, the hunter hoists himself to the desired stand height, pulls up his bow-shooting gear after him, and waits for deer to move within shooting range. Climbing down is equally safe and easy, requiring the hunter to simply depress a ratchet release that smoothly lowers him to the ground. Although only recently on the market, this sling is already being considered by the U.S. military because it is so well-designed and slick to use in forest reconnaissance situations.

The sling offers several unique advantages to stand-hunting deer enthusiasts: First, it can be carried out of the way and used spontaneously whenever an elevated stand seems to be a good idea. Second, it goes up a tree in less than a minute with little or no noise—something which cannot be said about other stand designs. Third, it allows effective tree-stand hunting for deer without the need to leave the stand out overnight where it might be stolen by unscrupulous opportunists. Fourth, it

(Left) The loose end of the rope is used as a hoist rope to tie up his bow and any other gear needed aloft. (Right) Using an easy pulling motion, Ted hoists himself up the tree.

(Below left) Once at a desired deer-hunting height, Poper pulls up his bow on the same rope he used to climb the tree. (Below middle) The "Ultimate" climbing tree sling allows bow-shooting in any direction and safely holds a hunter in place with a leg-and-waist nylon harness system. You cannot fall out! (Below right) To let yourself down again, simply depress the ratchet lever for a smooth, easy ride to the ground.

133

allows a hunter to quickly jockey around the stand location to meet the ever-changing habit patterns of deer. In my mind, the climbing tree sling by Hunter's Products, Inc. is a product every serious bowhunter should own. The model shown here is called the "Ultimate," and can be purchased direct from Hunter's Products, Inc., P. O. Box 2727, Reading, PA 19609. You can write these people for a free brochure on their products.

Semi-Permanent Commercial Tree Stands

In addition to tree stands that attach easily and/or help a hunter climb, there are many models on the market which must be physically hoisted up a tree after a hunter climbs aloft and then lashed, chained, or bolted in place to provide a semi-permanent platform arrangement. Although such stands are a bit of a nuisance to put up initially, they usually provide excellent stand-hunting comfort once installed.

The variety of semi-permanent commercial tree stands is much too wide to cover all models here. Most incorporate comfortable seats or stools for sitting and ample room to stand up and stretch the legs or shoot a bow. Check out the many semi-permanent tree-stand models at the archery or sporting goods store for an idea of what is currently available.

This semi-permanent tree stand features a comfortable bucket seat.

A homemade V-notch platform usually jams solidly between two or three stout limbs or tree trunks.

Putting up a large semi-permanent tree stand often takes two or three hunters, but the roomy results are worth it.

Homemade Tree Stands

A great many bowhunters erect homemade tree stands in their favorite deer-hunting areas. Such stands take as many forms as the imaginations of the hunters designing and putting them up.

Where it is legal and sensible, bowhunters often build roomy permanent tree-stand platforms overlooking time-tested deer trails or heavy-use areas. The platforms can be as large as trees and needs allow, and some I have seen are downright huge. One common design consists of two large trees connected by a frame of 2 × 4s or 2 × 6s with a plywood or slat platform on top. Another common configuration is a triangular platform built between three stout limbs of a single tree or three separate trees a suitable distance apart. Most of these have homemade nailed-on steps for easy climbing and simple safety rails at waist height.

Before erecting any homemade, nail-and-lumber tree stand, check local laws about doing so on public or private land. Some states prohibit any stand-building that damages trees with nails, and others prohibit stand erection altogether.

In addition to the hammer-and-nail type of permanent tree stand, some serious deer hunters build excellent portable tree stands which rope or chain to a tree. One very common design consists of a square or rectangular plywood board with a deep V-notch on the

(Above and left) A tower blind is quite effective on deer, but only when used against a brushy backdrop. As the author illustrates here, such a tower in open country silhouettes an archer for every nearby deer to see.

back that butts solidly against a tree. This stand is either wedged between two or three main limbs thrusting up from a single tree trunk or chained to a single tree trunk and held level with guy ropes or chains that extend from outer corners upward to overhead limbs. Such a V-notch board is relatively light in weight and very stable if put up in a location with stout limbs to hold it safely in place.

A resourceful bowhunter can tailor-make tree stands to suit particular locations in his favorite hunting territory. When trying for bottomland whitetail deer that characteristically travel the same basic routes from week to week and month to month, a well-placed permanent tree stand of the homemade variety can produce shots at deer year after year after year.

Commercial and Homemade Tower Stands

A tower stand differs from a tree stand because it at least partially supports itself instead of requiring a sturdy tree.

Several commercial tower stands are sold by outdoor companies. Most sit up like tripods on three wooden or metal legs with some sort of seat arrangement on top and are generally used in brushy areas where trees are sparse or completely nonexistent. A tower stand theoretically lets a hunter see down into brush where deer could hide from ground-level eyes. It also elevates a hunter somewhat above a deer's direct line of vision and tends to keep a hunter's scent above the level of sensitive noses.

I've had mixed results when using elevated towers for bowhunting deer. Unless such towers are tall enough to be *well* above a deer's field of vision, a hunter tends to stand out like a warning flare. This is especially true if the stand and hunter are both silhouetted against the sky. My best luck with tower stands has come when I've used them against outline-breaking walls of high brush or spindly trees. This approach provides the advantages of an elevated stand without letting deer clearly see what's going on.

One useful elevated commercial tower stand is the platform ladder. Basically a ladder with extension sections which lean against a tree, this stand provides a sturdy plywood platform the hunter can stand on or use in conjunction with a folding seat. Unless trees in a hunting area are too flimsy to directly support a regular tree stand but strong enough to hold up a leaning ladder stand, the only clear-cut advantage of a platform ladder is the sheer ease of climbing up such a design. This can be of major benefit to obese or physically handicapped archers who have the desire to hunt but lack the physical stamina or agility to use a hand-climbing tree stand, tree sling, or another commercial design.

There are several interesting home-grown solutions to the need for a tower blind in areas without suitable tree-stand trees. Bowhunters waiting for deer around livestock ponds in open areas with grass or low brush often erect plywood platforms on windmill frames high above the ground. One bowhunting friend of mine carries an extension stepladder in his pickup at all times for the sole purpose of putting it up among the stunted oaks in his favorite archery deer area. He sits on the top of this ladder with feet on a lower rung, and nails at least one deer per year from this unique tower stand.

Natural Elevated Stands

Because an elevated deer stand has undeniable advantages over a stand taken on the ground, a bowhunter should assume some kind of elevated stand whenever possible to improve his chances of fooling deer. A wide variety of options exist for taking natural stands aloft if a bowhunter uses his noggin. In alfalfa fields, harvested wheat fields, and other deer feeding hotspots, a stand taken atop a convenient haystack or stack of hay bales can be one of the best places to ambush unalerted deer. If a stack is composed of regular bales, a few of these can be lifted out of the top to form a sunken pit which is then rimmed by the pulled out bales. If loosely spread around the rim of the pit, narrow viewing slits are formed between the bales. Whitetail deer, mule deer, elk, and other deer that sometimes frequent agricultural fields are surprisingly docile around haystacks and sometimes make a beeline for the uncut growth near the bases. Haystack blinds need not be restricted to stacks with regular building-block-shaped bales. A loose-hay stack can be rearranged on top to form an excellent hiding pit for a bowhunter. Use your imagination.

In many situations, easily climbed trees can make dandy natural elevated stands for deer. A favorite

A blind in the top of a haystack often makes a comfortable, first-rate elevated stand for deer.

(Above and right) Screw-in tree-stand steps allow a bow-hunter to walk right up a limbless tree trunk to a desired stand height.

configuration of mine is a tree with a three-pronged crotch 15 or 20 feet overhead. Such a crotch provides safe standing and shooting if sturdy climbing limbs are present from the ground all the way up. I hunt whitetail deer regularly from two different tall, sturdy cotton-wood trees with elevated crotches, and have taken several nice bucks from those stands over the years.

One of the most bizarre elevated stands I've ever heard of was used successfully by a bowhunting friend of mine to nail a nice Montana mule deer buck. After watching the 3x4* deer for several days, my friend realized the animal was bedding during the warm, early-fall days in an abandoned old sheep shed near the hayfield where it was feeding each morning and evening. After fruitlessly trying to ambush the alert buck from the ground as it fed in early evening, my pal had a brainstorm. The next morning he entered the woods at daylight, sneaked upwind to the back of the sheep shed and climbed up on the roof. Less than an hour later, he shot the deer at 10 yards as it came tripping through the woods to the big door of its shady midday resting place.

Although shooting a deer off a sheep shed roof may not be the most aesthetic way to arrow your winter's venison, this stunt did require some imaginative thinking. Every bowhunter should use whatever stand possibilities present themselves to get well above deer in order to avoid their sharp eyes and sensitive nostrils.

Practical Accessories for Elevated Stands

A bowhunter who plans to spend plenty of time in deer stands should invest in a few accessories that ensure safety, comfort, and successful shooting.

---

*Indicating a buck with uneven antler points. In this case a main beam plus two points on one side and a main beam plus three points on the other.

Of foremost importance is a hoist rope to pull up and let down shooting equipment. It is unsafe to attempt to hold a bow and other gear in one hand while climbing, and much easier to simply tie a stout rope to this gear and haul it up after you reach the desired height. Any kind of rope will do provided it is long enough to let you climb with slack. I use a 35-foot length of ¼-inch nylon rope for this chore, and it works just fine. The only stand design that doesn't require a hoist rope is the climbing tree sling.

In most tree-stand hunting situations, it is highly advisable to use tree-stand steps or a rope ladder to make ascent and descent easy and safe. This is even true with rigid climbing tree stands, which can be a royal pain to inch up and down a tree each hunting day.

Commercial tree-stand steps take a variety of forms, from screw-in models to chain-on or rope-on varieties. Where it is legal, my favorite is a simple but sturdy screw-in design with a coarse thread that bites and holds no matter what. A pocketful of such steps allows a bowhunter to climb any tree on the spot, screwing in one step, climbing up on it, screwing in another higher up, stepping up on it, and so on. This lets a bowhunter climb to a variety of natural perches and places where he wishes to erect permanent or semi-permanent tree stands. Screw-in tree-stand steps are not legal to use in all states, so check state laws before rushing out and buying them for use in the deer woods.

In areas where screw-in steps are not legal, chain-on or rope-on steps work fine. Though generally more time-consuming to attach, they wrap securely around a tree to provide a solid foothold and can be attached higher and higher as a hunter climbs, the same way screw-in steps are used.

A safety belt is another smart investment. Top-notch tree-stand companies like Baker include safety belts

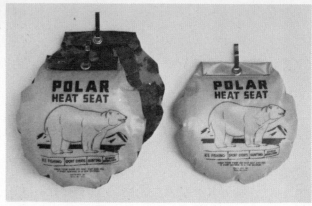

Warm padded seats are nice to have on stand in cold weather. These by Kolpin actually heat up when a bowhunter sits down!
(Left) An integral or separate tree-stand seat ensures bowhunting comfort and safety. This model has a handy storage pouch underneath.

(Left and opposite page) This tree-stand rack for bow and quiver is one of many such stand accessories sold at archery stores. ▶

with all their stands, but the do-it-yourselfer must purchase his own for safe hunting aloft. A safety belt should be made of strong nylon-web construction for comfort, and should fasten to the waist with a non-slip buckle to prevent tight cinching around a hunter's middle if he falls. One of the most common causes of bowhunter injury is careless movement about an elevated stand, resulting in slips and falls. This is particularly apt to happen when a hunter becomes highly excited in the presence of game.

As mentioned before, many commercial tree stands incorporate comfortable seats in their construction. However, some factory units do not, and all homemade tree stands also need seat additions for maximum waiting comfort. Standing up on a platform for hours on end is extremely tiring—often to the point that muscles become dangerously wobbly or too fatigued to produce accurate shots with a bow. For this reason, an inexpensive folding stool is a practical addition to any stand-platform setup.

For stand-hunting deer in really cold weather, a bowhunter is well advised to purchase a commercial insulated seat pad which keeps the posterior warm as a shooter patiently waits. Several companies offer such rear-warming seat pads.

Another comfort-ensuring item for serious treestand hunting is a rack for hanging up a bow, arrow quiver, hunting coat, and other miscellaneous items you might take aloft. This leaves the hands free and eliminates the need to grip a bow for hours on end. Several archery companies sell screw-in bow racks of various configurations. If noise is not a problem, such as when you build a permanent tree stand from lumber several months before bow season, a few judiciously driven nails or spikes make excellent hangers for bows and other loose tree-stand equipment.

One other elevated-stand accessory most bowhunters forget to use is a portable urinal in case nature calls in the middle of productive stand-hunting hours. Answering this call over the edge of a stand marks the stand area with potent ground-level human odor, and climbing out of the elevated stand and walking some distance away will also leave a scent trail guaranteed to scare off passing deer. This is not to mention the noise and hassle associated with interrupting prime hunting hours to go potty a long distance from a stand.

The best urinal I have found for tree-stand use is a plastic jug or bucket with a screw-on or press-fit lid. It weighs very little when empty and is easily pulled up a tree with other deer-hunting equipment.

(Right) A simple screw-in bow hanger makes a handy addition to any tree-stand deer-hunting setup.

A handy, flexible thumb-ring saw fits in a shirt pocket and lets a tree-stander remove small limbs that block easy viewing or shooting of a bow.

Ground Blinds

Although using an elevated stand is best for bow-hunting deer in most situations, this is not feasible in all cases. As long as the prevailing breeze and existing foliage conceal a hunter's presence, a stand on the ground can result in close-range, relatively easy shots.

I am not convinced that a regular commercial ground blind has much place in bowhunting deer. Archers can buy artificial blinds made of camouflage fabric stretched across stakes that press or hammer in the ground, but as far as I'm concerned a well-camouflaged bowhunter is a walking ground blind already, needing no artificial enclosure to hide him from deer. Carrying a blind into the woods and setting it up is a time-consuming chore, and the same ambush job can be better accomplished if a camouflaged hunter simply backs up against outline-breaking cover and patiently waits without moving around.

There are several built-in drawbacks associated with commercial ground blinds. For one, most deer are too smart and too skittish to simply ignore a large blind that suddenly appears in their favorite stomping ground. Forty-nine times out of 50, they'll give such a newly erected structure very wide berth. Another problem is the fact that archers inside such blinds must raise up to shoot over a blind edge, creating excess movement that often spooks a deer before an arrow can be released. On top of these arguments, the blind-sitting archer must peek periodically over the rim of the blind to gawk around—another source of unnecessary movement.

Despite these problems with a commercial ground blind, I do occasionally use *natural* blinds to good advantage in the deer woods. Such blinds vary considerably in configuration, but most allow easy, no-movement viewing out and generally allow shots to be taken with a minimum of motion. Among others, sparse bushes and tangles of roots or limbs make good outline-breaking barriers to sit behind if gaps exist to look and shoot through.

Elevated stands have a very important place in many deer-hunting situations, keeping an archer's scent above game and hiding him effectively from probing animal eyes. Natural ground blinds can also hide a hunter if they are intelligently chosen with looking and shooting ease foremost in mind. Every archery hunter should familiarize himself with available stand-hunting gear and choose wisely to make the most of efforts to waylay wary deer.

13/Scents and Lures

THE USE OF odor-masking scents and deer lures in bowhunting is a commonly debated subject among in-the-know deer hunters. As sure as one archer begins expounding the virtues of his favorite scent at a party, archery-club meeting, or gathering around a backwoods campfire, another hunter is almost sure to poo-poo the idea, claiming in no uncertain terms that *his* scent is best for deer instead. Some things like arrow accuracy or the ease with which a particular stand goes up a tree can be demonstrated clearly with little room for argument, but the effectiveness of various scents is a very subjective topic that every archer seems to have an opinion about. Whether or not a given fellow actually knows what he's talking about seems completely beside the point.

There are two basic kinds of scents commonly used by archery deer hunters. These are odor-masking scents—meant primarily to cover human odor—and deer lures, which are designed to attract deer like flies to honey. We'll discuss odor-masking scents first because these enjoy the most widespread usage.

Do Odor-Masking Scents Really Work?

It certainly is tough to objectively test and evaluate odor-masking scents. There are too many variables in the woods that cloud the issue of how well such concoctions work. A buck that runs away may indeed have smelled your telltale human odor, but on the other hand it may have seen you, heard you, or merely taken a notion to frisk away through the woods. It takes literally years of deliberately testing scents and using them incidentally on outings to develop a clear picture of what influence they really have on game.

The basic principle behind using scent is a sound one. A deer has a nose that positively identifies uncut human odor each and every time. The odds of a deer mistaking this smell or becoming confused by it are about as great as you or me confusing the smell of a juicy hamburger with that of gasoline. A deer may see something suspicious it can't quite identify, or hear a noise that concerns it but doesn't frighten it away; however, it will not mistake human odor for anything else and will run like gangbusters from that smell. For this reason, using some sort of scent to at least partially cover or change basic human odor makes sense.

The question is, is it really possible to cover human odor? In my extensive experience with deer, I'd have to answer this one with a qualified "yes." I say "qualified" because I'm not certain you can ever entirely hide your odor from a close-range deer that has normal olfactory nerves and a solid down-wind snootful of the air that's whistling around your ears. The smell the animal gets may be somewhat mixed up, but it will still likely ring a danger bell in the critter's head. I *am* convinced that odor-masking scents mix up or change human odor enough to confuse a deer instead of launching the animal like a rocket right out of the country. At best, at a distance, deer scents might actually hide human odor and allow a closer approach if the wind is reasonably cooperative.

To keep human odor away from a deer's keen nose, the best bowhunting bet is moving upwind whenever possible. However, unstable breezes sometimes make this ideal situation a sad, frustrating joke to contemplate. To cover the possibility of uncooperative breezes, I strongly urge the use of odor-masking scents as a backup strategy that just might yield a shot.

Covering Your Foot Trail

Though the primary use of scents is to mask human odor slipping along on breezes above the ground, they also have another vitally important function in the deer woods. A bowhunter who walks to a stand leaves behind a trail of odor which can be especially strong if there is moisture on the ground and/or if a hunter must wade through lots of grass and brush to reach his stand

The author took this fat mule deer buck after a long stalk in changing mountain breezes. He feels that using red fox urine helped hide his human odor from the animal.

(Right) Food scents like apple, sweet corn, and sunflower seldom lure deer in, but they do help cover human odor.

location. Odor-masking scent can have a decidedly dramatic impact on a deer's ability to smell a foot trail if a hunter squirts or rubs scent on his boot soles and pant legs prior to heading for his stand. I have seen whitetail reach a trail I walked along 2 hours before, stop as if electrocuted by the lingering smell, and nearly turn wrong-side out in a mad scramble to get away. I have seen deer entirely ignore a foot trail only 20 minutes old under similar moisture, foliage, and wind conditions when I bothered to mask my feet and legs with the smell of a judiciously chosen odor-masking scent. Try it—it works!

Which Commercial Scents Work Best?

There is a very wide variety of commercial odor-masking scents available through archery and sporting goods stores. Among the more common used by bow-hunters are wild grape, apple, sweet corn, acorn, sunflower, pine, cedar, skunk musk, deer musk, and earth scent. In addition, some archers use conventional trapping scents like fox urine with reported good results. As long as a scent is strong enough to overpower human odor, and as long as it is a natural odor in a particular bowhunting environment, it will probably help a hunter out.

Some scents I have tried do not seem to have an odor potent enough to do an effective masking job. Not being a deer, I can never know for sure what a deer smells on vagrant breezes, but experimentation with

them has supported my basic scent-using theories completely. These theories include the notion that if I can strongly smell an odor-masking scent, it should mask my own relatively mild body odor fairly well. The times I have deliberately circled upwind of deer during the off season—and I have done this quite a bit—the strong-smelling scents have seemed to confuse or completely fool deer while the weaker ones have triggered a more pronounced panic reaction.

No matter what sort of odor-masking scent you ultimately end up using, this scent should be manufactured by a well-known, highly experienced maker like Buck Stop Lure Co. to ensure potency and a realistic odor. Pine scent that smells like blueberries or deer musk that smells like vanilla extract will not help you

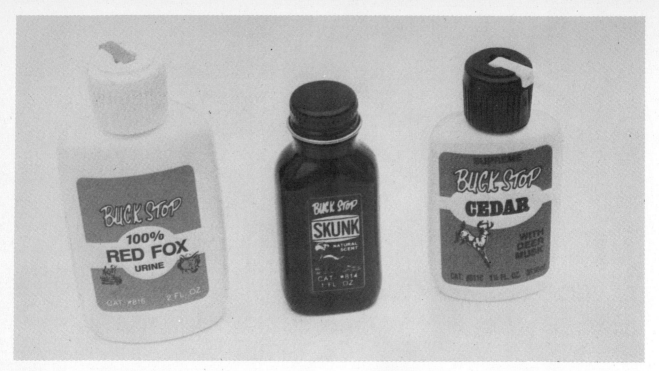

(Above) Odor-covering scents like red fox urine, skunk scent, and cedar scent at least confuse deer long enough to allow shots which might not otherwise have been.

(Right) Acorn scent from a reputable firm like Buck Stop certainly helps a deer hunter in areas with oak trees and ripe acorns on the ground.

out in the piney woods or fool a deer used to smelling other deer—not in 100 years! Not all scents smell the way they're supposed to smell, especially among the off-brands. Stick with name brands to ensure positive results.

Matching a particular odor-masking scent to a particular bowhunting situation is a relatively easy thing to do. Simply use common sense. When the wild grapes are hanging heavy in the fall bottomlands, wild grape scent is a natural winner. Around apple orchards where deer are used to gobbling up well-ripened fruit, nothing can beat apple scent for covering your own human odor. When stillhunting through the pines, pine scent is good, and if the surrounding forest is predominantly cedar, this odor is the obvious choice. When stand hunting deer around fields of sweet corn or sunflowers, match these crops with the appropriate scents. When the oaks are loaded with acorns and deer are feeding heavily in these areas, what better scent could there be than acorn? Choosing a proper scent is as easy as that.

Although many odor-masking scents are so-called food scents like acorn, apple, and sweet corn, these seem to function primarily as human scent-maskers instead of actually luring deer in. There are exceptions to this, the same as there are exceptions to almost

everything, but I've never seen a significant response difference in deer between the food scents and pure odor-masking scents like pine and cedar.

The four fairly universal odor-masking scents that can be used nearly everywhere with the same good results are skunk scent, the strongest-smelling, followed by fox urine, deer musk, and earth scent.

Skunks live almost everywhere, making *eau de polecat* a natural choice from sea level to high-country deer haunts. A few bowhunting pals of mine feel that skunk scent has the potential for *scaring* spooky deer because a skunk seldom sprays unless danger threatens it directly. Therefore, the theory goes that if a deer smells skunk, it knows that danger may be nearby. I have not found this to be the case, and I have seen hundreds of deer grazing peacefully with skunk odor saturating the air around them. However, I wouldn't rule out the possibility that a big old buck might slink away if it smells skunk scent, especially if it has had a bad

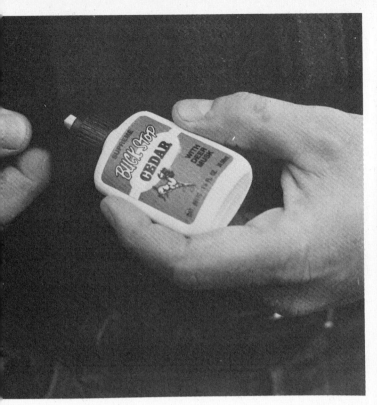

(Left and below) One method of using odor-masking scent is applying it directly to the fabric of hunting shirt or trousers.

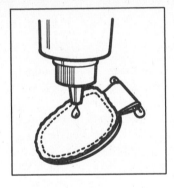

Soaking scent into a separate pin-on scent pad keeps clothes odor-free during non-hunting times of day.

experience associated with skunk sometime in its past.

A good reason *not* to use this product, from my point of view, is the terrible odor it has. I do use skunk scent in deer hunting, but only on bushes and trees near a stand—never directly on my person. I cannot think of a better way to bring about loneliness and possibly start divorce proceedings than regularly gallivanting around with the powerful odor of polecat permeating hunting clothes, tainting the interior of a hunting rig, and lingering on the skin!

Fox urine, coyote urine, and similar trapping scents have proven their effectiveness in fooling the very keen noses of these fur-bearing predators. Since predators abound in one form or another in most deer habitat, and since deer in such areas are used to smelling the by-products of these predators, using urine scent is a logical way to cover human odor. It can be obtained from larger scent manufacturers and distributors around the country.

Deer have a natural musky odor given off by the tarsal and metatarsal glands inside their lower legs. Deer musk can be purchased in bottled form and is strong enough in odor to at least partially cover body scent. Even many good-quality commercial scents of other types have a little deer musk added for good measure.

Earth scent accurately duplicates the pleasant smell of dirt dampened by a fresh rain. It can be used whenever this natural scent wafts up after precipitation and can also be used near any creek, slough, or lake that creates the same damp-earth fragrance. Earth scent is potent enough to help cover human body odor in most bowhunting situations.

Most of these commercial scents are sold in glass bottles or plastic squeeze containers and can be applied effectively to a hunter's clothing, the terrain around a stand, and/or some sort of separate scent pad or scent vent that clips or pins to a hunter's shirt or pants.

143

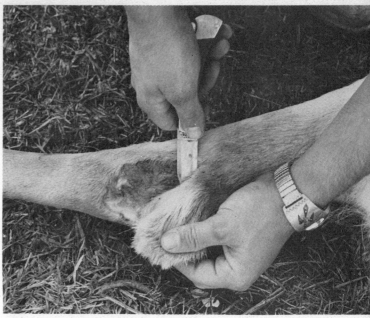

The tarsal glands from the hocks of deer produce their own natural odor and can be carried by a bowhunter to cover his human scent.

(Left) Pine needles crushed and rubbed on clothes provide a strong natural odor-masking scent.

Because most are strong-smelling by necessity, I prefer to apply scent to the lower half of my body. The tactic that makes the most sense is using a separate scent pad that soaks up and lets off scent but doesn't taint clothing in the process. When on stand, scent should be judiciously squirted around the stand site, too. Though many odor-masking scents are pleasant to sniff briefly, such as acorn and cedar, remember that constant breathing of this stuff can be disturbing if a hunter haphazardly douses it all over his body.

Natural Odor-Masking Scents

In addition to commercial scents, a bowhunter can put several natural scents to the same effective use. Certain deer areas have potent-smelling plants that help cover human scent. For example, parts of the western United States have stands of pepperwood—an oily, pleasant-smelling bush that absolutely reeks when the leaves are crushed and rubbed on clothing. Ordinary pine or cedar needles also give off a strong odor when crushed, providing you with a natural odor-masking scent.

One trick many deer hunters use is to cut the tarsal glands from the hocks of whatever deer species they prefer to hunt. Such pieces of strong-smelling hide can be frozen in ziplock plastic bags during off-season months, then thawed and tied to a belt during hikes around the hills. I have had particularly excellent success with this technique in remote areas on moose,

elk, and caribou, which have never smelled many commercial bottled scents and would probably bolt and run if they did.

One of the most effective natural scents for covering boot soles in farm country is found wherever dairy or beef cattle hang out. Prior to approaching a cattle-country stand, find a fresh cow pie and rub your boot soles thoroughly over it. As any farm boy knows, cow manure does not stink to high heaven like the droppings of dogs and other meat-eaters, making this boot-sole scent easy and not unpleasant to use. Not once have I had a whitetail deer smell my trail to a stand when I rubbed my feet in this natural barnyard odor-masking scent.

Other Ways to Hide Body Odor

Two other odor-masking procedures should be mentioned here. Using ordinary baking soda or commercial scent-reducing tablets can diminish your human scent. A thorough wash-down or even a partial sponge bath in baking soda in hunting camp will effectively cut human body odor the same way baking soda destroys odors in a refrigerator. An internal way to do the same basic thing is taking commercial chlorophyll tablets prior to a bowhunt.

Although baking soda and odor-reducing tablets might cut down the basic level of body odor, they cannot do a complete deer-fooling job because existing human odor is in no way masked. The uncut, telltale

A serious deer hunter stocks up on odor-masking scents like skunk, deer lures like doe-in-heat, and food scents like apple to improve his odds of success.

(Left) Rutting buck deer lose much of their natural caution and often approach the odor of doe-in-heat scent sprinkled around a stand.

smells of civilization clinging to a bowhunter's clothing, footwear, and shooting gear will still scare a deer into the next county even if direct body odor is entirely eliminated.

Bowhunting Deer Lures

When hunters talk about deer lure, they are talking primarily about doe-in-heat scent. Although the occasional hunger-driven or curious deer might come gallivanting toward the smell of food scent like acorn, sweet corn, or apple, the only smell that consistently draws deer is the odor of a doe in heat.

This lure is incredibly effective on buck deer at the height of the mating season—particularly whitetail bucks. At this berserk time of year, bucks cast away much of their normal caution and begin moving throughout the day in active search of mates. A hunter who takes a stand near scrapes, rubs, and other ample signs of deer and waits patiently all day can nail trophy bucks he'd probably never see at other times of the year.

Although it can be applied directly to a scent pad or clothes, doe-in-heat scent is most often sprinkled on bushes and the ground near a bowhunting stand. One whitetail-hunting enthusiast I know simply climbs to his tree stand during the deer rut and then tosses down a dark-colored handkerchief soaked with bottled doe-in-heat liquid. He annually takes a dandy buck as the sex-crazed critter buries its nose in the hanky and

thinks dirty thoughts.

The deer rut varies in exact timing, depending on the year and the part of the continent you happen to be bowhunting. Generally, late November and early December are the active rutting times in the lower 48 states. However, doe-in-heat lure works on deer that are not rutting heavily, too. The interest level in this lure rises steadily for a month or so prior to peak mating frenzy and tapers off again as the crazy time subsides. Surprisingly, I've had dozens of does and fawns walk in to the lure, lingering around to sniff before moving away through the woods. This natural scent never seems to scare away deer, even before or after mating activity, and helps archers who would be satisfied with a doe as well as died-in-the-wool trophy hunters.

Although not as commonly practiced, doe-in-heat lure will work on rutting mule deer every bit as well as rutting whitetail. Unfortunately, not too many mule-deer bow seasons coincide with the late-fall mule deer rut—a major reason deer lure is seldom employed by bowhunting mulie enthusiasts.

Odor-masking scents and deer lures have a definite value in bowhunting deer. They should not be regarded as a substitute for sneaking or stand-hunting skill, but they certainly can help put venison in the bag when properly used. As a result, well-selected scents should be a part of every serious archer's deer-hunting equipment checklist.

14/Deer Bowhunting Basics

SOME PEOPLE believe bowhunting and hunting with a firearm require entirely different skills. This is really not the case. Most of the same basic skills used by big-game hunting riflemen are also used by good bowhunters—they are merely refined in bowhunting to let an archer close the shooting distance from 200 or 300 yards to 20 or 30. A truly good rifle hunter can normally catch on to bowhunting fairly fast because he already has the basic principles of successful deer hunting firmly under control.

Despite the many likenesses between rifle and bow-hunting deer, the need to get truly close to animals with a bow-and-arrow really separates these two sports as far as hunting skill is concerned. The straight-shooting rifleman who gets within 150 or 200 yards of a broadside, stationary deer has virtually finished his hunt; a bowhunter in the same situation has only just begun. The last 150 or 160 yards that need to be covered toward a 200-yard deer might as well be 10 miles unless an archer refines his basic rifle-hunting skills into a delicate art. Bowhunting definitely separates the men from the boys, even when all concerned know something about basic hunting techniques.

Fooling a Deer's Basic Survival Senses

No matter what deer species is being bowhunted, one of an archer's primary concerns should be successfully fooling the animal's razor-sharp survival senses. Every deer is a fine-tuned machine with eyes, ears, and nose constantly on the alert for nearby danger. These senses are coupled with a nimble brain and excellent physical reflexes—innate qualities that let a deer interpret incoming danger data in a split-instant and race away before that danger has a chance to strike. A deer is not unlike a computer fitted with a variety of radar and other sensing devices—getting close to such a machine without being detected is seldom if ever easy.

The closer a bowhunter gets, the more likely a deer is to detect his presence and run or sneak away in fright. A deer's eyes are far more efficient at 30 yards than 300, its ears can clearly detect sounds at 40 yards it could not hear at all at 100, and its nose gets a far more saturated sniff of danger at 50 yards than the diluted smell it gets at 200. Penetrating the animal's danger-avoiding mechanisms is not easy even at 200 yards, but this is mere child's play compared to weaseling in to 20 or 30 yards without being detected. A bowhunter must be fully aware of a deer's ability to see, hear, and smell at both long and short range, and must take special measures to successfully combat these animal survival senses.

Avoiding a Deer's Prying Eyes

There is nothing second-rate about a deer's eyesight. Be it whitetail, blacktail, mule deer, elk, caribou, or moose, an antlered animal has the ability to see anything out of place in its home territory. A bowhunter should always respect the eyesight of deer and learn to avoid detection.

Just how good are a deer's eyes, anyway? Many casual hunters I've talked to entertain the mistaken notion that deer can only see them well if they move quickly and only when these animals are looking directly at them. Any experienced bowhunter knows better, and gives deer the infinite respect their seeing ability deserves. A deer can not only detect quick motion, but it can also see slow motion and anything that is more lightly or darkly colored than surrounding terrain. In addition, a deer can *recognize* a human shape that is not moving at all. The old wives' tale that deer do not pay attention to immovable objects is total, unadulterated bunk. I have had dozens of deer walk up to me in the woods—even when I was fully camouflaged—and spot my human shape for what it was. Invariably, the animals would freeze a second or two and then run, or whirl and run immediately. If you look like a human

(Left and right) A deer has sharp senses and a suspicious mind, quickly putting two and two together and running away from danger.

A deer has excellent peripheral vision, allowing it to spot danger to the sides and slightly behind.

and a deer spots you, the animal will know something is awry and get the heck out of there. Bowhunters who underrate a deer's ability to see and disregard their recognition of stationary objects will almost always be unsuccessful at their sport.

A deer has excellent peripheral vision. Like most prey species, they have eyes set in the sides of their heads, a setup that lets them see over 200 degrees of the terrain around them. A broadside deer that is looking straight ahead will see you if you move in from the side—will see you in a split-second! The only blind spots on a deer are almost directly behind it and sharply above its head.

To avoid a deer's sharp eyes a bowhunter should wear head-to-toe camouflage and carry camouflaged gear that accurately matches the terrain to be hunted. However, camouflaged clothing and gear is not enough. A fully camouflaged bowhunter who stands in the sunshine against a shady background or stands in the shade against a sunny backdrop will stand out dramatically, alerting even a half-blind deer to his presence. Similarly, the archer who cruises ridgetops, silhouetting himself against the sky, effectively cancels out the best-selected camo clothes and the most skillfully spray-painted hunting bow and shooting accessories. A bowhunter must be ever conscious of thwarting a deer's eyesight during every minute afield to give

147

Here are three progressive stages of putting camouflage techniques to good use. The archer in the white T-shirt (left) is partially in shadows, but his clothing gives him away. The archer in partial shade (middle) blends well, but will still show up if he moves. The camouflaged archer (right) in full shade blends the best of all.

A camouflage headnet is good insurance against being spotted by deer.

himself a decent crack at success.

If possible, it is best to completely stay out of a deer's field of view during most of a stalking or stillhunting situation. Cruise along the back sides of ridgelines and peek over the top once in awhile to look for game. Keep deer on the far side of natural obstacles like trees, logs, and rocks whenever possible. Stay well above your quarry if you can to take advantage of this blind spot. Deer do have good eyes, but they cannot see through solid objects and cannot see straight up or directly to the rear.

When moving through areas where deer might be able to see you directly, always minimize this risk by lurking in the shadows, screening your body with limbs and brush, or otherwise melting into the terrain. *Think* about how visible you might be at all times and try to remain unobtrusive. Do not skyline yourself or otherwise blow a setup that might pay off if you give a deer's eyes the full respect they deserve.

Move slowly; do not move fast. A deer spots fast movement better than slow movement, the same as you and I do. A hunter buried deep in the shadows can sometimes move slowly under a deer's very nose when fast movement would blow the setup—especially when the deer is standing in the sun and/or looking into the sun. A deer's eyes, like the eyes of man, must adjust to light levels—something a hunter can use to good advantage. A buck lounging in the warm, brilliant early-morning sun cannot see into the shadows any better than you can see in a dark house after coming in out of the sun, and the animal will have to squint to see even tolerably well if you move in with the low sun directly behind your back. Never blatantly challenge a deer's ability to see in such marginal circumstances if you want to put venison in the freezer—merely use these sight weak points to good advantage if no better strategy presents itself. You might get away with moving slowly in front of a buck's sun-dazzled eyes, but the same movement on a dull, overcast day would frighten the critter badly.

When bowhunting, use your common sense to thwart a deer's ability to see, always keeping in mind the strong and weak points of the animal's visual capabilities.

Thwarting a Deer's Sensitive Ears

A deer's ears never seem to drop their guard, even when an animal seems to be asleep. I have seen deer obviously snoozing with eyes closed and heads stretched out on the ground . . . deer that leaped up and took off at the sound of a pebble rattling down a slope or a leaf crunching underfoot. A deer can hear incredibly well, and uses its big, cupped ears for far more than flicking away flies. You must adapt to this fast and learn to move with absolute or near-absolute silence in the woods.

A bowhunter must develop techniques to prevent game-spooking noise. Most such techniques are common-sense moves an alert hunter automatically catches on to. He never wades through heavy brush,

dry grass, and other crackly plants if he can quietly sneak around. He learns to step down softly instead of charging through the woods and to pick routes that minimize underfoot debris. He learns to slow down in noisy areas, stooping over to clear quiet stepping places in rocks and leaves on critical stalks and never fails to look down before he steps. He learns to move his bow and other gear about a stand platform in a manner that prevents noisy collision with tree limbs and parts of the stand itself. Such moves become automatic when you fully appreciate how sensitive a deer's ears can be.

An archer takes advantage of situations that help to mask or dampen the noise of his movements in the deer woods. When it rains, a serious bowhunter heads for deer cover because foliage becomes soggy and the sound of raindrops helps drown out movement noises. When a deer is feeding noisily on bushes, a hunter knows the animal cannot hear quite as well as when it is bedded and motionless. When the wind blows hard, an archer uses this cover noise to good advantage. Even the drone of a passing airplane or the rumble of logging trucks in areas where deer are used to such noises can provide the necessary sound cover you need to take a noisy step or two undetected. Thwarting a deer's ears is never easy, but it is possible if a bowhunter learns his art.

There is one other thing you can do to keep deer from hearing you. Whenever possible, keep solid obstacles between the deer and you—obstacles that block out sound. If you have the option of stalking a deer up a ravine with a low ridge between you and the animal,

Rocky, noisy deer habitat like this makes approaching an animal very tough indeed.

take it so you can move faster without making noise the deer can hear. If you are stillhunting noisy terrain and can stay below a knife ridge except for occasional peeks over the top to look for deer on the other side, this technique is best. Similarly, sneaking up the bottom of a shallow dry wash will muffle walking noise, even if your upper body is above ground level.

Keeping Human Scent from Deer

As explained in Chapter 13, a deer has an incredibly keen nose. This is perhaps the animal's very best survival sense, because there is no mistaking human odor. A deer might linger around a bit if it hears or sees something suspicious, but smelling human odor always elicits the same response—they bolt and run immediately without any hesitation at all.

It never ceases to amaze me how keen a deer's nose really is. It can clearly detect a hunter's presence several hundred yards away, even if the hunter is freshly bathed and not reeking of deodorant, bath soap, or other odor the hunter himself can smell. A surprising number of hunters pay no attention to a deer's smelling ability, and by doing so severely handicap themselves every time they stumble into the field.

The best way to keep yourself from being detected is to be conscious of wind direction at all times and move directly into the wind or at least move in a cross-wind direction. Unless breezes take scent from you directly

to the nose of a deer, the animal will never smell your presence.

A truly dedicated bowhunter constantly monitors the wind because he knows that one whiff of human scent will scare a deer completely away. In strong, steady breezes it is fairly easy to keep track of wind direction. In lighter breezes, you must use special techniques to precisely check wind direction. One method is flicking on a butane cigarette lighter and watching which way the flame leans or bends. Another is to squeeze talcum powder from a commercial bow-hunting talc bottle or tap a little powder from a belt-carried powder pouch. The powder will visibly drift away on the breeze. A third method is to toss a little dust in the air and watch it float away. These tricks help the stillhunter stay more or less on the downwind side of deer, and tell the stand hunter from which direction he should approach his stand in order to prevent scent saturation of prime deer habitat, thus tipping deer off to his presence.

Unfortunately, in many deer-hunting situations the winds are not always stable. They swirl, blow from every point of the compass, or switch 180 degrees as temperatures warm up after sunrise and cool down after sunset. A bowhunter who knows his hunting area can learn to predict prevailing breezes caused by weather conditions or daytime temperature changes. He can learn that the wind blows downhill in his favorite deer

A flame of a butane cigarette lighter clearly shows the slightest breeze direction.

(Right) A little dust tossed in the air drifts away on prevailing wind currents to tell a bowhunter which direction to hunt.

An experienced bowhunter uses binoculars a lot to help him locate huntable deer.

hotspot until a little bit after sunrise, changes direction and blows uphill during the balance of the day, and then switches to a downhill direction again near sundown. Such "thermal" breezes caused by the heating and cooling of air are normal in mountain terrain, usually rising as air heats up and dropping as air cools down.

In some circumstances, unstable breezes make bowhunting deer almost impossible. A hunter cannot sneak up on animals when the wind is swirling 360 degrees, and a stand hunter cannot get far enough above deer when down drafts are sucking his scent to ground level from a high-up tree stand. Such situations can sometimes be avoided if a bowhunter simply decides to hunt someplace else, but the use of a potent, good-quality odor-masking scent can help if you find yourself in a situation where breezes suddenly become squirrelly in the middle of a stalk or wait on stand. There is nothing more frustrating or maddening than sneaking on a deer or waiting patiently on stand and then having a fickle breeze swirl, fan the back of your neck, and blow the setup completely.

Using Your Senses to Good Advantage

In addition to learning to fool a deer's survival senses, a bowhunter must sharpen his own senses of sight, hearing, and smell to improve his chances of detecting deer before they detect him. Knowing how to penetrate a deer's survival senses is well and good, but you cannot capitalize on this knowledge unless you see, hear, and/or smell game in the first place. Here's how.

Learning to See Deer

Developing a good "game eye" takes time and experience in the woods. Eventually, a bowhunter learns that deer frequent certain kinds of terrain and

foliage, and concentrates his looking in such consistently productive areas. However, being able to see deer also results from learning not only where to look, but what to look for.

As often as not, a good hunter spots a *part* of a deer—not the entire animal. Novice deer hunters head afield looking for deer poised neatly in the open like they are on magazine covers and postcards. In reality, hunter-wise deer seldom lounge around in such exposed positions. They are seen in the brush, among the trees, or partially obscured by ridgelines, cutbanks, and other irregularities in terrain. A hunter who spots a deer *might* see the entire animal, but more often he'll see the flick of an ear, the shine of an eye or wet black nose, the glint of an antler, or the curve of a lower leg. The good bowhunter concentrates on seeing such puzzle pieces instead of looking for the whole, complete puzzle picture.

In big mountain terrain, bowhunters often spend plenty of time scanning sidehills, ridgelines, and plateaus with good-grade binoculars. They look for spots of color that might be a deer's rump, head, or side exposed through brush or trees. They look for the stark white of freshly stripped antlers in late summer, and the telltale gleam of polished brown antlers in early fall. If a deer walks into wide-open view, the animal is *easy* to see for a hunter tuned to looking for smaller, less obvious animal clues.

In dense-cover stillhunting or stand hunting, using your eyes is every bit as important. A whitetail buck or big bull elk can stand or lie at point-blank range from an unobservant archer, either freezing like a pheasant until the nimrod passes by or exploding from cover and allowing no decent shot at all. By contrast, an alert hunter with practiced eyeballs can often spot such an animal before it spots him, giving him the chance to set up a decent shot.

LEARNING TO SEE DEER

There are one or two deer in each of these photos. How good is your game eye?

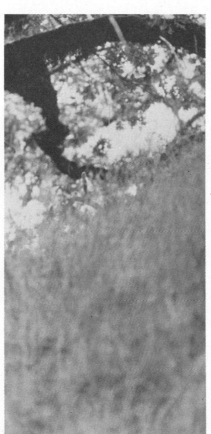

One major key to seeing deer before they see you is moving slowly in areas where you think deer might be hanging out. A hunter cannot walk steadily and observe everything around him—he must stop, look a bit, move a few steps, stop, and look some more. As will be discussed in Chapter 15, there are definitely times when fast movement helps an archer get a deer. However, taking time to carefully look is normally the best way to spot animals before they detect you and ruin your chances of success.

Listening for Deer

A bowhunter should use his ears to full advantage in the woods. As when trying to see deer, you really can't hear well when you're truckin' along at a moderately fast pace. It's far better to pause regularly to listen for various deer sounds which are not obscured by your own movement noises.

What noises do deer make, anyway? Actually, they make quite a few. They rustle, crunch, and crackle as they walk through dry woods—sounds a bowhunter stays tuned to hear. In dry weather, a deer that is feeding or moving along makes a surprising amount of racket.

Antlered male deer make sounds with their racks you can learn to recognize. This headgear sometimes clatters against foliage as a buck or bull moves along. When he's stripping off his velvet in late summer or sparring with bushes prior to the mating season, the ruckus created can sometimes be heard several hundred yards away. And when two males square off and lock antlers during the rut or just in pre-rut frolicking, the clicking and crashing of bone against bone is an unmistakable sound. I have often zeroed in on bucks stripping velvet from their racks in heavy cover and, during mating season, have shot several as they sparred with other bucks.

Deer make a variety of vocal sounds that savvy hunters listen for. Does and fawns softly bleat back and forth on a regular basis to keep track of each other. In elk, this sound between cows and calves is a louder chirp that can be heard several hundred yards away. Deer of all varieties sneeze, cough, and snort like humans do—sounds a slow-moving, observant archer can hear and recognize with experience. In addition, animals in full mating frenzy make noises peculiar to their kind. Bull elk bugle loudly, buck deer moan and groan, and cow moose utter a low, gutteral bawl. These and similar sounds become familiar to serious archers and help them locate the position of deer they cannot see or otherwise detect.

Learn to rely on your ears to hear and differentiate the sounds made by deer. You'll eventually come to know when a nearby deer is relaxed and feeding by sound alone, when the animal is stamping its foot in alarm, or when it is going through some sort of mating ritual.

Expert deer hunter Ron Hawkins nailed this dandy blacktail buck after first penetrating the animal's fine-honed survival senses.

Using Your Nose in the Woods

A human's sense of smell is grossly inferior to that of a deer. However, there are times when a hunter can actually sniff the presence of hidden game. Early American Indians had highly refined senses of smell, and some of these native hunters could reportedly smell a rabbit in nearby cover if the wind was blowing right. Few if any modern bowhunters can boast such highly refined olfactory ability, but almost any can occasionally smell game in the woods.

The most obvious example that comes to mind is the barnyard-like smell that elk let off. In dense cover, an archer can often smell elk at fairly close range when he cannot see or hear these animals. Rutting buck deer also secrete considerable musk from the tarsal glands near their hocks—an odor a human hunter can sometimes smell. The sense of smell is a bowhunter's least important animal-detection tool, but it can come in handy on occasion.

Learning the Habit Patterns of Deer

Aside from learning to combat a deer's three basic survival senses and to use your own senses to good advantage, you should also learn to quickly pattern the habits of deer through sharp observation. You should note how deer move, try to figure out why, and put such data to good use. In other words, you should *reflect* on what you see, hear, and smell to establish patterns of deer behavior you can take advantage of.

For example, on one of my recent summer caribou bowhunts, the weather in Alaska was unusually warm. The first morning out, I spotted several caribou at first light, and all were moving in a northwesterly direction. I knew that the annual migration would not start for another month, so I thought about the one-directional movement pattern of these big deer and decided they were all heading toward shady slopes where temperatures were cooler and insects were not so obnoxious. This spur-of-the-moment theory proved correct, and I shot a dandy bull later the same day as the animal lounged around on a shady northwestern slope.

Patterning deer is a basic bowhunting technique that is absolutely necessary for consistent success. If you don't know what motivates deer, you certainly can't find and fool them consistently. You must learn what deer are feeding on, where they are bedding down, and where their favored watering places are. Even more importantly, you must determine *why* deer eat, bed, and drink where they do. Such knowledge lets you accurately predict what they will do so you can find them in the first place. By and large, deer are creatures of habit—if you can map out these habit patterns, you can devise strategies to put animals in the bag.

Both reading about various deer species and intelligently observing them in the field will help you understand how and why they do what they do. A thoughtful, fully alert approach teaches a deer hunter myriad things about his prey that stand him in good stead when he tries to find game and devise specific bowhunting strategies. Rifle hunters devise strategies for taking deer, but bowhunters need far more intimate knowledge of deer to get within solid bowshooting range on a regular basis.

A bowhunter must learn to thwart a deer's fine-tuned survival senses, learn to use his own senses, and also learn to use his brain to absorb and interpret the data he collects through careful observation. These are basic requirements of successful bowhunting for deer—requirements that form a solid foundation for using the specific bowhunting techniques discussed later in this book.

15/Stalking & Stillhunting

AS FAR AS I'm concerned, there is no more challenging or interesting way to bowhunt deer than sneaking around on your two hind legs. It requires the highest level of hunting skill to penetrate a deer's survival senses and use your own senses and brain to locate your quarry and devise a successful approach strategy. Sitting on stand is an interesting and important method of taking deer, but a hunter who attempts to move in on a deer is actively probing the animal's senses instead of waiting like a stump until a deer moves past. To actually move, make noise, and still sneak within bow-shooting range is many times more difficult than passively waiting for deer on stand.

With a few exceptions, I believe a bowhunter who becomes adept at sneak-hunting has a much better chance of taking deer than a hunter who relies solely on the stand-hunting method. An archer who can move in on game is not glued to one location and left hoping something walks by—he can at least *try* to close the gap on any deer he sees, or actively slip around to find a deer when no animals are readily seen. An eastern whitetail hunter can take deer consistently from a stand because these animals have fairly predictable movement patterns. Other species like blacktail, mule deer, elk, moose, and caribou, which are not always predictable in the way they move, require well-developed sneaking skills for consistent bowhunting success. However, even the serious whitetail enthusiast can benefit by some deer-sneaking ability for effective bottomland bowhunting when rain or soft snow mutes noisy leaves and bushes. Many fine trophy whitetails have been taken in the damp, rainy woods. An archer who sticks to his tree stand and never develops sneaking skills might be severely handicapped if he ever decides to hunt another area or another kind of deer. I've seen this happen time after time when eastern whitetail stand-sitters have decided to try hunting elk or another western deer species. The result has generally been

complete shock and frustration as it dawned on them that they had to hunt on foot or go home empty-handed.

There are two basic forms of ground-sneaking techniques an archer should perfect—stalking and stillhunting. Although both share the need for quiet clothes, soft-soled footwear, and other standard items necessary in quiet walking, there are notable differences between these two bowhunting methods.

Stalking

Stalking is ideally suited for semi-open mountain or foothill terrain. On a stalk the hunter normally moves along ridgelines or sits on one elevated vantage point until he finds a distant deer he'd like to shoot. He then carefully studies the wind direction, the terrain between him and the quarry, other deer in the area, and similar factors that might come into play as he tries to move in. After devising an approach route and strategy, the bowhunter begins sneaking toward the deer and hopefully slips into good bow range for a solid shot at success.

There is nothing easy about stalking deer. In broken terrain with a view, wind currents are seldom rock steady from one ridge to the next or from one slope to another. Even if a hunter spots an animal at long distance—something that often requires careful looking through binoculars and with the naked eye—he must then worry about vagrant breezes that might ruin his stalk. He must decipher the best way to use the terrain to cover a stalk, choosing from several approach routes with wind and noise as well as adequate cover in mind.

Myriad factors can ruin a deer stalk even if a bowhunter chooses a quiet, well-covered approach route and lucks out on the wind. A deer can up and move even if it is bedded when spotted, leaving the hunter high and dry when he finally reaches the place

A stalking bowhunter spends much of his time glassing for likely deer to sneak on.

Bowhunting on foot in heavy cover requires quiet, soft-surfaced clothes for decent deer-getting results.

where the animal was. A deer seen feeding might continue feeding until the archer sneaks close, or it might wander away at a fast pace and ruin the bowhunter's well-laid plans. Even more frustrating is the strong possibility that you'll run into other deer on a stalk—deer that run away or linger and snort their heads off until every animal for miles around is fully alert and drifting for parts unknown. Stalking deer is challenging at best, taxing a bowhunter's skills to the utmost.

Despite the intricacies involved, this technique can be highly effective for a patient, confident archer. It is especially desirable for trophy hunters, who want to look over plenty of deer and then go after one specific animal with an oversized set of antlers. To bag a trophy mule deer, elk, caribou, or moose in mountain terrain, a bowhunter cannot simply take off through the brush and hope to achieve his goal. He must let his eyes do much of the walking until a trophy is found, and then map out a particular approach route that appears to allow a close-range sneak on the animal.

The most important ingredient in stalking, aside from wearing quiet, camouflaged clothes, is having *lots* of patience. You cannot become easily discouraged when stalking game because the odds are always less than 50-50 that a particular stalk will pan out. I once kept records on my stalks for high-country blacktail over a 5-year period, and the results were very interesting to review. I only took a decent shot at one in five bucks that I spotted and stalked because the wind, other deer, unexpectedly noisy terrain, or a variety of other negative factors spoiled many good-looking stalks. Sometimes, I'd be moving in for the kill when some old propeller-headed doe would stand up in her bed directly in front of me and either charge away toward my target buck or commence to stamp her foot and blow obnoxiously. Sometimes, the mountain air currents would swirl about my ears and then whistle my

(Left and below) A stalking deer hunter first plans a feasible approach route with the aid of binoculars and then executes the stalk as best he can with the stealth of a bobcat.

Stalkers often experience best results in remote backpack areas far from roads which require some simple wilderness camping equipment.

scent straight to the nostrils of the animal I was sneaking on. Sometimes, I would simply screw up and let the deer see or hear me before I could loose an arrow. Occasionally, the target would just be gone when I finally arrived where it had been, apparently taking a notion to wander away to eat, drink, or bed someplace else. In the face of such problems, iron-clad patience is a hunter's only salvation.

Fortunately, patience plus skill generally pay off big for the stalking bowhunter. There is nothing more satisfying than locating a target animal, deciphering a feasible approach plan, carefully weaving your way past several other deer without being seen, heard, or smelled, narrowing the gap to 20 or 30 yards, and then making a dead-center shot that drops the critter in short order.

When stalking animals, you should systematically formulate your strategy and devise alternate plans in case the original must be revised to accommodate changing wind patterns, other deer encountered, etc. First, locate a deer you want to stalk. Second, look over the terrain in between with a fine-toothed comb to see which approaches have the most merit. Are there little finger ridges providing total cover that you can hide behind? Are there stands of timber or rows of brush that will conceal your approach? Will running water on one side of the deer help cover any small sounds you might make? Will wind be blowing up the far-off slope where your target is, or will it be slipping downhill because of cooling evening temperatures? Ask such pertinent questions if there is time to do so, and formulate an approach plan that is likely to work.

In stalking, there is no standard ground speed you should strive to achieve. How fast or slow you move should be determined by every individual bowhunting situation. If a deer is up and feeding in late morning, you might decide to watch the animal awhile before going after it to make certain it plans to bed or lounge in the same general area. If an animal is moving steadily on a distant hillside, you might try to intercept its course by moving extremely fast. Speed of movement is no problem if footing is quiet and you can duck behind a ridge or heavy stringer of trees that fully covers your movement and helps mute your sound. In big, open country, I have shot several mule deer that I stalked for over 5 miles before moving into range. The old, standard "move one step and wait two" formula of walking in the deer woods doesn't work worth beans in such instances because it would be bedtime long before you reach your target animal.

As a general rule, I usually move as quickly as I can on a stalkable deer to minimize the chance that the animal will take a notion to move away before I reach it. If other deer are apt to get in the way and run toward the intended target, I go much slower than normal. It all depends on the circumstances. I once shot a feeding bull elk by running almost 2 miles to reach it across a canyon before it bedded up, using heavy timber to hide my approach. I covered all that ground in less than 45 minutes, but took another hour to cover the last 50 yards because once I topped a little ridge I was within sight of the elk from there on in. I arrowed the animal at 20 yards with a broadside hit through both lungs.

The ideal stalking situation as far as I'm concerned allows an archer to spot a deer at relatively long range, drop safely out of sight and hearing in a canyon or draw for most of the stalk, and then pop out near the animal for a slow, tedious final approach. Things are seldom ideal in bowhunting deer, but an active hunter can sometimes set up such a situation if he uses his noggin and formulates an intelligent approach.

The final portion of a long stalk on deer is invariably an exciting, pulse-pounding experience. You must keep close tabs on the animal, only moving when the deer is fully engrossed in eating or when its eyes are not able to see you move. This is indeed "take one step and wait two" sneaking. Sometimes you'll have to take one step and wait 30! The key to sneaking at close range is remembering the basic tips in Chapter 14—never let a deer see you, hear you, or smell you. This is accomplished by watching the animal and moving as slowly as a snail only when it is safe to do so.

A deer is a super-alert critter, but it drops its guard regularly when feeding or moving around. Let's take a feeding deer as an example. It will eat a little while, raise its head to gawk around, then eat a little more. If you have such a deer within 100 yards, keep your eyes on the animal and take a careful, quiet step only when the trophy has dropped its head to feed. Be sure that its sight is obstructed by what it is feeding on or that it is facing directly away before you move—a broadside deer with its head dropped and sight unobstructed will see you instantly with its peripheral vision. Hug the shadows and existing cover as discussed in Chapter 14, use a low sun behind you or other factors to help you out, and hope that everything goes smoothly.

Sometimes you'll have to wait for an animal to move into a different setting before you can complete a stalk. I've waited on bedded deer all day long because I knew I'd never take them where they were. On one old mulie buck I finally put in the bag, I watched the animal 3 full days until it bedded in a stalkable spot. I saw that deer every day, and finally it left the bare shale slide it was frequenting and bedded under a tiny ridgetop rim that allowed a stalk from the back side. Again, a bowhunter is seldom good at stalking unless he can be patient.

Spot-and-stalk deer hunting with a bow requires an archer to be in fairly good physical condition so he can negotiate broken terrain and move fast when fast movement is necessary. The out-of-shape bowhunter

Bowhunting deer on foot necessitates completely quiet gear. Rubber-coated binoculars, soft wool clothing, and neoprene-soled boots are excellent sneak-hunting choices.

(Left and below) A stalking or stillhunting archer must learn to avoid areas where quiet walking is impossible. This deer in the crackly wild oats was unapproachable except with a powerful telephoto lense. .

had best get in shape or forego this active method of taking deer.

Stalking is an exceedingly important bowhunting technique to master for two basic reasons. First, many bowhunting situations in open or semi-open deer terrain require this technique—without it, there is no hope at all of taking deer. Second, stalking is the only way a bowhunter can follow up and finish off a wounded animal that still has its wits about it and the capability to run away. Even the eastern whitetail deer hunter occasionally needs to sneak up and put the *coup de grace* on a hard-hit deer. Without basic stalking ability this hunter might very well lose the animal altogether. Enough said?

Stillhunting

Quite a few deer-hunting areas are choked with heavy timber or brush that prevents long-distance viewing of animals. This problem is complicated if terrain is gently rolling or flat. Mule deer, whitetail, blacktail, elk, and moose all sometimes inhabit such country, and the most productive hunting method is slipping along with the hope of bumping into an unsuspecting animal. This form of blind foot-hunting in heavy cover is called stillhunting, and produces deer like clockwork for those who master the technique.

Stillhunting is a more consistently slow-moving archery technique than stalking because a hunter never knows when a deer might be nearby until he actually sees it at fairly close range. He must ease along, a step or two at a time, looking and listening for deer and trying to avoid noisy bushes, trees, or underfoot debris which can completely spoil his efforts. Stillhunting is best used in areas with fairly heavy deer concentrations because the hunter is wandering blind into the wind with no way of deliberately homing in on a particular animal's position. This technique can produce nice trophies, but does not allow a hunter to look over lots of animals like stalking in semi-open terrain often does.

I think there is little question that stillhunting is the most difficult of all bowhunting techniques. An archer must be fully alert *all the time* for best results because he never knows when a deer might be lurking behind the next clump of brush or trees. He must constantly be looking for ears, eyes, feet, and other parts of deer in heavy cover, and must never relax and make unneces-

A bedded dear is fully alert and capable of hearing the slightest approach sound. Such an animal presents the ultimate foot-hunting challenge.

The author dropped this open-country mulie buck in its bed with a 60-yard shot. The stalk into position took over an hour.

sary walking noise.

Obviously, a stillhunter should sneak into the wind or in a crosswind direction to keep his scent from game ahead. He must wear head-to-toe camouflage for best results although the chances of deer seeing him in fairly heavy, close-range cover are less than when stalking in semi-open terrain. This clothing must be especially soft-surfaced to prevent noise when clothes brush close-growing foliage along a hunter's path.

The tendency of beginning stillhunters is to move along too fast, not allowing complete viewing of terrain ahead or ample time to listen for nearby animals. In uniformly scattered trees and bushes that prevent a long-range view but allow fairly quick walking, hunters often truck along at a steady pace and barge into deer that are feeding or lying down. A slower, easier, pace gets the game when an archer decides to stillhunt.

Unless the terrain to be hunted is rough, steep elk habitat or near-vertical mule deer country, a bowhunter need not be in spectacular physical condition to stillhunt along. When properly done, a morning's stillhunt seldom covers more than 2 or 3 miles of deer habitat—often much less.

One item a stillhunter should generally carry is some sort of marker material in case he drops a deer in monotonously uniform terrain with no outside view. It is painfully easy to take an elk in a huge expanse of dense timber or a whitetail buck on a giant brush flat and then not be able to find the animal again because every bush and every tree looks the same. I prefer to carry a roll of fluorescent surveyor's tape for marking a trail out of the woods once a deer is down.

Similarly, a stillhunter who is prone to get lost should carry a compass to ensure proper travel direction as he slips along. It is easy to become disoriented while concentrating on hunting out a large tract of flat, heavily timbered land . . . especially if wind direction is not constant and a hunter meanders around to keep breezes solidly in his face.

Bowhunting deer on foot is a challenging, extremely exciting technique. It requires the maximum in hunting skill, but allows an archer the most versatility to seek out and drop game he would probably never see on stand. Such hunting is especially effective on deer species which do not move predictably from day to day—which means every species but whitetail.

16/Stand Hunting

BOWHUNTING from a stand can be one of the most surefire ways to take a deer. A stand hunter has the advantage of waiting for deer to come to him, sitting or standing unobtrusively in one spot with eyes and ears alert for any sight or sound. In stand hunting, it is the deer that makes the movement and the noise, allowing the hunter to fade into the woodwork and only move when an animal is in ideal position to allow a clear, accurate shot.

Stand hunting is by no means easy. It normally requires more equipment setup than hunting on foot, and requires ample scouting and searching prior to the actual hunt to locate areas where stands might pay off big. In addition, it requires definite know-how to approach a stand properly, and requires a high degree of patience that some bowhunters simply do not have. When properly orchestrated, hunting from a stand is a deadly art that can produce extremely large, alert trophies which seldom allow foot hunters anywhere near them. Every bowhunter should use a stand when conditions dictate—stomping around the woods when leaves are ankle deep and cornflake crisp is foolhardy, and trying to stalk or stillhunt deer with fairly regular movement patterns is placing an unnecessary burden on yourself when you could simply wait in ambush.

When to Take a Stand

One primary, overriding key to success is knowing when to take a stand. A hunter who simply climbs into a random tree or hides behind a rock in a large area with a few deer of one species or another is likely to wait for weeks without so much as seeing one animal within acceptable bow range. An archer must take a stand only when he knows or suspects that deer will be using a particular area on a regular basis.

Some deer species are great about being predictable this way. Whitetail are tailor-made for stand hunting because they normally live in one small home territory

Bowhunting deer from an elevated stand is one of the best ways to put venison in the bag.

(Above and right) Well-used deer trails littered with tracks promise shots from a well-positioned stand.

and bed, water, and feed in the same basic places day after day after day. Although less predictable in general, other deer species have tendencies toward predictability a bowhunter can capitalize on. Blacktail and mule deer are sometimes drawn to alfalfa fields and other agricultural crops that concentrate their normal random feeding habits. Caribou migrate en masse during early fall over established routes, allowing them to be ambushed if an archer knows where to wait. Moose and elk sometimes feed or water regularly in places that are particularly comfortable to use. An alert hunter who notes such tendencies can often ambush animals that seem to be locked into convenient habit patterns.

The key to stand hunting to good advantage is noting regular habit patterns. To merely take a stand along a green meadow in elk country or above a waterhole in moose terrain is inviting failure because deer may not be using these particular spots at all. Take a stand only when you have strong evidence of regular deer movement in a particular piece of terrain.

Where to Take a Stand

There are several ways to determine if a specific area would be a good one to stand hunt, and several techniques for finding a specific stand location within this area.

First of all, consider the species you want to bowhunt and the general character of the countryside to be hunted. Is the species *normally* stand hunted, as are whitetail deer, or only stand hunted in unique circumstances, as in the case of mule deer and caribou? If you *aren't* after whitetail, is the country you plan to bowhunt conducive to drawing animals to specific stand areas like food fields or waterholes in dry, barren country? Mule deer, elk, moose, caribou, and blacktail do not frequent specific areas unless a unique food, water, or comfort circumstance exists to concentrate their activities. Unless you can think of some such

circumstance in the country you plan to bowhunt, stand hunting may be out. However, if there's a chance that stand hunting might help you get a particular species, by all means toss a tree stand in your pickup prior to heading for the hunting country.

A second thing to consider is what your direct observations of deer tell you once you reach a bowhunting area. If you actually see a little group of mule deer invading a farmer's alfalfa field each evening or regularly see deer from a distance belly up to a particular waterhole to drink their fill, you might want to dispense with your stalking plans. No matter what the species of deer being hunted, I always keep a wary eye out for situations in which animals seem to be consistently using areas where stands can be taken. Sometimes switching strategies and taking a stand will turn a potentially busted trip into a totally satisfying experience.

At times, a smart bowhunter can score from a deer stand by simply paying strict attention to especially

Glassing distant deer early and late will help an archer decide where to wait in ambush.

Waiting for deer on the ground does not work as well as taking an elevated stand, but does produce results on occasion.

heavy deer sign. Abundant tracks around a waterhole, pounded-out deer trails tattooed with fresh hoofprints, or small feeding meadows or brush patches littered with smoking-hot deer droppings all demand stand-hunting consideration, and an archer should always keep an eye out for such little "honey holes" of regular deer activity.

Choosing a Stand Location

Even if a bowhunter locates an area that deer are frequenting, he will not enjoy stand-hunting success unless he finds a specific, well-chosen location. To do so, he must survey the situation, decide where deer are most likely to move, and pick a stand site which allows a clear, uninhibited field of view, fairly easy shooting without limbs or bushes in the way, and downwind protection from a deer's ultra-sensitive snozzle. If possible, the stand should be elevated to take advantage of a deer's overhead blind spot, and to keep human odor safely cushioned on upper-air breezes.

To locate *specific* sites, you can often watch a potential stand-hunting area with binoculars for several days to establish exact deer-movement patterns. If animals move into the clear each evening underneath a big old cottonwood tree, you'll know where to erect your stand. If they always water on the north end of a large stock pond, the south end is definitely *not* the place to take a stand.

In dense cover that doesn't yield a decent view from a distance, a bowhunter can still dope out movement tendencies by dusting out tracks on likely trails, waiting 24 hours to see how many new tracks appear, and setting up a stand overlooking the more heavily used trail or trails. To dust a trail, simply blot out old tracks by sweeping a short section with a handy tree branch. On hard or wet ground, an ambitious bowhunter can actually carry a little dirt or sand to likely trails and deposit enough to clearly show any new track imprints deer put down.

Occasionally, deer sign is so heavy in an area that it is obvious where a stand should be erected. If this is not the case, or if dusting out trails is not a feasible or productive indicator of animal movement, a hunter can actually sit in an area prior to deer season to watch the animals and decide where to erect his "sure-nuff" hunting stand. Such preseason scouting takes time, but can be exciting and enjoyable.

Exact placement should in part be determined by your bow-shooting ability. If you are only proficient out to 20 or 25 yards, it is best to set up relatively close to where deer are likely to move. If you can shoot well out to 50, 60, or even 70 yards, you can cover more ground and should probably erect a stand that gives a wider field of view.

Use your common sense and your knowledge of deer when erecting any stand. Do not put a stand up in a tree that grows from the bottom of a ravine if the best deer trails run along nearby ridgetops. This would put you at eye level to deer and probably flood the area with your scent to boot. Do not choose a tree that doesn't allow clear shots at deer because of impeding branches or limbs. If you decide to take a stand on a tower blind, stepladder top, or other similar elevated setup, be sure to set it up against outline-breaking cover like tall brush or tight-knit trees to keep from being silhouetted against the sky. Make sure your stand is comfortable and quiet to sit on, and don't go pounding nails or spikes unless such a stand is erected several weeks before you actually plan to hunt.

If the only feasible stand is actually a natural ground blind at eye and nose level to deer, be sure the setup is on the solid downwind side of deer-movement areas and provides ample outline-breaking cover but with several holes to shoot arrows through, too. If you are adequately camouflaged and motionlessly standing or sitting against a solid wall of cover, you are often as well off *in front of* cover as behind it because you can see well without moving and because you can draw and shoot without impediments in the way. I personally prefer an elevated stand over a ground blind because most deer are so alert and so nervous that taking a shot from the ground can be tough unless the layout of bushes and trees is absolutely perfect for drawing when a deer's eyes are blocked off from this movement. In addition, sudden wind shifts can spoil the best ground-blind opportunities.

Tips On Stand Hunting

Once you've found a potentially productive location and set up a specific stand platform or location for a ground blind, all you really have to do is don proper camouflage and wait for deer to show up. The keys to successful stand bowhunting are waiting quietly and not moving around excessively as you wait. Even a tree stand erected 20 or 30 feet high will not fool deer if you make noise or move around a lot. Deer will look right up at a bowhunter in a tree if they hear or see something suspicious—especially deer that have been hunted from tree stands a lot. For this reason, I prefer stands a full 20 feet or more above ground level to give me an added edge.

Long waits can be boring if animals are not moving about throughout the day. You should normally take a stand at least 2 hours before you expect deer to pop out to feed—which means reaching a stand at least 3 hours before sundown when whitetail are the target and at least 2 hours before sundown on later-moving animals like heavy-timber elk. This allows ample time for nearby animals to settle down again if they have heard or smelled you approach a stand, and also lets any scent trail you have left fade away before peak deer-activity periods.

Morning bowhunting requires waits of at least an hour before sunrise for best results because climbing to a stand too late can disturb deer already moving back to bedding cover. Taking a morning stand too late can also leave a human scent trail that hasn't faded sufficiently to fool deer. Because of the problems with human odor on damp ground and deer-spooking noise associated with approaching a deer stand early in the morning, a few die-hard archers of my acquaintance sometimes spend the entire night in a roomy tree stand above a special hotspot or reach this stand especially early and suffer through 2 or 3 hours of predawn darkness.

For evening stand hunting with several daylight hours to kill, I often carry a good paperback novel with me to while away the dead hours. In all but damp weather, a bowhunter can usually hear deer coming toward him well before they actually walk within bow range. This lets the archer put down his book and get prepared for action if the odd deer walks past before peak movement periods when a hunter is normally holding his bow at the ready.

One vitally important thing every deer-stand archer should do is be ready for shots when they present themselves. Normally, this entails pacing off shooting ranges from the base of a stand tree to landmarks where deer are apt to appear, using a rangefinder to establish such ranges and/or actually shooting one or two practice arrows at likely deer-shooting distances from the stand. Pacing off distances is an acceptable technique if it is done well before deer are likely to appear, but using a rangefinder makes more sense because it prevents the possibility of leaving human scent on the ground near a tree and also takes less time and effort. I personally like to shoot one or two blunt-tipped arrows from a daylight stand as soon as I reach it to limber up my shooting muscles and double-check bowsight holds at likely deer-shooting distances. Such shooting also tells me if limbs are in the way of maneuvering a bow, or if parts of the stand platform squeak or groan when I shift my weight to shoot, etc. Practice arrows shot from a tree do not seem to hold human scent very long or scare deer walking by them, and can be retrieved after the sit on stand is over.

Because stand hunting is stationary hunting, be sure to dress warmly to combat temperature drops near sundown or to hold in body heat after arriving well before sunrise. By dressing in layers, a bowhunter can regulate his comfort level and hang any excess clothes over a handy tree limb or tie them around his waist.

For safety's sake, be sure all assembly bolts on tree stands are tight prior to using such stands.

(Left) A tree-stand safety belt is a must for safe, relaxed bowhunting high above the ground.

Whenever you climb to an elevated stand, do so carefully with feet firmly planted and hands hanging on tightly.

Tree-Stand Safety

Tree stands offer many advantages to the bowhunter, but also place a hunter dangerously high above the ground unless he carefully watches his Ps and Qs. A fall from 20 or 30 feet can be fatal, not to mention painful and crippling, and all too many bowhunters after deer *do* fall from trees each and every year. Most such falls can be avoided, provided you take the proper precautions.

The first step toward tree-stand safety is choosing a proper tree to begin with. Trees with slippery or icecovered bark should be avoided because they represent a built-in climbing hazard. Trees should be large enough and stout enough to safely hold a stand steady, even in a fairly high wind. Dead or dying trees are dangerous because branches can snap or dead wood crumble during the climbing process.

Dead trees in particular sometimes hold another danger bowhunters seldom think about. A variety of stinging and biting insects invade decaying trees, including ants, scorpions, and hornets. A bowhunter who mistakenly erects a tree stand in dead or dying wood can be suddenly attacked, an occurrence which can lead to an accidental fall, not to mention the bites or stings inflicted by the tiny attackers. Before erecting any tree stand, make certain your chosen tree is free of biting or stinging pests.

Be extremely careful when climbing and use your

166

Always climb to a tree stand first, *then* hoist up your bow and other necessary gear. Never attempt to climb while loaded down with shooting equipment.

equipment properly. A climbing tree stand improperly used can suddenly give way and plummet to earth, leaving you full of splinters in places you never even knew you had! Of particular importance is assembling a stand with stout factory bolts, making sure they are tightened down snugly to prevent bolt friction and wear that could eventually lead to breakage and a nasty fall out of a tree. Similarly, never rely on rickety tree-stand steps, a flimsy rope, or small-diameter branches to support your climbing weight as you erect your stand. Remember, anytime you are above the ground you are in serious danger if a handhold or foothold suddenly gives way.

When actually climbing up a tree, always tie your bow, backpack, and any other gear to a hoist rope and leave it on the ground until you have safely reached your stand. Carrying such gear upward can be dangerous because you can't climb as well, and if you were to fall, might find yourself landing on top of sharp hunting broadheads. To be on the safe side, leave your hands free for climbing and pull up shooting gear after you reach the desired hunting height.

The very first thing a bowhunter should do when reaching all but the roomiest of stands is to attach a tree-stand safety belt to the tree trunk and then strap it to his waist. The belt will prevent serious injury if a slip does occur aloft, perhaps jerking a hunter up short of breath but never letting him free-fall to the ground. Once the safety belt is firmly in place, a hunter can pull

his gear up using the hoist rope, arrange things as he sees fit, and settle in comfortably for a lengthy wait.

As mentioned in Chapter 12, some sort of comfortable seat is important because standing for hours can be dangerous as muscles become wobbly and tired. Bowhunters forced to stand up for hours can actually pass out from lack of blood circulation, and at *best* such standing is tiring and tedious unless animals come tripping by every 5 or 10 minutes.

According to surveys by this country's larger tree-stand manufacturers, the majority of tree-stand accidents occur when archers become highly excited in the presence of deer. One common stunt elevated hunters pull is shooting at a deer, then forgetting where they are and walking or running after the animal . . . and into vacant air space. Even with a safety belt attached, such an occurrence can result in scrapes and bruises, not to mention a somewhat damaged ego!

To prevent slips caused by carelessness, always try to remember where you are. Become familiar with where the edges of your stand platform are by walking around the stand a bit, and make a point not to stand in precarious positions near the stand's edge. First and foremost, try not to get so excited wher deer walk by that you forget the dangers involved in hovering 20 or 30 feet above the ground.

When climbing out of a tree after a hunt, reverse the aforementioned safety procedures. Let down your equipment by rope first, then unbuckle your safety belt,

When carrying any tree stand over rough terrain, it is wise to use backpack straps to free at least one hand for safe and comfortable travel.

Most whitetail deer are taken from well-placed tree stands. Shots are often under 20 yards.

and carefully climb to the ground. An excellent precaution whenever climbing up or down a tree is having one foothold and one handhold at all times, preferably *two* handholds unless reaching for a higher limb, tree-stand step, or rope-ladder rung. With this precaution, a handhold or foothold that suddenly gives way does not yield a dangerous or tragic result.

One other note on safe, comfortable tree-stand use. Bowhunters sometimes elect to put up stands in fairly remote areas where deer are abundant and other archers are seldom seen. To carry a bulky, full-sized rigid commercial stand a long distance over rough terrain, always tote it on backpack straps sold at archery or sporting goods stores for this purpose. Some of the better stands come from manufacturers complete with backpacking straps to facilitate easy carrying.

Using shoulder straps leaves at least one hand free to steady a hunter on uneven ground and lets him comfortably hand-carry other gear like a bow. In most cases, an archer can also shoot a bow with a back-packed tree stand in place if he happens to bump into a deer while walking to a stand location. Such an event is not unlikely in many good deer-hunting areas.

Tree-stand hunting for deer is safe, effective, and enjoyable when properly and systematically pursued. Every archery deer hunter should be constantly on the lookout for situations where stand hunting might pay off, and should never hesitate to use a stand when this promises to be the very best technique to use. If a deer exhibits predictable movement patterns, the animal can usually be ambushed by an archer with ample patience and adequate tree-stand hunting skill.

Other Hunting Methods / 17

The author's hunting partner, Bob Smith, jumped this gigantic Boone and Crockett Alaskan caribou out of its rock-protected resting place and bow-shot the animal at a full run less than 20 yards away. If no other shooting strategy is possible, jumpshooting can work like a charm!

ALTHOUGH STALKING, stillhunting, and stand hunting are the primary methods used by successful bowhunters, an innovative and dedicated archer uses other techniques as well to put deer in the bag. Such techniques must be carefully applied to unique situations where the standard methods will not work as well. The complete bowhunting deer enthusiast adds everything to his bag of tricks that he can find out about or think of to boost his versatility at consistently bagging deer.

The following methods take deer on those occasions when no other technique will work as well. What every archer must do is consider the standard bowhunting methods first, and then turn to alternatives if normally practiced deer-getting techniques are not likely to get the job done. In addition to being effective, these methods are also fun to use because they provide a novel and interesting change of pace from the norm.

Jumpshooting

As a general rule, it is advisable to wait for a stationary shot at a deer to help ensure a solid, vital hit. However, there are certain types of terrain and certain specific situations where traditional bow-shooting is simply not possible. In such cases, a flexible bowhunter can often "wing it" and shoot deer that leap up and bound or race away.

Let's say you're hunting a warm, brush-choked area where the deer are hard-hunted and prone to bed right at daylight. You spot a dandy buck slipping along a hillside well before sunrise, and watch it bed down beneath a small, brush-rimmed shelf of rock. The wind is right for a circuitous stalk around the deer, putting you on the little shelf right above it. However, once there you know you won't be able to see the buck to get a shot unless you actually jump it out of its bed. Do you walk away discouraged, or do you give the setup a whirl? As far as I'm concerned, the only answer is giving the setup a whirl.

(Left and above) Driven deer are generally alert and moving, making shots with a bow difficult at best.

You make your stalk and eventually tiptoe out on the shelf rock less than 10 feet from your quarry. You can't see it, but you know it's there. You pick up a fist-sized rock, heave it below the buck's position, and grab the bowstring to shoot. Nothing happens. You throw another rock, this time a little closer to the deer. Still nothing. Your third rock smacks the very bush the animal is lying under, and the brush explodes as the buck leaps up and charges away around the sidehill. You draw, swing in front of the deer, and let go of the arrow as the animal bounds between two widely spaced bushes. The shaft and the deer both disappear in a cloud of dust, and you sit down nervously to wait before checking out the result. Thirty minutes later, you are gutting out your buck, which took the arrow a bit far back through the liver and ran about 200 yards before piling up.

The foregoing scenario is not all that unusual in some parts of bowhunting country. The key to success is having the confidence to capitalize on a situation and also having the shooting skill to make the shot count.

Shooting at moving deer is absolutely *abhorred* by some writers and bowhunters who feel such tactics tend to wound too many animals. As far as I'm concerned, a bowhunter with some practiced snap-shooting ability and razor-keen broadheads will not lose any more deer by shooting at close-range, running targets than by shooting in other situations. Sloppy shooting on stationary deer and deer that "jump string" account for most wounded animals. Solidly hit deer are almost always recoverable if a bowhunter uses extremely sharp broadheads and learns how to skillfully track and trail. In addition, a jumpshooting bowhunter who is truly worried about poor hits can always put a game tracker unit on his bow. Shots at moving deer are seldom effective past 20 or 25 yards, anyway, and a jumpshooter never needs a second shot because unhit running animals are long gone after the first. For these reasons, a game tracker is fine for shooting at deer bounced out of their beds.

Becoming fairly good at jumpshooting takes specialized practice. Shooting at flying birds, like pheasants and ducks, is excellent practice, and so is bow-shooting fish like carp and suckers. Some bowhunters shoot at old auto tires rolled downhill past them by a friend, and others at hand-thrown styrofoam targets normally used for bird-shooting practice. Shooting at moving targets quickly teaches a bowhunter to use his bow much like a shotgun, swinging the sight bead ahead of the target and dumping the bowstring unceremoniously as the bow is still swinging. On a close-range, up-and-running deer, such shooting is really not impossibly tough. I kill at least one animal every year this way, and limit my shots to 20 yards or less to prevent horrendously long leads and the chance of misplaced hits.

In a few bowhunting areas, jumpshooting is about the *only* feasible method because cover is uniformly dense and deer always know that you are coming. The ones that do not run or slink away at once usually stick tight until a hunter is almost on top of them, and then leap from cover in a flurry of flying feet and flopping ears. The bowhunter prepared for such shooting can take deer with surprising consistency.

Drive Hunting

I've always regarded deer drives as the very *last* resort because driven deer are invariably alert, wound-up, and terribly difficult to hit with an arrow. However, in ultra-dense rainforest country or southern swampy jungles, driving deer is sometimes the only feasible way to produce open shots.

(Right) A commercial deer call sometimes lures animals to point-blank bow-shooting ranges—especially in heavy cover.

A bowhunting drive requires at least five or six archers for best results. Several stand hunters assume positions along routes that driven deer might take, preferably sitting high above the ground where alert animals are not as likely to see them draw and shoot. Several more archers walk out patches of cover to stir deer up and get them moving. Deer drives work best on whitetail inhabiting small, isolated patches of cover that they have to leave when pushed hard by hunters.

At its best, drive hunting requires an intimate knowledge of local deer and the terrain they inhabit. There are generally dozens of ways animals can leave an area when pushed by hunters, and only careful study of deer habits can tell a bowhunter which draws, trails, and saddles animals are most prone to use when running or slipping away from archers. This knowledge lets bowhunters erect stands in productive places and reap full benefit of the drive.

A driven deer is fully conscious of danger, edging along or running full-out on taut, nervous muscles. If it moves past a stand, it is highly prone to jump string even if the archer is lucky enough to draw and get off a deliberate shot in the first place. Plenty of deer are taken on well-orchestrated drives each and every year, but this method should be "left on the back burner" unless it is the only feasible way to hunt a particular piece of deer-rich habitat. In addition to the bow-shooting difficulties associated with this technique, it also requires several hunters to move through the woods with little or no chance of getting off shots of their own. Occasionally, drivers slip up on deer, but most driven terrain is too noisy and too dense to let the walkers do more than simply dog out the thickets for those waiting hopefully on stand.

Calling Deer

Most deer species can be coaxed into bow-shooting range at one time of the year or another if an archer knows how to do it. Calling deer to the bow has one major drawback—the animals moving toward the call are actually hunting the hunter, using their marvelous eyes, ears, and noses to detect what is making the sound that is luring them in. Unless a calling setup is absolutely right, this makes unobtrusively drawing a bow and shooting an arrow extremely difficult to pull off, and also boosts the chances that a deer will jump string and avoid the arrow or suffer a less-than-ideal hit.

Different types of deer require different calling techniques. Many blacktail, mule deer, and whitetail will move toward a properly blown commercial deer

call that imitates the bleat of a fawn in pain or terror. Blacktail are the most consistent responders, often running full-out to a bowhunter in heavy coastal rainforest terrain. Mouth-blown deer calls work best in very heavy cover where neither deer nor hunter can see very far.

Antler Rattling

The best way to call in big whitetail bucks is rattling together antlers during the fall rutting period, simulating the sound of bucks fighting over a doe in heat. Rattling is best accomplished with a pair of heavy, strong deer antlers that will not break when clashed together.

Make your rattling antlers by tying a couple of well-matched shed antlers together at the bases with an 18-inch nylon or leather cord, or by cutting the antlers apart from a big buck rack that has been taken by a hunter. The cord keeps antlers together so they can be hung from a nail or peg, and also allows them to be carried in and out of the woods while conveniently slung over a shoulder.

Rattling works best in areas with balanced buck/doe ratios because such areas do not generally have enough does to fully satisfy all the bucks. When antlers are clashed together repeatedly, sex-starved bucks move in to get a piece of the action. Although rattling up bucks was made famous in Texas, this technique works fairly well in many parts of the country where archery deer seasons overlap with the whitetail rutting period.

Bugling Elk

Perhaps the most in vogue archery calling technique these days is bugling bull elk. Because most archery elk seasons occur in September when elk reach their peak mating frenzy, bulls can be called to the bow by an archer who knows how.

Basically, an elk bugle is employed in two important ways. First, it is used to get responses from bulls as a hunter moves along, allowing the hunter to pinpoint bulls and move in for the kill. Second, bugling is used to

Rattling antlers can attract big whitetail bucks at the peak of the late-fall rutting period.

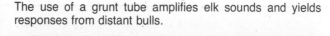

The use of a grunt tube amplifies elk sounds and yields responses from distant bulls.

Even young bull elk respond to well-blown elk calls. This fat spike bull was shot at less than 20 yards after being called by a turkey-diaphragm elk bugle.

How to Make an Elk Bugle

actually challenge and call in rut-crazy bulls that are belligerent and aggressive toward other bulls nearby. A bowhunter who is really good can set up point-blank shots at nice bulls that come stamping in with red, rolling eyes and angry, slobbering mouths.

There are several excellent elk calls currently on the market—calls that more or less imitate the multiple-note bugle of a rutting bull elk. Other elk calls imitate the grunt or chuckle of a bull, another vocalization bull elk often make when challenging other bulls and herding up their cows. In addition, a bowhunter can make his own simple elk bugle with a minimum of time and money—a bugle that imitates the whistling of a angry, rutting bull. For instructions on making a do-it-yourself elk bugle, see the accompanying photos and captions, courtesy of *Petersen's Hunting* magazine. For further information on elk calling, refer to Chapter 24.

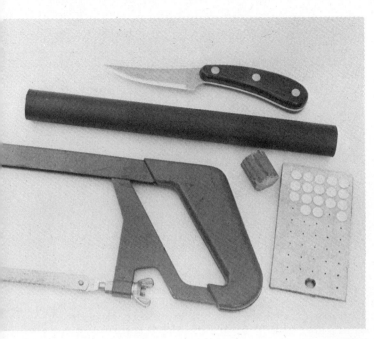

(Left) Tools and materials for making an elk bugle are inexpensive and easy to obtain—a sharp knife, common hacksaw, 12-inch piece of ¾-inch plastic water pipe, 1-inch length of wooden dowel of the proper diameter to slip snugly inside the pipe, and one or two thumbtacks. (Photo sequence courtesy of *Petersen's Hunting* magazine)

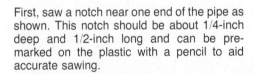
First, saw a notch near one end of the pipe as shown. This notch should be about 1/4-inch deep and 1/2-inch long and can be pre-marked on the plastic with a pencil to aid accurate sawing.

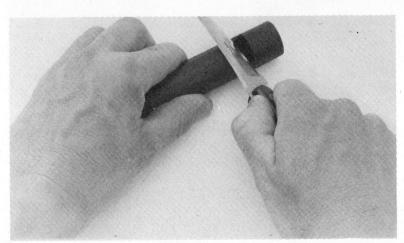

Smooth out the ragged edges of the sawed bugle notch with the knife, being careful not to make it any larger than it already is.

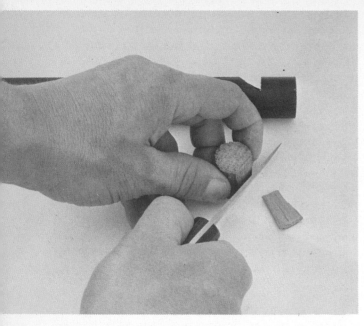

Shave approximately ⅛-inch off one side of the wooden plug as shown, then carefully smooth out the resulting surface with the knife until it is perfectly flat.

Press the plug into the notched end of the bugle with flat side up. If the plug is too large to fit, shave a little wood off the round sides with your knife until it slips in snugly. If the plug is slightly too small in diameter, a layer or two of plastic tape around the rounded (not flat) side of the plug will snug it up.

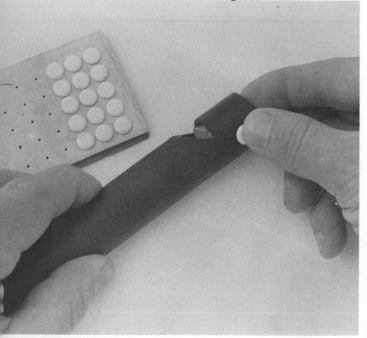

(Left) Once the best tune point of the plug is found, pin it in place by pressing a thumb tack through the pipe on one or both sides. Your elk bugle is ready to use!

(Right) To blow the bugle and tune it properly, cover the open end with your hand and blow through the other end, starting softly at first, increasing air volume, and then dropping off again in air volume rapidly. Move the wooden plug in and out until a point is reached where three full, strong notes are easily blown. This point should be near where the plug is flush with the end of the bugle.

Calling Moose

Moose become even more cantankerous than elk during their October mating season. A bowhunter can literally bring a bull moose into his lap if he accurately imitates the sound of a cow moaning seductively. This moan is generally produced by skillful bowhunters with the mouth alone—to my knowledge there are no commercial moose calls available to hunters. Expert old-time bowhunters, like Fred Bear, founder of Bear Archery, have often called moose by amplifying cow moans through a simple birch-bark funnel held to the mouth. Modern bowhunters can easily do the same using a piece of cardboard or newspaper rolled into a funnel.

Moose in rut can also be called in close by rattling antlers together or slowly pouring water into a lake, pond, or stream. The antler sounds work the same as they do on whitetail, luring in males that want to grab up a cow for themselves. The pouring water imitates the sound of a receptive cow urinating in water—a noise that can absolutely drive mature bulls crazy with lust. The moose is an extremely dense-minded deer at mating time. I once saw a nice bull cover ½-mile of ground to investigate the sounds of a hunting guide chopping wood with an axe. The sounds resembled antlers batting together, and the addle-pated bull came trotting in to check over the action.

The most successful deer-calling bowhunters carefully choose calling sites which give them ample opportunity to draw a bow and shoot without being seen. When possible, calling from a tree stand improves a hunter's odds of getting off shots at alert, incoming animals. If you are calling elk, moose, or other deer which require you to move around and quickly set up on the ground, always eyeball the terrain and stand or kneel behind a bush, tree, or similar cover that will hide your movement as you draw to take a shot. Remember, called-in deer are looking for you, and they have the excellent senses to spot you if you are haphazardly set up in an open or poorly chosen place.

Baiting Deer

Baiting is not a generally used technique with bowhunters—primarily because it is strictly illegal in many parts of the country. However, a few states do allow deer-baiting, and in these places the method can produce shots when no other strategy will.

Deer, like most other animals, have a weak spot for tasty, easy-to-get-at food. Special favorites are yellow corn, wheat, barley, and alfalfa hay. No matter what the deer species, good grub scattered near a stand will invariably draw in deer that have learned where they can find a free, easy meal.

In addition to food, certain minerals also lure in deer. Salt blocks put out for cattle attract them because they have a taste and a physical need for salt. Natural mineral licks with salt, sulfur, or other tasty substances in the mud or rock also attract a variety of deer. I have seen muddy mineral licks in moose and elk country that were literally open-pit mines from years upon years of deer eating up the good-tasting mud. Some are craters 20 yards across and 3 or 4 feet deep! Occasionally, mineral springs, when found in deer country, attract animals regularly. When it is legal to hunt over salt blocks, natural mineral licks, or mineral springs, these hotspots can pay off big for a patient tree-stand bowhunter or ground-sitter.

Other Bowhunting Methods

An imaginative bowhunter regards deer hunting as a problem-solving mission—the problem being how to effectively bag game in various bowhunting circumstances. Sometimes, the solution does not allow normal bowhunting techniques. An archer must devise special strategies despite the difficulty of doing so.

One bowhunting pal of mine takes whitetail deer in his part of the country by canoeing down sluggish sloughs and creeks between dense walls of ultra-thick foliage. He knows that deer drink at least once a day, and keeps on canoeing until he surprises a deer on a sandbar or mud-bank and manages to get off an effective shot. You won't read about this particular bowhunting technique in most deer-hunting textbooks, but it works best for my friend in the deer thickets near his home.

Bowhunting off horseback can be an exceedingly effective technique in big country where an archer must cover lots of ground to locate deer. I personally prefer to walk instead, but a bowhunter who will not or cannot walk long distances can take game by using a horse. Moose and elk are especially suited to bowhunting from horseback because they inhabit large country and because they can sometimes be approached within bow range. A hunter on a horse does not look like a hunter, and I know several archers who have shot elk and moose while still sitting in the saddle. More often, a bowhunter will spot game from horseback and make a final stalk on foot. Not everyone has access to horses, and deer in areas regularly hunted by horsemen are often scared to death of all beasts of burden. However, this hunting method does have merit in some situations.

Although a few states allow archers to hunt and shoot from vehicles, I would strongly recommend against this procedure for aesthetic and safety reasons. In areas where game is used to regular vehicular traffic, shooting from a vehicle can take deer if the animals decide to stand around and gawk. I personally dislike vehicle hunting, even where it is legal, because it requires little if any hunting ability and makes so-called "hunters" look like Neanderthals instead of skillful experts. Bear in mind that road hunting is positively forbidden in most states, partly because sharp broadheads and moving vehicles can be a dangerous combination. Keep this danger factor in mind before you do

Slipping along silently in a canoe can produce bow shots at deer near the water's edge. Famous bowhunter Fred Bear practices his canoeing technique here.

decide to hop in the back of your pickup truck and have your wife drive you over hill and dale.

One novel mule-deer hunting technique I recently ran across was being practiced by a bowhunting outfitter along the perimeter of a lush alfalfa field. This enterprising fellow had absolutely no trees or brush in his hunting area—only rolling, grassy hills dotted with occasional fields of grain and hay. As a result, his clients could not take advantage of a tree stand or ground blind, and had terrible trouble trying to stalk deer in the billiard-table terrain. With mulies aplenty and no standard way to bag one, the outfitter finally drove his tractor out to his favorite alfalfa deer field and dug a series of deep pits along the edge where deer most often entered. The wind was normally right for taking deer in these pit blinds, and the outfitter was enjoying excellent success as his clients hunkered down to wait for deer in the evening and raised up to shoot when animals walked nearby. A pit blind is a cold, damp place to sit, but it sure does work when prevailing breezes are right!

For best results, archers should master as many different standard deer-hunting techniques as they possibly can. In addition, they should devise unique strategies whenever the standard approaches will not do the trick. The best deer-hunting archers are pragmatic and flexible about bowhunting methods, using whatever will legally take animals the best.

Shooting at Deer/18

THE ACTUAL act of aiming and shooting at a deer takes only a few short seconds, but this single movement will determine the outcome of many weeks of careful pre-hunt preparation plus many hours of thoughtful scouting and hunting. As a result, a bowhunter should learn to shoot as well as he possibly can in a variety of situations as outlined in Chapters 8 and 10, and should also give some serious consideration to anticipated shooting situations on real-live deer.

Nothing can fully prepare you for the excitement-charged moment when you actually have the chance to shoot at a deer. At this moment, adrenaline shoots through your body and nervous shock is likely to cloud your brain. A deer is actually within your effective target-shooting range, and all you have to do is put an arrow through its vitals! Unfortunately, actually doing this is seldom as easy as it sounds.

Only the experience of shooting at deer will fully teach a bowhunter the ins and outs of this all-important move. However, you can at least partially prepare by considering the following facts. Using this knowledge, you will be able to shoot at the proper time, aim in the correct place, and at least have a decent chance of making the shot pay off with deer meat in the freezer.

When Should You Shoot?

When to shoot is a fairly complicated consideration because every deer encounter is a totally unique situation. However, there are basic principles which apply no matter who you are or what the individual shooting setup happens to be.

As a general rule, a bowhunter should never shoot if he thinks he can get closer or set up a higher-percentage shot. It is always easier to hit a 20-yard opposed to a 50-yard deer, all else being equal. A foot hunter or stand hunter who sets up a long shot should evaluate the situation carefully and get closer if he thinks he can. If the longer shot is most probably the only shot a hunter is likely to get, he should go for it and hope for the best.

Similarly, if a buck's body is veiled by branches that offer only small holes to shoot through, it is better to wait for a wide-open shot if such a shot is likely to materialize. If the shot is not likely to get any better, an archer should try his luck then and there after saying a little prayer.

There are seldom clear-cut answers for the decision of when to take a shot. It is a judgment call all the way—a call that is sometimes wrong no matter how much prior experience you have. A wide-open animal at 40 yards might wander off or smell you and spook if you decide to hold off for a closer shot, and then again, it might walk right into your lap. A 20-yard deer partially obscured by branches might step to the right and give you a beautiful open shot, or it might sashay to the left and eliminate the fairly good shot you opted to pass up. A bowhunter with experience learns deer habits and the limits of his own abilities to the point where he can make most of these judgment calls pay off, but a certain percentage always go sour no matter what.

A bowhunter who practices shooting a lot prior to season can get a pretty good handle on how far away he is likely to be deadly on deer. Know your effective shooting range to help you decide when to shoot. If you are sitting in an elevated stand and a deer walks past a 30-yard landmark, there is no point in hoping for a 20-yard shot if you can hit a grapefruit at 30 yards each and every time. If the shot is only a 50-50 proposition for you, you'll have to decide whether the deer is likely to come toward you and give you a 75- or 100-percent shot at success. Similarly, if a buck stops 15 yards from you behind a bush with a 4-inch opening directly in line with the animal's lungs, you'll have to decide whether or not to wait for a clearer shot based on your ability to hit a 4-inch-wide target at 15 yards. Some hunters can, and many cannot. Realistically assessing your own bow-shooting ability will help tremendously as you decide when and when not to shoot at deer.

Aside from assessing shooting distance and your own bow-shooting ability, you must always have a realistic shot at a deer's vital zone. If you don't, you should wait for such a shot. Vital zones are discussed later in this chapter. A surprisingly large part of a deer's body is vital if you are using a sharp broadhead, but shooting at a deer's neck, lower legs, or shoulder blade for want of a better shot is always a cardinal error. Wait until you can slip in a vital shot, or let the animal go until another day. Be sure to study the shot-placement illustrations with this chapter to help you decide when a particular shot possibility is vital and when it is not.

Let's assume you have somehow maneuvered within reasonable shooting range of a deer and can clearly see a vital area like the ribcage. The next thing to consider is whether or not the animal will let you draw and shoot. As mentioned in Chapter 14, a deer has exceptionally keen eyes, and unless they are completely blocked off by foliage, a log, a rock, or another natural

Shooting at a deer requires a practiced sense of timing as well as target-hitting ability.

object, the deer will probably see you draw even if it is exactly broadside or slightly angling away. A deer that is quartering away at a fairly sharp angle will not see you draw and shoot, and a deer sharply below you is not likely to see the movement, either. Never draw on a relaxed, unalerted animal unless its eyes are blocked off or its body position creates a blind spot in its effective field of view.

What about the deer that has you spotted, has its big, cupped ears swept forward alertly, and has its muscles bunched to run? Again, this is a judgment call with no pat solution. If the animal is only mildly disturbed by a slight noise you made or another deer's suspicious behavior, it might calm down if you remain frozen for a few long minutes. If the animal is thoroughly alerted and merely lingering to double-check its better judgment, it might be best to try a shot. At least 50 percent of the time, a deer that has you zeroed in will bolt before you can get the bowstring halfway back. However, a surprising number of alerted deer will stand pat and let a hunter shoot. After a shot, an alerted deer sometimes jumps the bowstring, but the shot is surely worth a try. I have nailed several elk, moose, blacktail deer, and mule deer that had me pegged, yet stood like statues as I drew, aimed, and watched the arrow sail into their vitals. I always cease and desist from shooting if I think there's a chance the target animal will calm down again, but as often as not a deer boring holes through you with its eyes presents a now-or-never shooting opportunity.

Where to Aim on Deer

No matter whether it's a big, 1500-pound moose or a smallish 100-pound blacktail, the animal will go down like a load of bricks if hit in the proper place by a well-designed, razor-keen bowhunting broadhead. A broadhead normally kills in one of two ways—either by instantly ruining a vital organ, or by cutting plenty of arteries or veins to promote the rapid loss of blood.

The primary target to aim for is the chest cavity. It extends nearly to the back of the ribcage, and houses both the lungs and the heart plus all major arteries branching away from the heart. An arrow placed here will usually hit one of these vital organs, and even if it doesn't, it will ruin the breathing action of the chest for a quick, clean kill anyway.

A hit dead-center in the chest will skewer one or both lungs. Normally the lungs will collapse, which in turn will cease the oxygen flow to the brain and result in death in less than a minute. A hit low in the chest cavity is likely to hit the heart or huge arteries branching off of it, which stops the heart quickly, robs the brain of blood, and again drops a deer in less than a minute. A chest-cavity hit that misses lungs, heart, and major arteries will puncture the breathing cavity, causing the lungs to collapse and producing a death almost as fast as if the lungs were actually punctured.

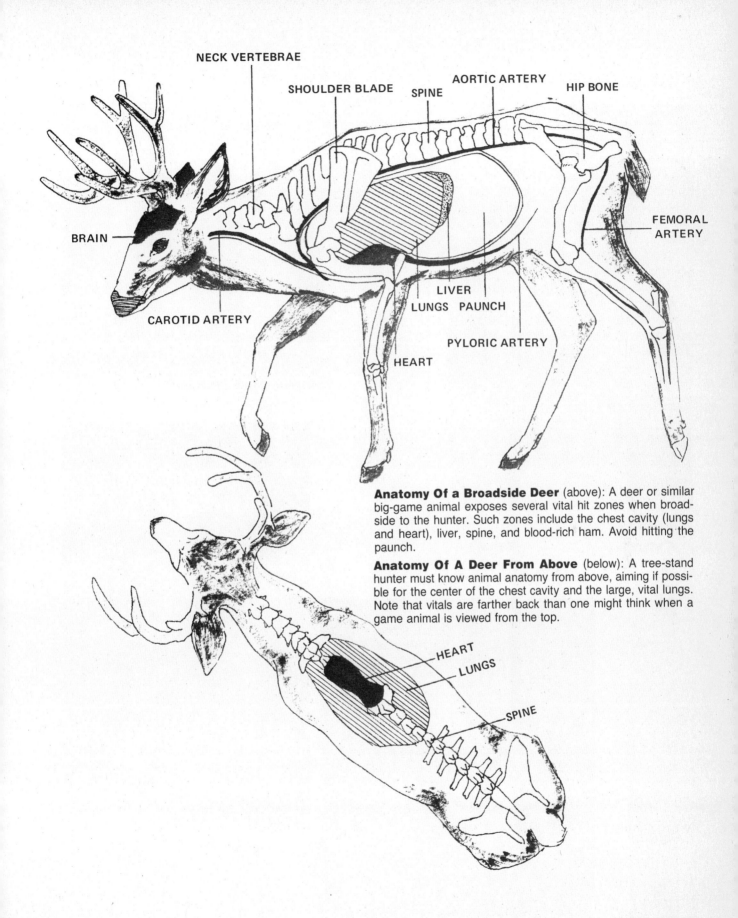

NECK VERTEBRAE

SHOULDER BLADE

SPINE

AORTIC ARTERY

HIP BONE

BRAIN

FEMORAL ARTERY

CAROTID ARTERY

LIVER

LUNGS   PAUNCH

PYLORIC ARTERY

HEART

Anatomy Of a Broadside Deer (above): A deer or similar big-game animal exposes several vital hit zones when broadside to the hunter. Such zones include the chest cavity (lungs and heart), liver, spine, and blood-rich ham. Avoid hitting the paunch.

Anatomy Of A Deer From Above (below): A tree-stand hunter must know animal anatomy from above, aiming if possible for the center of the chest cavity and the large, vital lungs. Note that vitals are farther back than one might think when a game animal is viewed from the top.

HEART

LUNGS

SPINE

Aiming Point: Chest-On Quartering

Aiming Point: Broadside

Aiming Point:
Angling
Slightly Away

Aiming Point: Quartering Away

Aiming Point: Chest On

Aiming Point: Rear End

The author dropped this fine record-sized blacktail buck with a 60-yard shot in the left ham. The deer was feeding directly away, allowing nothing but a long rear-end shot. In this case, the correct choice was obviously taking the shot.

The chest cavity can be hit from virtually any angle except from directly behind, and if a bow is powerful enough it will often drive an arrow into the chest even if it has to pass through the ham and paunch areas first.

Most fringe areas around the chest cavity are not especially good places to hit. The shoulder blade is a big, flat bone that is virtually impossible to penetrate with a broadhead. Stay away from it. The extreme bottom of the brisket is fat, meat, and bone with no vital tissue at all. The area above the chest cavity is composed of both vital and nonvital tissue. A direct hit in the spine will drop a deer on the spot because the spinal cord is ruined. A hit immediately below the spine will sometimes clip the aortic artery for lots of bleeding and a very quick kill. However, there is a large band of nonvital muscle between the spine and chest cavity that will take arrow hits without killing a deer at all. Many bowhunters who hit broadside deer behind the shoulder swear up and down that these "lung-shot" animals run for miles, but in reality they are hit in the muscle above the lungs and below the spine and normally recover completely with little or no discomfort.

A hit directly behind the chest cavity can be a good one if it skewers the liver. This large organ filters all the blood in a deer's body, and will bleed a deer out within 10 or 15 minutes if the hit is a solid one. Unfortunately, many hits too far back miss the liver and penetrate the paunch instead.

The paunch shot is one of the very worst a bow-hunter can make. Aside from one big artery that runs lengthwise through the lower paunch, most paunch tissue is not quickly vital no matter how sharp the arrowhead used happens to be. Bowhunters who accidentally hit the paunch can still recover their animals, but seldom without considerable trailing and tracking work.

Solid arrow hits in the rear end are amazingly effective on deer of all kinds. Many bowhunters scoff at "butt shots," but I'm here to tell you that they are highly effective because the ham region is extremely rich in large arteries and veins. A major femoral artery runs down the inside of each hind leg, and dozens of smaller arteries branch off from these major blood canals. If you cannot set up a chest-cavity shot, you'll make a mistake if you pass up a solid ham shot. If your broadheads are sharp, this hit will drop a deer within a few minutes—often much faster. I have hit them in the ham from many angles and have never lost a ham-shot deer in my life. Always aim at the biggest part of the ham that's visible—this is where the largest arteries are.

I hate the neck shot with a passion. Although the big carotid artery and the big jugular vein both course through the neck, there is lots of non-vital tissue around these pencil-sized blood canals. An arrow hit in the windpipe will not kill a deer for days and leaves absolutely no blood to follow. A dead-center hit in the spinal part of the neck will poleax a deer, but the chances of hitting the neck spine solidly or clipping the carotid artery or jugular vein are honestly fairly slim. The neck is a relatively small place to aim anyway, and at least 95 percent of it is nonvital tissue.

A deer's brain is a small, well-protected organ. If hit precisely, the brain will cease to function and an animal will collapse like a big sack of wheat. However, a brain shot is only advisable if no other shot presents itself. I've brained a couple of deer in the past, and this hit is a spectacularly good one. However, hitting the fist-sized target requires pinpoint shot placement and a bow sufficiently powerful to plow through cranial bone. Even with top-penetrating broadheads, bows under 65 or 70 pounds are not consistently effective on such shots.

The only rationale I can think of for shooting at a deer's head is when the animal offers absolutely no other option. The deer I have hit in the head were both peeking at me over heavy cover at fairly close range, and since I knew that no other shot would be possible, I aimed between their eyes. At least half the deer I've tried this on have turned and run away, but these two unfortunates stood their ground and took their medicine. They never knew what hit them!

Study the shot-placement illustrations on pages 179, 180, and 181 to get a good idea where to aim on deer in various body positions and various situations. There is always one *best* place to aim, and you should know exactly where this place happens to be for consistent kills.

How to Shoot at Deer

When shooting, always pick out one particular aiming point prior to drawing back your bow. As best you can, pay strict attention to the good shooting form you learned earlier in this book. If you have practiced a lot prior to bow season, this form should be almost automatic. However, be sure to aim precisely and follow through your shot to ensure accuracy.

The big mistake most beginning bowhunters make is shooting haphazardly at the whole deer instead of at a particular vital spot. Unfortunately, the exact middle of a broadside deer is where most haphazard shots are directed, and the exact middle is always the nonvital paunch. It's extremely easy to flail away without precise aiming—especially when you get excited—but such shooting results in poor hits or out-and-out misses guaranteed to sober you up fast. Try to remember bow-shooting basics anytime you find yourself ready to draw and aim.

Controlling Your Excitement

Buck fever can be a powerful thing. Rifle hunters are afflicted with this malady regularly, but bowhunters are especially prone because of close-range shots.

A case of the nervous shakes in the presence of game can cause all sorts of shooting nightmares to come true. Some bowhunters have reported being physically unable to pull back a bow at all in the presence of game, and many others get so wobbly they cannot keep the arrow on the arrow rest or aim solidly on target. After a shot is missed, some beginning bowhunters cannot even remember shooting at a deer, and the ones who can seldom know exactly what went awry.

The only sure cure for buck fever is lots and lots of bowhunting experience. The more time a person spends around deer, the calmer he tends to get when the time comes to take a shot. The thing to remember if you get excited is that this is a perfectly natural reaction. If you blow a few shots because of excitement, do not get discouraged or depressed. Even the best and most experienced bowhunters get excited when they see or shoot at a deer—if they didn't get excited, they'd probably be playing tennis, racing cars, or doing something else that *did* arouse their interest and excitement. Experienced bowhunters have simply learned to *control* their excitement and this is something a beginner can learn as well with enough time spent in the field.

Other Reasons for Missed Shots

Aside from excitement, bowhunters usually miss shots because they shoot at the wrong time or lack confidence in their ability to hit a deer. When to shoot has already been discussed earlier in this chapter, but

Shooting through a wire fence is a common test for deer-hunting archers.

freezes off the animal and lets go of the bowstring unceremoniously. This problem can be solved if a bowhunter recognizes it and has a good heart-to-heart talk with himself about his basic shooting ability. He must tell himself that shooting at targets and shooting at deer are really not all that different. He must somehow transfer some of his target-shooting confidence to shooting in the woods, convincing himself to bear down and concentrate on deer the same as he does on bull's-eyes. Most bowhunters with "deer panic" lose this malady after dropping a deer or two because their confidence levels go up.

One thing every bowhunter should realize from the outset is the fact that *everyone* misses shots at deer. As often as not, "deer panic" sets in after an archer misses a few shots and then develops a poor mental attitude. Frustration, dejection, and tension after missing shots tend to compound the missing problem. As in target panic, "deer panic" can be avoided entirely if you relax and enjoy every outing instead of flogging and chastising, yourself over missed shots. Bowhunting is supposed to be *fun*, so don't take it so seriously that you let the pressure to perform short-circuit your basic ability to hit deer once you set up feasible shots.

Shooting at a deer with another deer behind it can be risky business. If possible, wait until the target animal moves away from other deer before releasing an arrow.

we still need to cover the problem of mustering shooting confidence.

Many bowhunters who are deadly on targets cannot seem to hit a deer to save their lives. I call this inability "deer panic" because it is a lot like the "target panic" discussed in Chapter 8. The shooter simply cannot aim solidly on a living target because he is somehow convinced he won't hit the animal, anyway. As a result he either shoots in the general vicinity of the deer or

Special Shooting Problems

As a bowhunter perfects his shooting art, he learns to cope with various special shooting problems sometimes encountered in the field. Such problems must be solved on the spur of the moment or deer usually get away unscathed.

Learning to shoot past obstacles like bushes and tree limbs has already been discussed in Chapter 10. Other

(Left and above) To shoot or not to shoot? The deer with the tangled limbs in front of it would probably be impossible to hit in the chest cavity, but an arrow would slide through the grass in front of the other deer and neatly penetrate the chest. Bowhunters learn to make such judgment calls through trial and error.

less conventional obstacles can also hamper shooting performance unless a bowhunter figures out how to avoid them with his arrow.

In many hunting areas, fences can be a real bugaboo for archers. What do you do if a nice buck or tasty doe stands directly behind a wire fence and presents an otherwise perfect shot? Obviously, you try to shoot between the wires if you can see them clearly. If poor light or shooting distance prevent a clear view of wires, I generally shoot at the deer as if the fence wasn't there and hope for the best. The odds are strongly in a shooter's favor in such a situation, but I have hit wires on fences several times. It's a risk a bowhunter should take, and if an arrow hits wire it generally careens harmlessly up, down, or to the side instead of mis-hitting a deer. Don't panic—nine times out of 10 the arrow will fly through untouched.

What happens if another deer blocks a clear shot or stands behind your target animal? This is a far more serious problem than shooting through a fence because the wrong shooting decision might result in hitting the wrong animal or crippling more than one deer. A bowhunter should never take a shot that jeopardizes an unwanted deer or prevents a good shot at a wanted deer. Generally, deer will mill around until a clear shot at the target animal is possible. Remember also that a hunting arrow tipped with a proper broadhead will often whistle through the target animal like a hot knife going through butter. This can jeopardize another deer behind the one you are shooting at, and there have been several documented cases of two deer being killed outright with one shot. I personally killed two Spanish goats with one shot on a bet a few years ago, waiting for two big 150-pound billies to line up exactly and then shooting both through the lungs with a heavy, fast-flying arrow from a 75-pound bow. This stunt was perfectly legal, and both goats now hang on my trophy wall. Remember the superb penetrating ability of hunting arrows—if you don't, the local game warden might get mighty suspicious when two deer charge out of the woods near your stand and *both* drop.

One thing a bowhunter learns as he goes along is exactly what constitutes a shooting obstacle and what does not. For example, an arrow careens wildly when it collides with tree branches or brush, but the same arrow flies neatly through a barrier of brittle grass without significant deflection. A beginning hunter who has a deer at close range behind a wall of dry grass might hold off for a better shot, but an experienced archer knows there *isn't* any better shot and smokes the animal right through the grass. Similarly, truly dry, brittle twigs that are small in diameter often fail to deflect a hunting arrow's flight. The twigs and needles on a long-dead pine bough usually fall into this category. By contrast, small hardwood twigs often withstand arrow impact and ruin a shot. Lots of shooting experience afield teaches an observant bowhunter such things and greatly improves his ability to know when and where not to shoot.

Shooting at deer is partly art and partly science. Some aspects of this quick but important move are a matter of subjective judgment; others should be based on solid, proven fact. A serious bowhunter learns the science of knowing where to hit a deer, when a deer is able to see him draw, and other cut-and-dried facts about proper shooting. From there, he tries to exercise the art of good judgment, second-guessing deer as best he can and making snap decisions based on hunting intuition. At its best, such deer-shooting ability puts animals in the bag time after time after time!

After the Shot /19

THERE IS nothing more thrilling or gratifying than seeing your arrow hit a deer. All the hours of preparation, planning, and actual hunting pay off big at this moment, because you have actually accomplished what you originally set out to do. However, the hunt is not officially over until the deer is stretched out on the ground, and oftentimes there is a lot of legwork to be done before you can begin the field-dressing chore.

A successful bowhunter learns to shoot and hunt well, but he also learns a time-tested procedure for finding deer once an arrow hits the mark. Because an arrow does not have the energy to actually lift a deer upside-down and point its hooves permanently toward the sky, the majority of arrow-hit deer run or walk away after being hit—even if they are dead on their feet. Even a well-placed rifle bullet often produces "death runs" of 100 yards or more, but such runs are never a cause for alarm. To recover his prize once a shot is made, a bowhunter must proceed systematically according to a predetermined plan. Here is basically how it should be done.

Have You Actually Scored a Hit?

A bowhunter should alertly watch and listen once he releases an arrow to determine where that arrow hit. If the shot is immediately followed by a shower of sparks and a loud metal clang, the hunter knows he has hit the fence wire he was trying to shoot through. If the arrow makes a sharp thud and the hunter sees it quivering in a tree 2 feet above where the deer was standing, there can't be much doubt about where it hit, either. However, things are not always so obvious.

Sometimes a bowhunter actually sees an arrow hit a deer, and other times he merely hears an impact sound that promises venison in the bag. A hunter should look and listen to determine if he actually hit the deer he shot at. An arrow protruding from a deer leaves little doubt, but more subtle clues also tell an archer how his shooting attempt fared.

Normally, an arrow hitting a deer makes one of two sounds. If it collides with bone, it crunches solidly like a hardball thrown against a sidewalk. If it penetrates the ribcage or solid muscle, it plunks like a watermelon being tapped hard with a finger. Occasionally arrows pass through deer with little or no sound, especially on light fringe hits or hits in the paunch area.

Aside from actually seeing or hearing an arrow hit, you can often tell a lot merely by how the target deer reacts after the shot. If it prances alertly, mills in confusion, or gawks wildly around, it has probably not been solidly hit. If it runs away in normal fashion, it may be hit, and then again, it may not. If it charges off with body held low to the ground in a mad, frantically scrambling gait, it is probably hit through the heart or lungs. This hit is especially likely if the animal makes a beeline through bushes and other foliage blindly instead of weaving around these obstacles.

If a deer walks or hobbles slowly off with its back humped up and its hindquarters sagging, it is usually hit in the paunch or ham region. Deer shot through the liver area, lower neck, or fleshy edge regions of the body often run away as if unhurt. A bowhunter cannot always determine a hit by the way a deer reacts to a shot, but it is often a reliable clue.

What to Do Immediately After a Hit

If you think you have hit a deer, remain where you shot from to watch and listen for clues as to where the animal has gone. Obviously, if the deer stays in bow range, you should keep on shooting until it is down for the count or finally moves away. Once it moves outside of bow range, try to determine its escape direction, and listen to track it even farther by sound. Bowhunters often find arrow-killed deer exactly where they heard the last crash of foliage or the last crunch of a hoof. In addition, hard-hit deer often make breathing or cough-

After a shot is taken at a deer, a bowhunter should nock another arrow and try to see and hear where the target animal goes.

ing noises which can help you pinpoint your prize.

A smart bowhunter is seldom in a hurry to follow up a deer he thinks he has hit. The only valid excuse for following right away aside from a steady downpour that threatens to quickly wash away blood sign is when a hunter knows a deer is paunch-hit, and he feels he can keep a visual track of the animal without the deer seeing him and running away. A paunch-hit deer seldom leaves enough blood behind to trail, and I've sometimes carefully followed such a deer immediately after a hit *if* terrain allowed me to keep it in sight without being seen myself.

As a general rule, smart archers remain where they shot from for a minimum of 30 minutes. It makes no difference where the arrow has hit—if it has dropped an animal in 10 or 15 seconds, the deer certainly isn't going anywhere and the 30-minute wait won't hurt a thing. If the arrow has smacked less vital tissue, the

½-hour wait will give a deer time to expire or at least weaken and lie down. Some bowhunters operate on the misbegotten theory that a deer hit in the rear end should be pushed or chased to keep the wound open and bleeding, but in actuality it usually frightens a hard-hit deer to the point it runs away and leaves *less* blood per foot of trail than it would leave if it slowly moved away. The wound from a sharp broadhead does not quit bleeding with a solid hit anyway, so there's no need to keep an animal moving to ensure good blood flow.

Once you wait 30 minutes, clearly mark the place you shot from with toilet paper, a piece of fluorescent surveyor's tape, or another highly visible object. This prevents you from becoming disoriented in the woods and totally losing track of where the shot was made and where the target animal ran to. If you shot from a tree stand, get a clear fix on where the animal was when you hit it and climb down to have a look. Things appear differently from ground level than they do from an elevated stand, so study the terrain from your stand first to make sure you have not only the hit site pegged, but also where the deer was the last time you saw or heard the animal.

Next, proceed directly to where you believe you made your hit. Sometimes, you'll find the arrow you shot on the spot, and from this, you can usually tell a lot about where that arrow hit. If it is as dry as a bone and buried to the back of the broadhead in a stump or tree trunk, you'll know you missed the deer after all. If it is covered with fat, hair, blood, and/or other body fluids like intestinal acids or slime, you'll know you hit the animal and will be able to make a judgment about *where* you made the hit. If the only thing on the arrow is green, brown, or yellow paunch fluid with a peculiarly distasteful odor, you should probably wait at least another hour or two before beginning to track it down. I personally prefer to wait at least 4 hours before following up paunch hits unless I feel I can follow immediately, keep a deer in sight, and pinpoint where the animal beds down. A paunch-shot (gut-shot) deer invariably lies down within a short distance unless pushed hard by a hunter. Waiting a long period of time lets the animal expire or at least stiffen up to hinder its ability to get away once you do move in for the kill. The reason for keeping visual contact with a deer hit in the paunch area if at all possible is simple—the animal seldom bleeds enough to make blind trailing or tracking an easy job.

How to Follow an Arrow-Hit Deer

If you find your arrow covered or at least flecked with blood, fat, or hair, or if you find no arrow at all, clearly mark the place where the deer was hit with some more toilet paper or another strip of surveyor's tape. Cast about from this spot along the route the deer took looking for fresh running tracks and signs of blood.

A running track is generally splayed at the toes and often leaves distinct dew-claw marks behind the main hoofprint as the animal hits hard on stiff, running legs. Fresh tracks also tend to be darker in color than surrounding dirt, having penetrated to the moist, sub-surface earth. Running tracks on hillsides also tend to show skid marks here and there as a deer stumbles or slips. Such tracks can often be followed by an alert, patient bowhunter.

With a little luck, you will immediately find a wide blood trail that makes follow-up a snap. The most profuse blood trails are usually left by deer hit low in the chest or hit solidly in a major artery, and can often be followed at a fast walk or trot, usually leading to a downed deer within 50 to 150 yards.

Unfortunately, following up vitally hit deer is not always so easy. A hard-hit animal can often cover 100 or 150 yards in well under 10 seconds, which does not allow much time for blood to flow out and hit the ground. A deer hit high through the chest or punched solidly through a ham and on into the paunch will often

for blood squirted horizontally from an artery or smeared on surrounding vegetation. In heavy brush or trees, a blood trail is often above ground on foliage—not on the ground itself.

During the entire deer-searching process, you should move along quietly with eyes probing ahead and ears alert for sounds that might betray a nearby crippled animal. With any luck at all, you'll eventually find enough blood to follow and the deer at the end of the line.

One vitally important ingredient in any search is stick-to-itiveness. All too many bowhunters expect a wide crimson trail from hit site to deer, and when they don't find such a trail, they give up in disgust. The fact of the matter is, wide crimson trails are the exception—not the rule. I have shot deer through the chest on several occasions in open country, watched them run full-tilt until they piled up . . . and not found one speck of blood in between. Deer often bleed internally during the entire time period between the hit and death, requiring a bowhunter to go on hands and knees to

A deer usually moves away after being hit with an arrow—often at break-neck speed. Bowhunters should not expect animals to pile up on the spot. (Photo courtesy of Russell Thornberry)

(Below) A bowhunter often has to follow running tracks to recover an arrow-hit deer. Such tracks are usually deep, splayed at the toes, and characterized by dew claw marks behind.

leave *no* blood at first because initial bleeding runs down into the chest or abdominal cavity instead of out on the ground. This is the reason a bowhunter should watch and listen to a deer leave after being hit—a blood trail may not start immediately, requiring an archer to crisscross the country where he last saw or heard his animal to pick up a late-starting trail.

A bowhunter carefully studies the immediate hit site first for trail signs he can follow. If there is no initial blood, he tries to follow tracks. If there are no visible tracks, he proceeds in the direction he believes the animal went and continues to search for trailing clues. He not only looks for blood and tracks on the ground—he also looks higher on weeds, bushes, and tree trunks

A little snow on the ground can make animal trailing and tracking a lot easier than normal.

To keep track of a tough-to-follow blood trail, an archer should leap-frog sign markers as he slowly moves from one trailing clue to the next.

follow tracks and also requiring him to cast about to check different routes his animal *might* have taken. Searches for deer sometimes take *hours* in heavy cover, and a bowhunter should be mentally prepared for this tedious chore. If he looks long enough and hard enough, he'll find his prize if it was hit well to begin with.

Other Trail-Following Tips

Whenever you start out on a blood trail or running track, always move along to *one side of* the trail to avoid blotting out important sign. If blood spots are few and far between, leap-frog two white handkerchiefs or similar markers to keep track of a trail, marking the last blood found with one, casting ahead and marking the next blood found with the second, going back to retrieve the rear-most marker, etc. Careful marking lets you cast about to look for the deer itself or explore possible routes the animal might have taken without becoming disoriented and losing what little trail you have already found.

When following a trail, pay close attention to the direction the animal is going to formulate some idea about where it might be heading. I have found several non-bleeding deer stone dead by simply following hunches and canvassing country repeatedly until I finally walked into them. A keen-eyed deer-trailer can usually pick up occasional drips or flecks of blood here and there along an animal's escape route, but second-guessing a deer's direction of travel often pays off if sign is simply too skimpy to follow.

Blood is much easier to see in some areas than in others. Trailing a deer across a freshly mowed alfalfa

Blood from an arrow-hit deer is often found on bushes well above the ground—not just on the ground itself.

field or through an area of solid dirt and pine needles can be difficult even if blood is fairly abundant because it does not puddle up or contrast well with ground coloration. In such instances, it often saves time to cast ahead to areas where blood is easier to see. Rocks, logs, downed tree limbs, and dead leaves all show up blood extremely well because of the uniform color that contrasts well with red. I've sometimes kept on a blood trail other hunters lost by casting ahead for strips of rocky ground, areas with lots of deadful logs, and other locales that made sparse blood trails show up reasonably well. You can do the same.

A sharp bowhunter can tell a lot about where an animal is hit by the coloration and consistency of the blood it leaves on the ground. Pink, frothy blood invariably means a solid hit in the lungs. Bright red blood means a hit in an artery, especially if it has squirted out on the ground or foliage under obvious pressure. Medium-colored blood in very large quantity usually indicates a heart hit, and blood of the same color in lesser quantity often means a solid but possibly nonvital muscle hit. Dark red blood can indicate a surface nick, especially when it appears in big drops instead of sprays or spurts. Blood veins near the surface of a deer's body are not under high pressure, and hits here tend to well up and dribble. Blood from the liver is also fairly dark in coloration. Blood color is no surefire indicator of hit location—aside from lung blood, which is unmistakable—but blood-color clues can often reinforce your notions about where you've hit an animal.

One other blood clue can help you decipher where you have hit a deer. Simply note where blood is deposited in relation to where a deer has walked. Blood smeared high on tree trunks ensures that you haven't hit a deer in the lower half. Blood running down a deer's leg and collecting in a particular hoofprint might indicate a front or rear hit. The front hooves on deer are usually noticeably larger than the back ones, and if tracking conditions are good—as in soft snow or dirt—a bowhunter can sometimes differentiate a front from rear hoof-print that is full of blood. This little trick has let me know on several occasions that I hit a deer in the rear half instead of the front half where I originally thought the arrow had gone. This helps to mentally prepare you for a trailing job that might end up being longer and more time-consuming than you originally had figured on.

Special Trailing Problems

Sometimes bowhunters encounter trailing problems that require a deviation from normal follow-up procedures. The three that immediately come to mind are hitting a deer in a rainstorm or snowstorm, hitting a deer just prior to dark, and hitting a deer in the paunch.

Although the normal procedure is waiting 30 minutes before follow-up, such a wait is foolhardy if rain or snow threaten to blot out any blood, tracks, or other sign left by a hard-hit animal. In these situations a bowhunter must push the follow-up and hope for the best. With any luck, the deer has piled up dead within a few seconds of full-tilt running. Even if it hasn't, a rapid follow-up might allow an archer to spot where the animal has bedded, or jump it up and finish it off with a second shot.

A deer hit just before dark should be left the normal amount of time and then followed by flashlight or lantern-light. Blood shows up surprisingly well at night if a bright light is used, often allowing rapid animal recovery. Truly tough trailing or tracking jobs sometimes require a bowhunter to wait for morning light, but in the meantime a big, fat deer can bloat and spoil unless the weather is really cold. Smallish deer like blacktails can be left overnight and found the following morning, but mulies, whitetails, elk, moose, and caribou will often go bad within a few hours unless field dressed and hung up to cool. If you can, always try to find evening-hit deer to avoid meat-spoilage problems.

Paunch-hit deer are seldom easy to recover. However, I have had the misfortune to hit several deer here, and not one has gone to waste. When possible, I have followed them immediately to keep track of where they went. When this was not possible, I have carefully marked the place I shot from, waited several hours, and returned to ferret out the trail. A truly well-sharpened broadhead sometimes causes enough bleeding from the muscle layers encasing the stomach to allow careful, tedious trailing. Often as not, it must be accomplished with your nose nearly touching the ground to spot match-head size drops of blood.

If all else fails, a bowhunter with a paunch-hit deer

The end results of an accurate shot and proper follow-up procedures are a deer in the bag and the feeling of a job well done.

When You Don't Find Your Deer

It gripes me to no end when bowhunters automatically assume that a deer hit by an arrow is a dead, wasted animal if they do not find it. If a bowhunter exhausts every trailing, tracking, and searching option and *still* doesn't come up with his animal, the odds are extremely good that the deer will recover nicely. Many rifle hunters drop deer every year with healed-over broadhead scars in non-vital areas like the shoulder blade, lower legs, and brisket. All such areas bleed when hit, but they normally heal up quickly with little discomfort to the animal. One fortunate thing about a superficial arrow wound is the fact that it usually bleeds profusely to cleanse the wound, then seals up and heals without infection.

Many superficial arrow hits leave a lot of blood initially, giving hunters hope that they have dropped their deer. A blood trail from a creased brisket, clipped backline, or sliced lower leg will often leave more blood sign at first than a fatal chest hit, but the trail from a fringe hit gradually peters out over several hundred yards until there is no more blood at all to follow. A bowhunter who regards such a trail as evidence that the deer is "dead but lost" is usually mistaken. Paunch-hit deer do occasionally slip away and drop unfound, the same as they do when hit with a rifle bullet, but this doesn't happen very often if a bowhunter diligently works at recovering such animals. Deer hit in other vital places are almost always found by persistent, systematic trailers—if they are not found, they are usually hit too superficially to cause these deer any lasting problems.

To recover deer after shots are taken, competent bowhunters follow sensible, systematic, time-tested procedures. They do their best to determine where an arrow has hit, look and listen to tell what an animal does after a shot, wait patiently awhile if they believe they have hit their target deer, clearly mark both shooting and hit sites so these can be readily relocated, and then follow up hits patiently and thoroughly with confidence in finding their animals. The end results of such efforts are trophies on the meat pole and completely satisfying hunts.

should enlist the aid of others to help him comb the area. A thorough, crisscrossing search by several archers will often turn up the deer dead where it laid down or cause it to jump up, allowing a finishing shot. A gut-shot deer that has bedded for several hours is seldom in shape to travel and can generally be dispatched by a straight-shooting archer.

Field Care/20

BAGGING A deer is always a high point for any bowhunter—a time to celebrate and feel good. However, an experienced and responsible archer knows that dropping a deer creates a certain amount of extra work that needs to be done, and done quickly. A deer on the ground represents fine meals plus a nice trophy hide and/or rack, but only if a bowhunter takes proper care of that prize from the minute it is found until the meat is in the freezer and the trophy is delivered to the taxidermist.

Caring for a downed deer is not all that difficult, provided a bowhunter knows how to proceed. The basic steps of field dressing a trophy, transporting it out of the woods, caring for the carcass between hunting camp and locker, and cutting up the meat yourself if you are so inclined are all skills truly serious hunters are proud to exercise. This pride in a job well done stems from the knowledge that such deer-care procedures produce melt-in-your-mouth meat and trophies on the wall that look positively lifelike. A bowhunter who mismanages his deer between field and freezer suffers exactly the opposite results—spoiled or at least poor-tasting meat, and trophy hides that look ragged and scroungy at best. Every hunter owes it to himself to learn how to care for downed game to ensure good meat and first-rate trophy heads and hides.

Basic Principles of Proper Care

Once a deer drops to the ground, it is immediately in danger of souring or spoiling from bacterial action in the animal. As soon as anything dies, bacteria in the tissues begin breaking down the meat, hide, and other body parts. This is nature's garbage-disposal system, a system that can reduce a deer-sized critter to scattered bones and a few shreds of hide in a few short weeks if the weather is fairly warm. With the help of carnivorous insects like blowflies and maggots, meat-eating birds like ravens and vultures, and sharp-toothed mammals like bears, coyotes, and foxes, a deer is used up entirely if it dies of natural causes.

Nothing goes to waste in the woods, no matter how or where it dies. However, a bowhunter who selfishly wants to eat the meat and save the hide of a deer himself should do all he can to retard bacterial action, keep insects away from a carcass, and prevent meat vandalism by bears, coyotes, or similar animals. When this is properly accomplished, deer meat turns out sweet and the hides remain completely sleek and natural.

Bacteria thrive and multiply in a moist, warm environment. As a result, a hunter should try to keep deer parts as cool and dry as possible to counteract bacterial action. An archer should always think *cool* and *dry* anytime he handles meat, hides, trophy antlers and skulls, or any other parts of deer—this is a basic principle for handling any kind of downed game.

To avoid carcass damage by blowflies, meat bees, birds, and animals, a hunter must cover a deer with cotton bags or use other techniques described later in this chapter. Most are based on plain old common sense, and all stem from the basic knowledge that certain small and big pests can and will get to your deer if you let them. A bowhunter should never forget this threat once he downs an animal.

One other deer-care principle should be mentioned here. Although dirty meat can usually be cleaned up or cut away during butchering, it is far more convenient to keep a deer carcass relatively clean in the first place. It is impossible to keep a deer dropped in the woods white-glove spic-and-span, but excessive and unnecessary grit and grime from improper dragging, transport in the open over dusty roads, etc., only increases clean-up work later on and invariably wastes at least a little meat that is too packed with grime to save. Remember to keep meat clean to minimize meat-processing problems.

1. To begin field dressing a deer, slit the belly hide from genitals to point of brisket. Next, slice through the muscle layers lining the stomach to expose the paunch, being careful not to cut the paunch itself. (Field-dressing sequence courtesy of *Petersen's Hunting* magazine.)

2. Next, roll the innards out of the deer with your hands, cutting around the edges until everything comes free. Do not cut the paunch itself, or you'll have a mess.

Field Care

The very first thing a bowhunter should do once a deer is down, aside from a little bit of backslapping and picture-taking, is field dressing the animal to remove the stomach, intestines, anal tissue, and heart and lungs. A few hunters leave heart and lungs inside a deer until they reach hunting camp, and this is okay if temperatures are fairly cool and transport time is fairly short. However, the more completely an animal is cleaned out inside, the faster the natural body heat dissipates to cool down edible meat. Remember, heat accelerates the bacterial action that causes the meat to spoil.

On larger deer, such as elk and moose, simple field dressing is not enough to quickly cool a carcass unless temperatures are well below freezing. The areas between the shoulder blades and backbone, the neck, and the inner hams are most critical about retaining body heat and spoiling in the woods. As a result, it is usually a good idea to quarter a big deer in the woods or at least slice shoulders away from the carcass by cutting through the armpit area. Many conscientious bowhunters skin a big deer on the spot and cut it into pieces with a sharp knife and meat saw or hatchet to accelerate meat cooling. At the very least, they completely field dress the animal, roll it up on a bed of logs to allow cooling air to circulate between the animal and the ground, and make sure it is in the shade on a sunny day. On an elk, moose, or caribou, building a makeshift sun shade over the animal if it has fallen in a sunny place can sometimes make the critical difference between good meat and marginal meat.

In shirtsleeve weather, any deer over 400 pounds can completely spoil in 4 or 5 hours unless cared for as just described and transported out of the woods as fast as possible to be hung up and skinned.

The basic field-dressing process is too complicated to easily explain. As a result, study the accompanying photo sequence carefully to learn how this is done. My special thanks to *Petersen's Hunting* magazine for the use of these photos.

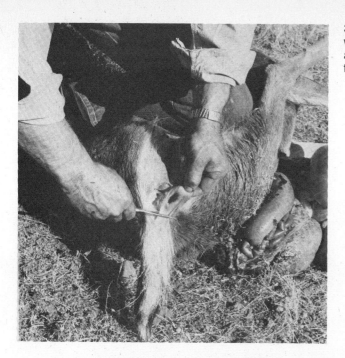

3. (Left) Cut completely through the hide around the anus with a very sharp blade and then ream deeply around the anus area like coring an apple and pull the entire anus out of the deer.

4. Remove the liver from the deer and save it if you enjoy eating this animal part. The liver lies in the body cavity just forward of the paunch area.

5. Your deer is now field dressed and ready to drag or carry out of the woods.

6. If transport grime is not a problem, you can accelerate carcass cooling by splitting the brisket on up to the chin with a sharp knife and some elbow grease.

7. Next, remove the heart/lung complex by whittling around it with your knife.

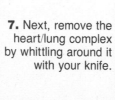

A makeshift sunshade of limbs and boughs can save the meat on a large animal that falls in a warm, sunny area.

Transport Out of the Woods

Unless a deer drops very near a road, getting it back to hunting camp can be simple but hard work. More often than not, you have to drag or backpack the whole animal or animal quarters out by yourself or with the aid of bowhunting friends.

Dragging a deer needs no real elaboration here. It is not very complicated to grab an antler or leg and begin pulling—just hard, hot, sweaty work. A few outdoor companies sell "deer draggers," which are rope-and-harness affairs meant to make dragging easier. Check these out at your local sporting goods store.

In areas congested by hunters, throwing a deer over your back and heading for hunting camp can be downright dangerous. More than one archer has mistaken a deer carried through heavy cover for the living thing and flailed away with an arrow. Carrying a deer on your back is often easier than dragging it, provided the animal is fairly small in body size. However, always tie fluorescent ribbons or surveyor's tape on any deer you plan to pack out.

If the backpack promises to be really long across steep or rough terrain, it makes a lot of sense to completely bone out a deer on the spot and pack out edible meat in some sort of backpack sack. I have done this many times, using the basic butchering technique illustrated in this chapter, discarding bones and unwanted parts of the hide. This can reduce carrying weight by at least a third, and makes packing out meat a whole lot easier than carting out ribcage, spine, leg bones, and other body parts you'll eventually discard anyway.

Using a four-wheel-drive vehicle or pack animal to carry out dropped deer in remote areas is by far the best way to proceed if this is possible. Using a bow-hunting outfitter for elk, moose, or caribou seems especially sensible once your big deer is down because such a professional normally has rigs or animals handy for transporting the meat and trophies back to civilization. In some kinds of terrain, such as heavily logged-over mountain areas, a do-it-yourself bowhunter can benefit by having a four-wheel-drive rig, a chain saw, a winch to get a vehicle over slick or steep places, tire chains for improved traction, and the perseverance to use these things to good advantage. By scouting feasible vehicle routes, cutting away downed trees and logs, and carefully driving in four-wheel-drive, an archer can often drive close to downed game and significantly cut down packing effort and time.

Whenever transporting a deer by any means, always carry it with the words *cool, dry,* and *clean* in mind. Hunters who drape a deer over the hot hood of an automobile and parade their prize around town are turning great meat into marginal meat or rotten meat. Hunters who wrap deer in plastic in an attempt to protect it are actually preventing the drying action of air circulation and are creating a moist environment for bacteria to breed and multiply. And those who toss game in the dusty, unprotected beds of pickup trucks or drag already-skinned carcasses across the dirt and leaves unprotected are grinding grime into prime steaks and chops. Cover animals with cotton deer bags or similar drapes that breathe air to help prevent dirt contamination.

Any deer with a head you wish to mount or a hide you wish to have tanned should be handled with special care during transport. An animal dragged over rocks, logs, and other forest debris can end up with bald spots or at best broken and tattered hair. Even a rough ride in a vehicle or regular rubbing from ropes on a horse or mule can damage the hair on a hide.

Carrying a small deer out on your back is safe as long as other hunters are not roaming the nearby woods.

Dragging a deer is easy on fairly level ground if there are two or more hunters to pull.

Pack animals can be a godsend when a big deer like an elk or moose is dropped well away from vehicular access points.

In really remote bowhunting areas, an archer is often best advised to bone a deer on the spot and backpack out the meat and antlers only.

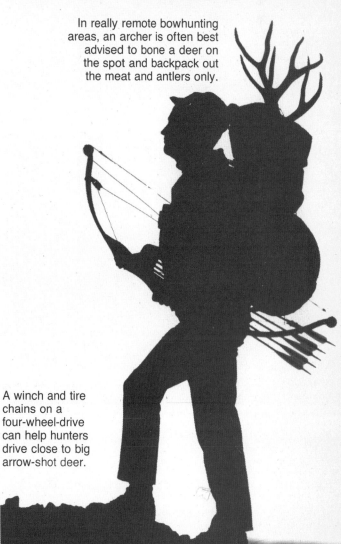

A winch and tire chains on a four-wheel-drive can help hunters drive close to big arrow-shot deer.

Care Between Field and Meat Locker

Unless weather is excessively cold, the first thing a bowhunter should do once he gets a deer back to his camp or home is hang it up by the head or hind legs to skin and trim up the carcass. Hanging a deer by the hind legs makes the most sense to me because this lets body heat rise directly out of the chest cavity and because it lets a hunter remove the head along with the hide during the skinning process.

Skinning helps the meat cool and lets the surface meat glaze over (dry out) to inhibit bacterial action. It also lets the hunter trim away bloodshot areas to prevent the blood from souring in these areas and tainting surrounding meat. In addition, certain inedible

(Left) A bow-shot deer should be hung up in camp to accelerate cooling of the meat.

1. To skin a deer, first slit the insides of both hind legs from crotch to lower leg.

2. Next, skin back the hide from the knee joints on the hind legs and remove the lower legs by cutting through these knee joints.

3. (Right) Split the pelvis with a sharp hatchet or meat saw.

parts of the deer are usually removed at this time to aid cooling and ready the carcass for butchering. These include the windpipe, the heart and lungs if these were not removed in the field, excess fat globules and surface meat which has inadvertently become dirty in transport. The accompanying photo sequence clearly details the entire skinning and cleanup operation.

To protect a hanging carcass until you take it to the locker or cut it up yourself for the freezer, cover it with a regular cotton deer bag unless weather is cold enough to eliminate the threat of blowflies, meat bees, and other flying meat menaces. In a pinch, meat can be covered with a mixture of lemon juice and black pepper to discourage such pests. Flies in particular will lay eggs or "blows" in an unprotected carcass—blows which

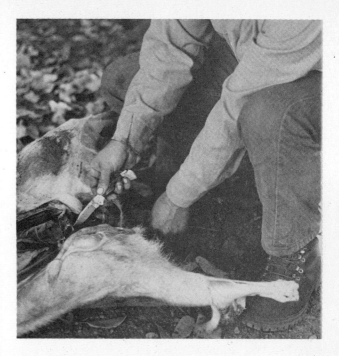

4. (Right) Unless you did it in the field, carefully remove the anus from between the hams by reaming around it with a knife.

5. Cut through the area between the ham and the hamstring to allow easy hanging from a gambrel.

6. Hook a meat-hanging gambrel in the hind legs as shown and hoist the deer up off the ground for skinning.

7. (Left) Begin peeling the hide away from the hams with the aid of your knife.

hatch into smelly, nasty maggots within a few short days. Fly blows which are found and carefully scraped away from a deer carcass cause no problem, but why be inconvenienced by the little white egg clusters when you need not be?

Meat which has already been cut up or boned out in the field can be hung up on ropes to cool and dry, or draped over the branches of a "meat tree" until transport to a locker is possible. These must also be covered with deer-quarter bags or with a lemon/pepper concoction to keep flies and bees away.

If you want to save the hide for the taxidermist, or if you cape out your deer for a head mount, remove as much flesh from the hide as possible and salt it well or freeze it at once in double plastic garbage bags. The salt

8. By pulling on the hide and slicing between hide and carcass, the skin should peel away smoothly.

9. (Right) Applying downward pressure to the hide, peel the skin away from the sides of the hams. In this area, the hide will often tear loose easily with hand pressure alone. With hand pressure and knife work, skin around the anus and pull the tail away from the tailbone.

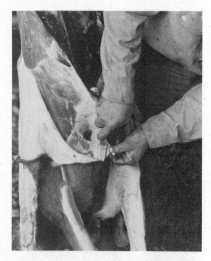

10. Sever the tailbone and continue skinning the deer downward toward the head. When you've denuded the carcass to the brisket, slice the hide on downward to the throat unless you already did this in the field.

11. Slice the hide down the back of each front leg from "armpit" to below the knee. Free the hide from the front legs with hand pressure and careful blade work.

12. (Left) Skin one shoulder and down toward the neck. The skin adheres to the body tenaciously near the base of the neck. Skin the other shoulder in similar fashion.

dries a well-fleshed hide to prevent bacterial action, and several resaltings will dry it out nicely. However, unless you have handled hides before and have a knack for this sort of work, you should preferably rush a hide to cold storage for immediate freezing and let your taxidermist worry about fleshing, caping, and other tanning preparation. If you wish to head-mount a nice antlered deer, be sure to skin it according to photo instructions in Chapter 27—*do not skin it as shown here.* If you do not immediately freeze the hide, or completely flesh and salt it, or rush it to your taxidermist, it will quickly spoil, the hair slipping out and the skin developing a decidedly rank odor. Once this happens, a deer hide or cape is ruined for good.

A hanging carcass and hide or hide/head combina-

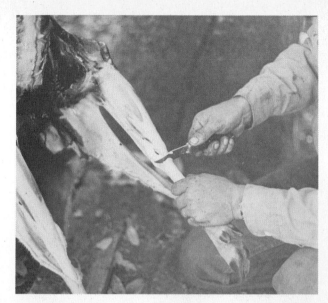

13. (Right) Cut the front legs off at the knee joint with a probing knife blade.

14. Skin out the neck with careful knife strokes. The hide here is impossible to pull free with hand pressure alone.

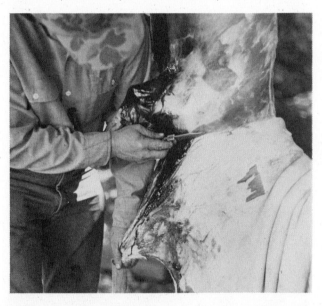

15. (Above right) Remove the hide all the way to the base of the deer's head.

16. (Below) Slice through the neck meat to the bony joint where head and neck meet, then girdle the entire neck in this area with your knife.

17. (Right) Twist the deer's head free, cutting any remaining muscle with your knife until the head is separated from the carcass.

tion can be safely kept in camp for 2 or 3 days in cool weather, provided it is left hanging in the deep shade. In warm weather—60 degrees or above—they can still be kept a day or two in camp if a hunter lets them hang out in chilly nighttime air, gets out of bed at dawn, and covers meat and hide on the ground with a good-quality sleeping bag to *insulate in* the coolness acquired during the night and *insulate out* daytime heat. At dusk, the meat and hide should be hung up again to allow drying air circulation and recooling of the meat. Despite the success of such temporary precautions, a deer hunter should transport meat and hide to a cold storage facility as soon as possible to ensure sweet meat and an undamaged trophy—preferably on the same day the animal is killed.

18. Split the brisket meat down the center with your blade, continuing the cut right down the center of the throat, exposing the windpipe as you go.

19. (Left) Split the brisket bone with a sharp hatchet along the knife cut you just made.

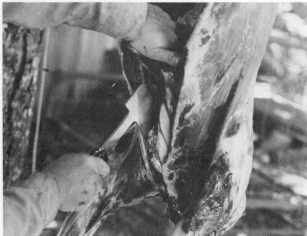

20. If the heart and lungs are still inside the chest cavity, these can now be pulled out downward along with the windpipe in the neck.

21. (Left) Carefully wipe away any blood remaining on the carcass with clean paper towels. If blood is especially bad, scrub the meat with damp paper towels and then dry off all meat surfaces.

22. Cover the carcass with an insect-proof deer bag and transport the animal to a cold storage locker as soon as you can.

A deer hide which is not properly handled will quickly sour and spoil, and hair will pull out by the handfuls. When hair begins to slip, the hide is ruined for good.

Meat Processing at Home

Some experienced bowhunters prefer to cut and wrap deer meat themselves, either to save butcher-shop prices or simply to enjoy the do-it-yourself experience. As long as meat is well cleaned and wrapped correctly to prevent freezer burn (drying out in the freezer), meat processing at home produces first-rate food for the table. If home meat processing appeals to you, study and duplicate the accompanying step-by-step photo sequence.

Unless deer meat is cut up at once, a hunter should hang a deer in a cold-storage plant until he is ready to tackle the cutting and wrapping chore. Some bowhunters feel that venison should hang in cold storage for 7 to 10 days to let meat "age" or tenderize prior to cutting. Others feel aging does not contribute to meat taste or texture at all. I honestly cannot tell the difference in meat cut and wrapped at once and meat hung a few days in a cold box, but hanging 7 to 10 days does not hurt anything, and doesn't cost much either.

One other advantage of home-processing deer meat is the ease with which a hunter can convert venison to *(continued page 206)*

1. Separate both hams from the carcass of your animal, first using a sharp knife to cut the flesh and then a meat saw to sever the backbone.

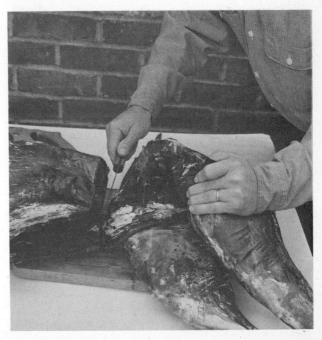

2. Separate one ham from the pelvis by cutting deep with the knife till you hit the ball-and-socket hip joint. One twist of the ham should pop this joint loose. Then cut the ham completely free.

3. Separate the back shank from the ham with knife and saw.

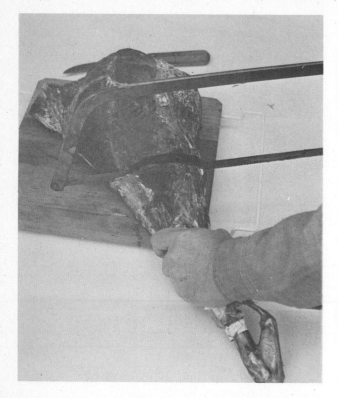

4. (Right) Remove the bone from the ham by making a vertical incision on the outside of the ham and carefully cutting around the bone with your knife.

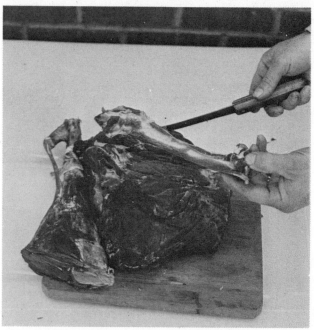

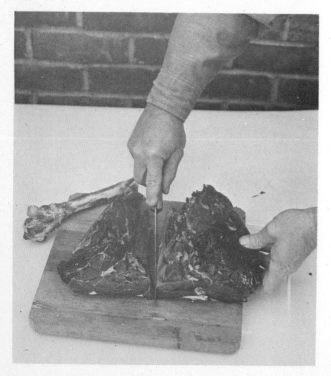

5. (Left) Separate the round steaks (right) from the heel of round steaks (left) by cutting the deboned ham in two lengthwise. (The heel of round is the front half of the ham.)

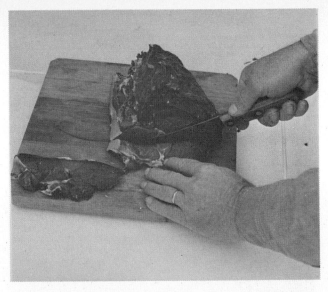

6. Slice off the round steaks, making them about ½-inch to 1-inch thick. Steak thickness is largely a matter of personal preference. Repeat the process with the heel of round.

7. Bone out the back shank. This meat can be diced up for stew or ground into hamburger.

8. (Left) Split the pelvis from the top with a meat saw, then bone out the resulting cut to make a boneless rump roast. Repeat steps 2 through 8 with the other ham.

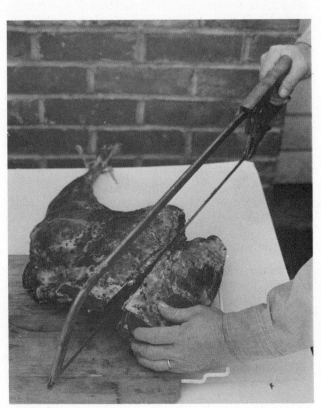

9. (Above right) Remove both shoulders and front legs from the carcass with a sharp knife. A deer's shoulder "floats," which means there's no bone to saw through here—simply insert your knife behind the shoulder blade and start cutting.

10. (Right) Remove the front shank from each shoulder with knife and saw.

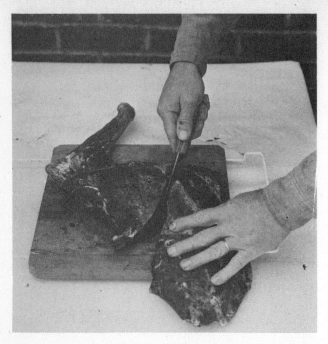

11. Separate the shoulder (right) from the shoulder blade (left) using knife and saw.

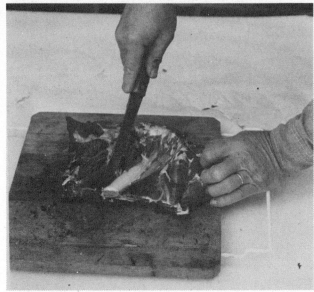

12. (Above and left) Bone out the shoulder, then slice the boneless meat into shoulder steaks. This piece of meat can be left intact as a roast if you prefer.

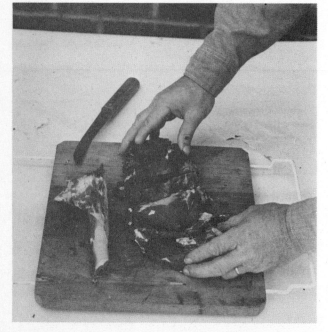

13. Bone out the front shank for stew or hamburger.

14. (Left) Separate the shoulder blade bone from the meat with a knife. This cut of meat can be used in one piece as a roast or cut up for stew.

15. (Left and below) Remove the *backstrap* from each side of the backbone. This is some of the best meat on any animal, and should be sliced into thick *loin steaks*.

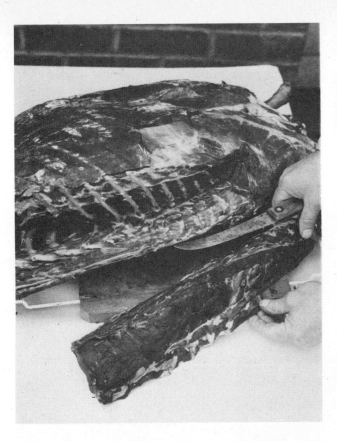

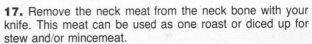

16. (Left) Strip all surface meat from the ribcage and brisket. This meat can be used for stew, hamburger, or jerky.

17. Remove the neck meat from the neck bone with your knife. This meat can be used as one roast or diced up for stew and/or mincemeat.

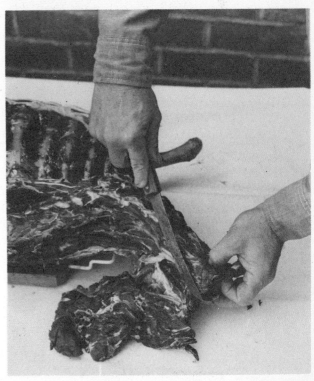

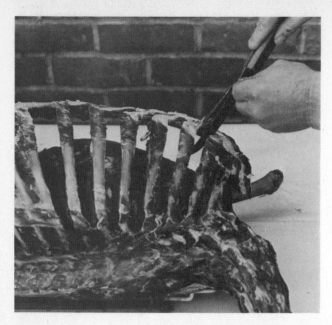

top-notch jerky if he likes dry, seasoned meat. Deer meat boned at home can be packaged in chunks, frozen, and thawed at a hunter's leisure to cut it in strips and process it in a stove or meat smoker. The accompanying photos show how to make excellent oven jerky—which I, personally, enjoy eating a great deal.

Caring for your bow-and-arrow deer is relatively easy if you know how to proceed. Field dress your animal at once, transport it quickly out of the woods, know how to handle the carcass around a hunting camp, and rush the meat and hide to a cold-storage locker as quickly as possible or cut up the meat yourself before spoilage can occur. As long as you protect the carcass from heat, moisture, grime, and egg-laying or meat-eating pests, the end result should be top-notch meat and a sleek trophy hide!

18. Strip the meat from the ribs for hamburger or jerky.

19. Your buck is completely boned out, and not one shred of meat is wasted! With practice the whole procedure takes less than one hour.

THE WHITETAIL is America's most popular bow-hunting animal, primarily because it is the most abundant and most widespread of all the deer species. However, this "everyman's deer" is also a difficult, cagey customer to bowhunt, providing a challenge as great as any North American big-game animal. The whitetail has learned to adapt to human encroachment incredibly well, and as a result can hide on a postage stamp, slip away unseen through very sparse cover, and otherwise elude hunters with ease. The whitetail may be a common animal across the country, but there is no finer or more taxing deer available to archers.

General Description

Odocoileus virginianus, is a distinctive-looking deer no serious hunter could mistake for any other species. Although they vary considerably in body weight from one part of the continent to another, the average mature whitetail stands about 38 to 40 inches high at the shoulder, measures about 65 to 70 inches from nose tip to tail, and weighs about 150 pounds on the hoof. Exceptionally large trophy bucks can weigh up to 400 pounds, and the world record weight was well over 400 pounds. By contrast, small desert whitetails, called Coues deer, and Florida Key deer, which are also a small race of whitetail, seldom weigh over 100 pounds on the hoof.

Whitetail are clearly distinguished by several physical traits. The most obvious is the large, fluffy tail, which is gray-brown on top and snow white underneath. When whitetails run in alarm, they usually raise their tails and wave them like large white flags. Such flagging is peculiar to this species, and can be seen hundreds of yards off as a whitetail bounds away.

The basic coloration varies a lot from area to area and individual, to individual, with the average body color being a medium grayish brown. Whitetails are darkest in coloration along their backlines, shading lighter down the flanks and turning abruptly white under the belly and inside the legs. A whitetail's head is uniquely colored with a jet-black nose backed by a solid band of white, a uniformly gray-brown face and ears, eyes distinctively rimmed by white, and a large, pure-white throat patch and underchin. No other deer has such facial markings, making the whitetail exceedingly easy to identify.

A buck's rack is every bit as unique as its overall coloration. Unlike the antlers of other deer, all tines on a normal whitetail rack branch upward from a single main beam. This beam rises from the head and then thrusts abruptly forward over the nose, the points rising directly upward from the beam like dinner candles in a row. Whitetail racks normally have "eyeguard" points which are longer than those on mule deer and blacktail near the bases of the beams. In some cases, the eyeguards actually project above the height of the rest of the rack.

When discussing whitetail racks, most deer hunters count all points on both sides of a rack, including eyeguards. In other words, a buck with one eyeguard plus three main points per side is called an eight-point, a buck with an eyeguard plus four main points per side is called a 10-point, and so on. By contrast, in other deer species, hunters count only the number of points on *one* side of a rack *without* including eyeguards. For example, a mule deer buck with four main points and one eyeguard per side is called a four-point.

Distribution and Preferred Habitat

Whitetail are our most widely distributed deer, ranging from Atlantic to Pacific coastlines and from central Canada south into Old Mexico. At present, California, Alaska, and Hawaii are the only American states without healthy populations of these fine deer.

They tend to be lowland deer when compared to the muley and blacktail. However, whitetails are incredibly

The whitetail deer is a handsome, alert trophy.

A whitetail's "flag" is a distinctive physical trait.

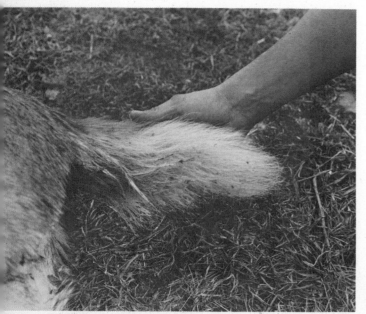

An average mature whitetail buck usually weighs about 150 pounds field dressed. (Photo courtesy Russell Thornberry)

adaptable and sometimes take up residence in thickets along streams at elevations of 6,000 to 7,000 feet. As a general rule, whitetails prefer heavy forest or forest-edge cover, especially that running along rivers and streams in valley bottoms. Their choice of habitat contrasts sharply with that of most mule deer, which prefer higher, semi-open country unless cold weather drives them down.

Because whitetail are smart, highly adaptable animals, they are often seen living in the very shadows of large cities and towns. If there is a little cover, ample water, and plenty of brush or farm-crop food to eat, they are completely comfortable.

It is widely believed that most whitetail live and die within home territories seldom larger than 1 or 2 square miles. However, there are notable exceptions to this, and exact habitat size largely depends on food availability. There have been recorded instances of whitetails moving 10 or 15 miles in one steady direction, either in search of wintertime food or during the rut when bucks are roaming to find does. Most normally, though, a bowhunter can count on finding the same whitetail deer in the same general area day-in and day-out.

Basic Behavior Profile

Whitetail are the most predictable of the deer clan, partially because they do prefer to stay in one small home territory instead of roaming about large tracts of ground. Their living routine is more or less the same from day to day except when heavy hunting pressure or

Summertime whitetail deer often wade into ponds and sloughs to eat tender aquatic vegetation. This big-racked buck would satisfy the most nitpicking trophy bowhunter. (Photo courtesy of Russell Thornberry)

During the late-fall rut, normally sane whitetail bucks chase does about the woods with little regard for their personal safety. (Photo courtesy of Russell Thornberry)

the late-fall rut causes them to deviate from the norm.

A whitetail usually beds in extremely heavy cover during midday hours, rising once or twice to go to water in warmer weather but otherwise staying more or less put. Normally, it rises around 4:30 or 5:00 PM to feed, moving slowly toward the edge of heavy cover and popping into the open sometime between sundown and complete darkness. The average adult requires about 10 pounds of food per day to remain healthy, and browses on an extremely wide variety of brush to satisfy this dietary requirement. Some common natural foods include red willow, acorns, fir, snowberry, oak brush, sweetfern, and white cedar. In warm weather, whitetails often feed on aquatic vegetation like lily pads, sometimes actually wading into deep water to get at these tasty treats. In addition, they absolutely dote on agricultural crops like alfalfa, apples, yellow corn, wheat, and barley. In cropland areas, whitetails tend to rise in late afternoon and rapidly browse through heavy cover toward open agricultural ground where they eat off and on all night.

Feeding most heavily near first and last light of day, the bulk of the night is spent lazing around chewing on cud in relatively open areas. Where it is legal to do so, a sportsman with a strong spotlight or merely the headlights of a car can scout agricultural areas at night and see hundreds of deer. Night hunting for deer is not legal anywhere, but a sportsman can sometimes locate hunting hotspots at night where night-scouting is legal, letting him find and concentrate on big bucks or large groups of deer that are not so readily located during daylight hours.

Whitetail vacate open areas soon after the first light of day, slowing this pace once they reach heavy cover again to leisurely browse toward favored bedding areas. This same basic bedding/watering/feeding cycle goes on day after day as long as deer are left relatively undisturbed.

Except during the mating season, mature bucks tend to hang to themselves or in the company of other bachelor bucks. Does and fawns live their own separate lives until the rut commences in November and December. The rut changes a whitetail's normally docile existence. Mature bucks begin chasing does all over the place, their necks swelled from glandular action within their bodies. They rub brush and trees vigorously with their antlers, scrape out shallow ground depressions to urinate in and mark their territories, and provoke fights with other bucks. At this time of year, the largest trophies, seldom seen at other times of year, come out of hiding and give bowhunters the best chance to nail a truly fine rack for the wall.

It is important to note here that although most whitetail follow set habit patterns, the biggest bucks are often loners with less discernible movement habits. This is often how these trophies got so big. In addition, no whitetail follows the *exact* same routine from day to day, meandering somewhat and using slightly different routes to and from bedding, watering, and feeding grounds.

Typical Whitetail Sign

The most common forms of whitetail sign are regularly used trails pounded out by fresh hoofprints, lots of soft, fresh deer droppings, and washtub-sized deer beds in heavy cover. Such unmistakable signs pinpoint areas deer are using, and help a bowhunter concentrate his efforts in productive hunting locations.

(Left and below) Whitetails leave lots of tracks along heavily-used trails through the dense foliage they prefer.

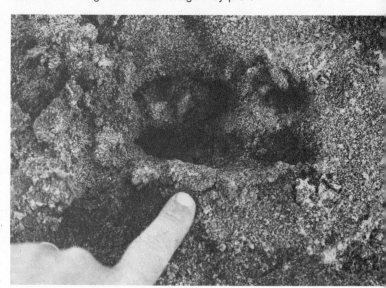

Other forms of whitetail sign observed by sharp, experienced bowhunters are shed antlers on the ground, fresh rubs on bushes or trees made during the rut, and fresh scrapes on the ground. All three of these signs are particularly important to trophy hunters. Shed antlers can give a good indication of just how many big bucks happen to be in a particular area, because they will be hanging around the same general locale each and every year unless they are bumped off by successful hunters. Fresh rubs and scrapes indicate that a buck is on the prod in the general area, and mark an excellent place to wait on stand.

A scrape is a clearly visible pawed-out area on the ground—an area a buck urinates in to mark its territory, then rolls in to cover itself with vile-smelling mud. Bucks visit such territorial markers regularly throughout the rut, making them hotspots for bowhunting ambushes.

Perhaps the most beneficial form of whitetail sign for the average hunter is the deer itself. An archer who glasses brushy edges of fields at first and last light will see most of the whitetail deer in a particular area, and will also be able to formulate notions about where the most and biggest deer are moving out to feed. This visual data lets an archer set up productive tree stands.

Antler rubs on low-growing shrubbery (arrow) are sure signs of nearby rutting whitetail bucks. (Photo courtesy of Russell Thornberry)

Shed antlers can tell a bowhunter plenty about the size and number of whitetail bucks in a particular patch of bottomland.

A stand atop a haystack can be a dandy ambush point for whitetails feeding in agricultural fields.

A truly huge buck can sometimes be located from a distance and ambushed a day or two later by a hunter who eases up a tree near the area the buck seems to be frequenting.

Productive Bowhunting Techniques

Because whitetails usually inhabit dense, extremely noisy terrain, because they are incredibly nervous and alert by nature, and because they display relatively consistent movement patterns, the majority of whitetail bowhunters sit in tree stands or other elevated blinds in wait for them. Especially productive stand areas are the edges of alfalfa, corn, or grain feeding fields—constant food sources draw whitetails from all around.

Because most whitetail bed well back in the brush and move quite a ways before actually popping out in the open, many archers prefer to place stands well back from cover edges to ambush deer in better shooting light and also catch deer before they build up maximum caution and alertness prior to stepping into an open field. Whitetails—and larger bucks in particular—tend to move about inside heavy cover until the last light of day, increasing the chances of a hunter who erects a stand well back in the brush and trees.

During the fall rutting period, dedicated whitetail bowhunters strongly improve their chances of success if they sit on stand all day long. There's no predicting when a buck or doe might stroll by during this crazy time of year—it may be sunrise, noon, early afternoon or sundown when the best bow-shooting chance materializes. As already discussed in previous chapters, a little doe-in-heat scent squirted around a stand and some antler-rattling to stimulate bucks fighting over a doe can lure in trophy whitetail bucks during the rut. Especially good areas to stand hunt in the mating season are those with fresh antler rubs on saplings and fresh scrapes pawed in the ground.

Stillhunting in damp, quiet weather is a decent technique for a skillful archer, sometimes producing midday shots when stand hunting is not very productive. Drive hunting in ultra-thick whitetail cover can also be effective if no other technique seems to be getting the job done.

How to Judge a Trophy

A buck has ears which generally measure 16 to 17 inches from tip to tip when they are cupped alertly forward. This ear-tip to ear-tip measurement is a dandy rule of thumb when judging the relative size of whitetail heads.

points average 6 to 10 inches long. The antler-bases on a good representative whitetail head should be at least as big around as a broom handle, and the mass should be fairly good right out to the antler tips. When viewed from the side, main beams will normally thrust at least to the white band behind its jet-black nose.

By contrast to such a fine, mature representative, bowhunters occasionally nail truly monstrous whitetails, large enough to thoroughly impress the most nitpicking trophy hunter using bow *or* rifle. Racks in this rare class are more massive, have more points, have longer points and main beams, and/or are wider-than-normal. Such super-bucks, which often score high in the bow-and-arrow record books, generally have

(Left) Glassing likely whitetail habitat from a distance near dawn and dusk is an excellent way to locate concentrations of these wily deer.

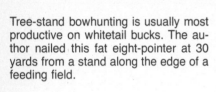

Tree-stand bowhunting is usually most productive on whitetail bucks. The author nailed this fat eight-pointer at 30 yards from a stand along the edge of a feeding field.

Many bowhunters feel that any whitetail deer is a first-rate archery trophy. They are perfectly correct. However, the fellow who wishes to take an especially nice whitetail head for the wall should carefully size up antlers on various bucks to ensure that he isn't disappointed once a deer is dropped. By paying attention to how wide a rack is in relation to the ears, and noting other antler traits, an archer can ensure a top trophy on the ground.

Although trophy size varies considerably from the tiny Coues deer and Florida Key deer on up to fat, large-antlered whitetails found in agricultural parts of the Midwest, the average, nice, trophy buck sports a rack 16 to 20 inches wide, with at least 8 points altogether—two eyeguards plus three main points per side. Better yet is a buck with 10 points, provided these

antler bases up to 6 inches in circumference, at least 10 long, massive antler points, often 12 or 14, and outside antler spreads of 18 to 26 inches. A buck of this general description is the trophy of a bowhunting lifetime.

Other Important Facts

There are several other traits displayed by the typical whitetail which are vitally important to bowhunters. One is the strong tendency to bed on a slight rise during midday hours to take advantage of any thermal updrafts caused by the earth's surface heating up when the sun is out. A deer so positioned has the best chance of smelling an approaching human and can also see surrounding terrain better than one bedded in a draw or on the flat. The elevated animal also has myriad escape routes to choose from, merely ducking down the

A mature whitetail buck makes an excellent bow-and-arrow trophy.

(Left) Well-known bowhunter Mick Roberts took this handsome 10-point whitetail after watching the buck for several days and devising a feasible ambush strategy.

back side of a ridge or hill in the opposite direction from where potential danger is lurking. A bowhunter who recognizes this tendency can concentrate still-hunting efforts in elevated places, at least attempting to penetrate the strategic places occupied by wary deer.

Although whitetail that leap up and run away appear to be carrying the mail to the next country, they usually stop in the first heavy cover they come to so they can watch their backtrails for danger. Whitetails generally try to circle behind a stillhunting archer instead of running dead ahead toward stand hunters—something to keep in mind if setting up a deer drive in heavy cover. Often the best deer-drive stands are to the sides or behind the walking drivers—not directly in front.

Whenever bowhunting whitetails, an archer must keep in mind that these are extremely wary survivors. If hunting pressure becomes too heavy or food conditions change, the deer automatically adapt to the circumstance by moving someplace else. For instance, many

whitetail spend their summers and early falls in standing yellow-corn fields, never leaving these until the corn is harvested and the artificial cover is destroyed. After that, the deer move into natural cover along the edges of these feeding fields. Similarly, if a rambunctious group of bowhunters decides to drive patches of prime whitetail cover, they should be aware that such activity is likely to relocate deer to other areas if drives are repeatedly conducted. It is usually better to wait silently to capitalize on the regular movements of whitetails —not to disrupt these movements with less sophisticated techniques.

The whitetail deer is a fine bowhunting animal. It is alert and extremely nervous but is also abundant and widespread. Whitetail meat is incredibly good stuff, and mature bucks are decidedly handsome, striking trophies. It's little wonder these deer are so overwhelmingly popular with bowhunters across the North American continent!

22/The Mule Deer

MANY SERIOUS eastern whitetail hunters regard the mule deer as a big, dumb galoot, a sort of imbecile brother to the sharp, cagey whitetail. The main reason for such feelings is the fact that there are no mule deer in the East for these skeptics to match wits with. As far as I'm concerned, a big mule deer buck is a *tougher* trophy than a whitetail to come by, mainly because of the terrain big mulies prefer and the fact that these deer are seldom bowhunted from stands. The average whitetail may be more nervous than the average mule deer, but typical mule deer terrain and necessary mule deer hunting techniques more than even the odds that deer will win and hunters will lose.

General Description

Odocoileus hemionus is a stout, stocky animal with heavier-boned features than the average whitetail. A mature adult stands about 40 inches high at the backline, measures somewhere around 75 inches from nose tip to tail, and weighs in the neighborhood of 175 to 200 pounds on the hoof. Especially fat, large-framed bucks have been recorded at over 400 pounds on the hoof. As with other deer species, mulies vary somewhat in average size from area to area. As a rough rule of thumb, these deer are the stockiest and heaviest in the northern parts of their range and the leanest and lightest in the southern parts.

The mule deer got its name from its overly large ears, which average about 22 inches from tip to tip when alertly cupped and flared. These ears project from a blocky head that is quite distinctive in appearance, the forehead being dark gray or black, in sharp contrast to the uniformly colored face of the whitetail. The balance of the face is a lighter gray, with muted gray-white highlights around the eyes, along the cheeks, and under the chin. The throat usually has two off-white patches divided by a dark-gray bar—patches which merge into the basic steel-gray color of the deer's body. The belly and inner legs are fringed with light gray merging to white near the center.

A very distinctive and easy-to-see coloration is the very large, prominent white patch covering the majority of the rump—a patch extending from the top of the tail right down to where the belly begins. The tail, white, except for a jet-black tip about 2 inches long, is much shorter and more ropelike than the fluffy tail of the whitetail, and the black tip stands out dramatically against the white rump, like the bull's-eye on a target.

The mule deer has the potential to grow absolutely breathtaking antlers. They are entirely different in shape than those of the whitetail, taking a typical "bifurcated" formation with two beams branching from the base area, then forking again like slingshots. A typical mule deer buck has an eyeguard near the base of each antler, generally much shorter than that on a whitetail.

Distribution and Preferred Habitat

Mule deer inhabit the western half of the United States in excellent numbers. Their range stretches from the central Dakotas and central Texas west to within 200 miles of the Pacific coastline, and from the northern edge of British Columbia, Alberta, and Saskatchewan all the way south into central Old Mexico.

Mule deer are quite adaptable within their range, inhabiting alpine peaks of 12,000-foot altitudes to low sage-brush flats and broken river-bottom badlands. The average mule deer lives at a higher elevation than the average whitetail, preferring more open terrain with a view. However, there are notable exceptions to this, for mule deer are sometimes seen feeding with whitetails in western farmland country and are sometimes found inhabiting ultra-dense juniper or cedar thickets even whitetails might find constraining.

Mule deer do not seem as compatible with human-kind as whitetail, with the majority of these animals

Many western mule deer inhabit high, semi-open mountain terrain with a view.

A typical four-point mulie's antlers double-branch like slingshots from a relatively short base section. Eyeguards are not always present.

(Right) The mule deer is a magnificent and distinctive-looking animal. (Photo courtesy of Russell Thornberry)

found in relatively remote locales well away from major towns and cities.

Mule deer in general have much larger home territories than do whitetail. Some mule deer are so-called "residents" living out their entire lives in fairly low-elevation country and moving around to find food within several square miles of terrain. Others live in loose-knit migrating herds, spending their summers in high, cool country and migrating to low winter range when snow becomes deep or high-country feed is killed off by frost. A few herds migrate up to 100 miles between summer and winter range, but the average migration is something closer to 10 or 20 miles.

Basic Behavior Profile

A mule deer is a calmer, more docile animal than the high-strung whitetail. However, this animal is less predictable about how and when it moves, making bowhunting primarily a stalking or stillhunting proposition. Add to this the fact that mule deer tend to stay in

Mule deer bed in heavy cover in some locales, but tend to prefer fairly open areas to feed. (Photo courtesy Russell Thornberry)

Mule deer sometimes live in agricultural bottom-land terrain, waxing fat on the same kinds of feed as farmland white-tail deer.

open or semi-open terrain where they can use their eyes to best advantage, and the chore of taking a nice specimen with a bow becomes a definite challenge. To top all this off, most mulies inhabit steep mountain terrain or at least prefer foothill terrain with plenty of draws, ridges, and small peaks. Such country is often extremely tough to move around in quietly, and the breezes in areas with broken topography also tend to be frustratingly inconsistent. Because a mule deer prefers such difficult-to-bowhunt country, the animal represents a definite test of skill.

Mule deer generally feed heavily during early morning and late evening hours, bedding the balance of the day in the same area where morning feeding occurred and perhaps rising once or twice during daylight hours to eat a bit more or to change positions to be more physically comfortable. These deer usually prefer to bed on high ridges where they can see and smell danger from afar. They are extremely comfort-oriented, choosing warm, sunny slopes when temperatures are chilly, choosing cool shady slopes when temperatures are warm, and generally lying on the calm, wind-protected sides of hills when breezes really gust up. They drift around from day to day, perhaps remaining on the same mountainside for an extended period of time but seldom bedding, feeding, watering, and moving in the same places from one day to the next.

Mule deer eat a wide variety of grasses and brush types. Among the most common foods are snowberry, cedar, oak, mountain mahogany, sagebrush, and bitterbrush. In addition, they sometimes home in on western ranch crops like alfalfa and wheat if the fields are adjacent to typical semi-open foothill or mountain habitat where the mulies can bed during midday hours.

As with most deer species, mule deer bucks usually hang off by themselves in bachelor groups until the mating season commences late in the year. Quite often, the prime big-buck hotspots are several miles away from the areas frequented by does, fawns, and immature yearling bucks. As a general thing, the bucks prefer higher, more rugged terrain than the does and youngsters do.

Although young, small mulie bucks can act downright dumb at times, the truly big-racked animals between 4 and 7 years of age can become astonishingly alert and wary when subjected to regular hunting pressure. There is nothing dumb at all about a mature, hunter-wise mulie, and nothing particularly calm and complacent, either. Such a deer is a fine-tuned survival machine for sure!

Mule deer rut after most bow seasons are closed, but rut-crazy mulie bucks leave antler rubs (above) and scrapes the opportunity to try for rutting late-season mule deer. (Photo courtesy Russell Thornberry)

(Right) A truly fine mule deer like the author's makes a first-class bowhunting trophy.

Typical Mule Deer Sign

Mule deer litter their favorite areas with plenty of big, boxy tracks and lots of small, oval droppings. Such sign is scattered all over—mute testimony to this deer's random movement peculiarities. Deer trails often lace their habitat, but they are seldom as heavily pounded out or as consistently used as the freeways whitetails follow to move from one place to another. The one exception to this is during the migration where movement between summer and winter ranges is often on well-established trails. However, very few bow seasons coincide with mule deer migration time, so trails offer little value to bowhunters.

Similarly, mule deer move around far too much to make shed antlers from previous seasons worth much to bowhunters seeking information about their whereabouts. An area with resident mule deer and lots of nice shed antlers can promise great trophy bowhunting, but more often a shed antler from the winter before belonged to a deer that may be 20 miles away during open bowhunting season.

Unbeknownst to most bowhunters, rutting mule deer leave scrapes and rubs the same as whitetail. Such rutting signs aren't quite as helpful to an archer if he's hunting one of the few open bow seasons at rutting time, mainly because mulies move around more and are less likely to revisit scrapes and rub areas on a regular basis.

As is the case with whitetail, mule deer are often best located by finding the deer themselves. A scouting bowhunter who doesn't mind cruising ridgelines early and late in the day can usually spot plenty of them feeding in good areas with the aid of top-quality binoculars. These slate-gray deer (reddish in color during really early summer bow seasons) stand out well in most forms of foliage, especially their large white rumps.

Productive Bowhunting Techniques

The traditional method of bowhunting mule deer is spotting animals from afar, planning a feasible approach strategy, and then stalking in with the hope of making a kill. A bowhunter in good physical shape can make this technique pay off regularly in semi-open mountain and foothill terrain. The keys are spending time along high points and ridgelines until deer are spotted with binoculars or the naked eye, and then adhering to sound stalking techniques outlined in Chapter 15.

217

Mule deer have the exasperating habit of bedding in all directions to prevent danger from slipping in unawares.

(Left) An exceptional buck like Lyle Dorey's No. 1 Alberta bow-and-arrow record mule deer is truly the trophy of a bowhunting lifetime. (Photo courtesy of Russell Thornberry)

In some areas with rolling hills dotted by scattered shrubs and trees, a bowhunter can also successfully stillhunt mule deer. This particular technique also works well in areas where they retire to evergreen thickets early in the morning, then feed some more under the cover of trees prior to bedding down for the day. Though still hunting does not allow an archer to size up trophy heads prior to moving in close, it certainly does produce deer on a regular basis for archers who hunt areas where mulies are hard-hunted by riflemen and are prone to stay in heavy cover.

Although stand hunting is not traditional for mule deer hunting, a few tree-stand specialists do exceedingly well on them in areas with heavy mountain mahogany, juniper, cedar, or oak brush. Some of the biggest mule deer bucks in the West stick close to such heavy cover, and a bowhunter who locates a concentration of nice bachelor bucks can sometimes waylay one by sitting in a heavy-cover stand day after day until the right deer walks by.

In certain circumstances, jumpshooting, driving, calling, and other specialized techniques can put bow-and-arrow mule deer in the bag. However, stalking, stillhunting, and stand hunting account for the majority of mulies taken by bowhunters every year.

How to Judge a Trophy

A mature mule deer's heavy, wide-flung rack makes a magnificent sight for any hunting archer. The rack on an average buck is apt to astonish an eastern whitetail hunter because it absolutely dwarfs an average white-tail rack. Truly outsized mule deer antlers will leave the most experienced western archer either speechless or babbling incoherently about the gigantic trophy. From an antler standpoint, the mule deer is hard to beat.

Using its ear span measurement as a guide, a reasonably close assessment of a head-on mule deer's rack can be made. The average mature buck usually sports a rack of ear width or slightly wider—a rack with an outside spread in the neighborhood of 24 or 25 inches. The rack typically has three or four points per side plus eyeguards, although eyeguards are often absent from even large mule deer antlers.

The magic antler-spread measurement for many serious mule deer hunting enthusiasts is 30 inches. Some truly nice deer are taken every year with spreads between 26 and 29 inches, but a buck with a spread an honest 30 inches wide is spectacular to see, provided the deer has four or more points per side, point length of 6 to 12 inches, and antlers with bases nearly as thick as axe handles. If the antlers are reasonably high as well, it will score well up in bowhunting record books.

The truly cream-of-the-crop mule deer bucks are staggering to see. These fellows vary an awful lot in antler conformation, from typical 4x4s with massive beams, long points, and spreads between 30 and 40 inches to non-typical monsters with antler points sprouting every which direction. Most such racks are incredibly massive, resembling elk antlers as much as those of mule deer. A typical once-in-a-lifetime bow-and-arrow mule deer from a top trophy-producing state like Colorado, Utah, Idaho, or Wyoming will have

(Left and above) When field dressed and transported to a meat locker promptly, a fat mule deer is hard to beat on the table!

antler bases 4 to 6 inches in circumference, an outside spread of 28 to 40 inches, at least 5 or 6 antler points per side, and individual points 10 to 15 inches long.

Other Important Facts

A mule deer's ears are big and impressive looking, and they work every bit as well as they look like they would. However, they still trust their noses more than their ears or eyes. A bowhunter cannot make serious stalking errors, but he can occasionally get away with showing himself briefly or making slight noises if he'll hide for awhile after making such blunders. A mule deer that sees or hears something suspicious and doesn't vacate the area post-haste will often freeze for 5 to 30 minutes to check out the countryside thoroughly, then relax and continue feeding or lie down to rest and chew its cud. At this point, the bowhunter can carefully resume his stalk. By contrast, the mule deer that smells a hunter invariably runs or sneaks away at once.

In first-rate mule deer habitat, one of the primary problems with stalking is an overabundance of animals. In areas with mixed bucks and does, getting past multiple does and fawns to set up a shot at a target buck can be darn near impossible with all those noses, ears, and eyeballs in the immediate vicinity. Even when stalking a group of bachelor bucks without does nearby, the two to six mulie bucks that normally hang together invariably lie down facing different directions with a very good view of most approach routes a bowhunter can take. The best way to foil such wary groups of bucks is to somehow get above them on a hillside—these deer normally bed on a slope so they can gaze downhill and to the sides. If no immediate approach is possible, a bowhunter must bide his time until the deer move, or come back another day and hope to find a better stalking setup.

Bowhunters who wish to try for mule deer should practice their long-range shooting skills, and also practice shooting up and down hills. Although I have shot mule-deer bucks as close as 7 feet, the average shooting on my personal trophies has been 40 to 50 yards—and almost always sharply up or down a hill. You can expect the same accuracy test when in mule deer mountains.

One other tip on bowhunting mule deer. These animals are often most abundant a fairly long hike away from roads—a fact necessitating some pre-planning on a bowhunter's part about how he intends to transport the meat and trophy if he happens to score. A big deer is too heavy to backpack out in one piece, and mulie terrain is seldom flat enough or consistently downhill to allow dragging the carcass. As a result, most taken a ways from roads are either boned out and carried in a backpack sack or transported on horses or mules.

The mule deer provides top-notch archery sport. Within its range, this deer is very abundant, allowing an archer to see quite a few per day if he gets out and walks around. Mature bucks of this species carry magnificent racks, and the topography they inhabit is often breathtakingly beautiful. Add to these things the basic difficulty of setting up a shot at a mulie in its steep, broken habitat, and the whole hunting experience is very interesting indeed!

23/The Blacktail

The blacktail deer is a small but very challenging bow-and-arrow animal.

THE BLACKTAIL is a small deer by any standard, but this little runt makes up for its physical size by offering absolutely top-notch bowhunting sport. The blacktail is in many ways a pleasant, pint-sized combination of the whitetail deer and mule deer, offering the unpredictable foot-hunting challenge of the mulie coupled with the extreme alertness and love for heavy cover displayed by the whitetail. Because of its far-West habitat, the blacktail is often overlooked by otherwise savvy bowhunters. However, this animal is becoming a solid entry in the deer-hunting lists of more and more archers as modern sportsmen discover the challenge and excitement associated with hunting this wily Pacific-Coast prize.

General Physical Description

Odocoileus columbianus is a small, fine-boned deer by mule-deer standards. Resembling the mule deer in overall body configuration, it stands about 38 inches high at the shoulder, measures about 60 inches from nose tip to tail, and weighs an average of 120 pounds on the hoof. Blacktail tend to be heavier and stockier in the northern part of their range, lighter and lankier to the south. A few northern blacktails from Alaska and British Columbia have been unofficially estimated at 200 or 250 pounds on the hoof. By contrast, mature bucks from California sometimes weigh no more than 100 pounds on the hoof.

A blacktail is an extremely handsome customer with finely etched facial features. Its ears are more like those of the mulie than of the whitetail, perhaps a bit less prominent but still wide and deeply dished.

Because the blacktail is most often bowhunted in the summertime instead of fall, its typical body coloration is a summer rust-red when archers see it. This reddish summer hair is replaced by mousy gray winter hair in September and October. The facial coloration also resembles that of the mule deer, except the forehead is

The blacktail got its name from its solid-colored tail, which varies from a dark brown in the summer to jet black in the fall.

mulies the same age, and often sprout only three points per side on adults plus fairly small eyeguards. Blacktail racks are generally handsome and nicely formed—merely pint-sized to fit the deer wearing them.

Distribution and Preferred Habitat

Blacktail deer are strictly Pacific Coast animals, inhabiting a narrow coastal band over 3,000 miles long but averaging less than 200 miles wide. Four American states harbor blacktail deer—Alaska, Washington, Oregon, and California. In addition, the coastal Canadian province of British Columbia has a large blacktail population.

Most sportsmen who have not actually hunted blacktail regard these animals as inhabitants of thick, lush coastal rainforests. It is true that many blacktails do inhabit exactly this kind of terrain in coastal Washington, British Columbia, and Alaska, but many more reside in completely different environs. You see, the

Blacktail deer inhabit a wide variety of terrain. There are over two dozen blacktails in this one herd seen feeding in semi-open grass-and-oak habitat.

(Right) A really large blacktail like the author's fine 4×4 trophy is extremely difficult to come by. This particular deer was shot over 10 miles from the nearest road after a long backpack trip over rugged terrain.

not as dark on the average. There is less white encircling the eyes and marking the throat, neck, and underparts on a blacktail, and the distinctive white rump patch of the mule deer is entirely missing. There is often the faint suggestion of double white patches in the frontal neck area, but the patch under the throat is usually predominant.

The blacktail was named after its distinctive dark-colored tail, which varies from solid dark brown in the summertime to jet black in the fall. The tail is short like the mule deer's, but fluffier with a faint strip of white rump hair bordering it.

The antlers double-branch in mule deer fashion when mature bucks grow four main points per side. However, they are easily ⅓ smaller than those of

(Below and right) Blacktail deer often live in "edge" areas with heavy bedding cover but sizable openings where they feed.

Basic Behavior Profile

Blacktail are alert, relatively nervous animals falling somewhere between whitetails and mule deer in basic temperament. They are every bit as unpredictable about movement as mule deer, perhaps inhabiting a large home territory but wandering about this range willy-nilly to conform to feed and weather conditions. In typically brushy or heavily timbered habitat, this lack of predictability makes bowhunting one trophy buck a real problem because you cannot glass large open tracts to locate it wherever it might be on a particular day. Unless the terrain being bowhunted is high open ground or grassland mixed with heavy patches of brush, an archer after blacktail usually sees a particular deer once and only once in the course of several hunting days.

Like other deer, blacktails feed most vigorously near dawn and dusk. They tend to loaf in the open near brushy edges throughout the night, alternating between contented cud-chewing and getting up now and then to grab a few more bites of food. Unless weather is particularly cool or foggy, they disappear into heavy bedding thickets for the balance of the day or bed in openings adjacent to heavy cover.

Blacktail seem to have a more pronounced tendency to move about and feed sporadically during the midday hours than most other types of deer. These animals might disappear in ultra-heavy cover at the crack of dawn, but a bowhunter who haunts rainforest thickets or sits high and glasses hillsides covered with brush throughout the day will usually spot blacktails off and on as they rise to feed briefly and then lie down again.

Primarily browsers, blacktail will eat certain grasses if ample nutritious brush is not easily found. Blacktails love to eat ceanothus, chamise, mountain mahogany, oak brush, and a few other bushes common within their range. They also love acorns and freshly blown-down oak leaves in the fall. When regular browse is scarce,

blacktail is an extremely adaptable animal and can be found in hot brushfields, tree-choked river bottoms, grass-and-oak savannah country, and high alpine mountain terrain as well as rainforest habitat. Black-tails seem well adapted to living near human habitation, adopting living habits not unlike those of farmland whitetail. In some cases, blacktails migrate between high summer range along mountain peaks and low winter range at the base of these mountains. It seems that along the western coast of North America, the little blacktail deer has filled both the high-elevation niches normally held by mulies and low-elevation niches usually held by whitetail. The reason for this remains a mystery, but the accommodating little blacktail seems at home anywhere near the ocean if ample food, water, and bedding cover are handy.

Glassing and stalking is one favored method of taking brush-country blacktail deer. The hunter in this photo is Bob Brandau, well-known archer and deer enthusiast.

(Below) A large, mature blacktail buck like the one skylined here is seldom easy to get close to. As often as not, when a bowhunter spots such a buck, the animal is already staring suspiciously at the archer.

these little deer can survive nicely by eating wild oats, bromegrass, and ferns. It is difficult to fully list all foods blacktail eat because their range is so long and flora varies so much.

In the summertime when blacktail are often bowhunted, the mature bucks are clustered in little groups of two to six. These animals do not seem as judicious about bedding on high ground so they can look in all directions as mule deer do, perhaps because they prefer less open bedding areas where they rely to a greater degree on sound and smell to flush out potential danger. Like mulies, blacktails prefer to bed in a comfortable place with a cooling breeze and shade in warm weather or warm sunlight in cold weather. They usually bed high on ridges or points where daytime thermals tend to sweep up the scent of predators and man.

As with any type of deer, the young bucks in any blacktail herd tend to be the least alert and most naive. By contrast, an older trophy-sized buck with several hunting seasons behind him is noticeably jumpier and is seldom seen a second time if a bowhunter gets in close, blows his chance, and spooks the animal badly.

Typical Blacktail Sign

Blacktail leave the same wandering tracks and scattered droppings seen in good mule deer habitat. However, the tracks are smaller, daintier imprints to match these smaller creatures.

In well-used blacktail areas, heavy cover is often tunneled with frequently used trails. The same deer might not show up on these trails from day to day, but the most convenient ones are used frequently by all blacktails in the area.

The very best way to locate blacktail in mountain country with even a partial view is glassing for them throughout the day. Once an animal is spotted, some sort of bowhunting strategy can often be devised. Blacktails stand out particularly well against typically

green coastal habitat during late-summer bow seasons because they are still yellow-red in color at this time of year.

Productive Bowhunting Techniques

Every traditional deer-hunting technique can be used on blacktail somewhere within their 3,000-mile-long range. The most commonly employed is probably stillhunting, mainly because the bulk of their habitat is dense rainforest or fairly dense brush mixed with trees. Stillhunting can be a particularly productive endeavor in blacktail haunts if coastal fog is thick—this cool, damp stuff makes walking quiet, lets a stillhunter slip close to deer, and keeps deer up and feeding longer than they would be on days that quickly become warm.

Stalking is another suitable method in high alpine terrain or any other semi-open habitat. Jumpshooting is sometimes the end result of stalks on blacktails seen in fairly heavy cover, because once an archer leaves a vantage point and drops into cover, he often completely loses sight of the game he is stalking and discovers the animal can only be shot at if booted out of a heavy brushpile.

In heavily timbered habitat, bowhunting from a tree

Blacktail-hunting weather is often warm, necessitating prompt drives to nearby meat lockers.

stand can be an excellent approach, provided the area being hunted is densely populated. In such a situation, a tree-stand overlooking a well-used trail or several trails will generally produce shots as deer wander through the immediate vicinity. This sort of bow-hunting will probably seem hit-and-miss to the archer accustomed to setting his watch by the regular movements of whitetail, but patient waiting will pay off on blacktails in a well-chosen stand.

One of the most popular hunting methods in heavy coastal rainforests is calling these animals with a commercial or homemade deer call which imitates the bleat of a fawn in pain or distress. Calling often produces spectacular results for archers if camouflage clothing matches terrain well and hunters set up where they can draw and shoot without incoming deer seeing them and running away. Deer-calling is especially effective on blacktails when two archers work as a team with one calling and the other sitting farther upwind to ambush incoming game.

Drive-hunting sometimes produces decent shots in areas where archers literally surround brush patches or isolated stands of timber. However, blacktails are less prone to follow established escape routes when spooked than whitetail and are more prone to take off running and *keep on* running rather than sneaking out cautiously around the drivers. As I always say, drive hunting is a bowhunting technique to be used only when all else fails.

How to Judge a Trophy

A big blacktail looks small to a hunter used to looking over mule deer bucks. A blacktail carries a rack seldom measuring over 18 inches wide, often higher then it is wide, and almost never non-typical with points sprouting every which way like some whitetail and mule

deer racks. It is generally a nicely formed, extremely symmetrical basket with several very even points per side.

The blacktail's ears measure an average of 18 inches from tip to tip, which provides a good means of judging the width of trophy racks. Any buck with ear-wide antlers is a dandy. If the rack has four points per side, not counting eyeguards, it will score quite well in any bowhunter's record book. The antlers tend to be less massive than those of mule deer and whitetail, although thick-beamed blacktail racks are occasionally taken by bowhunters. Any 4x4 blacktail buck with an average point length of 3 inches or more is a very good trophy.

Any rack measuring over 20 inches wide must be considered huge, provided it has other characteristics to match. If a rack this wide has four points per side, nice little eyeguards, bases at least 3½ inches in circumference, and even tines 3 to 6 inches long, it is a once-in-a-lifetime blacktail trophy with bow or gun. Racks measuring 25 or 26 inches wide (outside spread) have been recorded, but these are rare as hen's teeth no matter where you go in blacktail country.

Other Important Facts

Because blacktail are usually fairly small in body size, hunting them for the first time can completely ruin an archer's practiced ability to accurately estimate shooting distance by eye. The usual tendency is to shoot high because they appear farther away than they really are.

Since they often hunt in warmer than normal temperatures, early-season blacktail buffs must dress accordingly and be prepared to rush any downed deer to a meat locker as soon as possible. The blacktail's relatively small body size contributes to quick heat dissipation from meat, but this doesn't do one iota of good if daytime temperatures are hovering in the 90s or low 100s. Hot temperatures are especially typical of California, which can be positively sweltering during the normal July and August blacktail bow seasons.

Camouflage T-shirts, brim-full bota bags, cool footwear, and other warm-weather gear are definitely par for the course when bowhunting during the hot, humid Pacific-Coast summer. If you plan to bowhunt blacktail, find out about temperatures to be expected and prepare accordingly. Ordinary bowhunting garments can positively cause heat stroke in some environments.

The blacktail is one of the most sporting deer in North America. This animal is smart, wary, and full of surprises, a combination that taxes any archer's skills to the utmost. The blacktail may not be particularly large in physical size, but no deer is bigger in terms of challenge and archery-hunting pleasure. This animal has a nervous temperament and heavy-cover preferences similar to those of the whitetail, yet also displays the notable lack of predictability inherent in mule deer. Combine all three survival traits in a single species of deer, and the result is an exceptionally difficult but enjoyable animal to hunt!

(Right) A blacktail buck may not be huge in antlers or body, but archers who have hunted this animal regard it as a top-notch bowhunting trophy.

24/The Elk

IN MANY bowhunters' minds, a mature bull elk is America's most desirable big game trophy. This animal has an abundance of attributes to support this notion, including a spectacular rack, several hundred pounds of beef-quality meat, and an overall grace and majesty other deer are hard pressed to match. Add to these traits the spine-chilling sound and raw animal belligerence of a mature herd bull during the rut, and the elk is truly a stand-out deer worthy of any bowhunter's attention.

General Physical Description

Aside from the moose, the elk is America's largest antlered animal. A mature bull 3 to 5 years old will weigh 600 to 800 pounds on the hoof, measure about 9 feet from nose tip to tail, and stand a full 5 feet high at the shoulder. At times, an elk can weigh considerably more than the norm, with a few officially recorded body weights of well over 1,000 pounds. Most of the heaviest-bodied elk have been so-called Roosevelt elk, which live only along the Pacific Coast of North America. Cows are generally about 20 to 30 percent smaller in size and weight than their male counterparts.

Elk vary somewhat in basic body coloration, from a medium reddish brown in cows and young bulls to an off-white silver-gray in older herd bulls. The average body color is a medium gray-brown. In contrast to whitetails, mule deer, and blacktails, the elk has very dark underparts and inner legs. Its neck and head are normally a very rich chestnut brown, the neck usually being a little bit darker than the head. The neck is characterized by a slight bearding or fringing of longer hairs from under the chin down to the point of the chest. The rump is distinctively marked with a large cream-yellow patch of hair shaped similarly to the rump patch on a mule deer. The elk's short, stubby tail is this same cream-yellow color.

Sometimes an elk looks to be somewhat awkward because it has relatively long legs in relation to its body. However, this animal moves with the smooth grace of a professional track runner, walking, galloping, and running full out with the same basic agility and fluid economy of movement.

The ears are fairly small compared to the size of the elk's head and body, its face broad, its nose wide and massive. However, this animal still has finely cut features with a definite look of alertness and intelligence—traits an elk certainly does have.

A bull's antlers are large and beautiful—enough to stagger the sensibilities of any bowhunter accustomed to trying for smaller species of deer. Even a juvenile "raghorn" 2 or 3 years of age sometimes carries a rack with five or six points per side and overall dimensions guaranteed to put any mule deer buck to shame. A typical mature bull annually grows a rack with five, six, or seven long, heavy points per side, a main beam over 4 feet long, and a spread over 3 feet wide. Such a rack makes a spectacular trophy for any hunting archer.

Distribution and Preferred Habitat

The elk, *Cervus canadensis*, inhabits a spotty range across the western United States. This animal was once found over much of the lower 48 states and was primarily a grass-eating plains dweller when white men first arrived in North America. However, this smart, adaptable animal quickly vacated more open ground and took up residence in thick, protective mountain forests in the face of hunting and shooting pressure plus increased open-ground human habitation.

Today, elk inhabit every Rocky Mountain state from Montana and Idaho south into Arizona and New Mexico. In addition, there are thriving herds of elk in the Canadian Rockies along the British-Columbia/Alberta coastline, along the Pacific Coast from central California into southern British Columbia, on Alaska's Afognak Island, and in a few other scattered locales

Elk are magnificent animals with big bodies and oversized antlers to match!

The modern elk is primarily a forest dweller, although it prefers to eat grass instead of browse. (Photo courtesy of Russell Thornberry)

(Right) A decent trophy bull like the author's nice 5×5 requires careful bowhunting technique and pinpoint shooting. Adams called in this bull and shot it through the heart at 58 yards.

like the Black Hills of South Dakota.

Typical habitat consists of heavy evergreen timber and mountain aspen thickets interspersed with occasional grassy openings or meadows. Modern elk are primarily mountain dwellers, but still require grass to eat as they did in their plains-dwelling days. In some uniformly timbered areas, elk can survive quite nicely on grass underneath the trees, and in such places they seldom stray far from protective cover.

Despite the preference for the type of terrain just described, these animals also inhabit some pretty off-beat environments. For example, lightly hunted elk on some large Rocky Mountain ranches have reverted to former habits and can be seen feeding on sagebrush flats or out in the middle of open, grassy plains. In the

Southwest, some gigantic-antlered bull elk are taken by bowhunters on a regular basis in out-and-out desert terrain complete with cactus, scrub mesquite, and other non-typical elk cover. As long as elk can get to water and find some grass to eat, they seem to do okay in a variety of terrain and climatic zones.

Basic Behavior Profile

Elk are probably not quite as alert and nervous by nature as whitetail, blacktail, or even mule deer. However, they make up for this by spending most of their time in herds of 3 to 200 animals. The herds are generally led by a mature, especially wary cow, and this old crone plus all the other eyes, ears, and noses in the herd protect the group from various forms of danger.

(Above and opposite page) Rutting bull elk leave large, easy-to-spot antler rubs on trees within their breeding areas.

(Left) Elk leave large, distinctive tracks slightly less boxy than those of cattle.

Most large trophy bulls tend to hang off by themselves except during the September rutting season and are difficult to find in the vast maze of blow-down logs and densely clustered trees where they make their home. The very best time to find bulls is during the September rut, and fortunately a good many archery elk seasons occur at this time of year.

Elk are primarily grass eaters, their favorites being bluegrass, wheatgrass, and bromegrass. In addition, elk will occasionally eat oak brush, conifers, and willow brush if such browse is handier than grass or if grass is deeply covered by snow. Elk seem to have a definite weakness for aspen bark, peeling this off with their teeth and chewing it vigorously.

Unless hard-hunted by riflemen, they tend to feed fairly late into the morning and begin feeding again fairly early in the afternoon. If hunting pressure is on, elk usually vacate open areas fairly early and do not pop out again till fairly late. However, the animals feed for several hours each day under cover of trees and brush. They seldom sleep in midday, lying in heavy timber and brush to chew their cuds and relax. Such midday resting areas are usually on high slopes or points where an elk has the best chance of hearing or smelling nearby danger. In most mountain areas, elk generally feed downhill in the evening and move upward again from daylight until mid-morning hours.

Elk, like most other deer, are extremely comfort- and food-oriented animals. They seek shade in hot weather, lie in little sunny openings when it is cold, and hole up in the heaviest timber available to ensure protection when it rains, snows, or blows. Since elk prefer grass, they are usually found where this food is most readily accessible—if grass is sparse or completely covered with snow, the chances of finding elk are slim.

In many ways, elk resemble large, antlered cattle in their basic habits. They eat grass, lounge away the bulk of the day, and bed where temperatures and wind conditions are most comfortable. In addition, they have a definite weakness for salt, mineral licks, and mineral springs found within their territory.

Inhabiting fairly large home ranges, elk often move 5 or 10 miles in one direction if danger or lack of food necessitates such moves. In addition to normal movement, lone bull elk on the prod cover lots of ground throughout the day during the peak of the rutting season.

Typical Elk Sign

Elk leave a variety of sign important to a serious bowhunter. Of primary significance are the large, somewhat cow-like tracks of these big deer, and the thumb-sized, oval-shaped droppings they scatter about their feeding areas. Elk tracks are a bit more slender

An elk wallow is a territorial marker which a bull will visit repeatedly over the course of the September rutting period.

than those of cows, with slightly more pointed toes. Where fresh tracks and soft droppings abound, elk are seldom very far away.

In a heavily used area, a faint barnyard odor pervades the air in the quiet, heavy timber. Part of this odor comes from abundant elk droppings, and part from the animals themselves. Bull elk smell particularly rank during the rut, the tarsal glands on their hind legs smelling especially pungent.

Elk tend to wallow across cattle fences instead of jumping these cleanly, and since they often inhabit the same basic terrain as range cows, fences are commonplace in most good elk habitat. Broken-down fences with telltale elk hair caught in the wire can mark regular crossing places—places a hunter can set up effective morning or evening ambushes.

During the September rut, bulls clearly mark their territories in two basic ways. First, they leave large, bare antler rubs on trees—rubs that stand out clearly for all to see. In addition, bulls create large mud wallows near springs or flowing creeks, they roll in these to cool down their overheated, hormonally accelerated bodies and urinate in them to clearly mark their personal rutting districts. Fresh rubs and wallows are sure signs that bulls are in a particular area. These animals are apt to return to rubs and wallows regularly as they cruise about their rutting territories, something good bowhunters know and capitalize on.

Carefully moving along and glassing the forest edge will often reveal elk invisible to the naked eye.

229

much can sometimes take elk from tree stands or ground blinds placed near heavily used trails, fence crossings, natural mineral licks, or mountain crops like alfalfa or grain. Elk sometimes frequent specific areas, although these animals do not display the consistent movement patterns of whitetail.

The most exciting and most productive method of bowhunting elk is calling them during the September rutting period. Depending upon the year, the weather, and the locale, bull elk sometimes begin tuning up for the rut as early as late August and often finish the mating season as late as mid-October. However, the red-hot rutting peak occurs sometime in mid-September in most areas and lasts at least 2 weeks.

A bowhunter can go after rutting bulls in one of two ways. Because they are bugling regularly with long-distance, piercing notes, an archer can simply cruise good elk habitat, home in on the bugles of bulls, and stalk these sounds until a shot materializes. However, rutting elk move around a lot, which can make such sound-stalking a time-consuming, strenuous, and often frustrating endeavor.

A better way, in most circumstances, is learning how to call in rutting elk for a good shot. There are several

(Above and right) Calling elk with a turkey diaphragm is a very effective bowhunting technique. Several companies sell diaphragms, grunt tubes, instructional manuals, and how-to-call tape recordings with the bowhunter specifically in mind.

Productive Bowhunting Techniques

Before or after the September rut, elk are best bowhunted in their heavy-cover habitat by stillhunting timber or walking high ridges to spot distant animals and formulate stalking strategy. Elk move around a lot in big mountain country, requiring the most successful bowhunters to cover plenty of ground during a hunting day. It is not uncommon to cover 15 or 20 miles on foot between first daylight and dark in search of stalkable elk, and much of such terrain is fairly steep and rugged to boot.

Bowhunters who do not wish to exert themselves so

instructional tapes on bugling elk currently available through archery shops and sporting goods stores—tapes that tell you how to hunt, and also tell you how to imitate the sounds of rutting bull elk. The best of these include segments of actual elk bugling and grunting to help archers perfect their techniques.

There are two basic calls used by bowhunters. The most successful archers learn both. The first is a simple multiple-note bugle consisting of two, three, or four notes that rise to a peak and then fall back instantly to the lowest note again. The homemade elk whistle illustrated in Chapter 17 makes this basic bugle, and so do a variety of commercially available calls.

A truly big bull elk is a breathtaking bow-and-arrow trophy. Jeff Shimizu, the author's bowhunting friend, poses here with a tremendous five-point he arrowed in northern New Mexico. The bull is unofficially the largest 5×5 ever shot with a bow.

The grunt is another call a serious elk hunter should master. This is often called the chuckle and is made by an elk all by itself or after it lets out a series of regular bugles. The grunt consists of several hoarse, medium-pitch hiccups made in quick succession, and signals ultimate aggression and belligerence on the part of a riled-up bull. Some bowhunters have learned to produce realistic grunts by sucking air through a plastic or rubber "grunt tube," but most make this sound with the help of a turkey diaphragm call.

The turkey diaphragm is really the ultimate elk-calling tool for a bowhunter because it is capable of making the hoarse bugles of an old bull, the higher-pitched bugles of a younger bull, the sound of an immature spike bull barking, the assembly chirp of a cow calling her calf, and the very effective grunting of a hopping-mad bull. When used with a grunt tube to amplify sound, the diaphragm will elicit responding bugles from bulls that would be silent otherwise, and when a bowhunter presses such bulls by sneaking within 100 to 200 yards and then bugling, grunting, and smashing trees with a stick to imitate antlers thrashing, these pressured bulls often respond by running or sneaking to the hunter and presenting point-blank shots. At close range, a turkey diaphragm can be used effectively without a grunt tube, making it the only elk call which leaves both hands free to shoot a bow. This is a major advantage in all sorts of elk-calling situations.

Bull elk are especially easy to call early in the rut when they have not yet gathered their harems. Once the bigger bulls have gathered their harems, they still answer a bowhunter's artificial bugles but tend to be more reluctant about actually leaving their cows and pressing a fight with an intruder. However, an expert elk caller who presses a big herd bull closely can often draw the animal into point-blank range no matter how long the rut has been going on.

All kinds of commercial and homemade elk bugles elicit responses from nearby bulls, letting a bowhunter plan his strategy once he has pinpointed animals by sound. Purchase a reputable elk-calling tape at your archery shop or sporting goods store to perfect calling techniques. One of my favorites is sold by Rob Hazlewood, the well-known Montana elk-hunting enthusiast. For information on this particular tape, call or write Rob Hazlewood, 1540 Hayes Drive, Missoula, MT 59802/(406) 721-5538.

How to Judge a Trophy

Any mature bull looks huge to the average bowhunter. However, a prime, stand-out bull has certain characteristics that a serious trophy hunter looks for.

The nicest trophy bulls have five, six, or seven points per side—sometimes more. However, more important than point count is how long the points are, how heavy the main beam is, how widely the antlers are spread, and how symmetrical the overall rack happens to be.

A good, mounting-size bull elk generally has main beams at least 40 inches long, five or six points projecting from each beam that average at least 10 or 12 inches long, antler beams as large around as a man's wrist near the base, and an inside beam spread of at least 30 or 35 inches. To judge such a bull on the hoof, a bowhunter should objectively count the points on each side, determine their length as best he can, and try to realistically evaluate the beam mass, spread, and main beam length. A bull viewed from the side is a good one if its antler tips reach at least a foot beyond the highest point of its shoulder when it rocks its head back to bugle or sniff the air. A few real "rumpscratcher" bulls with beams 50 to 60 inches long can actually reach their frontal rump areas with the tips of their antlers. To judge elk-antler spread, a bowhunter should try to get a front or rear-end view of a bull's body. The average is about 30 inches wide, which means any rack that appears wider than an elk's chest, rump, and paunch should make a decent trophy.

A real top-class bull elk is almost always a 6x6 or better with antler beams too large to reach around with the fingers near the base, long, heavy points with plenty of white "ivory" showing near the tips, main beams extending to the middle of an elk's back or beyond when it throws back its head, and an inside antler

To preserve elk meat during warm September bow seasons, a hunter should quarter an animal and skin the quarters to promote rapid meat cooling and drying.

Other Important Facts

Because bowhunters can go after elk during the rut in most states, they have the very best chance of seeing wary old monsters that seldom expose themselves at saner times of the year. Such bulls are in a class all their own, approaching solitary whitetail trophies in their wariness and preference for heavy, remote cover. Only during the mating season do such "lunkers" lose some of their inherent caution to allow looks and potential shots.

Shooting at elk requires well-chosen equipment and well-practiced bow-shooting skills. An animal this large should be hunted with bows of 60 pounds or more, and many strong-armed archers use bows of 70 to 80 pounds to ensure arrow penetration. Even more important than a bow's draw weight is using a hunting broadhead of streamlined, sharp-nosed design to enter and slice through an elk with minimal friction.

Because they generally inhabit heavy evergreen cover, an archer must often shoot around pine boughs, over deadfall logs, or between fairly tight-knit branches. Such shooting is usually up or down hillsides as well. Mastering such shooting skills is fully covered in Chapter 10.

One other note on elk. These animals spoil very quickly unless promptly gutted, quartered, and skinned. A do-it-yourself archer who drops an elk several miles from the nearest road must be immediately prepared to cut up the animal in the field and begin ferrying out 100-pound quarters plus the head and/or hide.

An elk is a big, regal deer offering unsurpassed bowhunting thrills to any hard-working archer. With a little luck plus a lot of patience and skill, the end result of a bowhunt is fine meat on the table, a spectacular set of antlers on the wall, and a lifetime of memories about the excitement of the outing and the lofty grandeur of the country where the hunting took place!

spread significantly past the edges of the body. Such a rack usually has a very big "Y" between the last two points although this is not always the case. A bull of this caliber is seldom seen in the woods, but when such an animal appears there is no mistaking the ponderous, rolling rack, the uniformly long points, and the overall sense of tremendous antler mass.

The Moose/25

THE MOOSE is the heaviest-bodied deer species in the world. This huge animal carries a very large rack to match, making a mature bull moose one of the most exciting sights a bowhunter can ever see. A moose is also surprisingly difficult to bowhunt except during its October mating season, lurking in dense thickets of brush and trees and hiding incredibly well considering its size. There is no finer deer meat on the continent than that from a moose, and many expert hunters prefer it over any other outdoor game meat. The bowhunter who successfully penetrates a moose's eyes, ears, and ultra-sensitive snozzle will have a shot at the widest rack and the biggest chunk of game meat he'll ever take in North America.

General Physical Description

Alces alces is a ponderous, long-legged giant of a deer. A mature bull will normally stand 6 to 7½ feet tall at the shoulder hump, measure a full 10 feet long from nose tip to tail, and weigh well in excess of 1000 pounds. The largest variety, the Alaska moose, often weighs 1500 or 1600 pounds on the hoof, and a few exceptionally large bulls have been estimated by biologists at a full 1800 pounds. Canada moose are a bit smaller, but still weigh 1100 or 1200 pounds. The Shiras or Wyoming moose, the "runt" of the species, usually weighs a bit over 1000 pounds.

An interesting-looking animal to say the least, the moose appears to be assembled from the spare parts of other creatures. It has a hammer-shaped head tipped by a great, bulbous nose and topped by extremely short ears. The large, muscular neck tapers into tremendously powerful shoulders topped by a prominent hump of fat, gristle, and hair. Beneath the neck hangs a long stringer of hair-covered skin called a bell. The moose's body tapers down from the shoulders backward to lean, narrow hips. This body is supported by long, large-hoofed legs that keep the moose's chest and stomach

The moose is by far the largest deer in the world.

233

well over 3 feet above the ground. It is predominantly a dark-colored animal, ranging from deep gray to near-black reddish brown. The inner legs and inner ears are lighter gray to break the color monotony.

A moose moves with awkward jerky strides reminiscent of those displayed by a camel. However, it can eat up ground incredibly fast on its long legs, and can lope or run like a freight train in easy, graceful strides.

The cow is seldom considered a pretty animal because her homely head seems out of place on the strongly tapering body. However, add a set of wide-flung antlers and presto, the animal is transformed into a downright handsome brute! A set of antlers 50 to 70 inches wide seems to balance out a moose's looks considerably.

The antlers are entirely unique in shape and configuration. Basically, they consist of relatively short main beams which branch near the ear tips into wide palms to the rear and multiple, palmated points to the front. The rear palms on a moose rack are usually fringed with a series of points like dull teeth on a saw blade. A large rack will often weigh 75 or 80 pounds all by itself, making it the heaviest grown by any kind of deer.

Distribution and Preferred Habitat

Strictly a north-country animal, the moose inhabits the majority of Alaska, Canada, the Yukon Territory, and the Northwest Territories. In addition, the Wyoming or Shiras moose inhabits the northern Rocky Mountain states in huntable numbers in Idaho, Montana, and Wyoming. Shiras moose are also seen in northern Utah and Colorado, and Canada moose sometimes stray south into northern Maine, Michigan, and Minnesota. These big animals do not survive well

Moose enjoy wading in lakes and streams during summer months to ward off insects, cool down, and eat aquatic plants.

(Left and opposite page) Typical north-country moose terrain is a scenic mixture of big mountain valleys and steep, timber-studded slopes. ▶

near heavy human habitation, and are usually found in remote, roadless locales.

The general picture most non-moose hunters have of "old paddlehead" is one of a moose standing ankle-deep in swamp-water with lily pads and bullrushes all around. It is true that the moose has a definite affinity for water and loves to wade in lakes and streams to get at tender aquatic plants. Its long legs and overly large feet both allow it to wade water and walk in soft mud without sinking up to its eyeballs. However, this animal spends less time around moist, swampy areas than most people imagine.

In reality, the moose is largely a creature of forests and mountains, and is often found many miles from the nearest lake, preferring to feed and bed in dense brush or trees on steep, rocky slopes. Moose can and do live virtually anywhere there is plenty of brush to eat and timber to hide in. They enjoy rivers and lakes when these are handy, but by no means *need* to live along such water bodies at all times. Moose are most commonly seen around water in the summertime because wading and swimming in the cool stuff wards off both heat and obnoxious summertime flies. Aquatic vegetation is most luxuriant at this time of year, too, making it prime food.

Basic Behavior Profile

Moose are not as alert or as wary as elk or the smaller deer species. This might be due in part to the lack of steady hunting pressure in places where they abound. They have fairly good ears and eyes, but this animal's keenest survival sense is its nose. A moose can smell as well as any deer, and never lingers around when it gets a solid whiff of human odor.

Throughout the summer and early fall, moose are relatively sedentary animals, moving about very little except to water and feed. In August and September, they bed in extremely heavy cover throughout the day, chewing their cuds and whiling away daylight hours thinking whatever thoughts a moose normally thinks. When they rise to feed or water at this sluggish time of year, they seldom travel far and seldom stray more than 100 yards from very heavy cover. Moose before the October rut are often found bedding and living well up on mountain slopes—especially mature bulls, which tend to stay off to themselves or in the company of one or two other bachelor bulls.

Unlike elk, moose are browsing animals. They eat a variety of brush, including aspen, willow, fir, birch, snowberry, and mountain maple. This diet is supplemented by many other secondary kinds of plant growth because a moose is not too particular about what it chews up and swallows. As already mentioned, they also eat most forms of tender water-growing plants.

With the onset of the rut in late September or early October, a bull will drift away from its steep mountain habitat to lower elevations where cows are most apt to be. Most rutting activity occurs in well-watered valleys and draws. Bulls in the full swing of the rut are extremely dangerous and antagonistic toward other bulls, humans, pack horses, or anything else that invades their domain. There are documented instances when rut-maddened bull moose actually attacked automobiles and freight trains, with the consequences usually being a dead moose and damaged equipment.

Though moose are somewhat dangerous during the rut, this time of year is the very *best* time to locate trophy bulls. The animals are constantly on the go throughout the day and have lost much of their natural caution. This makes finding and arrowing a nice bull easier than normal.

No matter what the time of year, moose have a strong attraction to mineral springs and licks. They absolutely love the taste of salt, sulphur, and other natural minerals, making licks and springs excellent places of ambush.

Typical Moose Sign

Moose leave long, gigantic tracks all over their range which can be of special importance in locating heavy-cover animals prior to the rut. The tracks normally show deep dewclaw marks behind the main hoofprints,

A moose leaves a huge track often measuring over 10 inches long.

(Right) Shed moose antlers are sometimes important clues to the whereabouts of these big but elusive north-country deer.

(Left) A big bull moose makes a first-rate bowhunting trophy. The author dropped this 60-inch Alaska moose after spotting the animal's antlers from afar and making a long, time-consuming stalk.

and often exceed 10 inches in overall length. Moose also leave oval droppings in prime feeding areas—droppings a bit larger than the average man's thumb. Wandering more or less aimlessly as they feed and go to water, moose do not seem to follow set travel patterns. Since they often eat the very brush and trees they bed in, well-used trails are pretty much nonexistent except near mineral licks and springs.

During the rut, bulls paw out large circular scrapes or wallows in their mating territories. Bulls urinate in these, then roll in the mud until their bodies are thoroughly caked. Wallow areas mark where mature bull moose are likely to be and are one form of sign an early-fall bowhunter should keep a sharp lookout for.

Although not a surefire indicator of moose in every case, these animals often winter in the same areas where they rut, making shed antlers important signs bowhunters can read. A valley area littered with nice shed moose antlers might very well harbor trophy-sized rutting bulls as well.

A truly stand-out trophy moose has wide palms, heavy bases, and at least a dozen points per side. This shed antler more than fills the bill.

236

During late summer and early fall, sitting high and glassing is an excellent way of locating trophy moose.

A young bull moose carries spindly antlers with little or no palmation.

A birch-bark horn like the one being fashioned here by Fred Bear will make the rutting moans of a cow moose—sounds which often bring a big, rut-crazy bull running in like a locomotive.

Productive Bowhunting Techniques

The majority of pre-rut moose are spotted from a distance and carefully stalked. Such bowhunting can be very difficult—for two important reasons.

First, a late-summer moose tends to spend most or all of its time in extremely dense foliage. This makes the animal exceedingly difficult to spot in the first place—far more difficult than one might think when the animal involved is every bit as big as a horse. As often as not, a bowhunter who gets up high and glasses throughout the day will only see a moose's ear flick, spot it rise to shift its resting position or briefly feed, or locate the white flash of a freshly stripped antler palm. A bowhunter after a trophy bull can sometimes spot white antlers when finding a moose any other way would be darn near impossible. After a bull sheds his velvet in early to mid September, his rack stands out dramatically for several weeks until he soils it by walking through foliage and rolling in mud wallows. I

have spotted the white antler palms on moose up to 5 miles away with good-quality binoculars.

The second reason spot-and-stalk hunting for late-summer moose can be darn difficult is the fact that foliage is generally dense and terrain noisy to traverse. An archer who spots a distant animal cannot always find it in thickets after making a stalk, even if the quarry is still in the very same position. As often as not, crackling undergrowth and a heavy carpet of noisy leaves reduces a stalk attempt to an out-and-out waste of time. Such bowhunting is never easy, and the sneaky bowhunter who does take a September moose by stalking can pat himself on the back.

Stand hunting is a feasible bagging technique, but

This mature Canada moose was shot by author Adams at the peak of the rut. The animal had antlers over 50 inches wide–a dandy for this particular sub-species.

(Below and opposite page left and right) Because a moose is so darn big, it must be butchered at once, carried out of the bush on horseback, and rushed to cold storage via bush plane. For this reason, most bowhunters opt to try for moose with the help of a reputable outfitter.

only when an archer takes his stand within bow-shot of a northern mineral lick or spring. Such mineral moose attractors are quite common in some parts of Canada and Alaska.

Calling rutting bulls is a very effective bowhunting method at the height of the rut. Calling is an art which requires plenty of practice, but the hunter who learns what the moan of a love-sick cow sounds like and uses a birchbark horn or similar amplifier can end up with mature, wide-racked bulls storming toward him with vigor. Because most moose are taken with the help of bowhunting guides, the majority of archers leave the skillful calling work to hired professionals. A less difficult calling technique some archers have used with good results is rattling two small shed moose antlers together to simulate two bulls sparring over a receptive cow. When a bull is in close, pouring water into a lake or stream further provokes aggressive behavior because it resembles the sound of a cow moose urinating.

Moose during the rut can also be stalked quite successfully because they are often seen in semi-open terrain. However, these animals move about a lot, making it difficult to plan a stalk because the target bull is apt to be elsewhere when the hunter finally arrives.

How to Judge a Trophy

A bull moose is one of the most difficult of all deer to accurately trophy-judge on the hoof. Most bowhunters emphasize the widest spread of a moose rack when they talk about trophy size, but for the record book the spread is really less important than the width and length of the palms, number of points per side, and circumference of the antler bases.

A trophy-sized Alaska rack generally measures somewhere between 55 and 70 inches in overall spread. A Canada moose is a good one if it has a spread of 45 to 55 inches. The Shiras or Wyoming moose, which has the smallest rack of the three varieties, is hard pressed to measure past 35 or 40 inches.

When judging a rack, try to estimate overall spread in relation to the length of a yardstick. A moose is so large and ponderous that accurately judging spread can be difficult. However, one hint besides merely mentally yardsticking a rack is looking to see where the antler tips come in relation to the shoulder hump when the animal is broadside and looking toward you or looking the other way. If antler tips come even with the very top of the shoulder hump, the rack will probably measure 45 inches wide. If antler tips stretch to the back of the shoulder hump, it is probably in the 55- to

65-inch category. It takes plenty of practice and experience to accurately judge the spreads on bull moose.

A first-rate trophy has wide, long palms no matter what the subspecies being hunted. Obviously, narrow palms mean a poor-scoring target. A good, mature bull normally carries at least 10 points per side on its rack, and often 12 or 14. Bases of antlers between the antler burr and the beginning of the palmation normally measure 6 to 8 inches in circumference regardless of the kind of moose being bowhunted.

One thing to do when judging racks is looking at the basic way a rack sits on the head. Larger, more trophy-sized moose tend to carry racks with palms that lay back over the shoulders more or less parallel to the ground. Smaller, less impressive bulls often have palmations that sit up at a higher angle to the head, making them more visible when the bull looks directly at you.

cannot be backpacked very far, even if the animal is tediously butchered and cut into manageable pieces. A bowhunter might carry out meat ½-mile or so to a remote airstrip, but longer treks are real backbreakers and some of the meat will usually spoil before it can all be lugged to a pickup point. An outfitter with horses or mules can quickly carry moose quarters out of the woods, get them on a bush plane, and have them at a cold-storage plant in relatively short order.

Although the moose is extremely large, this animal drops very quickly when hit properly with a sharp, well-designed broadhead backed by a fairly heavy, deep-penetrating arrow shaft. I personally feel that bows much under 70 pounds are on the light side, but a 60-pound bow will kill moose if ribcage hits are made and broadheads are the sharp-nosed slicing variety.

The moose is a big, uniquely built deer with truly gigantic antlers atop its head. The remote, scenic

Other Important Facts

The vast majority of bowhunters engage the services of a licensed guide or outfitter. There are two basic reasons for this. First, moose live in remote, tough-to-reach terrain a do-it-yourself bowhunter simply cannot reach by automobile. Savvy outfitters know where they are and have the airplanes or pack strings necessary to get you there. Second, a moose is a huge beast which

northern country this animal inhabits is well worth a hunting trip all by itself, but a bow-and-arrow moose on top of the wilderness experience yields 500 to 700 pounds of edible meat plus a trophy rack that will cover most of an entire den wall. Getting this animal will most likely require plenty of walking and looking plus careful bowhunting technique, and such challenge adds value to the overall archery experience. A bowhunt for moose is an adventure every deer enthusiast should seriously consider!

26/The Caribou

THE CARIBOU is without a doubt North America's most spectacular-looking deer. The reason for this is simple enough. You see, a caribou carries the largest set of antlers in relation to its body size of any American deer, making them stand out dramatically and bob bewitchingly above the animal's head. That veritable brushpile of beams and points atop a mature bull's noggin is enough to blow any bowhunter's mind, and the frosting on the cake is the caribou's sleek, beautiful gray-and-white hide. Add to these basic trophy qualities the elegant, graceful way it moves about its range, and it is no wonder this animal is a favorite of many bowhunters in the know.

General Physical Description

A mature bull caribou, *Rangifer tarandus,* stands about 50 inches high at the shoulder, measures about 7 feet from nose tip to tail, and weighs between 300 and 350 pounds. Cows are considerably smaller in size and weight. The very largest bull, while still carrying summer fat prior to the September mating season, will sometimes weigh 400 pounds or more. A caribou is the only North American deer species in which both males and females carry antlers. The antlers on the females are much smaller and far less massive than those on the males.

Caribou vary in basic coloration depending upon the time of the year, the subspecies being considered, and the individual animal. However, most summer caribou are basically slate-gray with white nose-tips, a strip of white down the front of the throat, a white rump patch complete with stubby white tail, and white rings just above the hooves. The antlers on summer animals, although fully formed by mid-August, remain encased in gray velvet until sometime in late August or early September. The caribou's short, functional warm-weather coat is replaced by heavier winter hair in early fall. At this time of year, the creature carries its

prettiest cape, which is basically a rich chocolate brown with the white highlights already mentioned. At the same time, most of the neck hair on many of the biggest bulls turns nearly pure white, and these white neck manes can be seen clearly a very long distance away.

Caribou have somewhat homely faces when viewed at close range, featuring broad nose tips, elongated snouts, and fairly short, jug-handle ears. They move with a ground-eating, ambling sort of gait on long, efficient legs, seldom seeming to hurry but always covering plenty of landscape.

A big bull's antlers are simply huge in relation to its body. These antlers do not display the weight or mass seen in those of elk or moose, but the beam length and number of points is truly impressive. A mature trophy caribou's rack usually stands a full 50 inches above its head, spreads over 3 feet wide, and often sports 15 or 20 points per side. Such headgear rocking and bobbing as the animal moves is enough to blow any hunter's cool!

Distribution and Preferred Habitat

The caribou is strictly an animal of northern regions. The overall range of the four basic types recognized by record-keeping organizations and biologists spans the continent from the western Alaska Peninsula eastward to Newfoundland and from the southern Arctic south to the U.S./Manitoba border. Caribou often move hundreds of miles in the course of one year, making them difficult to locate unless an archer has carefully studied their movement patterns prior to a bowhunting trip.

They are primarily open-country animals, although they often feed and bed in thickets of cover near more open stretches of northern tundra. It is difficult to talk about a preferred habitat because it varies so much depending on the herd under consideration and the time of year. In general, caribou spend their summers

Caribou are unique, big-racked animals well worth trying for with a bow.

in high, relatively barren mountain terrain or at extreme northern latitudes where temperatures are relatively cool and insects are least abundant. They usually migrate to lower elevations and/or lower latitudes in late summer or early fall to escape the coldest winter weather. Caribou rely primarily on their eyesight for protection from predators, which is one reason they prefer fairly open terrain.

Basic Behavior Profile

Caribou can safely be considered the least alert and wary of North American deer. However, these animals are often maligned too much by riflemen who can bump off critters at several hundred yards. A caribou

The gray velvet covering a late-summer caribou's antlers can be left in place or stripped away at a bowhunter's discretion. Antlers are fully developed by late August or early September.

A gigantic bull caribou is an impressive trophy indeed. The author's Alaskan barren ground caribou green-scored well enough to make the top five in Pope and Young—a dandy trophy for sure!

(Below and right) As these aerial views show, caribou prefer open or semi-open terrain with a view.

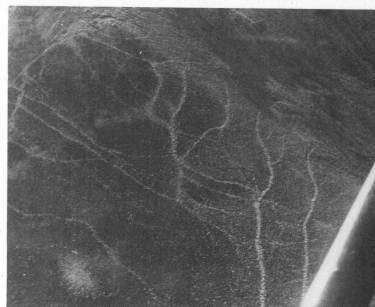

Productive caribou country is heavily laced with deep, meandering trails in shale and tundra.

can be a really tough customer to stalk within good bow-shooting range, especially in wide-open summer terrain where bulls often lounge around without moving very far. They are somewhat easier to take if a bowhunter manages to locate a major migration trail and sits on it for several days as hundreds of animals file by. However, taking caribou often requires long bow-shooting, ticklish stalks, plenty of physical exertion, and bout after bout with frustration.

Among the most unpredictable of animals, caribou meander over large tracts of real estate with no apparent plan of action in mind. Their tendency to lie down, stand up, and relocate long distances without warning makes them extremely difficult to locate and closely approach.

They prefer to feed off and on throughout the daylight hours, and can be seen in open areas throughout the long north-country days. These handsome deer lie down wherever their bellies happen to become full, chewing their cuds and flicking flies with their ears.

During the late summer and early fall, caribou are easily vexed by the stinging and biting insects that inhabit tundra areas, and usually choose to lie in snowbanks on shady slopes if snow is available in a partial attempt to avoid heat-loving flies. If a strong breeze is blowing, caribou often climb out on exposed ridgetops or peaks and stand with their tails to the wind to cool off and rid themselves of insects, or they will often run several miles along ridgelines in a futile effort to get away from the bugs.

Before the rut and migration period in September or October, bulls tend to hang apart from herds of cows and calves in small bachelor groups. As a general rule, the bulls favor the highest ground they can find at this time of year.

Caribou eat a variety of things, but lichens found in their northern habitat are their favorite food. They also feed on convenient bushes like blueberry and willow.

These deer almost always bed down throughout the nighttime hours, and animals spotted at dusk will usually be in the same place at dawn. This is important knowledge for the spot-and-stalk bowhunter because he can locate evening caribou and confidently plan early-morning sneaks.

With the onset of the early-fall rut, bulls become downright daffy, gathering small harems of cows and fighting frequently in heated battles. At this time of year, there is no telling when or where a caribou will move, although rutting animals generally cease their major migrating patterns until the rut has subsided.

Typical Caribou Sign

Caribou sign is of little value to bowhunters because these animals move such great distances and seldom display discernible, repeatable movement patterns. Any good caribou country is absolutely laced with trails where these animals have been—deep-cut trails formed by thousands of footfalls over hundreds of years.

A bowhunter can often scout the country by bush plane prior to a hunt, and sometimes areas with lots of trails are also areas with lots of caribou. However, in such scouting endeavors it makes far more sense to look for the critters themselves rather than trails which might or might not have been used for months.

It is encouraging when walking around your chosen hunting area to see plenty of fresh caribou tracks and lots of droppings. On summertime hunts, before animals actively migrate, such fresh tracks meandering every which direction do help keep a bowhunter's spirits high and give him the assurance that at least a few "bou" are in the area.

The track is a completely unique imprint consisting of a main frontal hoofprint with deep dewclaw impressions behind. The main frontal part is almost perfectly round and clearly shows the two curving parts of the deer's cloven hoof. The overall track of a mature bull

A caribou leaves a completely unique track with a near-round frontal section and deep dew-claw marks behind. The tracks of bulls measure about 7 inches in overall length.

(Left) Although shed antlers and winter-killed trophies are interesting to look at, these have little bearing on where caribou are apt to be during open hunting season.

A stalking caribou hunter lets his eyes do much of the walking in the vast open terrain these animals prefer.

Migrating caribou can often be ambushed along deep, wide migration trails.

measures nearly 7 inches long.

Caribou droppings are uniquely shaped as well. The pellets dropped by other deer are merely oval with rounded ends, but caribou pellets are oval on one end, flat and indented on the other. This bell-like shape clearly differentiates caribou droppings from moose droppings in areas where both species are found.

In many caribou areas, the plains are littered with shed antlers and bleached remains from winters gone by. However, such sign has no value because caribou during regular summer and fall hunting seasons may be many miles from their antler-littered wintering areas.

Productive Bowhunting Techniques

Caribou are either spotted from a distance and stalked or ambushed from stands along well-used migration trails. Which technique a bowhunter employs on a particular hunt depends primarily on the time of year and the resulting movement tendencies of the animals being hunted. In the summertime, game that is lounging around must be stalked. Once these animals begin their yearly migration to comfortable wintering grounds, it is best to find a point they are moving past and simply wait for a good shot. A caribou moving out toward a distant destination is virtually impossible to catch up with on foot, making stalks impossible.

As mentioned already, stalking is by far the more difficult of the two bowhunting techniques. As often as not, summertime caribou haunts are steep and physically demanding to walk around in. On top of this, summering bulls are generally scattered out instead of hanging together in large, accessible herds. This means a stalking bowhunter must often cover many miles of terrain per day to locate approachable animals, and even after animals are seen the approach routes to these trophies are often several miles long.

A bowhunter who tries for summer caribou in places like Alaska must strap on his hiking boots, carry

(Below and right) Bowhunting for caribou requires long treks by bush plane and/or pack animal to reach remote caribou haunts and carry out any animals taken.

top-notch binoculars for clear, distinct scanning of huge tracts of land, and be fully prepared to hustle toward animals seen a long distance away. This type of bowhunting is physically taxing, but is also extremely enjoyable. The vast tundra plains and lofty naked mountains typical of summer caribou haunts are wildly beautiful, and the prizes that inhabit such big, open country give it a definite life and excitement guaranteed to please any serious archer.

Ambushing animals along migration routes is a relatively easy sport, provided an archer is situated in the proper place to begin with. Most good caribou outfitters carefully monitor movement patterns to ensure that bowhunting clients *are* placed where plenty of animals will move by. In some areas, if the timing is just right, a bowhunter can see literally thousands of caribou per day, his only problems being which animal he wants to shoot and how to get a shot at the animal as it moves by in a herd of 20 to 200. The sheer excitement

of seeing game by the hundreds and having the animals move past at ranges as close as 5 yards is difficult even to imagine, but many bowhunters experience this thrill each and every year.

How to Judge a Trophy

A caribou is the most difficult trophy in North America to judge. There are over 40 different measurements involved in officially scoring a bull's brushpile rack—a mind-boggling task when a bull trots past at a ground-eating pace or feeds on a naked slope several miles away.

The best way to size up a head is to gain as much experience as possible at looking over caribou before a bowhunt actually begins. An archer can do this in two basic ways. First, he can find as many books as possible with good photographs and descriptions of these animals. Second, he can arrange to look at mounted heads in sporting goods stores, museums, taxidermy houses,

Do-it-yourself Alaskan bowhunters can do well on caribou, but only by researching hunting areas thoroughly and choosing camping and hunting gear with care.

and private trophy rooms to get a "feel" for how a decent head looks. Such looking coupled with a copy of the Pope and Young Record Book's caribou-scoring system will help a bowhunter prepare for judging them on the hoof. Any bull past the yearling stage looks big to a neophyte north-country hunter. However, a truly serious trophy bowhunter guards against taking a bull that looks big but really falls in the mediocre to normal size range.

When judging any bull, look for the following antler characteristics: First, the overall rack should rise approximately as far above the head as the animal stands from hoof to shoulder. In other words, the rack itself should be as tall as the animal's back. Second, check out the flat shovel section of the rack, which protrudes directly out over the nose. It normally juts out even with or nearly even with a big bull's nose, and often measures a foot or more from top to bottom. In rare instances, bulls carry two shovels instead of one, and such "double-shovel" bulls are highly desirable prizes. Third, look at the middle beams that branch forward off the main antler beams—these are called the bez formations, and should ideally thrust forward even with a bull's nose, too. The bez should have at least two points per side, and preferably three to six. Fourth, check out the tops of the caribou's antlers. These should have a minimum of five or six points, and hopefully seven to 10 or more. Two of the top points on each side should be fairly long for a good record-book score—preferably over 15 to 20 inches each. If the main beams atop a caribou's head are heavily palmated, too, the trophy score goes up even more.

To get a really good idea of how to dispassionately judge a rack, a bowhunter should study Pope and Young measurement diagrams with care. A symmetrical caribou rack scores better than an uneven rack, and a more massively beamed rack outscores a more lightly beamed rack. A bowhunter who is not consumed with

the desire to "make book" with a caribou can take a suitable trophy by simply looking at some bulls on the hoof and then trying for a head that seems especially large or handsome. Any mature bull with a body-high rack and plenty of points per side makes a fine trophy for the wall regardless of its official record-book score.

Other Important Facts

Shooting at caribou is often long shooting, requiring a bowhunter to carry a fairly flat-shooting bow/arrow combination plus an accurate, long-range rangefinder. Many caribou are taken at point-blank range in both stalking and stand-hunting situations, but many more are taken at ranges over 50 yards.

Most are bagged by bowhunters on fully guided hunts. However, it is legal to bowhunt caribou on your own in Alaska, and a few adventurous woodsmen try do-it-yourself bowhunts each and every year. The key to making such hunts pay off is carefully researching productive areas, locating a dependable Alaskan flying service to transport you in and out of caribou country, and fully preparing to camp in a remote location, transport meat on your back to the airplane rendezvous point, and ship meat and antlers all the way back home.

Caribou are not particularly tenacious for life, and solid arrow hits usually drop them quickly. A bowhunter in most caribou areas also has the advantage of being able to keep track of a wounded animal in the very open terrain.

The caribou is a truly magnificent deer with awesome headgear and a gorgeous trophy hide. In addition, the meat is second to none, having a fairly tender texture and a mild, pleasant taste. A bowhunt for caribou offers ample excitement and challenge to satisfy anyone, and the vast, unspoiled northern wilderness where this animal resides is a pure pleasure to visit. The caribou has a lot to offer any dedicated bowhunting archer!

Trophy Deer Hunting/27

A huge trophy deer like this whitetail is the dream of most serious hunting archers.

TAKING ANY deer with a bow is an accomplishment well worth being proud of. However, the bowhunter who perfects his art and accounts for several archery deer often becomes more selective about which deer he wishes to shoot. Selective bowhunting is not everyone's cup of tea, and an archer who is completely satisfied with the first piece of venison he can arrow need not apologize for his recreational preferences. However, there are several reasons why many experienced bowhunters become selective archers—reasons well worth considering here.

Why Be a Selective Bowhunter?

One of the primary reasons seasoned bowhunters become selective is the fact that selectivity gives them more hours of sport per year than dropping the first deer that walks into range. An archer who prepares for months in anticipation of deer season, and then fills his deer tag the first morning out, is often frustrated by the quick conclusion to his annual bowhunting experience. Archers with some self-discipline and the anticipation of several enjoyable bowhunting weeks ahead of them often prefer to be selective about the deer they try for to milk maximum pleasure from their deer-hunting vacations.

Aside from simply increasing the amount of hunting time spent afield, selective hunting also increases the challenge of an already challenging sport. A bowhunter who sets his sights on a buck instead of a doe or a big buck instead of a small one is placing an additional restriction on his killing efficiency on top of using a primitive bow-and-arrow. This increases the excitement and fulfillment of scoring on a deer even more, and also lets an archer watch deer at close range that he'd be shooting at if he hadn't decided to be selective. Deer watching is highly enjoyable in its own right, and also teaches an archer many useful things about basic deer behavior.

A tender, tasty chunk of meat is ample reward for many archery deer hunters.

What Makes a Bowhunting Trophy?

As far as I'm concerned, a trophy deer is any animal a bowhunter is fully satisfied with. Any arrow-shot deer on the ground is a bonafide trophy to a beginning bowhunter, and a fat young doe whitetail or cow elk is a trophy to the hunter who loves well-prepared meals. If the archer who takes such animals wants a lasting memento of his accomplishments, he can always have a taxidermist tan the hides of these animals or do this job himself. Hides make excellent decorations on the floor or on the wall, and bring back pleasant memories every time a hunter admires them.

For many, any male deer with antlers is a first-rate trophy. As mentioned in the introduction to this book, North American deer grow an infinite variety of antler sizes and shapes, making each individual head a unique and interesting trophy. The head need not be especially big to be worthwhile, and even a spike or two-point deer rack can be converted into a dandy little hatrack for the den or office wall.

Most experienced bowhunters I know especially appreciate a rack that is exceptionally large for the area it was taken in. A bowhunter who lives in a whitetail area with mainly spikes, forked horns, and smallish eight-point bucks regards any 10-point deer as an outstanding trophy, whereas a bowhunter in an area with ample 10-pointers will probably be looking for a buck offering something extra in antler size or number

Basic ingredients needed to produce a home solution for hard-tanning a deer hide are (left to right): borax, alum, plain salt, and washing soda.

Aside from the challenge of actually *finding* a big buck to shoot, a selective archer after a trophy-sized deer will also experience the intense challenge of trying to fool such an animal. A mature male with outsized antlers is usually over 4 years old and did not reach middle age without developing finely honed survival skills. Older deer are far more difficult to bag than younger, smaller-antlered animals, testing a woodsman's skills to the maximum.

A third reason for selective bowhunting is the extreme desirability of a truly large or unusual set of antlers. The bowhunter who annually pots a big, fat doe enjoys his trophies on the dinner table, but an archer who holds out for nice antlers can end up with both meat and a lifetime trophy on the wall. Big antlers fascinate most hunters and are well worth passing up lesser animals for in the minds of many.

1. Stretch out your deer hide flesh-side up and carefully cut away all fat, meat, and other tissue clinging to the hide.

TANNING YOUR OWN HIDES

2. To form the tanning solution, add 4 oz. washing soda, 8 oz. plain salt, and 16 oz. alum to 1 gallon water in a container with a lid. Shake well to dissolve the chemicals.

3. Pour the tanning solution in a 5-gallon bucket, then add another ½-gallon water to the solution.

4. Fully immerse your deer hide in the tanning solution and leave it about 5 days. If the hide tends to float to the surface, weight it down with a large brick or rock.

5. After the prescribed soaking time, remove the hide from the soda-salt-alum solution, lay it out, and spray it down thoroughly on both sides with cold water.

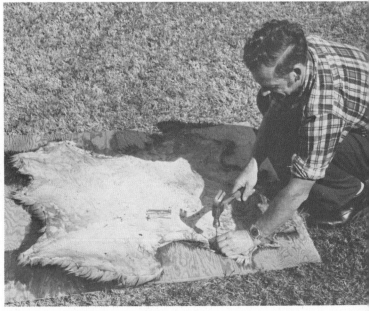

7. Stretch the hide tightly on a large sheet of plywood with hair down and tack the edges in place with nails spaced an inch or two apart.

6. Wash out your mixing container and bucket, then add 8 oz. borax to 1 gallon of clean water and immerse the wet hide in this solution for about 2 days. After 48 hours or more, remove the hide and wash it again with a hose.

8. (Opposite page) Allow the hide to air-dry until it is completely hard and stiff. This normally takes 1 to 2 weeks. Remove the nails from the board and comb or brush the hair to smooth it out. Your deer hide is hard-tanned and ready to hang on the wall!

of antler points. A bowhunter after local deer knows darn well what a trophy animal is in his area, and even if the buck does not remotely qualify for the official record books, it is still a trophy to the fellow who took it.

Organized Trophy Competition

Although a trophy deer is any animal that completely pleases the bowhunter who took it, there are several official bowhunting trophy clubs that provide a basis for state or continental trophy competition. They use widely accepted antler-scoring systems that help bowhunters compare the relative size of trophy deer taken throughout North America. Although not important to everyone, official bowhunting trophy competition does give many hunting archers a goal to shoot for whenever they match wits with deer.

The largest and most revered bowhunting trophy organization is the Pope and Young Club, founded in memory of Saxton Pope and Art Young, two early American archers who helped make bowhunting popular today. This club carefully compiles the trophy scores of deer and other North American big-game animals, holds semi-annual conventions for the purpose of recognizing truly outstanding trophies and the bowhunters who took them, and publishes periodic record books

Any antlered deer, whether large or small, can make a handsome bowhunting memento if the rack is plaque-mounted for the wall. Every archery deer is special!

(Left) Serious bowhunters pay close attention to the record-book scores of their better bucks and bulls. Here, well-known elk outfitter Rick Martin (left) and master bowhunter Jeff Shimizu measure a record-sized bull Jeff took in New Mexico.

Jim Dougherty, well-known bowhunter and president of the prestigious Pope and Young Club, often pores over topographic maps of top trophy areas to improve his odds of success—even when riding en route in tiny bush planes. Such dedication gets the game!

Careful research into state-by-state deer-hunting regulations and specific geographic areas noted in record-deer listings will help an archer find trophy-hunting hotspots.

listing top-scoring North American trophies and the minimum antler scores necessary for entry in these books. Many bowhunters feel that "making book" is the ultimate deer-hunting challenge, and set their sights on deer that have a chance of meeting Pope and Young standards. The Pope and Young Club and similar record-keeping trophy organizations provide a standard by which all bowhunters can compare their bucks and bulls, and thus provide a legitimate service to the bowhunting public at large. How involved a bowhunter decides to become in club activities and purist record-book bowhunting is his own personal business, but most deer-hunting archers are at least aware of record books and how big a rack has to be to qualify as an official record contender.

How to Locate Trophy Deer Hotspots

If the thought of taking bow-and-arrow deer with really big antlers turns an archer on, he owes it to himself to find out where such outsized deer are usually found. Certain parts of the continent produce larger-racked deer than others, and these trophy deer hotspots are the best places to fulfill a bowhunting dream. A skillful archer can hunt a lifetime in a decent deer area and never once see a record-sized buck or bull, whereas he can see big-antlered trophies regularly if he bowhunts someplace else instead. Both animal genetics and special minerals in grass or brush can make certain parts of the continent trophy producers while other areas without these antler-producing ingredients yield few if any impressive-sized deer at all.

One of the very best ways to locate hotspots is carefully studying entries in various bowhunting record books. They normally tell when and where entered animals were bagged, and a close look at the record lists for various deer species often shows clearly where bowhunters should go to take their own large-antlered trophies. For example, in Alaska the majority of truly huge caribou are taken in the southwestern peninsula region, while more northern parts of this state produce few if any top-scoring racks. Similarly, Colorado and Utah dominate the Pope and Young record book in the mule deer category, and this record book shows that virtually all the top Columbian blacktail deer racks taken by bowhunters have come from Oregon. The Pope and Young record book goes one step farther by listing the specific counties where record-sized heads were bagged. A close study of the counties where record mule deer, blacktail, and deer of other species were taken will let any archer further zero in on areas where he is apt to meet his trophy-hunting goals.

Another way is to call state or provincial game-department offices and talk to deer-management experts within these departments. They know where the biggest-racked deer reside within their states or provinces, and can point a polite bowhunter in the right direction.

Top trophy-producing areas tend to change from year to year and decade to decade with shifting deer-food and weather conditions, changes in hunting pressure and harvest regulations, etc. A serious bowhunter constantly keeps in touch with the changing trophy situation in America, checking out the latest big-deer entries in record books and regularly talking to deer biologists and other trophy bowhunters. Finding trophy deer hotspots and dreaming about upcoming trophy bowhunts can be nearly as much fun as the actual bowhunting turns out to be!

Displaying Your Trophy Deer

A bowhunter who does take an exceptional trophy usually wants to display the head for all to see. However, too many hunters do not know the first thing about preparing a trophy head for the taxidermist. Unless the head is properly caped immediately after a deer is dropped, the hide can spoil or at best end up ragged

CAPING OUT YOUR TROPHY

1. To cape a deer for the taxidermist, first slice the hide along the exact top of the neck from back of skull to top of shoulders.

2. Next, girdle the body behind the shoulders and peel the skin from the shoulders with your knife.

3. Make a straight cut up the back of each foreleg, girdle each leg at the knee, and remove the hide from the upper legs.

4. Skin out the brisket area of the deer with careful knife work. The hide clings tenaciously to the carcass here.

5. Skin out the base of the neck, being careful not to nick the hide. No more incisions should be made in the cape.

6. (Right) Skin on down the neck to the back of the deer's head. Slice through the meat completely around the neck behind the head.

7. Twist off the deer's head at the joint where neck and head meet. If the head won't pop loose, whittle through more neck tissue with a probing blade.

8. (Right) Place the cape and intact head in double plastic garbage bags and freeze them immediately. Transport to a taxidermist as soon as possible.

Expert outfitters often skin out trophy heads—most archers should freeze their animals' heads and capes and leave the ticklish head-skinning jobs to the professionals.

and scruffy instead of sleek and natural. If you wish to have a deer head shoulder mounted for the wall in traditional fashion, carefully study the accompanying photo sequence on proper caping.

A good-looking alternative is displaying the antlers on a plaque. A bowhunter can easily mount deer antlers himself by using one of several commercially available rack-mounting kits, or he can take the antlers and skinned-out skull to a taxidermist for a professional-quality rack-mounting job. Either way, he should freeze an entire deer head until he decides to mount it himself or have this done by a taxidermist. An alternative to this that requires no freezing is completely removing the hide from a head, carefully cutting away the eyeballs plus most of the meat and cartilage from the skull with a sharp knife, removing the lower jaw, scooping out the brains through the spinal hole in the back of the skull, heavily salting the skull inside and out, and letting the skull dry naturally in the open air. A salted skull will not smell at all when dry, and can be mounted or sent to the taxidermist at your leisure.

If you decide to have a taxidermist shoulder-mount your deer head or put the antlers on a plaque, ask him to show you alternate ways the mounts can be done. In mounted heads, a variety of head forms are available, including head-down sneak mounts and head-up alert mounts that look straight ahead or turn left or right. Deer antlers can be plaque-mounted in several different ways, including mounts with velvet or leather over the skull cap and natural European plaque mounts with the complete bleached-white upper skull fully exposed instead of cut down and covered with fabric or leather.

Selective bowhunting is the most advanced form of archery deer hunting, producing an unmatched outdoor challenge plus handsome trophies on the wall. When correctly cared for and attractively displayed, the antlers and hides provide lasting reminders of exciting and fulfilling hunts gone by.

The end result of A-to-Z bowhunting preparation is a nice trophy deer on the ground!